Orchids and their Conservation

Harold Koopowitz

TIMBER PRESS
Portland, Oregon

Dedication

This book is dedicated to all my friends and enemies in the 'orchid world' who have immeasurably enriched my life and made it so interesting. It is also dedicated to members of the American Orchid Society's Conservation Committee who work against great odds.

First published 2001

© Text and images Harold Koopowitz 2001

All colour photographs and line drawings are by the author unless otherwise stated

Printed in Hong Kong

Published in North America 2001 by
Timber Press, Inc.
The Haseltine Building
133 S.W. Second Avenue, Suite 450
Portland, Oregon 97204, U.S.A.

ISBN 0 88192 523 3

A catalog record for this book is available from the Library of Congress

Contents

Acknowledgements

I have tried to write a book where each chapter stands alone and they do not need to be read in sequence. If there is some repetition in the chapters, then please do forgive me and bear with me.

This book has undergone an unusually long gestation period and during that time a large number of people have helped me in various ways, ranging from discussions to critically reading portions of the manuscript. The person to whom I owe the deepest debt of gratitude is Philip Cribb who encouraged me to write the book and then took the time to read most of the manuscript. He helped tone down much of my rhetoric, although I have not always followed his advice. Others who kindly read and commented on parts of the book are Ernest Hetherington, Ned Nash and William Rhodehamel.

Over the years I have had many conversations with various people about different aspects of orchids and orchid conservation. These people included Leonid Averyanov, Eric Christenson, Margaret Dix, Eric Hágsater, Gren Lucas, Jack Fowlie, Cordelia Head, Alex Hertz, Ann Lauer Jesup, Alasdair Morrison, Otto Tinschert and Alan Thornhill.

Several people expedited my travels to examine orchids growing in the wild, which helped to formulate some of my ideas and attitudes. Among these are Ant Cambitzis in Zimbabwe; Hendrik van der Hoven, Gavin MacDonald and Gerit van Eede in South Africa; Michael Ooi in Malaysia; and Hendrik Vorster who helped organize an expedition to Malagasy. Tito Marchant accompanied me to Costa Rica and Nikolaas van Zyl helped me in Malawi.

I owe a debt to several people who went out of their way to find or provide information on specific topics. Shelagh Kell and Wendy Strohm cheerfully provided information when I needed it. Among others were Cassio van den Berg who provided information on the Piracicaba orchid collection; Calway Dodson for the update on *Epidendrum ilense*; Robert Gabel and Molly Sperduto for helping me find information on *Isotria medeoloides*; Hubert Kurzweil and Peter Linder answered questions about *Acrolophia ustulata* and David Given updated information on *Danhatchia australis*. Ernest Grell discussed efforts to re-establish *Paphiopedilum rothschildianum* in the wild. Otto Mittlestaedt Villela kindly provided me with information on the status of *Lycaste skinneri*. Sathish Kumar contributed his observations on *Paphiopedilum druryi* while Keeshab C. Pradhan gave me an overview of his plans to re-establish *Paphiopedilum fairrieanum*. Others include George Marcopulos, Earl Ross and Russ Vernon who talked about their experiences trying to maintain orchid collections.

Yves Aubry went out of his way to look for references for me, discussed conservation problems, and accompanied me on several expeditions.

The ideas expressed in this book, while colored by my interactions with the above people, do not necessarily reflect their opinions. I am solely responsible for the views put forward and any mistakes are definitely my own.

Harold Koopowitz, March 2001

CHAPTER 1

Introduction

The planet Earth is currently in the middle of one of the most critical events in its entire history. The diversity of life on the planet is the richest that it has enjoyed during its whole geological record. However at the same time this diversity is threatened and is undergoing one of the most alarming extinction spasms of all time. This event threatens to surpass even the great Permian extinction crisis, when the world lost the majority of its life forms. We are now at a similar transition point, but this time it is not being caused by an extraterrestrial source, such as the meteor that wiped out the dinosaurs at the end of the Cretaceous. The problem is caused by the unchecked growth of our own species, which, like an unrestrained disease, is overwhelming its host. Like any disease, when the host dies, the disease organisms will die as well. Our exploding numbers are making similar demands upon the world's resources, just as germs do on a host.

The growth in the human population is affecting the world's biodiversity, partly because of the need to produce ever-increasing amounts of food, but also to provide housing for these new people. Indirectly the population explosion is producing an increased quantity of waste products, which are affecting the planet's ability to sustain its ecosystems. These indirect effects include global warming, erosion of the ozone layer, oceanic pollution and increasing amounts of atmospheric carbon. These feed back into the world's ecosystems, perturbing them and making it increasingly difficult for the planet to maintain its eroding base of biodiversity.

In order to understand why so many groups of organisms are under threat, one needs to have a clear grasp of the way in which the planet is undergoing change. The world has never been a static place with a constant environment; it has fluctuated through the ages. Many of the changes in the past have been profound and these have wiped out entire groups of organisms. However, there have been few biologically induced events to equal the current paroxysm that the planet is now undergoing. Perhaps the only other one was the potentially poisonous atmosphere created as a byproduct of algal and bacterial photosynthesis. This toxin, a highly reactive gas, threatened most of the earlier life forms. It was oxygen.

As oxygen accumulated in the atmosphere the world became inhospitable for most of the early species. A new biota had to evolve that could cope with this new atmosphere; it would eventually become reliant on the oxygen. The forms of life that evolved to utilize this new chemical gained the advantage and, ultimately, became the dominant life forms. The earlier forms of life were relegated to the relative backwaters of rarer anoxic environments. That ancient world was very different from the present, and we can expect that any future atmosphere will be different from that of today.

I have chosen the orchid family to examine, but I could just as well have selected any other group of organisms. Orchids merely represent a model that allows one to understand events that threaten general

1   *Cattleya trianae* 'Brecht's', the classic orchid that epitomizes the general public's idea of an orchid. (Photocredit: Richard Clark and the American Orchid Society)

biodiversity. Irrespective of the group of organisms considered, there are similarities in the underlying factors that have placed them at risk and similar solutions exist to deal with them effectively. Money is usually used to save large and spectacular animals, such as tigers or giant pandas. These species are considered to be charismatic and attract more resources than plants, but in the long run, the latter are more important. We can only guess at what is the total number of species on the Earth. While there may be as many as eight million species of animals, there are probably only a quarter of a million species of flowering plants. As each plant species becomes extinct it may drag a large number of animals (about 32 on the average) after it, into oblivion. There are very few organisms, including our own, that are not threatened in one way or another by man's activities.

Orchid plants have a mystique about them. Steeped in legend and fable, most lay people think of them as bearing large exotic and gorgeous flowers, enormously valuable and only to be possessed by the upper classes. There are other large and glorious flowers such as dahlias, *Hibiscus* and chrysanthemums, but they have never attained the same pre-eminence as the orchids. Their flowers, while colorful and beautiful in some species, can be bizarrely shaped or even insignificant in others. In some respects they are the ultimate expression of plant evolution, in others there is nothing special about them. But all can instil a respect for the possibilities of organic evolution and the myriad forms that have been produced. It is important that we understand orchids and how they relate to the real world, if we are to be successful in our attempts to save them for future generations. We need to leave our children something that is worth marvelling at, that is a product of the natural world, so that perhaps in comparison they can appreciate their own realistic place in the universe.

The one human activity that most directly affects the ability of orchid species to persist in all their diversity is tropical deforestation. The tropics are being converted from forested lands to other uses at an alarming rate and, as these are cleared away, suitable habitats for orchids are being lost. There are many different reasons for the loss of the tropical forests. Some are scavenged for firewood, others are cut for timber and finally large tracts are cleared to provide pasture for cattle. Besides habitat clearance, some orchid species are also threatened because of their horticultural desirability and are being collected while their habitat remains otherwise undamaged.

There are also many indirect results of man's activity that have negative consequences for orchid conservation. One of the more important of these has been the worldwide over reliance on chemical insecticides. Nearly a half

century ago Rachel Carson raised the cry against the indiscriminate use of chemicals to control agricultural pests. She pointed out that there were unexpected side effects to the build up of those pesticides in the environment. Many enlightened First World governments banned their use within their own national boundaries, but they did not ban the continued manufacture and sale of those noxious chemicals to the developing Third World countries. We still face the consequences about which Rachel Carson preached. The survival of orchids and many other plants is dependent upon the presence of specific pollinators. Honeybees are poor pollinators for most, if not all orchids. If anything should happen to the natural pollinators, the affected orchids are also doomed. The continuous and heavy use of chemical insecticides and indiscriminate spraying of tropical areas kills both helpful and harmful insects. The orchids are tied into and dependent upon the healthy continuance of the habitats of which they are an integral part. There is increasing concern that many natural pollinator populations are in a state of serious decline. In their wake a great number of wild plant species may suffer extinction.

Another serious problem is that we lack the background information to be able to manage orchid populations effectively, either in the wild or in captivity. This is especially true of tropical orchids. There has been little work on the ecology of natural populations of orchids. There are so few studies that we are unable to draw reliable generalizations from them. Much of the current work in orchid ecology is pollination orientated, but that is only one of many components of knowledge that we need. We have no idea of what it costs a plant to replace itself in a natural population, that is, how many seedlings have to be produced in order to replace one mature plant that dies or is removed from the forest. We don't have life cycles that show which are the most vulnerable parts of an orchid's life cycle. We don't really understand the role that is played by mycorrhizal fungi and why they seem more important in temperate terrestrial orchids than tropical epiphytes.

How do epiphytes on exposed branches of trees get their nutrients, such as nitrogen and inorganic phosphate? We assume that the trees might leak nutrients in rainstorms but critical studies are few and far between and how do orchids perched on exposed rocks get enough food? It is difficult to believe that sufficient nutrients dissolve from the rocks during a rainstorm. Do the surrounding lichens or mosses also leak nutrients when they are wetted? And, if so, are these important to the orchid? Are there patterns of population growth and loss in the wild? How are orchid populations distributed and how are they founded, how do they grow and then disappear?

It is important to understand how orchid populations are founded and if there is a genetic interchange between discrete populations of the same species. Orchids are often found in disturbed areas. Epiphytes grow on the soil of road cuttings, as do many terrestrial species. How long do such populations persist at any one place? Much of this is knowledge that we will need if we ever want to manage populations of orchids the way we do animals, but we don't have it. Getting this information does not require big science; it is performed with relatively cheap fieldwork. But science is a slave to fashion and journals want to publish 'cutting-edge' research. The basic ecology of orchids is not considered such cutting-edge research. But even relatively inexpensive fieldwork still requires money and unfortunately most orchid ecology is not high on the priority list of funding institutions. Unfortunately, knowing how orchids exist in their natural habitats is not considered exciting and hardly 'important' enough to prompt ecologists to encourage their graduate students to go out into the field to find the information. And it is unlikely that the situation will improve. Yet this information is critical if orchid biodiversity is to be saved.

In the course of the world's history most species have become extinct or have evolved into other species. Ninety-nine percent of all species that have ever existed no longer live on the Earth and we can expect that the majority of our current species will also eventually disappear. Why then the concerns about biodiversity loss if these species are fated to become extinct anyway? The answer is complex and has many facets, which will be addressed in the various chapters of this book. However there is one important and overriding fact. The present rates of extinction are thought to be many times greater than normal background losses that have occurred until recent history. In the past, extinction losses were balanced or even surpassed by the emergence of new species. Now extinction is outpacing new emergence and current losses proceed at a faster rate than the formation and appearance of new species. In the face of all of this it is inevitable that we will lose an appreciable fraction of the world's species, including many orchids. The world will become poorer as biodiversity diminishes, but because human populations are so urbanized and cut off from the natural world, few will miss them or even be aware of what has disappeared. Perhaps after man has passed from the scene a rich biodiversity will once again emerge, but can anyone be certain of that?

We have known about the population explosion for the past half-century, but despite much hand wringing, the world has yet to deal with it effectively. Our models have predicted human population growth, but in fact the real growth has outstripped model predictions and there are no assurances that it will end. Optimistic predictions project that there will be a leveling of the human population at between 11 and 15 billion, possibly by the middle of the next century, but there are no real reasons why this should be. Problems are compounded by real increases in human longevity as medicine makes significant advances in that direction.

The strain that humans are putting on the planet is real. There are few places on the earth where one can escape pollution. A sample of ocean water from anywhere in the world is bound to contain cellulose fibers derived from toilet paper and chemical pollutants can be measured nearly everywhere. It is not unusual for smoke from fires in one country to damage the health of citizens in another. Rising average annual global temperatures keep breaking records but the naysayers still raise their voices to protect special interests and big business. Detractors claim that the entire meteorological community is wrong and that we are merely witnessing part of a natural warming trend. The lawmakers and politicians like this, as they prefer to take the easy road and ignore the hard questions.

It is our generation that has to take the responsibility for what happens on our world. We have had long and fair warning, but our attempts to ameliorate the situation have been piddling at best. Man's history has shown that it is possible to mobilize entire nations to achieve important goals that range from fighting wars to fighting AIDS. We have put several people on the moon – why are our attempts at saving our planet so half-hearted? When our grandchildren point accusing fingers at us for destroying or allowing the destruction of their heritage will we merely shrug our shoulders and blither desperately that we knew not what we did? Well we do know – it is just that most of us do not really care.

Professional biologists, who should be at the forefront in the crusade to save the world's biodiversity, deserve a great deal of blame. They were laggard in joining the fight and reluctant to commit themselves to more than lip service. These biologists, in the course of their teaching, come into contact with enough young people at the universities and colleges of the world that they could have mobilized an important and educated segment of the population. But for the most part, biologists have shied away from this or have been ineffective in their attempts. Even ecologists from some of the most prestigious institutions have shirked their responsibilities, claiming that conservation is an applied science, while their interests focus on pure science. Meanwhile the communities and ecosystems that they purport to study and want to understand have deteriorated and are perturbed by the hand of man, to the extent that there is very little in community ecology left to study that is still pure and uncontaminated.

Where does this leave us? There is no going back to Eden. In fact a pristine Eden that would reassert itself if man were obliterated from the face of the Earth is a myth. Systems and communities change with time and it is unlikely that the old concept of a stable community in some sort of equilibrium, that would emerge as a climax at the end of a succession, is correct. Ecosystems appear to be mosaics and when they are damaged they rarely reassume the same configurations they originally possessed, instead the systems will change, sometimes in subtle or at other times in drastic ways. Setting aside nature reserves will not be enough to save more than a fraction of the world's biodiversity. More importantly, as the global climate alters, the animals and plants jailed in those areas may become trapped in unsuitable environments. When climate changed in the past it was relatively gradual and whole forests and their attendant organisms migrated, following their preferred temperature regimes. Now the changes taking place are too rapid for forests to accommodate them, but even more important is the fact that the open landscapes that were available in the past and into which the forests could move no longer exist. As man continues to affect the earth he will be forced into actively manipulating it, in an effort to save even a small portion of the natural world. And then unfortunately, for much of the world, man will have neither the information nor the deep comprehension of the systems that he needs in order to reconstruct or maintain them.

In recent years a new and unexpected barrier appears to have erected itself that will interfere with maintaining biodiversity. This impediment stems from the conservation movement itself. With science's increasing ability to perform genetic engineering, all sorts of organisms that had received very little attention in the past have now assumed a new potential value. Their genes might be used to make products, such as new medicines, with profound economic value. Those concerns were raised at the 1992 Rio Convention on Biodiversity. This was one of the largest conservation events in the world's history, convened to review and raise concerns about imminent biodiversity losses. Instead of formulating strong plans to protect the world's organisms attention was switched to protecting each nation's economic interests. First world countries have the finances and expertise to carry out effective conservation. Developing countries on the other hand, contain many of the endangered species but in order to protect their resources from exploitation by the first

world countries they have become reluctant to allow those resources to leave the country. Mounds of bureaucratic red tape have been introduced and while this may protect economic self-interest it seldom promotes conservation. Genetic exploitation also seems to have led to ideas about sustainable harvest. Ideally sustainable harvest recognizes that it is possible to selectively exploit a certain level of biodiversity without endangering it. In reality recommendations for sustainable harvest are rarely followed and it has been used as an excuse to go out and rape and pillage the natural environment.

There appear to be few institutions or governments committed to saving significant fractions of the biodiversity available. Preference is given to agricultural crops and some attention is also given to medicinal species. Our response to this crisis has been a call for cataloging organisms, rather than saving them. In the end we may know some of what has been lost but that will be poor compensation for the extinction of those organisms. For most plant species we know how to preserve seeds almost indefinitely, but many of the attempts to set up seed banks for wild species in different parts of the world have failed. This is a pity for the technology involved is very simple and requires a minimum of training. We know how to do it and it is relatively cheap, but few governments are committed to setting up seed banks. For orchids, seed bank technology is not impossible but we still have to figure out how to do it properly. There is very little research focused in this direction and yet orchids comprise about 10 % of the world's plant species.

If significant numbers of orchid species are to be saved for future generations, the success of those endeavors will not be due to the efforts of governments or institutions. Hope rests with non-governmental organizations and the voluntary efforts of individual men and women, working singly or in groups, for the survival of their favorite plants. Gardeners and plantsmen will have to assume the responsibility for the continuance of their favorite plants. This will also be true for most of the other hobby plant groups based on wild species such as aroids, succulents and cacti, gesneriads, *Narcissus*, etc. Private collections and the passing on of species from hand to hand will be the way many species will survive in the face of environmental degradation. Yet the long term prospects for species in collections is also fragile. Few have worked out methods for protecting the contents of important collections amassed during the lives of individuals.

The picture drawn above is clearly quite pessimistic but it does not mean that everything is totally hopeless or that one must or should even consider surrendering to the situation. There are many things that can still be done to retard biodiversity loss and even if we do lose many species, the correct actions can still save significant numbers of species for our future enjoyment and contemplation. But it is important that one clearly understands the severity of the situation if one is to carry out effective rescue operations. We know what to do and we know how to do it. What is now needed is to gather the will for effective action. We are going to lose many species but the rate and total numbers that go extinct will depend on what we do during the next two decades. Twenty years is not a long time. It is the blink of an eye. Time is critical and unless concerted activity is forcefully initiated within the next few years, or sooner, we will miss the only window of opportunity left to slow the coming cascade of extinction. If we do not stem the tide, we will experience a loss the like of which this planet has not seen since the great Permian extinction event some 248 million years ago.

There are a number of models that predict rates of species extinction (Frankel and Soulé, 1981; Shafer, 1990; Koopowitz *et al.*, 1993). These are based on area changes that occur as natural landscapes are converted to other uses. These models tell us how much land we need to set aside as reserves in order to save significant numbers of species. Essentially the models suggest that between 50 % and 62 % of the species can be saved if 10 % of the land is set aside for conservation. In fact about 10 % of the tropical rainforests have already been dedicated as preserves of various kinds. There are also uncounted preserves on private property and municipalities that probably increases the number somewhat.

The same models can also make predictions about rates of extinction and how many species should already be extinct. With 45 % of the tropical forests already cut we should have lost approximately 22 % of all orchid species (Koopowitz, 1992) and our model (Koopowitz *et al.*, 1993) suggests that as many as 402 of the 3405 pleurothallid species may already be lost. However closer examination reveals that relatively few species have actually been lost at this point in time. And it is extremely difficult to be absolutely sure that any species have been totally obliterated. At best, one might be able to say that one has not been able to find that particular species for several years. Two prime examples concern the Slipper Orchids, *Paphiopedilum delenatii* and *Paphiopedilum druryi* that were both thought to be extinct for many years, but have been rediscovered. *Paphiopedilum delenatii* still occurs in substantial quantities, and over 3,000 specimens of *P. druryi* are known from one extant population. There are additional examples for other genera ranging from *Acrolophia ustulata*

to *Odontoglossum crispum*, as well.

How does one reconcile the assertion that many orchids are on the verge of extinction with the paucity of numbers and examples of orchid extinction? Biologists recognize that when a population is reduced in size below a certain number (often thought to be about 500 individuals) extinction becomes almost inevitable, unless man steps in and artificially rescues that population. Individual orchid plants are, for the most part, long-lived and can continue to exist for decades, although they may only constitute part of a non-viable population that will eventually die out. These species have received descriptive terms such as representing the 'living dead' or being called 'functionally extinct'. We think that enormous numbers of orchids fall into this category. And those that one can still find (if we search hard enough), will all vanish unless we do something about the situation. Fortunately, orchids produce so many seeds that we could probably save any species in dire situations. If we really wanted to, we could save nearly all of the endangered orchid species. One could not have made that statement ten years ago, when germinating terrestrial orchid species presented special problems. However this is no longer the case, easy and reliable methods of germinating terrestrial orchids have now been worked out (Wodrich, 1997). Many of the previously recalcitrant terrestrial species can now be germinated using aseptic media.

There are many preserves which, while not specifically set up just for orchids, do contain and protect appreciable numbers of those plants. These preserves may hold as many as 50 % to 60 % of the world's 30,000 orchid species. Orchids are also one of the few plant groups that tend to get blanket protection in most countries, where they exist. We have the knowledge and ability to grow and propagate most of the other species that do not have protection in nature. In addition, there are hundreds of thousands of amateur orchid growers that could hold substantial numbers of species safely in cultivation. Furthermore, we could develop efficient methods for storing orchid seeds and this is probably one of the most powerful methods of species conservation that has yet to be applied to orchid conservation. There are problems with all these approaches to saving orchids and they will be discussed in this book, but while difficulties exist, none of them are insolvable and they can all be managed.

What is missing is the will to do the job. It is still possible to save the world's orchids, but we will need to want to perform that task. It will need focus, commitment and guts. And it is still possible, but the opportunities to save the world's orchids are running out. Now is the time for action.

CHAPTER 2

What are Orchids?

There is enormous diversity in the plant kingdom. The number of all the different flowering plant species is usually given as 250,000 species but many tropical species have not been officially recognized and there may be as many as 300,000, or even more, distinctly different types. These numbers also reflect the species concepts embraced by taxonomists. The definitions that they use vary among authorities and this leads to considerable debate – leaving the actual numbers in a continuous state of flux. The fraction of flowering plants that are accommodated in the Orchidaceae, the orchid family, is considerable. Somewhere between 8% and 10% of all flowering plants are considered to be orchids. That is a figure between 20,000 and 30,000 different species and may give the orchids the distinction of being the largest plant family. The other contender for the largest plant family is the Asteraceae, the daisy family. Orchids are cosmopolitan and found naturally in nearly all parts of the world from Tierra del Fuego at the tip of South America to the edges of hot springs in Greenland, but they reach their greatest development and diversity in the tropics.

Orchids are classed as monocotyledonous plants, or more familiarly as monocots. The monocot families share several common features including a single seed leaf or cotyledon in the seed and other features such as parallel leaf venation, a stem with scattered vascular bundles for transporting fluids and flower parts in multiples of three. Orchids share many of these features but they have seeds that are so small that there is no cotyledon. The seed is merely a microscopic ball of cells.

Modern concepts of monocot families dictate quite small groups. The old family, the Liliaceae, has now been broken down into some 20 to 30 smaller more uniform families. Despite attempts, in the past, to bring the orchids into conformity with other monocot families and break it apart into several distinct families there has been enough resistance so that for the present, a single concept has been retained. What should probably be separate families are still considered sub-families of the Orchidaceae.

Currently, orchids are defined by a suite of only three morphological features (Dressler, 1981). Not one of these characteristics is unique to the Orchidaceae but the three together are constant features of all members of the family. The first feature concerns the stamens, which are arranged so that they open up and shed their pollen towards one side of the flower. This is a common arrangement in many families where the pollinator lands or crawls on only one portion of the flower. We also find this in the *Iris* family, in many *Gladiolus* species and other related genera; the mint family in the well-known genus *Salvia*; and most members of the Bignoniaceae. These are only a few examples. A second common feature of all members of the Orchidaceae is the partial to complete fusion of the stamen filaments with the style, to form a column. This feature has also been elaborated upon in the milkweed family, the Asclepiadaceae, where it can be argued that an even more complex system than that found in the Orchidaceae has evolved. In the monocots, some of the shell gingers such as *Alpinia*, have evolved a pseudocolumn which bears a remarkable resemblance to that of the orchid column, except that the style is not fused to the filaments but rather runs through and is supported by a narrow filament cavity. In the dicotyledons we find that *Impatiens* also possesses a structure that approaches the orchid condition. Here the stamens are fused at their tips and tightly surround the ovary and style, forming a combination that superficially resembles a column. The third feature is the microscopic nature of the seed. All orchids produced large numbers of very tiny seed. The numbers can be mind boggling. Ruschi (1986) estimated that a single fruit of *Cyrtopodium punctatum* produced over seven and a half million seeds, he measured four million for *Laelia harpophylla* and 1.6 million in a pod from *Cattleya guttata*. The fruit with the smallest number of seed was *Barbosella australis* with only 25,000 seeds and even that is a respectable number that puts other non-orchid flowering plants to shame. Orchid seeds develop into a structure called a protocorm on germination. Many other families also make microscopic seeds, among the dicotyledonous plants we find them commonly in the Gesneriaceae

and several of the carnivorous plant families. In the monocots, tiny seeds are also found in the Burmanniaceae, once
thought to be a sister group of the orchids. Therefore none
of these features is unique to the Orchidaceae, but it is a
combination of features that defines the group. With the
absence of endosperm we find that orchids have also for-
saken the double fertilization that is a normal characteristic of all other flowering plants and this sets them apart
from other flowers in the plant kingdom.

Other commonly identified orchid features (such as
tuberoids, the labellum, flower resupination and pollinaria) are structures and arrangements that are only found in
certain of the subgroups that make up the orchid family,
but they may also occur in other families. Within the family there are clear groups of related plants but while the
boundaries between groups are generally acknowledged,
their relationships to each other are not uniformly agreed
upon. Here we recognize five subfamilies and follow
Dressler's (1993) treatment of the family. A brief discussion of each subfamily will give a feel for the diversity in
this enormous assemblage of plants.

The first of the major sub-groupings is the Apostasioideae, containing only two genera, *Apostasia* and
Neuwiedia, each with 8 species. This is the smallest
group and these are the least 'orchid-like', having starry
regular flowers with either two or three stamens. The
pollen is loose and there are no pollinia. Molecular evidence does indicate a close relationship with the rest of
the family but this group represents a clade[1] that
evolved from the basal ancestral stock before many of
the more obvious 'orchid-like' features evolved. These
are terrestrial plants confined to the tropics.

The Cypripedioideae are a relatively uniform group of
four to five genera containing probably no more than 200
species. Also primarily terrestrial, these are the familiar
lady-slipper orchids. One genus *Paphiopedilum* has long
been an important component of orchid collections. This
sub-family has species that possess two fertile stamens and
one sterile staminode.

Another sub-family of terrestrial plants is the
Spiranthoideae, with nearly 100 genera. For the layman
these are usually the terrestrial orchids, which do not have
tuberous roots. The familiar jewel orchids, such as
Luidisia and *Goodyera*, belong here. Relatively few other
members of this group are cultivated or found in general
collections. To a large extent they tend to have relatively
small and insignificant flowers, but anatomically the flowers may be quite complicated.

The Orchidoideae is the fourth subfamily, also containing primarily terrestrial genera. Most of these plants

have tuberous roots or tuberoids that are a curious mixture of root and stem, characteristics that are peculiar to
this group of plants. They also have some of the most
advanced and highly evolved sex organs in the family. If
the subgroups are to be elevated to family status this is
the section that would retain the name Orchidaceae.
Familiar genera within this section are *Disa*, with approximately 100 species and *Habenaria* with 600, making the
latter one of the largest genera in the Orchidaceae. Many
of the sub-family are terrestrials of Mediterranean climate zones and their tuberoids are adaptations to surviving summer drought. Columns in this group are among
the most advanced and here the single stamen can be split
into two widely separate and independently acting units;
even the stigma itself may be divided into two independently placed and acting units. In some species fusion
between the stamens and pistil may be difficult to discern.

Dressler (1993) included over 550 genera in the
Epidendroideae, which includes most of the orchids in
cultivation. These are the orchids with which most gardeners are familiar and it includes approximately three-
quarters of all orchid species. The vast majority of the
plants in this section are epiphytic. The largest genera,
which have 300 or more species, are listed in Table 1. It
is interesting that half of the genera on this list (it includes
the two largest, *Pleurothallis* and *Bulbophyllum*, with
1,120 and 1000 species respectively) tend to have quite
tiny and highly specialized flowers.

Genus	Number of Species
Pleurothallis	1120
Bulbophyllum	1000
Dendrobium	900
Epidendrum	800
Habenaria	600
Maxillaria	420
Oncidium	420
Liparis	350
Malaxis	300
Oberonia	300

Table 1 The largest orchid genera: after Dressler (1993).
Note that only one, *Habenaria*, does not belong to
the Epidendroideae.

The Epidendroideae contains several major assemblages and there is some argument as how to divide this
subfamily. There are two major groupings, the epidendroid (all sympodial) and the vandoid (mono- or sympodial) orchids.

[1] A group of species sharing a common ancestor

The Spiranthoideae, Orchidoideae and Epidendroideae, all possess the typical features that one normally associates with the orchids, namely flowers with a column formed from the complete fusion of a single stamen with the pistil. Nevertheless, if the orchids were to be brought into conformity with other monocot families and broken into a number of smaller families, all of the preceding taxa would end up as separate plant families. The Orchidaceae would be strictly a small group of terrestrial species and our familiar orchids would be members of the family Epidendraceae. The Slipper orchids would belong to the Cypripediaceae. If the orchids did not enjoy such a large following, primarily among horticulturists, there would not be so much resistance to the move. But this appears to be one place where amateur interests are holding scientific values in check. All the families, however, would belong in the same order, the Orchidales. For a more detailed accounting of modern orchid taxonomy and classification the reader is referred to the excellent work of Robert Dressler (1981,1993).

Orchid distributions

Though orchids reach their peak diversity in the tropics, they are not evenly distributed. Within the Neotropics, Ecuador, Panama and Mexico appear to be particularly rich. Africa has much less variety, both in color and form, than either the neo-tropical or Southeast Asian orchid floras. This is particularly true of the tree dwelling species, though less true for terrestrial orchids. There are some unusual quirks in their distribution. Slipper orchids are found in South and Central America as well as Europe, Asia and as far south as Papua New Guinea and the Solomon Islands. There should be slipper orchids in Africa and Madagascar but they seem to be missing from that area. However, Central Africa does have a few other genera, such as *Epipactis*, that are primarily Eurasian in distribution.

The New World is rich in epidendroid genera and species and this appears to be where they have developed their greatest diversity. The Subtribe Laeliinae is renowned for the large flowers in genera like *Cattleya* and *Laelia*. For the layperson these plants epitomize orchids. Perhaps even more successful are the pleurothallids, with their myriad species of primarily small fly-pollinated flowers. There are, however, epidendroid taxa that are well developed in other parts of the world. Africa has *Polystachya* and Asia *Dendrobium*, two groups that superficially resemble each other very closely. Another large genus in this Tribe, *Bulbophyllum*, perhaps the ecological equivalent of the New World pleu-

rothallids, is cosmopolitan in its distribution, but has most of its members in the Old World.

The monopodial vandoid orchids are primarily Old World, with only a few species and genera in the New World. The angraecoid types are most developed in Africa, where their subdued moth-pollinated flowers have led to the credence that Africa is impoverished orchid-wise. The large colorful flowers of the terrestrial genera *Eulophia* and *Disa*, are little known but do have Africa as their main center of diversity.

Orchid flower evolution

The ancestral plant from which the orchids evolved is thought to have had flowers with five whorls (rings) of organs. Each whorl is a circle of three similar parts i.e.

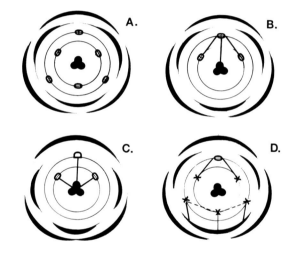

Fig 1 Floral diagrams showing the arrangement and derivation of various floral parts.

A. Hypothetical ancestral flower. The outer whorl of three parts represents the sepals, the next whorl is the petals; there are two inner whorls of three stamens each and a central tripart ovary. Note that each row of parts alternates position with its adjacent whorls.
B. Apostasioideae with three stamens joined to each other and the gynoecium.
C. Cypripedioideae with one sterile outer staminode and two fertile stamens in the inner whorl.
D. Monandrous orchids. Here there is only one fertile stamen. 'X's represent hypothesized structures derived from the other five stamens, dashed lines indicate structures to which the stamen has been incorporated.

2 *Pecteilis radiata* (syn. *Habenaria radiata)* this orchidoid species is a Japanese terrestrial that bears a remarkably fringed labellum.

sepals, petals, stamens and carpels. There were two whorls of stamens. Although there are no reliable fossils of these flowers and the exact early stages of orchid evolution are unknown, any member of the family can be derived from such a flower. How can biologists be so sure? Modern orchids usually have three sepals and the same number of petals. While the ovary also has three fused carpels there is only one single stamen, so why do we think the primitive ancestor had two whorls with a total of six?

Fundamental to understanding this is the following concept. In nearly all whorled flowers, each succeeding circle of parts, alternates with the one before it, thus the petals are situated in the gaps between the sepals. The first ring of stamens should be in the gaps between the petals, while the second ring of stamens is expected in the gaps between the first stamen whorl. If the first ring of stamens is missing the second whorl will be situated opposite the petals. The three compartments of the ovary are positioned between the gaps of the second ring of stamens. A hypothetical ancestral flower is illustrated with a floral diagram in Fig. 1a.

In the Apostasiodeae (Fig. 1b), the three stamens are derived from both of the stamen whorls. One stamen is derived from the outer whorl and the other two from the inner whorl. All three of these stamens are joined together at the base and they produce dry powdery pollen of separate grains, like that of many other plants. The next step in complexity can be found in the Cypripedioideae (Fig. 1c) where the outer stamen is no longer able to produce pollen and becomes a sterile appendage. This sta-

minode is interesting as it has been retained in all species except one (*Phragmipedium exstaminodium*) and has evolved into a variety of forms and shapes. The actual function of the staminode still needs to be investigated. There has been speculation that it might be a visual attractant or perhaps a landing platform for the pollinator; but there have been few experimental studies to determine the real functional significance of the staminode. In this group the pollen grains are still separate grains but united into a waxy or mealy mass that can be deposited *en masse* onto the pollinator. In the other orchids there is a single stamen (also derived from the outer whorl of stamens, Fig. 1d). In certain orchids there are sometimes two projections – one on each side of the column. Some workers consider these to represent two staminodes, derived from the inner staminal whorl and homologous with the two lateral stamens of the Apostasiodeae. Pollen can be powdery and merely deposited on the pollinator, as in *Chlorea* species, or may be elaborated into a variety of complicated structures produced, in part, from both the style and the anther.

What happened to the other stamens? There is some debate that they may have been incorporated into the labellum. The lip or labellum is one of the petals and is usually divided into three portions, a mid-lobe and two side lobes. There have been suggestions going back to Brown and Darwin in the early 1800s (Endress, 1994) that the labellum represents the fusion of three staminodes and the median petal. Thus the two side lobes would be derived from stamens and the crest on the labellum may also represent a third stamen. There is also the suggestion that the petal has been lost altogether and the labellum evolved from only the 3 stamens (Nelson, 1967). Totally opposite is the assertion that the labellum is not of staminoidal origin and may merely be an elaborate petal (Kurzweil, 1987).

In some of the more complicated labella there is also a fusion with the lateral sepals, which is clearly evident in genera such as *Polystachya* and *Dendrobium*. In some other flowers such as *Stanhopea* and *Coryanthes*, the labellum is amazingly complex and special anatomical terms have had to be developed to allow accurate descriptions of its various parts. In the very large genus *Epidendrum*, the column may be fused to the labellum along its length.

The shape of the labellum and the way that it develops in different species reflects the important role that this structure plays in guiding pollinators under the sex organs. The diversity is truly amazing. The labellum can be modified into a trap and tunnel in the slipper orchids, a swimming pool in *Coryanthes* or a beckoning 'fungus' in *Dracula*. Few species, even within the same genus, have identical labella. The labellum can also have a function other than assisting in pollination. In the African genus *Bonatea*, the labellum is folded in the bud so that it protects the sensitive stigmatic surfaces from herbivorous insects during development. It can be adorned with ridges, crests, hairs and/or a variety of other outgrowths. In some species of *Bulbophyllum* these new structures may be hinged and vibratile. The labellum may have spots, blotches and areas of contrasting color. In all, this is a truly amazing structure, scarcely matched by any other petals in the plant kingdom.

The labellum frequently produces nectar in a specialized structure, called the nectary. Moth-pollinated flowers, such as many of the angraecoids, have very long cylindrical organs that can accommodate the moth's tongue. The record holder for length appears to be *Angaecum longicalcar* (syn. *A. eburneum* var. *longicalcar*), where the nectary is reputed to reach as long as 50 cm. In the terrestrial genus *Satyrium*, which is widespread through Africa and Asia, each labellum has two nectaries.

The labellum is usually either the landing site for the pollinator or the main target for its attention and its position relative to gravity is important. Developmentally the labellum is produced in the adaxial position but in order to be effective it must assume an abaxial orientation. This is achieved by resupination where the ovary supporting the flower twists through 180° to move the flower into the correct position. In pendant flowers, however, no resupination is required. One wonders if the primitive orchids had pendant flower sprays.

In orchids with arching flower sprays the basal flowers on the erect portion of the spike may be resupinate but terminal flowers where the inflorescence is drooping will usually not be twisted – so all flowers have their labella on the ventral side of the flower. Resupination appears to be a gravity response that was confirmed by early Russian experiments when developing flower sprays were taken up into space.

The sepals usually have two functions, they protect the inner petals and column in the bud but they are also usually petalloid and add to the attractive function of the petals. In some genera such as *Stelis* and *Masdevallia*, the sepals take on the major attractive function and the petals have become reduced and insignificant. Many slipper orchid species have one of the sepals enlarged and it may be brightly colored (e.g. *Paphiopedilum charlesworthii*), patterned with contrasting spots (*P. insigne*) or striped (*P. rothschildianum*); so as to be the main advertising agent for the flower. Sepals may fuse with each other or to other flower parts. In genera where the sepals and labellum are fused together (as in some *Eulophia* species and most members of the genus *Dendrobium*) the arrangement may lend mechanical support so that the flower can accommodate the weight of the pollinating vector.

The two lateral petals tend to be larger than the sepals and seem primarily to be 'advertisers' for the flower. However there are many exceptions to this and the petals can also be much smaller than the labellum, as in genera such as *Miltonia* and *Tolumnia*. In certain species the petals can be so reduced as to be insignificant.

Many orchids have spotted or blotched flowers, particularly in the *Oncidium* and *Odontoglossum* alliances. Astute observers will notice that patterns vary from flower to flower, even on the same inflorescence, and the two petals of a single flower will often not have identical markings. It may seem odd that a flower can be built with the remarkable precision needed to effect pollination and yet be 'sloppy' with regard to pattern placement. The reason for this may be something to do with the way in which an insect's eye works. Compound eyes are not very good at discerning shapes in space but they are exquisitely sensitive to changes in light intensity and respond to 'flicker' rather than images. Markings on orchid petals are registered as changes in light intensity as the insect eye passes across the pattern and the exact placement is unimportant. Thus evolution has not had to select for placement, but rather degrees of contrast on a blotch or flower part where the light intensity changes. Insects also tend to follow converging lines and here placement of nectar guides, usually on the labellum, is more critical but even this does not need to be exact. Because of the physiology of insect eyes, smooth circular and overlapping flat flower parts are less effective than wavy, twisted or uneven edges with distinctly separated sepal and petal bases. The idealized orchid flowers that connoisseurs prefer are quite 'unnatural'. In addition, orchid breeders select for large, flat and rounded flowers, rejecting those that have recurved or reflexed petals and sepals. If such flowers occurred in nature those plants would be selected against. Three-dimensional flowers can be perceived by the pollinators from much wider angles than two-dimensional flattened blossoms and are consequently more effective at attracting them. Very large flowers, while easier to see at a distance, can confuse a smaller insect when it gets close.

Orchids have inferior ovaries i.e. the ovary is situated beneath the tepals. The ovary is attached to the flower stem by a solid pedicel. The ovary is composed of three carpels but most of the orchid ovaries have a single central cavity. A few genera such as *Apostasia* and *Phragmipedium* have three cavities, one for each carpel, making up the ovary. Seeds tend to be mixed with long hairs called elators, which are thought to help disperse the seed from the ovary. In many orchids the ripe capsules split along a suture that runs down the middle of each carpel, but other patterns of dehiscence are known.

A flower can tell one much about its pollinator even without ever observing the plant in the wild. Flowers that receive nocturnal visitors tend to be white, cream, pale yellow or sometimes very pale pink. These are colors that reflect moonlight the best and are usually pollinated by moths. Such plants need to offer a reward and will have nectar to entice the visitor. Moth-pollinated flowers also have pleasant scents that help entice and guide the pollinator at night. Brightly colored flowers are pollinated by diurnal insects. Butterflies and birds prefer red and/or orange colors. While butterfly eyes are sensitive to red light, bee's eyes can not perceive that color. The visual spectrum for bees is shifted to shorter wavelengths and they see from orange-yellow through to ultraviolet. The various insect groups have different color perceptions.

Many orchids have fragrances as an additional inducement to promote visits by their pollinators, but butterfly and bird-pollinated flowers do not. Neither of those two vectors use or possess well-developed senses for floral odors and subsequently, red colored orchid species very rarely emit fragrance. Fly-pollinated flowers often have dingy colors, e.g. reddish-purple and brown, and may have vibrating hairs, e.g. bulbophyllums and pleurothallids. They may have putrid or the even worse scents that flies seem to appreciate. Floral scents can be important to the various bees that visit them. Floral fragrances in the *Stanhopea* alliance have received a great deal of attention and analysis. Male *Xylocopa* and other related bees actively seek out and collect the fragrances, pollinating the flowers while doing so, but the importance of the substance to the individual bees have not been determined. In European orchids of the genus *Ophrys* the flowers produce a scent that mimics the pheromones of female wasps. Males actually copulate with the labellum and while doing so also pollinate the flowers. Different *Ophrys* species are pollinated by different wasp species and each produces the appropriate pheromone. The system is not exact, however, and many hybrids between various *Ophrys* species have been recorded.

Many orchids are deceptive flowers; they offer no reward, but depend on the pollinator confusing them with other nearby plants that do offer a reward. One system that has been recorded involves *Cymbidium insigne* and *Dendrobium infundibulum*, which grow and flower together with *Rhododendron lyi*. Bumble bees visiting the large white *Rhododendron* flowers for rewards also visit and pollinate the cymbidiums and dendrobiums growing among them (Du Puy and Cribb, 1988). The orchid flowers offer no rewards. This system will only work as long as the number of deceptive flowers is modest. Another famous example is in Central America, where the orchid *Epidendrum radi-*

3   *Ophrys bombylifera*, an orchidoid species from southeastern France. The labellum has evolved to mimic a female bee.

thought of as the delivery system for the pollen and it can be a quite complicated structure derived from a combination of stamen and pistil components. It is sometimes helpful when thinking about the evolution of the pollinaria to first consider one of the more highly evolved systems and then later examine some of the less developed types. In Figs. 2a and 2b, pollinaria from *Phalaenopsis* are illustrated. The structure can be divided into three components. At one end is a sticky disk called the viscidium. This is the part that is attached to the vector. The viscidium is usually considered to have been derived from part of one of the stigmatic lobes. The glue on the disc is thought to be homologous with a modified stigmatic secretion (the glues produced by some orchids are extremely tenacious).

At the other end of the structure is a pair of pollen

4   A *Telipogon* species from high altitudes in Costa Rica. The central column resembles a fly mimic.

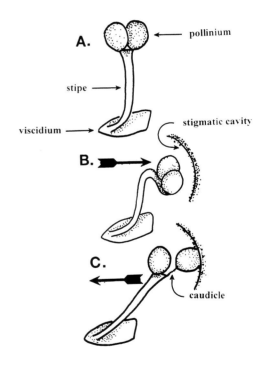

Fig. 2   Pollinarium of *Phalaenopsis lindenii*. **A**. Pollinarium freshly detached from the column. Three main parts are obvious, the basal sticky viscidium, an erect linear stipe and two terminal pollinia. **B**. In the air the stipe bends to assume the correct configuration to facilitate positioning the pollinia on the stigmatic surface. **C**. The vector moves away from the stigmatic cavity leaving one pollinium trapped. The caudicle is stretched until it breaks. Arrows represent direction of pollinator movement.

cans grows on roadsides, close to plants of *Lantana* and *Asclepias* (neither of which are orchids). All three species have red and yellow flowers that are favored by butterflies, but only the *Lantana* and *Asclepias* offer a nectar reward. The butterflies confuse the epidendrums with the other plants and, while probing and searching for the non-existent nectar, pollinate the flowers.

There is enormous diversity among species in the structure of the column; much of it tied to variations in the structure of the pollinarium. The pollinarium can be masses, known as pollinia. The pollinia are compact bodies containing an enormous number of pollen grains. In most other non-orchidaceous plants each stamen has an anther composed of two halves and each half is further subdivided into two cavities where pollen is produced. Primitive orchids would be expected to produce four pollinia and in fact that is what one finds. In more advanced cases the pollinia can be either subdivided to increase the number of pollen masses (e.g. *Laelia* has eight pollinia) or it can be reduced to two as in the case of the *Phalaenopsis* species in Fig. 2. Between the viscidium and the pollinia is a section of supporting tissue called the stipe, which is derived from a strip of columnar tissue. Between each pollinium and the stipe there is a short, relatively fragile section called the caudicle, which is usually derived from anther tissue. The viscidium and stipe are held in position by a beak of stigmatic tissue called the rostellum. In *Phalaenopsis*, after the pollinarium is removed, the stipe looses water as it dries up and bends into the correct position (Fig. 2b). This facilitates the placement of the pollinia into the stigmatic cavity. Once this occurs and the pollinia are held fast by the stigmatic 'glue', the structure tears apart between the pollinia and the stipe, leaving the latter still attached to the insect vector and the pollen in the female orifice.

Nearly all variations of these structures that could be imagined have already evolved. They range from primitive situations such as those found in *Vanilla*, where the viscidium as such does not exist and the vector merely receives a droplet of stigmatic glue onto which the pollen is deposited. A similar situation can be seen in *Epidendrum* where there is no discrete viscidium. By contrast there is an increase in complexity in the genus *Cattleya*, where there is a caudicle and an obvious rostellum. In many orchids the viscidium is differentiated into a sticky pad on one side and caudicles (or stipe) on the other side. Despite the complexity, there are many examples that show how the more complicated structures evolved. The process has been repeated on many, completely separate, occasions.

Getting pollen from one flower to another involves many factors. The effectiveness of doing this is male success. Unlike most other flowering plants, male success is an all-or-nothing event. Either one flower contributes all of its pollen towards the seed production of another flower or none of it gets to the right place. By contrast, we can judge female success by the number of fertile seed capsules that the plant produces. The same flowers can have different male and female success rates and within a species some plants may be better at being male or female. It stands to reason that not all of the pollen that a flower donates actually finds its way to the appropriate recipient. Some gets lost along the way. We have found, for example, that in the African orchid, *Aerangis verdickii* approximately 75% of the flowers are successful as males i.e. they give up their pollen, but only about 20% of the flowers make seed pods. More than two-thirds of the pollinaria never make it to the stigma of the next flower. While there are a number of studies on fruit set in orchids, there is much less data on male performance.

The fruit of an orchid can hold tens or even hundreds of thousands of seeds. The number of pollen grains deposited in the pollinia must equal that, but most probably they exceed the number of ovules. Pollination is an all-or-nothing event. Depending on the species involved it can take months for the pollen tubes to grow into the ovary and release sperm to fertilize the eggs. Some *Phalaenopsis* species appear to take at least three months for this to happen. Almost nothing is understood about the competitive events that take place in the ovary, as the pollen tubes vie for available eggs. We have counted nearly 50,000 pollen tubes in the ovary of *Aerangis verdickii* at a single moment!

Because the number of seeds produced is so great, each seed is microscopic and is only provided with a minimum of nutrient reserves. Consequently seed life is short, often no more than a few weeks or months. During that time the seed must land in the appropriate microhabitat where it can germinate. Germination requires invasion of the seed by a mycorrhizal fungus, which will provide essential nutrients during early development. The probability of a seed being lodged in a moist crevice on a branch and in the presence of the correct fungus is remote and the greater majority of the seed produced never germinate. Of those that do germinate, only a few ever reach reproductive maturity. It is essential therefore that plants produce enormous numbers of their seeds during their lives in order that a few might survive to continue the species. Not all plants succeed in contributing towards the next generation. The orchids are caught in a tight spiral of events. They must produce enormous numbers of seeds but in order to do that they cannot package much in the way of seed nutrient resources and therefore in order to increase chances of success they must produce even more seeds with even less nutrients. At the same time to ensure that the numbers of seeds can be produced the pollen must be packaged in pollinia, but this means that they must evolve precise pollination mechanisms. Interactions of these two parameters during natural selection have probably helped to ensure the rapid evolution and radiation of the family, producing the myriad forms for which the family is renowned.

Vegetative growth

There are several aspects of the growth forms of orchids that set them apart from other families of flowering plants. As with the flowers, much of this is not unique but there are combinations of features that tend to set them apart or are common within sections of the taxon.

Roots: The majority of orchids possess aerial roots and these have special adaptations that optimize their two main functions, clinging to branches or rocks and absorption of water and nutrients. The roots must deal with conflicting needs. Because they are exposed to the air they must be adapted to prevent water loss by evaporation to the surrounding air and at the same time facilitate the absorption of water into the root. The roots achieve this by having a multicellular layer of dead cells called a velamen. In mature velamen the cell contents are dead and the layer merely consists of cell walls. Cells making up the layer are not uniform but they may contain islands of differentiated cells that become visible on watering. This is especially noticeable in some of the African Angraecoids (such as the genus *Mystacidium*) after the roots have been wetted. After wetting these specialized areas are seen as lighter colored patches and they may reflect hydrofuge zones consistent with piping air into the roots. A variety of micro-organisms have been recorded from within the velamen and these include mycorrhizal fungi and blue-green algae. It has not been determined whether the latter contribute towards the nutrition of the host. The velamen is not unique to orchids but is also shared with a few species of other monocot families.

In other plants' roots there is an area behind the growing tip, which produces unicellular hairs that are used to absorb nutrients. Typically such root hairs are very rare in orchids, although multi-cellular hairs can be found in some terrestrial groups, particularly the Cypripedioideae and the Orchidoideae.

Many of the epiphytic orchids have chloroplasts in their roots and this is particularly noticeable in actively growing root tips; chloroplasts may also occur below the velamen on the exposed sides of the root. There appears to be a trend that has evolved independently, on several occasions, among the vandoid orchids where certain genera i.e. *Chilochista*, *Microcoelia*, etc., have lost their leaves and rely exclusively on their roots for photosynthesis. In most of those cases the roots also act as the main storage organs for water and nutrients and the stem becomes reduced as well. The proportion of root to shoot biomass can be very large. On the other hand, in saprophytic species such as *Eulophia longisepala*, the-

roots are reduced to small stubs, one to two cm long. As with other organ systems the Orchidaceae shows an enormous range and variation. In a few species, such as *Phalaenopsis stuartiana* and *P. philippinese*, the roots are flattened and ribbon shaped and the velamen takes on a metallic silvery sheen – the significance of this is unclear.

Tuberoids: Most orchids have thickened roots, when compared to other monocotyledonous plants where they are often thin and fibrous. In the Spiranthoid subfamily there is usually a mass of thickened roots, but in the Orchidoids the roots range from thickened tubers to a curious type of structure known as a tuberoid. Tuberoids contain a mixture of both root and stem anatomy and are unique to the orchids. They appear to have evolved as adaptations to dry seasons and are particularly well developed and common in Mediterranean climates, which have wet winters and hot dry summers. In those regions tuberoids allow the plants to survive in a dormant state. Tuberoids are also well adapted to tropical monsoon climates with their alternating wet and dry seasons. The success of these adaptations can be seen by the large number of species in some genera that possess these organs. One genus, *Habenaria*, is one of the largest of all orchid genera. Other successful genera include *Disa*, with probably more than 200 species, *Cynorchis*, a spectacularly diverse Malagasy genus and *Satyrium*. In addition countries such as Chile, South Africa and Southwestern Australia possess a myriad of tuberoid species in smaller taxa.

The tuberoid is usually a single bulbous organ with an apical bud at the dorsal end. This grows into a shoot, sometimes a single leaf, but more often a rosette that can elongate into a central terminal inflorescence. Mature tuberoids usually contain enough resources, not only to let the plant flower, but also sufficient to contribute sufficiently to allow the plants to produce a second tuberoid for the following season. If one were to dig up a plant in the middle of its growing cycle, one would find two tuberoids. The larger one will have developed during the previous year and will be supporting the current season's growth. By its side will be a smaller one, which is being built by the current shoot and with resources translocated from the older tuberoid. This behavior is typical of geophytes in other plant families, which have adaptations such as bulbs, corms and rhizomes that may have to persist over several seasons of drought.

Stems: Epiphytic orchids possess two main types of growth. There are monopodial orchids that continue to grow season after season with indeterminate stems and produce their flowers from a lateral outgrowth. Vandoid orchids exhibit this type of growth pattern. Sympodial orchids on the other hand have shoots or stems that complete their growth in a single season and then produce the following season's growth from a lateral bud. In sympodial orchids the inflorescence may be either terminal or lateral. Epidendroid orchids are sympodial. There are a few species that appear to be intermediate such as *Cymbidium suave*. In many of the sympodial orchids we find the evolution of pseudobulbs. These are thickened portions of stems that act as storage organs and have evolved into an enormous variety of sizes and shapes. Usually, above ground pseudobulbs are green and are capable of photosynthesis. In rare cases such as *Vanilla perrieri* and *V. roscheri*, there may be no leaves and the plant relies entirely upon its green stem for photosynthesis. In particularly xeric environments, the leaves may be deciduous for many months of the year and during that time the plant can be solely dependent on its pseudobulbs or roots for nutrients.

Leaves: Leaves are the main photosynthetic organs of most plants and that is also true of the majority of orchids. Orchid leaves come in a variety of shapes but can be grouped into three major types with a few exceptional unusual ones. There are thin textured, folded or plicate leaves best known from *Calanthe* and *Lycaste*, but also occurring in a wide variety of other genera. Then there are thick leathery leaves like those of *Cattleya* and many *Dendrobium* species. A few genera such as *Eulophia* may have some members with plicate leaves and others with leathery leaves. Leathery leaves are adaptations to xeric climates and usually last for several seasons, while plicate leaves are more mesic or are shed at the onset of the dry season. A third category contains fleshy succulent leaves such as those of the jewel orchids and many orchidoids, such as *Satyrium*. Among the most bizarre are leaves of the xeric Australian *Dendrobium* – orchids that range in shape from cylindrical whips to forms that approach the shapes of stunted gherkins. Epiphytic plants often suffer from a great deal of water stress unless they exist in Cloud Forests and the leaves have a range of adaptations to prevent water loss. These adaptations range from fattened succulent leaves used as water storage organs, to leathery cuticles needed to prevent evaporation. Thin-leafed species may become deciduous during dry seasons. Even some terrestrial orchids may have water storage areas of leaves. The leaves of both *Paphiopedilum* and most *Satyrium* species have upper layers of cells that are specially adapted to store water. In the latter case much of that moisture is probably shunted into the tuberoid at the end of the growing season.

Many of the terrestrial orchids have leaves with disruptive coloration i.e. patterns that allow the plants to blend in with their environment and presumably protect themselves from herbivores. The jewel orchids are a group of plants that have leaves with contrasting refractile veins. If the leaves are bronze then the veins glisten with a metallic golden sheen. The plants often nestle among the dead leaf litter on the forest floor and consequently are difficult to spot. Green leaves tend to have silver veins, which break up the contrast of the leaves against a background of grayish-white dead leaves. These patterns have developed independently in a number of genera from both the orchidoid and spiranthoid sub-families. Heart-shaped greenish blue leaves with silver veins can be found in *Holothrix aspersa* (from Southern Africa) and several species of *Corybas* (from Southeast Asia); both belong to the orchidoid alliance. Similarly sized and shaped leaves also occur in the North American spiranthoid, *Goodyera pubescens*.

Oeceoclades maculata is one of the most widespread of all orchid species in the world. It is found on all tropical continents and has leathery marbled leaves that make the plants difficult to discern among the dead vegetation, under the trees and shrubs where they prefer to grow. In Madagascar other related species of *Oeceoclades* have leaves with even more elaborate camouflage coloring.

Growth Patterns: Many orchids have stems that branch, or they make numerous offsets, which can produce enormous clumps. The stems can be elongated into thin rhizomes, which connect the various branches. Old clumps of *Paphiopedilum micranthum* can be nearly a meter across and consist of many individual growths. In time the individual parts of the plant (called ramets) may loose their connection and become separate entities. If the plant is in a situation where slippage occurs, as may be found on a steep slope, individuals may become widely separated. In another slipper orchid species, *Paphiopedilum druryi*, the rhizomes between growths can extend many meters from where they originated (Kumar, personal communication). Riparian orchids grow along riverbanks. Floods may tear parts of the bank loose and wash the plant downstream. It may eventually re-establish itself further away from the mother plant. Thornhill (1996) has not only observed this with *Epipactis gigantea* in Western North America but, by genotyping ramets along the edge of rivers, he was able to demonstrate genetically identical individuals established at a variety of points along the river bank considerable distances from each other.

In captivity many terrestrial species with tuberoids

can produce considerable clumps (e.g. *Habenaria rhodocheila* and *Stenoglottis fimbriata)*, but in the wild one almost never finds such large clusters of plants. This suggests that mortality among the various ramets must be quite high. Asexual reproduction is an effective means of perpetuating an individual, however the various herbivores with which the plants must contend in the wild must destroy many of the offshoots.

Orchid Seeds: Orchids have remarkable seeds. They are microscopic in size and even the largest seeds, such as those of *Disa uniflora*, only weigh a few millionths of a gram. The seed is essentially a ball of undifferentiated living cells, surrounded by a single layer of dead cells. There are no cotyledons. Orchids are considered to be monocots because their leaves have parallel veins and their flowers are based upon a trimerous pattern (the whorls each originally contained three parts). Developing seedlings of a few genera are said to have a vestigial cotyledon, but the distinctions between a cotyledon and the first real leaf can be very fine in a developing new seedling and are subject to interpretation. The cell walls of the testa (the seedcoat) can have a variety of thickenings. Perhaps the major function of the coat is not so much to protect the living cells inside but to create friction with the air and prevent the seed from falling to the ground too soon. The overall small size and lightweight nature of the seed also lends itself to buoyancy. Provided the seed manages to rise up into the air column it can be blown great distances. Some of the riverine orchids, such as *Disa uniflora*, and its close relatives appear to have seeds that are dispersed by water. Dressler (1993) discusses some 21 distinctly different types of seed in the orchid family.

If the seed lands in the correct microhabitat, and is invaded by the correct mycorrhizal fungi, it begins to swell and undergoes cell division. It then develops into a small turnip-shaped body called a protocorm. Epiphytic orchids tend to produce green protocorms but some terrestrial orchids produce achlorotic protocorms and are dependent on their symbiotic fungi for nutrition for extended periods of time. This phase can last a considerable time, often in excess of many months. The top of the protocorm differentiates into a series of embryonic leaves; while at the bottom are a series of hair-like rhizoids. The latter presumably have two functions; on the one hand they anchor the developing seedling, while on the other they aid in the absorption of nutrients. A stem develops at the base of the leaves and from this the first adventitious true roots will grow.

Orchids often take many years to reach maturity and flower, but there are a few exceptions to this rule. *Psygmorchis* (syn. *Oncidium pusillum)* lives on leaves and must be able to complete its life cycle during the life of the individual leaf that it lives upon. Several other genera are known as 'twig orchids', because they are nearly always found perched on small (and therefore presumably young) branches. Many species of *Comparettia* and *Rodriguezia* belong to this category. Among terrestrial orchids, such as *Cynorchis fastigiata*, seeds can germinate and produce a flowering mature plant within the space of a year.

CHAPTER 3

Orchids and their Ecology

We are abysmally ignorant of the ecology of tropical orchids. Nearly all attention has been focussed on their taxonomy, the distribution of orchid plants or how they are pollinated. We know very little about how they 'fit' into their environment, the way in which these plants manage themselves or their needs in the wild. Our ideas about the ecology of orchids are often based on the extrapolation of evidence derived from studies on other plant families.

To preserve and manage orchid species in the wild it is necessary to monitor the plants in question to see how well they are faring. In order to do this it is important to understand how the species is normally able to maintain itself in the natural state. Unfortunately, we have relatively little information on how orchid populations fit into and interact with those ecosystems in which they are an integral part. For example, we have little idea of what it costs an orchid plant to reproduce. How much energy is necessary to maintain the plant in a fit living condition and what proportion of its resources need to be set aside for it to become pollinated and what does it cost a plant to make a single seed? How many seeds does it need to produce to ensure the survival of a single offspring, which can reach maturity and flower? This must surely be the most important element in determining whether the population can be maintained at a constant level.

In plant and animal ecology the concept of 'metapopulation' presupposes that plants and animals occur as scattered patches or distinctly separated populations, which can interchange genetic material amongst themselves. An orchid species often exists as distinctly separate populations, which can interact genetically with each other to varying degrees. The gene pool of a population (the genetic material) can be changed by the arrival of seed or pollen from other populations. Not all of these populations are equivalent. Some populations (called sources) are more successful than others and may produce seeds that can found new populations or contribute to other distant populations, when pollinators carry pollen to those populations. Seeds from one group of plants can be disseminated to other populations and

thus change the gene pool of that other population. There are also less successful populations, called sinks, and these may sometimes go extinct. If a population is cut off from the other populations and there is no change of genetic material, it may change randomly with time. Metapopulation effects are important in maintaining genetic diversity and as a hedge against inbreeding. Therefore it is important to know how much gene flow normally occurs between isolated populations of orchids, if only one patch is to be maintained in a preserve. For conservation purposes it is important to identify and protect sources and not waste efforts trying to maintain natural sinks. But, almost none of this information is known for tropical orchids, although there are some studies on temperate orchids. The morphological differences which are often seen in isolated orchid populations suggests that there may be relatively little gene flow among populations and this itself could be important for understanding the rapid evolution of new orchid species.

Whether orchids grow perched on the branches of trees in tropical forests, or barely holding their leaves above the water in temperate marshy meadows, they are well adapted to survive in their own particular environment. If these environments become drastically changed (as occurs when a forest is felled or a swamp is drained) then the plants are faced with a crisis to which they cannot adapt and they will ultimately die.

There is no argument that the best way to preserve an orchid species is in the wild, in its normal and natural environment. But just fencing off an acre of forest or meadow is not sufficient to ensure the survival of a species. Ecosystems are complex interacting sets of species in specific environments and the ecosystem itself must be sufficient to maintain the orchid species in question. No organism can exist indefinitely in an ecological vacuum; they constantly interact with other members of the ecosystem. Some of these interactions will work to the detriment of the plant, but it will benefit from others. One obvious dependency that most orchids have is for their pollinators. Without the pollinators sexual reproduction would halt and the species will die out. There are, however, whole constellations of other organisms on which an orchid species may depend. These range from the host trees on which they perch, the lichens and mosses that provide microhabitats for their seed to germinate in and finally the microorganisms that play a role in the nutrition of the plant. It is often easier and cheaper to let nature provide those needs than to engineer or manage them for the plant that needs protection.

Most orchids only exist in a few localities and these sites are often outside large nature preserves. Small reserves tend to be fragile and require active management. But we cannot manage a reserve effectively unless we have a good understanding of the needs and requirements of the particular species that we want to save. This is the crux of the problem. In recent years, Ackerman and his co-workers have described reproductive success in several neo-tropical orchids and while that is a great start there is still much that needs to be discovered. Unfortunately for many, if not most orchid species, we may never understand them fully before they become extinct.

Epiphytes, lithophytes and geophytes

Orchids are often classified according to where they grow in the ecosystem. Species that are rooted in the ground like normal plants are often called geophytes or terrestrials, but most orchids in the tropics live perched on the branches of trees, high in the canopy of the forest. These plants are called epiphytes, which means that they live attached to other plants. Epiphytic orchids are not parasites on their host trees, their roots only take up nutrients resulting from decay in, or on, the bark layers of the branches where they grow. Some orchids grow on exposed rocks and their roots cling to the rock itself for support. These orchids are usually termed lithophytes, but they are also referred to as being rupiculous, both terms refer to plants occurring on rocks.

Epiphytes find themselves in an unusually harsh environment. High up in the canopy, water is only abundant when it rains. Even though it may rain regularly, there are often times when precipitation is reduced. In the tropics, although the air can be very humid, there is no conclusive evidence that orchids can avail themselves of this type of water. However, the high humidity retards the loss of water from the leaves, either by slowing transpiration or direct evaporation. Nearly all exposed epiphytic orchids tend to have heavily waxed leaves or a thick cuticle, which helps to conserve moisture (only the epiphytes of

5 Tree festooned with epiphytic orchids, mainly dendrobiums, Western Samoa (above).

6 Tree at the forest's edge with epiphytes, La Selva, Costa Rica (below).

7 A lithophytic *Bulbophyllum* species, Chimanimani Mountains in Zimbabwe (above).

8 A lithophytic *Cyrtorchis* species, southern KwaZulu-Natal, South Africa (below).

high mist forests seem to have mesic leaves). In addition plants may also possess swollen storage organs, where water and food products can be sequestered for times of need. The most conspicuous of these are the swollen stems, known as pseudobulbs. Where pseudobulbs are not present we find that the leaves themselves often act as storage organs. Epiphytic orchids share many of the same physiological characteristics that are found in desert succulents and cacti. Most of the orchids grown by hobbyists are epiphytes.

Lithophytes tend to live in the harshest environments, where water is often at a premium. In addition, on the exposed rock faces, which might have no more than a thin layer of lichen, surface temperatures can be hotter than those of tree branches, high off the ground. Lithophytes also have less available resources in the way of humus and detritus. In the lithophytic Australian dendrobiums, leaves are among the main storage organs

and they can take on a variety of weird shapes. The southern races of the African *Ansellia gigantea* have solved their humus problem by producing two kinds of roots. One type, which are not very branched, holds the plant firmly to the rocks, while the other is a finer, more wiry root that is heavily branched. These second type point vertically up into the air. Bits of dried leaves, twigs and dust get trapped in the roots, which then collect their own soil and compost. *Grammatophyllum* species in South-East Asia and *Cyrtopodium* species of the New World have a similar life style and show a remarkable degree of parallel or convergent evolution.

Tropical forest geophytes tend to live in shaded or sheltered areas, where water is usually not a problem. Often they occur on the forest floor itself. The majority of temperate species of orchid are geophytic, in some sense or another, and they can live in sunny bright areas, often growing in meadows or swamps. Among the best known of the geophytes are the slipper orchids. There are temperate species, which belong to the genus *Cypripedium* and live in the Northern Hemisphere, other genera such as the Asian *Paphiopedilum* and the American *Phragmipedium*, are found in the tropics. Paphiopedilums are among the most favored orchid plants and are grown by hobbyists all over the world. Although their habitats do vary, many are from very densely shaded forest floors and do well in cool shaded greenhouses, or even in the dimmer light inside some homes.

There is a tendency to reserve the term geophyte for orchids and other plants, which have underground storage organs that allow the plant to survive during harsh climatic seasons. For example, in Mediterranean climates the winters tend to be wet and this is the best time for growing. The summer is, by comparison, dry and the terrestrial orchids that live in those climates often resort to dormancy and the use of underground tuberoids, tubers and/or pseudobulbs to survive the unfavorable conditions.

There is a progression between these three types of life style, because occasionally geophytes can be found growing on trees. In many areas of the tropics, one can find epiphytes growing successfully along the sloping edges of road cuttings. The plants grow either on rocks or even in the ground, despite the fact that they normally grow on trees. Frequently after the forests have been cleared the road cuttings are the only places where one can find orchids. Fence posts or even telegraph poles are often utilized as 'trees' by orchids, especially at higher elevations.

Of the three lifestyles, it is the tropical epiphyte that is the most successful in terms of both biomass and numbers of species. In all of temperate North America there are probably only some 153 species of orchid (Dressler, 1981) and the majority of these are terrestrial, while the much smaller territory of Central America has several thousand species. The epiphytic species do not seem to have adapted so successfully to very cold climates. Among the New World epiphytes *Encyclia conopseum* extends the furthest north. Correll (1950) describes collecting *E. conopseum* from trees along the shore of Lake Waccamaw in North Carolina, where the plants were subjected to winter frosts. In the Old World, the most northern epiphytic species is *Dendrobium moniliforme*. This is found just north of Tokyo in sheltered places by the sea, where frosts are uncommon. In the colder regions there are several geophytes that are related to epiphytic species. These include species belonging to the genera *Pleione*, *Cymbidium*, *Liparis* and *Malaxis*. *Pleione* is an interesting example, for while some of the species are truly terrestrial there are other species, such as *P. praecox*, *P. humiliis* and *P. chunii*, which can be found growing as epiphytes, geophytes or even as lithophytes. The latter seem to grow on rocks among mosses and do not seem to have the xerophytic adaptations that we find in other lithophytes, such as *Dendrobium*.

Temperate orchid species

Many of the temperate species of orchid are geophytes that live either in grasslands, meadows or marshy wetlands. Others inhabit shady forest floors. Orchid hobbyists cultivate relatively few of these species. In Asia, the temperate orchids seem to be most appreciated. Many of the small cymbidiums are grown all over the Orient, for their scent or stylish leaves. The Japanese have made an art of cultivating many of their geophytes, such as *Poneorchis graminifolia* and *Cypripedium japonicum*, as pot plants. The Australian flora, particularly in those areas with a wet winter-dry summer climate, is rich in geophytes and here many species and even hybrids are cultivated.

In North America the orchids of the more arid regions of the country are, for the most part, confined to the sides of streams or seepage areas. Temperate marshy and boggy areas, especially those of a seasonal nature, seem to be rich in orchids. The vegetation assemblages that grow in these wet areas are among the most productive in the world, rivaling that of the tropical rain forests. It is unfortunate that the bogs also harbor many insect pests and man has made a conscientious effort, through the recent centuries, to drain as many bogs and marshes as possible. These wetland ecosystems are now recognized as being among the most critically

9   Mauve spikes of a *Dactylorhiza* species flowering in a glade, England (above).

10   *Satyrium membranaceum*, a terrestrial geophyte, South Africa (below).

endangered in the world. Orchids can be significant members of the wetland communities and Correll (1950) records that they can be the dominant flowering plants in the community. He recorded 14 species and varieties of orchid in Henderson County in North Carolina, growing in a *Sphagnum* bog of only one-acre in extent. In eastern Wisconsin, Fuller collected twenty species in a single Tamarack swamp. Frequently, when the orchids are found, they are in large numbers. *Cypripedium regina* occurs in colonies of over a thousand individuals and Correll recorded hundreds of plants of *Habenaria flava* in alluvial woodlands, where he thought that orchids were the principle herbaceous species. I have seen colonies of *Cypripedium calceolus* var. *pubescens* interspersed with *Orchis rotundifolia*, in *Sphagnum* bogs of Western Alberta, where we counted over 76 plants in 30 square meters.

Many temperate geophytic orchids are meadow plants, growing among low grasses and other forbs. In Europe and temperate Asia, calcareous grassland or open scrub is often very rich in species. A single one-acre slope in Crete yielded 22 species of orchid in five genera; ten of the species belonged to the single genus *Ophrys*. In Southern Africa orchids of the genera *Eulophia*, *Satyrium* and some of *Disa*, occur in association with other meadow plants. While they can occur in dense colonies, their distribution is rather disjunct, meaning that the plants occur in patches often separated from each other by great distances, and therefore they cannot really be classed as dominant parts of the vegetation.

Orchid distributions

Not all species are distributed in nature the same way. Some are common and others are rare. In a conservation sense rare species are at far greater risk than common species because their smaller numbers make them more vulnerable to chance events that can wipe out the entire species. Population numbers are also reduced by anthropogenic factors. Man destroys available habitat or over collects some species. However there are a myriad of other ways that man can affect species numbers, ranging from death by pollution to unintentionally disturbing other essential components of the community. Besides man induced problems there are also species that are naturally rare. Ecologists have enumerated seven different forms of natural rarity. At one end of the scale are species only known from one or a few small discrete populations and at the other end of the spectrum are species that are so widely dispersed that one hardly ever encounters them and when one does they may exist as single individuals. In the first category are the many orchids we shall discuss below. At the other end are species such as *Eulophia odontoglossa* and *E. orthoplectra*, which are widespread over a continent but never occur together in very great numbers.

It is a truism for most tropical animal and plant species that there are more rare than common species and this is the case for orchids as well. If one collects information on the number of different places where a particular species has been found, one finds that most orchid species have only been recorded from a single locality and nearly three-quarters of the species are known from three or fewer sites (Koopowitz, 1992). Distribution profiles plot the number of species in a group known from single, two, three and more sites. These profiles allow one to compare different group. When we compared the profile of epiphytic orchids with that of terrestrial species, for Central and East Africa, we found that epiphytes have proportionately more single site species than terrestrial orchids (Koopowitz, *et al.*, 1994), in other words terrestrial orchids tend to have more populations than epiphytic orchids. The greater endemism for epiphytes should place them at higher risk of than terrestrials. This does not mean that grassland species are safe. Heather Campbell (personal communication) suggests that many of the savanna species from East Africa have become increasingly rare due to the conversion of those grasslands for agricultural uses. In some groups of epiphytes such as Dracula, (Koopowitz, *et al.*, 1993), which has particularly high levels of endemism, as many as three-quarters of the species are only known from a single locality. Wiping out the forest patch where they occur will mean that species is doomed to extinction.

At the other extreme there are a handful of weedy orchid species, which appear to have cosmopolitan distributions. There are several that occur naturally in nearly all parts of the tropics and others that have followed man. The terrestrial species, *Eulophia alta* and *Oeceoclades maculata*, are found in the tropical Americas and tropical Africa, while the latter also grows in Madagascar. The tropical epiphyte, *Polystachya concreta*, is known from South and Central America, Africa, Madagascar, mainland Asia and the Southeast Asian islands. *Eulophia puchra*, is found in Central Africa, Madagascar, Southeast Asia, the islands of the South-west Pacific and Australia. Three tropical species *Phaius tankervilliae*, *Spathoglottis plicata* and *Arundinaria graminifolia* have followed man from Southeast Asia across the Pacific and established themselves as roadside weeds. *Spathoglottis plicata* has also escaped in East Africa. What makes these so successful is the fact that they are either self-pollinating or able to accept a variety on non-specialist insect pollinators. In temperate climates *Epipactis helleborine*, a European species, has established itself as a North American weed. I have seen it growing in cracks in the sidewalks of Toronto and in also in the wilds of California.

Reasons for rarity

There are several natural reasons for rarity and small population size, beside the fact that populations could be reduced by mans' perturbations. Small populations could exist because one is dealing with a newly evolved species that has not had enough time to spread. Conversely the population could be reduced in size because the species is naturally proceeding towards extinction. Some species are restricted by substrate preferences, such as aspect (which side of a slope faces the sun) or the presence of a rain shadow, which can also limit their distribution. Besides being ecologically restricted by many edaphic factors, there are also biological factors such as mycorrhizal associations or a pollination syndrome that can limit a species occurrence.

Understanding the forests

There is more to a tropical forest than the trees. The forests that straddle the equatorial regions of the globe are intricate networks of living organisms existing in a unique equilibrium with the physical environment of the region. It is ironic that only now, at the start of the 21st century, as the world's tropical forests are being decimated and destroyed, that biologists have started to appreciate and understand the multidimensional ecology of the forests.

Tropical forests are very different from temperate forests. Both, from the outside, appear to be lush but closer examination reveals that temperate forests are only made up of a relatively small number of different tree species, sometimes only one, whereas the tropical forests comprise an almost unimaginable array of different species. According to some scientists more species of tree have been counted on a single mountain in the Philippines than all the tree species in the whole of the United States. In tropical American forests the numbers of tree species per hectare can be over 300. Here the diversity of tropical trees is mirrored by the diversity of other plant species that live in association with them. If temperate forests can be likened to a lawn with a few dandelions and a moth or two, then a tropical forest is a wild meadow with myriad different flowers and butterflies.

A tropical forest ecosystem is similar to an orb spider web. Imagine walking into your garden one morning and there, between two shrubs, is strung a newly spun web. It is not only a thing of beauty and symmetry but also a finely engineered functional construction perfectly designed to do its job. A spider web is built upon a few major strong dry threads that hold a radiating series of guy spoke lines that are also dry. Festooned and attached to these radii is a spiral of finer silky thread, which in turn carries regularly spaced and evenly sized droplets of sticky glue. An orb web is two-dimensional and forests are much more complex, but nevertheless our web will illustrate some important concepts.

How much of the web would one have to damage before the entire structure collapses in an ungainly mess? Certainly one could cut many of the finer strands without affecting the whole. Sever one or two of the radii and the web can still catch insects. Cut three or four radii and a section will collapse, yet except for a blank space the structure will retain much of its integrity and still be able to ensnare prey. However, if a major support is damaged then the web will be lost. On the other hand, if one were carefully, to spray the web with glue solvent the structure would retain its apparent integrity but still be totally useless. In a tropical forest the trees are the major supporting radii and spokes, but it is the festooning assemblage of both animals and plants, which make up the essential 'glue' that gives the ecosystem its functional integrity. These organisms include lianas and moss, ferns and creepers, the aroids, the bromeliads, the fungi, the myriad insects and many birds and the orchids. As we cut down the trees in the tropics and they fall, one by one, with ever-increasing speed, the forests collapse and with them will disappear, forever, the greatest diversity of life known on this planet.

Replacing the tropical forests with a man-managed plantation of timber trees is the same as trying to replace a spider's web with a strip of flypaper. A plantation in the tropics does not support the diversity of life found in a natural virgin forest.

Energy flow in forests

The plants and trees of forests trap the energy of the sun by means of photosynthesis and package that energy in a variety of organic molecules, the simplest being perhaps the sugars. Later on the energy in the sugars is used to drive a large number of additional chemical reactions – many of which are used to produce other more complex molecules.

In temperate forests when the trees die or their leaves fall, the organic matter is turned into humus that builds up in the soil. The organic matter can accumulate in the soil for years, if not decades and centuries. It becomes a bank of energy that can be tapped decades later when fungi and other microorganisms break down the humus. In moist, warm, tropical forests, on the other hand, once an organism or part of the organism dies it is very quickly converted back to smaller molecules, many of which are rapidly absorbed and taken up by other organisms. An entire tree can be reabsorbed in a matter of months. One does not often find the build up and reservoir of organic matter in the soil of tropical forests that one gets in temperate forests. In the wet tropical forests, the branches form a platform upon which the epiphytes grow. The bark supports a variety of mosses, ferns and orchids, etc. These in turn catch detritus, bits of leaves, dust and, together with fungi and other microscopic bits of life, form a layer of humus on the branch. Small animals, primarily arthropods, live in the humus layer and work it further. While all trees eventually do die in their entirety, frequently only bits of them are lost. This happens when leaves are dropped or new layers of bark sloughed off. Very often small or larger branches are broken off the tree. Wind, heavy rainstorms and animal activity are the usual causes.

In tropical forests these fallen twigs or branches may have orchids still attached to them. It is quite common to find many broken branches and their attendant orchids forming a considerable layer mixed into the litter on the forest floor. One of the common fates of tropical orchids is to fall off onto the ground and that may be the main cause of orchid death for mature orchid plants. While we have not measured this, being eaten by a herbivore is a fairly rare occurrence for wild mature orchids. Presumably their hard leathery leaves, often considered as adaptations against desiccation, are also an effective protection against many arboreal herbivores. We have seen more orchid biomass littered on the ground, in neo-tropic and African forests, than parts of leaves lost to insect or other damage. The fate of an orchid on the ground is usually death, the result of falling into the litter and then slowly dying among the other rotting forest debris.

Recycling in the tropics is so fast and important that some trees actually produce roots from their branches that course through their own decaying bark, ready to reabsorb the organic matter layered on their branches as soon as it becomes available. There is fierce competition for the meager supplies and the trees have to fight the epiphytes for a share of the forest's available assets. It is ironic that the lush tropical forests, that seem to carry an overabundance of life, are caught in a tight spiral forced to recycle resources. When a forest is cleared away, one also loses the major part of the organic matter of the forest. Tropical soils often only have a limited fertility, the soil is degraded and its usefulness lost after the forest has been cut. In the tropics, unlike the temperate regions, decomposition is very rapid and nutrients are continuously recycled through the living organisms. This is why many tropical soils are nutrient poor and virgin soil will only support one or two years of crops.

Inorganic nutrients such as salts and metals can be rare and limiting nutrients in forests and it is important that these be continuously recycled. There are several ways this recycling happens. The tree can drop leaves or branches, returning those components to the soil but there is another way. When it rains, leaves leak solutes and these run down the branches or fall directly to the soil as the water drips off the leaves. Decaying leaves also release their component parts, which can be absorbed by the same tree. By catching leaves and siphoning off dissolved salts from the rainwater by their root systems, epiphytes are able to subvert some of these nutrients for their own use. They have in fact been called "nutritional pirates" (Benzing, 1980), stealing from the host trees. Some of the epiphytes, such as mosses, also leak nutrients, sugars and complex organic molecules that run down the bark and feed the tree and possibly other epiphytes as well. Orchid plants need appreciable quantities of nitrogen, potassium and phosphate to grow and how this is achieved by a plant sitting on a branch twenty feet above the ground becomes an interesting problem, which is not easily understood. Many epiphytic orchids have their roots hanging directly in the air. Other species may have clinging, but bare roots, exposed on the bark, not organs rummaging through a fertile 'garden' of mosses, lichen and decomposed bark. In both cases, there is little chance to absorb nutrients released from decaying material from the branches. The best that they can hope for are nutrients in rainwater running down the branches. We have measured the dissolved charged ions in water collected from leaves or branches in a forest in Zimbabwe and found that levels ranged from between 30 and 70 parts per million (Koopowitz and Aubry, unpublished).

Eventually when the epiphytes or their parts die, they in turn decompose and their nutrients become available to other living beings. The numbers of epiphytes growing in the canopy of a forest is substantial and they add in a very real sense to the forest's economy. In a 10 km² or section of Amazonian rain forest there can be between 300 to 750 different species of trees, with an equal number of non-tree higher plant species. In the neo-tropics one quarter of all plants in natural habitats are epiphytes (Gentry, 1990).

Populations

We can think of orchid populations as comprising a number of individuals, growing in an association that can potentially interact with each other for reproduction. These populations can be arranged in a number of ways and these will have important consequences for conservation. At one end of the spectrum will be species where all of the members may be found in a single population with only a limited number of individuals. Such species are relatively common in the orchid family. At the other end of the spectrum are species that are never found in concentrations, but are thinly spread over vast areas. We have little information that shows exactly how large orchid populations can get, but the number of individuals may be surprisingly large. *Aerangis verdickii* seems to be found in small, localized areas, with five to six hundred plants in each local population (Koopowitz, unpublished), which are scattered several kilometers apart. *Paphiopedilum sanderianum* is also known from small discrete populations of approximately 100 plants each and separated from adjacent populations by 10 or so kilometers (Rogers *et al.*, 1998). Cribb (personal communication) reports that in China *P. micranthum* and *P. malipoense* occur in populations with less than ten to over a thousand plants, separated from each other by one to fifty kilometers. On the other hand, populations can also attain enormous size. Ruschi (1986) reports the results of a 1942–43 survey of orchids in the São Miguel swamp in Espirito Santo (Brazil) where 253,168 plants of *Cattleya warnerii* and 387,216 individuals of *C. harrisoniana* were collected. These plants were noted in a portion of the swamp that was only 350,000 square meters in extent, or put another way, approximately one third of a square kilometer!

Orchids and biodiversity

It is in the tropics that orchids come into their own in terms of biodiversity. Where people have actually counted the numbers of plant species for flowering plant families in samples of tropical forests they usually find that it is often the orchid family that has the largest number of species. The late Alwyn Gentry (1990) compared the floristics (numbers of plant species) for several neo-tropical rainforests. He noted that La Selva, a famous lowland forest reserve in Costa Rica, contained 114 different species from the Orchidaceae but the largest tree family, the Leguminosae, had only 79 species. On Barro Colorado, a biological reserve and study area in Lake Gatun, Panama, there were 90 species of orchid and 112 species of legumes. There are exceptions. In Reserve Ducke, a central Amazonian forest, there are only 24 species of orchid and that family ranks thirteenth in regards to richness (Prance, 1990). But, even there, orchids dominate the epiphyte biodiversity. The fact that orchids are so successful in evolutionary terms and that the family has the greatest diversity of species, among the flowering plants, itself suggests that they play an important role in those ecosystems where they abound.

The role of orchids in forests

Orchid plants are not merely fabulously beautiful or bizarre creatures that grow in tropical forests; they also play an integral part in the functioning ecosystem of the forests. It may not be apparent that epiphytes play an important role in tropical forest ecology, but they do fulfil a variety of different functions. In their photosynthesis they contribute to the overall carbon fixation of the forest. Converting carbon dioxide into sugars and other molecules, they add to the organic wealth of the forest. In addition, epiphytes provide both food and shelter for animals.

Many orchids secrete droplets of sugar solution, especially from the flower stalks. These are collected by ants, which in return protect the developing buds and flowers from other animals that might browse or damage them. Of course, other insects or browsers, by eating parts of the epiphyte are gaining organic matter produced by the host, which then becomes part of the cycle too. A number of orchids, in the tropical Americas (such as *Schomburgkia* species) have hollow stems, which provide nesting sites for ants. Even orchids that do not provide constructed shelters can have colonies of ants and other biting insects living among their roots, as almost any orchid collector can vouch. Ants are very important components in the tropical ecosystems. Despite their small individual size, they occur in astronomical numbers. A myrmecologist (ant specialist) once collected 800 ants of 50 different species from only one square meter of forest floor litter. Imagine how many ants occur to the hectare! The biomass of ants and termites accounts for the major proportion of animal biomass in a tropical forest. These small insects outweigh both the birds and mammals combined.

Orchid seeds and fungi

The germination of orchid seed requires the presence of a mycorrhizal fungus. This is a fungus that invades the developing seed and sets up a symbiosis with it. It is generally thought that the fungus provides several important nutrients that are essential for the growth of the developing seed. Thus, in order for a seed to germinate in the wild, it must be blown so that it lodges against a branch and there must be a nearby living fungus of the correct species. The fungus invades the tissue of the embryo and eventually sets up residence within the protocorm (the developmental stage of the orchid before leaves, and roots are produced). It appears that there may only be a limited number of fungal species that can act as mycorrhiza (the term given to this type of fungus). Two factors, becoming lodged on a branch and being in the presence of the correct fungus probably accounts for the high mortality of orchid seed. Parasitic fungi probably invade and devour much of the seed. The probability of the favorable juxtaposition of these two factors accounts for why orchids have evolved a system that needs to produce thousands of seeds in a fruit. If an orchid plant is reproductive for 25 years, and produces only one seed capsule a year it will, during its lifetime, produce somewhere between a quarter of a million and two and one half million seeds. The fact that the world is not covered with wall to wall orchids demonstrates the enormous mortality of the seed. The need to produce such vast quantities of seed has also driven the evolution of bizarre and intricate pollination mechanisms for which the orchids are renowned.

It does not take much of a breeze to get orchid seed carried away by air currents. A hundred species of orchid are found in Samoa, all are related to or identical to New Guinea species. In the western part of the United States, *Epipactis gigantea* populations are always found associated with water. These places range from springs at the bottom of cliffs along the beach, to margins of ponds in desert oases, the edges of strongly flowing rivers, to still bogs and even the margin of hot springs in colder climates like British Columbia. The one common thread is water. In order to achieve this distribution the entire western portion of the continent must have been blanketed with a fall of orchid seed and only a small percentage that fortuitously fell in the right places could establish. *Epipactis gigantea* has a European cousin *E. hellebore*. About 200 years ago one of these plants was carried by settlers, or with their produce, to the northeastern parts of Canada. It took less than two centuries for the plants to make their way westwards to California. And that is in the opposite direction of the wind in jet stream. It is easy to see how new, isolated, populations can become established. This is borne out by those other orchid species that have managed to establish themselves on Pacific islands, hundreds or even thousands of miles from their nearest neighbor.

There is an important concept from the mortality factor that needs to be considered for conservation. Not all the seeds in a pod are equal. They all have different combinations of the genes inherited from their parents. Normally natural selection determines that the majority of those combinations will not survive. The very few that survive to maturity are adapted to a variety of factors and are best suited to their environment. These survivors are individuals that have successfully passed through the filter of natural selection. Under artificial conditions the rigors faced by the seeds and seedlings

are relaxed and most can grow up to sexual maturity. This underscores why it is so difficult to re-establish a species in the wild after it has been in artificial cultivation for a while. In fact a surviving artificially propagated population is merely a hollow image of reality. Of course, one might argue that it is a case of 'half a loaf is better than none at all'.

Terrestrial orchids seem more closely tied to their mycorrhizal (fungal) symbionts than the epiphytic species. Epiphytic orchids were the first orchids where we developed methods for germinating the seeds in the absence of the fungus. Only recently have similar methods been developed for terrestrial species. When one looks at mature plants, one finds that most temperate region terrestrial orchid species maintain an association with a fungus symbiont. However, the few studies that have been carried out on tropical epiphytes indicate that mycorrhiza are quite rare in mature orchid plants (Richardson *et al.*, 1993). It may be that tropical epiphytes lose their fungi after the seedlings become large enough. We need more studies on the interactions of tropical orchids and their fungi.

More orchid interactions

The way that orchids are pollinated and their interactions with pollinating insects, birds and bats have fascinated scientists and laymen alike for centuries. Darwin wrote a book on the subject, probably one of the most

11   An unidentified *Encyclia* species from very high altitudes in the Cerro de la Muerta, Costa Rica, displaying red flowers that are typical of humming bird pollinated flowers.

readable of his many and sometimes ponderous works, and even today many scientists still investigate the various contrivances by which orchids are pollinated. If a species of orchid depends on a single species of animal (the 'vector') for its pollination then if that vector disappeared the orchid would also be doomed. In only a few cases would the demise of the orchid threaten the vector; in other words, the orchids are more dependent on their pollinators than the pollinators are on the flowers. There are many remarkable instances where orchid flowers have evolved intricate mechanisms to attract and guide their pollinators. That subject has been the topic of several books but we might look at a few fascinating examples.

The genus *Stanhopea* has large, bizarre blotched flowers that are short lived. They hang down from the branches below the plants and the flowers themselves dangle in the air, where the breeze can pick up their heady scent and waft it through the forest. Each species produces its own typical scent and is visited by one species of bee. Many of these bees are wonderful creatures with a burnished metallic sheen of green or blue. Taxonomists have given the bees euphonious names, such as *Eulaema, Euplusia* and *Euglossa*. As a group they are called the Euglossine bees. Darting about the forest the male bees become enticed by the scent of the *Stanhopea* and many other related genera. They land on the flowers and then engage in some curious behavior. The bees scratch and rip at the scented parts of the flower and in the process appear to become intoxicated. Their tarsi (feet) have special pads that absorb the scent. Only the male bees engage in the scratching behavior. How the bees actually use the scent is not known although many hypotheses have been put forward to account for the selective advantage of this behavior. It has been suggested that the scent might act as some kind of vital chemical rather like a vitamin, or perhaps it could be used to mark territories or is even chemically changed and used as a pheromone to attract the female bees. Whatever the scent's function, the bees, while intoxicated, are used by the flower to effect pollination. Each species of bee appears to be specific to one species of orchid. If the bees must have the flower scents for their own survival then both the species appear to be mutually dependent on one another. Natural hybrids are found within these groups of orchids so one must presume that the bees do make occasional mistakes. However, it is likely that if either the bees or orchids become extinct the other will follow too.

A feel for the inter-relationship of the species in an ecosystem can be obtained by considering the following.

Brazil-nut trees are not cultivated, but the nuts are harvested from wild forest trees. The same Euglossine bees we have discussed above also pollinate Brazil-nut flowers. Peccaries (wild pigs) feed on Brazil-nuts but they are rather messy feeders and in the process of eating, tend to trample and bury some of the nuts. These in turn grow and produce new trees. If the loss of the orchid species leads to the loss of the bees then Brazil-nuts will stop reproducing and a major peccary food source dries up. Thus the loss of an orchid could jeopardize the fate of a pig species.

Perhaps the most bizarre and best known pollination mechanism is that of pseudo-copulation. While this has evolved independently on several occasions in the tropics and temperate regions, it is best studied in the temperate European species of *Ophrys*. In this genus of terrestrial orchid, each species has a labellum that mimics the shape of an insect (a solitary bee or wasp). The flowers only attract male insects and they do this by secreting a chemical scent or pheromone that closely resembles the pheromones produced by receptive females. The males visit the flowers and actually attempt to copulate with the flowers' labellum, which has patterns and hairs that resemble a bee's body. During this process pollen is received or deposited on the stigmatic surface. Generally, one species of *Ophrys* is visited by its own species of insect. They seem to be able to distinguish between different *Ophrys* species by the coloration, shape and positioning of the hairs on the labellum. The males are, however, able to distinguish between the flowers and the real females, because they will select the female wasps in preference to the flowers, if given a choice. Nature is a two-way street and while it is obvious what the orchids derive from the pollinator it was not at first clear what benefits the insect species received from this peculiar relationship. Female insects, generally, only mate once. If a male insect is to be successful in passing his genes along to the next generation he has to be effective at mating. Like so many things in life practice makes perfect. The orchids flower about two weeks before the female insects emerge. During this time the males flit around the fields of orchids practicing! Some of the insect mimicry involved with pseudo-copulation is remarkable. The Central American genera *Telipogon* and *Trichoceros* have fly mimics formed from the base of the labellum and column, which can hardly be distinguished from real flies.

The bias in orchid distribution profiles towards large numbers of rare species is probably related to their reliance on specific insect species. If one compares the distribution profiles of tropical flowering plants with those of tropical spore-bearing plants (which are not dependent on animals for their reproduction) one finds that the spore-bearing plants have significantly less endemism than is true for insect and bird pollinated species (Koopowitz, *et al.*, 1997).

Our obsession with pollination syndromes tends to distract us from the other kinds of interactions that go on between orchids and their different partners in the community. For several years I have studied a population of *Aerangis verdickii*, a pretty epiphytic orchid which grows in dry forests near Harare, Zimbabwe. These flowers have the typical long nectaries of the taxon, measuring some 14 to 15 cm long, and only half-filled with nectar to reward the hawk moths that pollinate them. There is a quite large weaver ant, a *Polyrachis* species, which patrols the trees and their epiphytes in the forest. In dry years the ants rob the flowers of nectar within a day of opening, but in wet seasons, when there is abundant moisture, relatively few of the flowers get robbed. In the wet years the ants seem as plentiful and active as in the dry years. During dry years, on an average, approximately 20% of the flowers make seed pods but in a wet year as many as 63% of the flowers may produce fruits. We think that *Aerangis* provides an important liquid and food source for the ants in stressful conditions, but this in turn depresses the orchids' fecundity, although not to the level that jeopardizes the orchid's ultimate existence. In one dry year, not only were the ants stealing nectar, but also during the first evening that the flowers were open another predator ate most of the tepals. That year pollination success was half of that found in other dry years. It is actually quite unusual to find undamaged flowers for most orchid species in the wild. While an animal may not be totally reliant on a particular plant species for its survival, utilizing some of the plant's resources may give the animal an edge. This may enable it to survive despite other disasters, which could otherwise have spelt its death.

This brings us to a more general point about the animals' dependence upon the plants in the ecosystem. There are many species of animal for each species of plant. Exactly, how many animals per plant is not known but while there are probably no more than 300,000 different species of plants (of which perhaps 30,000 are orchid species) we think there are at least as many as five to ten million or (even more) species of animal. The vast majority of animals are insects. On average each species of plant provides for 15 to 30 animal species (in reality some plants, such as the European oaks, harbor hundreds or thousands of insects, while others harbor few). We can also assume that the extinction of a single species of plant will also lead to the loss of several animal species. Does this mean that if some little insignificant orchid species disappears, it may take with it an entire constellation of animal species? We don't really know.

Reproductive costs

There is an entire body of knowledge concerned with how much effort is put into reproduction and how much is required merely to maintain a plant in its vegetative state. A plant must also be able to grow vegetatively. Successful reproduction actually takes quite a lot out of a plant. Primach and Hall (1990) found that if *Cypripedium acaule* was pollinated and produced a pod, it would still flower the following year. However, if the plant's flower was pollinated again it might then be several years before the plant recovered enough to flower a further time. We have noted two tropical orchids, *Aerangis verdickii* and *Paphiopedilum sanderianum*, which are relatively successful at producing seed capsules. After studying them we found that only about two-thirds of the adult plants flower each year, suggesting that on the average they rest for one in every three years. We do not know what the situation is for other tropical orchids. For plants of other families we do know that plants may abort seeds or entire pods if too many flowers are pollinated.

Most orchid studies suggest that less than ten percent of the flowers usually make seed capsules, and this is normally due to a lack of pollinators, rather than fruit abortion. However, only a handful of the 25–30,000 orchid species have been studied. When we hand-pollinated all the flowers on several *Aerangis verdickii* plants we found that they did one of two things. If all the flowers produced mature fruits then the plant did not flower during the following season. Some plants aborted most of the fruits and these orchids did flower during the following year. Reproduction was clearly imposing a cost on the plant, but they had some flexibility in how they dealt with the problem.

Orchid demography

If we want to conserve orchids in nature reserves then we need to have some way of measuring the health of the population in the reserve. That can only be done if one already has an understanding of the population biology of the particular orchid species under natural conditions. Unfortunately we have little information about those aspects of tropical orchid life and certainly not enough is known to allow one to draw broad generalizations on which one can base actual conservation practice. We need basic knowledge about the age structure of natural populations, including how long plants can live and what is the mortality of different stages. We need to appreciate how numbers of individuals in a population fluctuate in nature and that can take decades to determine. We don't really know how new populations of orchids are founded. Some evidence from investigations of the genetic structure of isolated populations of the temperate *Epipactis gigantea* suggests that there is more variation between, rather than within populations (Thornhill, 1996). This indicates that there is little or no gene flow between populations and that they may only have one or two founding members. Is this true of tropical orchids too? The age structure of epiphytic orchid populations has received almost no attention. Are new individuals added gradually and continuously to the population or are there lucky batches of seed that contribute a substantial number of new plants all at once? Our observations on *Aerangis verdickii* in Zimbabwe suggest that the latter might be the case. There is a need to understand recruitment into wild populations in a forest reserve.

It is also important to understand to what degree two separate populations of the same species normally interact with each. There are two ways that different populations might influence each other. Pollinators can carry pollen from one population to another or seed from one population could become established in the other. The net result either way is the possible influx of new genes into the population. The importance of this is that gene flow promotes vigor and decreases the possibility of inbreeding depression and drift. Drift refers to changes in the gene pool merely due to random chance and in the absence of natural selection. Some scientists believe that much of the variation and production of new species that we find in orchids can be ascribed to drift, involving small isolated orchid populations. But there is little direct evidence for this. Somebody needs to go out and look.

In most orchids with widely spread populations the probability of a new seedling being established from a seed source outside of the population is remote. The possibility of the pollinator carrying in new pollen is dependent on the type of pollinator and the distance between the populations. Nilsson and his coworkers (1992) carried out a very ingenious experiment in Madagascar. They glued a small microdot, carrying coded information, onto the pollinia of *Aerangis ellisii* and then retrieved the microdots after pollination. From this, they could determine the site of the pollen donor. They found that the vast majority of the pollen traveled no more than five meters but that there was a small, but appreciable fraction, which must have come from a population outside of the study area. Other plant studies suggest that very low levels of gene flow are sufficient to maintain gene pool variation and this may well be sufficient for orchids too. Unfortunately the Nilsson experiment is only one case and needs to be repeated with other orchid species and genera. In this way we can determine if there are similar patterns of gene flow, which can be applied to all orchids in general.

Conservation and ecology

If we are to manage orchid populations and preserve them in the wild then we need to be able to understand them and their needs in some detail. Orchid populations can be ephemeral, especially populations that are sinks. We know nothing about the longevity of populations in the wild and this is of vital importance in reserve design.

Much of the information that we need is of a simple nature, it is easy to collect and does not require sophisticated apparatus or facilities. Following populations for several years and counting their components is relatively easy to do and it and can be carried out by nearly anyone with a minimum of training or instruction. Yet, we have almost none of this sort of data for wild tropical orchids and it is needed if we are to actively monitor and protect orchid species in the wild.

It is time for orchid biologists to start gathering the information that we need to carry out effective conservation.

CHAPTER 4

Forests and Deforestation

Because most orchid species are epiphytic their distribution is intimately associated with the fate of tropical forests. For the last half-century the world's forests have been cut at an alarming rate and, as the area of forest is reduced, their associated flora and fauna become depleted. It is unlikely that all the forests will be lost, but the forested lands held as heritage for the next generation will be a small percentage of their former glory and even these remnants will not be untouched by the hand of man. In 1995 the tropical and sub-tropical forested area of the earth was estimated to be just shy of 1,727 million hectares (ha). Between the years 1990 and 1995 the world lost about 13.7 million ha each year. Tropical rainforests are now approximately half of their original extent and continue to shrink at an appreciable rate. The topics of deforestation and the state of the world's rain forests could fill several volumes. Here we will try and summarize the current state of affairs.

Some terms

Tropical rainforests are usually closed forests, which means that the trees form a continuous layer, as opposed to open forests that may have patches of trees interspersed with savanna. Closed forests have a continuous canopy or layer of branches that may or may not be stratified into distinct layers. Rainforests grow where there is abundant rainfall throughout the year, usually in the order of at least 100 mm per month. Where rainfall drops below 60 mm per month for several months, seasonal or monsoon forests grow. This tropical forest often contains trees that are deciduous during the dry season. The two kinds of forest can grade into each other and the term tropical moist forest is used to include both types. Orchids are found in all kinds of forest but often attain greater species diversity in rain forests, especially those that are at higher altitudes. Most attention has been paid to the plight of rain forest, but people are usually unaware that tropical dry forests face problems of equal magnitude.

A short history of tropical forests

Over the history of the earth its forested lands have changed following the natural climatic swings of the globe. Until comparatively recently tropical forests covered some 14% of the total land surface. It is now estimated that this coverage has been reduced to less than half of the original amount. The forests contain about 60% of the planet's animal and plant species but a much greater portion of the world's orchid species. The future of the world's orchids therefore rests upon the fate of the forests.

No one is exactly sure when modern rainforests first appeared, but fossil evidence suggests that they were already present at the end of the age of the dinosaurs, some 60 million years ago. They have probably been around for an even longer period of time. There is fossil evidence that forests similar to tropical rainforests existed well away from the present equatorial regions of the world. It would appear that during the Paleocene (65-55 million years B.P.), Alaska had rainforest, with evergreen tree species related to the tropical forests of modern Malesia (Wolfe, 1972). Malesia is the region encompassing Malaysia, Borneo and the Philippines. It is not known if there were epiphytic orchids in those ancient forests, but the forests were rich in liana species and had the types of leaves associated with modern rainforests. In those times, global temperatures must have been much warmer than they are at present. However by the end of the Eocene (38 million years B.P.) global temperature seems to have dropped, because the fossil record in Alaska shows the replacement of evergreens with deciduous species. These were in turn lost when conifers took over in the Pliocene, between 5 and 2 million years ago.

In more recent times periods of glaciation and drying led to the fragmentation of tropical forests, both in South America and Africa. This led to a dramatic reduction in their extent. After the last glacial maximum, some 20 to 10 thousand years ago, there was a rapid expansion phase, with the forests taking over much of the Amazonian and Congo basins. These phases of forest expansion and contraction into fragments have probably been very important in the evolution and radiation of the orchid family. One of the major questions, which still has to be answered, concerns the plethora of orchid species. Why does this family have so many different species? Why are so few species widespread and why do most of the species have such restricted distributions. Twenty thousand years is a short time in evolutionary history and hardly enough time for the myriad orchid species to have evolved. This leads to another question. The fragmentation of the forests, concomitant with glaciation, must have been accompanied by a massive die off of all sorts of species in many different tropical families.

In Malesia, the situation during the last ice age was probably somewhat different. So much water was locked up in the glaciers that global sea levels had dropped nearly 200 ft. This meant that many of the present islands of the Malesian region were joined to the Asian mainland. One could have walked from Thailand to Borneo, and New Guinea was probably joined to Australia. The paleoclimates of that region are not well known, but it seems feasible that at that time much of the lower altitudes were covered by forest. As the glaciers melted and sea levels rose, 15 to 10,000 years ago, the Malesian forests became fragmented and isolated on the individual remaining islands. The pattern here was then the opposite from other parts of the world. In Malesia the forests were probably spreading while those of Africa and America were being reduced and fragmented. At the end of the ice age the American and African forests expanded, while the Malesian forests were reduced.

It seems that the history of tropical forests has been one of dynamic change, which continues to the present day. Because fragmentation means a reduction in forested area, one might expect species extinction to occur during those periods and because the events happened so recently there should not have been sufficient time for new species to emerge and replace those lost. Was the orchid family even larger in the past than it is today and is the wealth of current orchid species also only a remnant of an even more glorious past? There appears to be no way of knowing for sure because the Orchidaceae do not leave good fossil traces. An alternative explanation, which does not sit well with most modern biologists, is that there has been an extraordinarily rapid burst of orchid evolution, much faster than that encountered in other taxa. Speciation, especially in long-lived organisms, such as orchids, can be expected to take hundreds of thousands, if not millions of years. Certainly many orchids today appear to be in the midst of speciation. This is true of many widespread species that are

very variable and possess distinctive differences between their populations, but the differences are not really distinct enough for them to be considered separate species except to the most ardent splitters. Species such as *Ansellia gigantea* and *Paphiopedilum callosum* are two of many orchids in that situation. Give them several more tens of thousands of years with the right conditions and those complexes should each split into a number of distinct species. But the time since the last ice age does not seem long enough to account for the present orchid diversity.

Not all forests are created equal

Tropical forests in different parts of the world are not of a uniform type. They differ not only in the kinds of species found in various regions but also in their overall structure and physiognomy. The structure of a forest is a complex four-dimensional system. It is four dimensional in the sense that the forest and its component species also vary with time and age. A mature tropical forest is not uniform in structure; it is made up of interlocking clumps of vegetation, each of a different age and formation. The death of individual trees, land slippage, etc., produces gaps or clearings that are re-colonized by species that can take advantage of the increased sunlight in the gap. The size of the opening itself is important in determining how a gap is filled back in with trees. In a small gap the trees growing around the edge may simply extend their branches and fill in the space, shading it once more. In a very large gap totally different species of tree may come in and compete for the light. These pioneer trees are fast growing, relatively short lived species, but as the pioneers grow, they in turn shade the space and other more shade tolerant tree species will then become established. Because gaps occur all the time in a mature forest it becomes a mosaic of different aged patches.

Besides those factors, the kinds of forest produced and the component species are also dependent upon the distribution and amount of annual rainfall. In addition, mean temperatures as well as the range and pattern of temperature fluctuations have a profound effect not only on the structure of a forest but also upon the component species that are able to establish themselves. Temperature differences depend on the physical location of the forest. As one proceeds north or south from the equator mean annual temperature decreases. It also decreases with altitude above sea level. Finally, warm or cold ocean currents can have a marked effect upon the ambient temperature. The effects of temperature are quite similar to the structural changes produced by variations in available water. Fig. 3 shows how

12 Pristine forest, Langkawe island, Malaysia.

an idealized forest's structure would change in the face of declining rainfall.

 Many of the earlier ecologists interpreted forests as consisting of a number of layers of canopy (the canopy is the layer of branches occupying approximately the same height above the forest floor). As many as four different layers have been described in the most complex lowland forests, but these become reduced in number at higher altitudes, with very high montane or temperate forests having only a single canopy. Other workers have questioned whether or not such stratification is real. It is certainly difficult for a casual observer to see clear evi-

dence for stratification in most tropical forests. It is only in recent years that ecologists have started to study the canopy in any detail and it turns out to be far more complex than originally thought. For example not all branches in a canopy are equal. Some trees in the forest are larger than others and because rain tends to fall from a particular direction, a tree can produce a rain shadow. This creates heterogeneity in the amount of rainfall an adjacent tree or different branches may receive.

 Orchids perch in the branches of the canopy where there tends to be higher levels of light. There has been little work on the arrangement of orchid plants among the strata of the most complex lowland forests. While many orchid growers are aware of species' preferences for different shade and light regimes there is little published work on how those plants naturally occur in the canopy.

 Not only do totality and patterns of rainfall and/or temperature alter the arrangement of trees, but other components of the forest, such as the lianas and epiphytes, vary depending on those conditions too. Orchids seem to be most profuse in montane and pre-montane forests, with smaller numbers of species found in the lowlands or higher altitudes. This has been fortuitous for

Fig. 3 Effects of rainfall on tropical forest formation for lowland forests. Note the increasing epiphytism with increasing rainfall. (Redrawn after National Research Council, 1982).

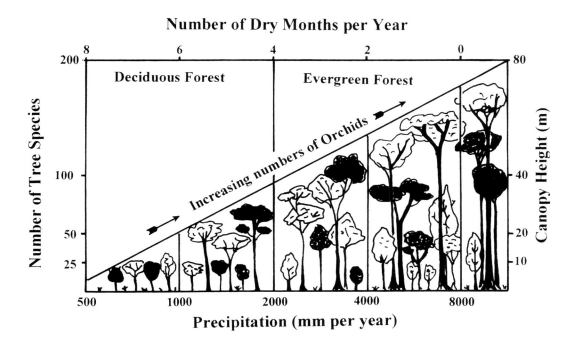

the survival of the family, as most tropical deforestation has involved destruction of lowland forests. But today much of the low altitude forest has been harvested and as attention is being focused on higher altitudes, more and more orchids are now brought into risk.

Kinds of tropical forests

It is generally not apparent to the armchair traveler or even the active tourist that there are many different kinds of tropical forests. The forests themselves can be classified in a number of different ways and they range from complex multi-layered structures to relatively simple organizations. There are two major factors that control the kind of forest that grows and there are also several minor parameters that can modify the type of forest that results. The main factors are the average temperature and the amount of rainfall, although position on the continent, soils, prevailing winds and evolutionary history can also modify the end result. A simple overview can be obtained by considering only wet forests and dry forests.

Wet forests

The humid tropics occur in those areas of the planet where the annual mean temperature is greater than 24°C and the rainfall is greater than the amount of water returned to the atmosphere, through either evaporation or transpiration from the plant cover. Typically, the rainfall will be in excess of 1,500 mm per year, and there will be no more than two dry months each year. In addition, these areas are frost-free. The humid tropics tend to be confined to a belt that lies between the Tropics of Cancer and Capricorn but the actual distribution is also modified by the shape of continents and the sea currents off their shores. An obvious way that the wet forests are modified is seen as one ascends to higher altitudes. As the altitude increases the average temperature drops and even though the rainfall may be as great, the forests will change their composition and complexity.

Tropical lowland forests

In the moist lowlands where the average temperature is maintained at the hottest levels one finds that the trees are tallest and the most complicated forest structures occur. The upper canopy is usually about 60 meters above the ground but it sometimes reaches 80 meters. A few trees reach beyond the upper canopy and these emergent trees can be even taller, approaching 100 meters. The number of different tree species is enormous, up to 400 different species have been counted in a single square kilometer of forest. The presence of different tree species means an increased diversity of habitats, not only for the animals, but also for the epiphytic plants as well. About 80 percent of the world's humid tropical forests were originally of the lowland type.

Forests at different altitudes

With increases in altitude the average temperature drops and the nature of the forest will change (Table 2). Typically when the mean annual temperature ranges between 18°C and 24°C one finds a type of forest which is intermediate between those of the lowlands and the woodlands associated with mountains. These are often called pre-montane forests. The number of tree species in the forest drops down to a maximum of about 110 species per square kilometer. The trees themselves are shorter and the top of the canopy is between 20 to 40 meters above the soil. Epiphytes are still generally quite abundant. Unfortunately, the pre-montane zone is ideal for agriculture, much of it has been logged and areas are often very heavily farmed.

As one ascends into mountainous regions, one first encounters lower montane forests; these are usually also rich in epiphytes despite the fact that tree diversity is even lower than the pre-montane forests. The mean annual temperature is now between 12°C and 18°C, with tree diversity down to less than half of that found in the pre-montane forests. There are still large numbers of orchids that grow under these conditions. Ten percent of the tropical forest area is pre-montane

Table 2

Altitude (m)	Ave. Biotemp. (°C)	Forest Formation	Canopy height (m)	Orchid abundance
3,500 – 4,000	6 – 3	Subalpine	1.5 – 9	common
2,500 – 3,500	12 – 6	Montane	15 – 18	abundant
1,500 – 2,500	18 – 12	Lower Montane	15 – 33	abundant
500 – 1,500	24 – 18	Premontane	20 – 40	common
0 – 500	24	Lowland	25 – 45	sparse – common

and five percent lower montane. Unfortunately, they both occur in regions of maximum disturbance, where man has settled, because those regions have more equitable temperatures.

The highest and coolest forests are the montane forests with mean annual temperatures between 6°C and 12°C. About 2% of the tropical forests are of this type. Relatively few tree species are found and the canopy will not always be continuous. Often there is only one layer of trees and in many regions it has been disrupted and changed into open woodland. While these forests are naturally the most impoverished in terms of numbers of species they can also contain some of the most spectacular orchids. Because of the low mean temperatures, insects are not as abundant nor do they function as well in the montane forests as they do at lower and warmer altitudes. Birds take over much of the job of pollinating and consequently one finds more flowers with the orange-pink-red colors that are typical of bird pollinated flowers and which the orchid hobbyists like so much. Orchids such as *Cochlioda noezliana* and *Comparettia speciosa*, from the Andean states, provide the brilliant oranges and red colors for the *Odontoglossum* alliance-hybrids. The scintillating orange-red *Dendrobium cuthbertsonii*, from New Guinea, also falls into this category. The tree line ends when the mean temperature drops below 6°C but there may still be a few geophytic orchid species to be found in the higher alpine regions. However, few of these are presently cultivated.

Dry forests

As the rainfall decreases, because there are dry and wet seasons or just because there is decreased precipitation, the diversity and complexity of the forest will also decrease. The number of canopy strata, as well as the height of the canopy will lessen. If there are more than four dry months in the year or if the average total precipitation is less than 2,000 mm then the forest will change its nature from being evergreen to being deciduous and the trees will shed their leaves during the dry season. Still there are some exciting epiphytes to be found associated with the drier forests and these are often easier to grow than their cousins from the wetter areas. Many of the orchids have become so adapted to dry seasons that they will not grow or flower properly unless forced into dormancy. Often the orchids themselves are also deciduous. Many of the Asian species of *Dendrobium* fall into this category. In the New World, orchids such as *Cyrtopodium* sp., *Cychnoches* sp. and *Catesetum* sp., from decidu-

ous forests, have also adopted a deciduous habit. Dry forests have been given little attention compared to the wet forests, so few people realize just how badly they have fared in the face of man's advance.

Distribution of tropical forests

Until recently, the extent of tropical rainforest was a band lying roughly between the equator and the Tropics of Capricorn and Cancer. The forests seem to extend farther north than the tropic of Cancer and just short of the tropic of Capricorn. The belt of forest is irregular and also dependent on local and continental conditions. Most attention is paid to rain forest but there are other kinds of forest in the tropics that are also important orchid habitats. These include monsoon forests and tropical dry forests. However, most conservation attention is focussed on rain forests, despite the fact that other types are also equally or perhaps even more critically endangered. Within the tropics there are basically four regions of rain forest that share similarities in their tree flora. All four regions are rich in trees of the Caesalipinodeae, a subgroup of the Fabaceae (Leguminosae) and other families such as the Annonaceae, Euphorbiaceae, Moraceae, etc., but there are distinct differences as well. Members of the family Dipterocarpaceae are prominent in western Malesia and the Lecythaceae (the Brazil-nut family) is typical of the Americas. Plate tectonics provide an adequate explanation for the present geographical distributions and differences of most tropical tree families.

- The smallest of the tropical floristic regions is the Australian rain forest, found in the northeastern part of Queensland. This shares some similarities with the forests to the north but it is botanically distinct. This region contains interesting orchids but has relatively low orchid diversity.
- The forests of the New World extend from Mexico in Central America to about 15°S in Brazil and Bolivia. The largest expanse of continuous forest in the world is in the Amazon basin. Overall the Americas are an extremely rich area, as far as numbers of orchid species are concerned.
- African rain forests are mainly confined to West Africa and the Congo region and are only a fraction of the size of their American counterparts. In East Africa, only isolated remnants of forests exist. As a whole the continental African sector is relatively poor with regards to epiphytic orchid diversity. However, geographically associated with the African continent is the island of Madagascar. This is

extremely rich in species, although the variety is confined to a relatively few groups. Estimates as high as 1,000 different orchid species for Madagascar are probably conservative.

- The Indo-Malayan region stretches from southern India across South East Asia down to Papua New Guinea. Despite being one floristic group, this region is separated by the Wallace line. This separates the zone into two distinct sub-regions, when regarding the distribution of animals. Orchid diversity in this region is legendary. Rainforests are also found on some of the more remote islands of the western Pacific.

Forest myths

The increased urbanization of man, even in the tropics, lends itself to a growing ignorance of the true nature of tropical forests. Much of modern man's forest experience is vicarious and based on the nature shows seen on television, in the movies, pro-conservation picture posters or lurid novels. Even in countries where forest occurs, only a tiny percentage of the populace experiences its wonders directly.

Mabberley (1983) listed and examined some of the more common rain forest myths. He included the following examples in his discussion. People believe that rain forests are an impenetrable jungle. Usually when tourists gaze at the edge of a forest they see a dense wall of vegetation, a tangle of fast growing vines and large leafed plants. It is indeed difficult to get through that mass of vegetation but those plants make up secondary vegetation taking advantage of the increased sunlight at the edge of the forest and it does not represent the condition that one finds inside the forest proper. Once one gets through the edge one finds a relatively sparse understorey of smaller plants and little impediment to walking across the forest floor. Forests are often described as being habitats where there is little difference between seasons, in terms of temperature or rainfall and in this uniform environment plants flourish. In fact there are diurnal fluctuations in temperature and rainy or dry seasons are fairly predictable. There are humidity differences between the forest floor and various parts of the canopy too.

Televised nature programs unintentionally suggest that forests are a riot of colorful flowers and rampant animal wildlife, but reality is different. Birds can be heard, but they are hard to see while mammals are very rare and flower displays are exceptions. The dominant impression is of green and as Mabberley points out it is rather monotonous. But the orchids are there and they may have stunning flowers, although often the petals and other parts have been chewed by insects or damaged by rain. We once counted eight different orchid species in bloom on a single branch in a Costa Rican forest but this was not obvious except on close inspection.

Orchid shows and greenhouse displays are concentrations of color that one hardly ever experiences in forests in the wild. In a similar vein people expect that forests are dripping with venomous snakes, nasty stinging insects and hungry leeches. Of course encounters with these creatures do happen, but they are actually quite rare. I remember a forest on the slopes of Mt. Mulanje in Malawi, south central Africa, where several green mambas were as anxious to get away from me as I was to get away from them! But I have also bashed my way through forests in Costa Rica, Malaysia, Queensland in Australia, Taiwan and Zimbabwe, among other countries, without confronting snakes. There are exceptions, Madagascar has no poisonous snakes and there is also no tradition of hitting nearly every snake over the head with a club. As a consequence the snakes are not afraid of people and I saw a number on that island. Lizards always seem frequent, but the snakes are probably too wary to get in the way. California and Baja California, on the other hand, always seem to be awash in snakes and we seldom go into the field there without encountering a rattler or two. Over the years, insects have appeared less and less of a problem in the tropics. Perhaps that is an unwelcome testimony to excessive worldwide use of chemical insecticides.

Another myth that Mabberley discussed was the perception that if the forest appears to be lush that the soil must be nutrient rich. In temperate forests that is often the case. Temperate regions with their lower average soil temperatures often have a build up of organic matter in the soil. There can be more organic matter in the soil than the forests. The microbes that break down leaves and bits of wood work much more slowly at cold temperatures than warm. The tropics, which have warmer soils throughout the year, have very rapid decay cycles. Leaves may be broken down into their component chemicals is a matter of weeks or months and wood takes scarcely longer. Most of the organic matter in a tropical forest resides in the living tissues of the trees and their epiphytes. If the forest timber is harvested, most of the organic matter and inorganic chemicals in the trees leaves the area but if the forest is burnt all of the organic matter is converted to carbon dioxide and water, leaving a residual ash of inorganic salts. In the latter case the salts can provide fertilizer for crops for a few years. Once that is depleted the plot becomes unproductive and must be abandoned. If the plot was small and surrounded by forest there was a good chance that the forest might regenerate. This slash and burn agriculture could be tolerated in the past when human populations were small but the exploding populations are now so large that there is not enough time or space to allow proper recovery.

A final myth is that there exists a state of the forest, often called virgin, primary or climax forest, that has been untouched by the hand of man and exists in some pristine and primeval form. Mabberley concludes that most forests have been disturbed although some more than others. The land around the famous Temples of Angkor Wat, in Cambodia, was abandoned about 600 years ago, but the forests that invaded that area seem different from other forests nearby. It has been suggested that it might take over 1,000 years for the forests to reach their 'climax' condition. Much of the forested land in Central America is of even more recent origin and less than 500 years old. It is estimated that the forests in Venezuela more than doubled in extent between the years 1825 and 1950 (Myers, 1980). Such forests cannot be considered as primeval. The lowland rain forest at La Selva, a biological reserve and famous tropical study area has traces of fire from earlier peoples, living in what was considered pristine rain forest.

Deforestation

There is general agreement in the world that tropical moist forests are under a high degree of threat but there is very little agreement on the details of rates and amounts of deforestation. Trying to get accurate and reliable data about the actual extent of deforestation is often like trying to measure a smoke ring. The general effect is obvious but the ring formation evaporates before one can apply the calipers.

The crucial study that alerted the world to the general threat of deforestation was an assessment carried out by Norman Myers and published in 1980 as a report from the National Academy of Sciences. He examined tropical forests in most areas of the world and in the report he tried to project the ultimate fate of the various forests and how long it would take to reach them. Myers was rigorous in how he defined virgin forest and considered disturbed, although still partially wooded areas, as being deforested. This brought his study under attack, but it did not lessen the impact that his projections had on the field of conservation biology.

Rates of deforestation were considered to be so enormous that many authors projected a staggering loss of species by the year 2000. Myers (1983) thought that up to a quarter to a third of the world's plant and animal species might be lost. A quarter of a century ago Peter

Raven (1976) projected that by the turn of the millenium, all of the world's tropical forests might have been logged and with them much of the precious tropical biodiversity would be lost. Later, the entire demise of the tropical forests was pushed back to the middle of the twenty-first century.

The first international attempts to collate information on forested areas, in a global sense, were initiated by FAO (the Food and Agricultural Organization of UNESCO) and over the years their data has been updated every few years. The FAO data has shown a surprisingly steady and constant rate of decrease in forested areas over much of the face of the planet. Individual governments submit the FAO data and critics consider that much of this data is suspect, overly optimistic or not strictly comparable between countries. Other estimates usually produce figures that show higher rates of deforestation (Collins *et al.*, 1991; Saywer and Whitmore, 1991). Critics think that the situation is much more severe and that the FAO rates are overly conservative. FAO data suggested that forest is being lost at 0.62% per year but most other studies suggest that the figure is probably closer to 1%. In absolute terms this means that we lose an area of forest approximately equivalent to the country of Switzerland each year. Although these figures encompass a wide variety of deforestation, ranging from clear cutting to selective tree harvesting, the figures are often interpreted as total conversion from forest to agriculture or other uses. This degraded forest may be an important refuge for orchid species. In recent years, the realization that the pattern of forest fragments remaining and the possibility that these can act as refuges for species has become more apparent (Lugo, 1988; Laurance and Bierregaard, 1997) and the utility of fragments in conservation has assumed increasing importance.

As forests are destroyed, those that are not clear-cut and utterly obliterated are reduced to fragments. There are two kinds of these fragments. The small islands of trees isolated from each other by the surrounding fields are called 'patches'. The other type consists of long remnants of forest, edging the banks of rivers or fields. These elongated remnants are often connected and form a network. The term 'shreds' has been applied to them to differentiate them from island patches. Shreds may also be found along mountain ridges in those countries wise enough to protect their watersheds. Ecologists have expended a great deal of effort trying to understand island patches, how they might loose species after they are formed and the factors dictating how many species a patch can hold. Almost nothing is understood about shreds and they have only been recognized as a distinct condition in recent years (Feinsinger, 1994).

Fire and forests

Look out of any plane flying over tropical forests anywhere in the world and you will see smoke rising through the canopy. Throughout the world, in normal non-drought years, it has been suggested that between 630 and 690 million ha of forest are destroyed each year by fire (Stott *et al.*, 1990). Following fire and sufficient rain there can be some recovery. But if the fire was severe the entire area may be totally devastated and, despite normal forms of vegetation succession, may never develop tropical forest again. Less severe forms of damage may regenerate faster, but there are few studies on the length of time it takes a forest to regenerate or how biodiversity is affected by the trauma. One of the rare studies to consider fire-regimes in the Amazon (Cochrane *et al*, 1999) found that initial fires, if not severe, opened the forest to additional and more devastating fires. They also assert that accidental fires have affected half of the remaining forests in the eastern Amazon and were responsible for more deforestation than deliberately set fires for that region.

The burning of tropical forests has been strongly implicated in increases in atmospheric carbon dioxide

13   Forest fire in Mpumalanga, South Africa.

and is thought to be a major contributor to global warming. The actual area lost was astounding in both years 1987 and 1988, when 1.6% of the South American forests were burnt. This included 8 million ha, each year, which were lost to fire on the southern fringes of the Amazon. In 1983 there was a great fire on the island of Borneo, which destroyed 3.0 million ha in Kalimantan and 1.0 million ha in Sabah. Drought and previous logging activity had left a great deal of dead wood, which fed the fires. Illegal immigrants who had settled along old logging roads had accidentally started that fire.

During the same period fires in the peat forests of East Sumatra created an additional haze of smoke, which blanketed much of the area. History repeats itself. In 1997, fires in Indonesia blazed out of control, covering adjacent countries in a pall of smoke that lasted for months on end, burning hectares of forest. Here the fires were started deliberately but soon got out of control. That year was an *el niño* season and the accompanying drought with dry forest conditions greatly exacerbated the problem. The percentage of forest lost has not been accurately determined but is thought to be between 81,000 ha and 688,000 ha. The truth is probably somewhere in between. Certainly the former number, the official government figure appears to be too conservative. By mid-1998 it was estimated that 7,700 sq. miles (20,000 sq. km) had been burned (Linden, 1998).

The same *el niño* event lasted well into 1998 and also had devastating effects in Central America. While the season brought three times the normal rain to California and other northern states, Mexico and further south suffered from a drought. A series of fires broke out in May of 1998 and devastated large sweeps of forest including rainforest as far south as Costa Rica. Some biosphere preserves such as Las Chimalapas in the southern state of Oaxaca, suffered losses of pristine cloud forest and in the neighboring state of Chiapas even rain forest was burning. Smoke drifting north caused problems in Texas and even further away. The Mexican government realized that this was an exceptional environmental tragedy and obtained help from the USA but, when it came, it was too little and too late. In a normal year Mexico has 7,000 fires. In 1998, the number was over 11,000 fires and the country lost 1,500 sq. miles (4,000 sq. km) while further south, Guatemala, Honduras and Nicaragua also lost forest (Linden, 1998). In all, Central America is thought to have lost at least 3,650 sq. miles (9,500 sq. km) and countless species. That may seem to be a lot but Brazil itself suffered a conflagration ten times that amount in the same year. The numbers of lost species of all kinds including orchids has not been estimated.

Originally ecologists had thought that primary tropical forest was immune to fire but there is not only recent but also historical evidence in the form of buried charcoal, that indicates that fires do occur in those areas. However, the 1998 fires in moist, high montane cloud forests in Mexico came as a shock. No one could imagine that those mist-shrouded dripping forests could become dry enough to burn. Was this drought only caused by the *el niño* conditions of that year or was it symptomatic of something even more serious, a permanent climate change induced by global warming and a general decrease in moisture, resulting from previous deforestation? In East Africa the pattern of savanna, with small forest patches surrounded by savanna, also appears to be anthropogenic and the result of fire. It is also likely that man influenced the pattern of forests in West Africa.

Drowned forests

Trees can be killed in many ways. If they are spared the blade and the fire, then there is always water. In the twentieth century man has had a penchant for building enormous dams to control and tame rivers. Extensive valley systems become inundated with water to make gigantic artificial lakes and in the tropics the usual result is a drowned forest. Even if the trunks and branches extend above the water, air cannot get to the trees' roots and they will die. Because many of the dams become recreation areas there is relatively little outcry about this form of forest extermination, although it accounts for a substantial percentage of forest loss. In addition, hydroelectric schemes are relatively pollution free

14   Lake Temenggore in Malaysia is a man-made lake that covers a drowned forest valley.

sources of cheap power generation and that often outweighs concerns about countryside destruction. The Bakun dam in Malaysian Sarawak serves as one of many examples. This dam has not yet been built, but in preparation over 400 square miles of rainforest were cleared, with additional areas of forest to be drowned.

There are parts of the world that have a special significance for orchid growers. They are either particularly rich in orchids or are places where orchid collectors traditionally sought plants for the hobbyist markets. In the following sections deforestation and how it affects some of these regions which will be examined.

Deforestation and Malaysia

Deforestation has reached critical levels in some countries. All of the significant lowland forests of peninsula Malaysia have now been cut and what highland forests still exist are now protected as reserves. Malaysia also occupies nearly half of Borneo (Sabah and Sarawak), one of the largest islands in the world. While there is still some lowland forest there, it is being destroyed at a fast rate. Peninsula Malaysia was very rich in plant species, containing well over 8,000 species with approximately 2,600 species of tree (compare this to all of North America, a vastly larger territory, but only containing 700 native tree species). The orchids are probably the largest plant family with about 2,000 species in Malaysia (Polunin, 1988). Peninsular Malaysia is thought to contain at least 846 orchid species (Aiken and Leigh, 1995), while in the Malaysian part of Borneo orchids probably number well over 1,000. Mt. Kinabalu National Park is thought to carry over 700 species of orchid. If that is true, then the current orchid biodiversity has been underestimated. How many of these species have been lost through deforestation is not known.

As one drives through the lowlands and even into the foothills around the small mountainous portion in the center of the country one is struck by the monotony of the landscape. There is mile after mile of rubber or oil palm plantation, broken only by vast stretches devoted to rice paddies. Teak, once the staple timber-tree of the country and famed for its long-lasting qualities, has all been cut and, except for some small stockpiles of timber, almost impossible to obtain. Teak seedlings are now planted along the freeways and tollways of modern Malaysia. Socially Malaysia is not typical, while there is poverty, its citizenry are comparatively well off and urbanized. The population is currently approaching twenty million people (Aiken and Leigh, 1995). This is not that excessive and much of Sarawak and Sabah are under-populated. The demands on the

15   Rubber and oil palm plantations in northeastern Malaysia. Originally rubber replaced the natural forests but now oil palm threatens to replace the rubber trees.

remaining forests are therefore also somewhat reduced. The country now has relatively strict protection of its natural resources and mounting public awareness about conservation issues. The native orchids that are left are probably relatively safe.

The Philippines

The Philippines represents a different side of the mirror. Here the human population appears to be doubling out of control but the population explosion had relatively little to do with deforestation rates. Conservation biologists, when asked about that country, either shrug their shoulders or lift up their hands in despair. Geographically also part of Malesia, the Philippine archipelago is also exceptionally rich in orchids. As long ago as 1875 there was concern that more than a quarter of the islands' forests had been felled. If we look at the various assessments of remaining forest cover plotted against the year that the assessment was made, we find wide variance (Fig. 6 on page 49), with the estimates often differing by as much as 20% of the original forest cover. FAO estimates were that about 30% of the forests still existed in 1988, but less conservative estimates suggest as little as 20% of the forest cover remained by that year. Forest cover decreased at a steady rate of between 0.74% to 0.8% of the original cover per year. By the year 2000 only 15% was expected to remain; the projection is that by the year 2030 all of the remaining forests will have been cut down. Workers in the field (Somer, personal communication) consider these estimates are quite optimistic and

believe that in reality only 2% of the original forests remain undisturbed.

Computer models that link deforestation and species distributions with extinction (Koopowitz *et al.* 1998) predict that probably a quarter, to one third of all Philippine plant species have already been lost. What this means for the orchids on those islands is that possibly as many as 300 of the countries 1,000 species are already extinct or can no longer maintain themselves in what remains of the wild forests.

It is usually stated that deforestation is an important byproduct of overpopulation, but Kummer (1992), who studied the situation in the Philippines, is convinced that large scale deforestation was not inevitable for the archipelago but rather forced on the country by a small group of corrupt elitists. He does not see the population explosion as driving deforestation but merely exacerbating the problem. Similarly, Caufield (1984) thought that the elite upper class and not the peasants drove deforestation in South America. She also calculated that most of the land converted from forest to pasture was controlled by only a small percentage of the people. There is relatively little information to allow one to decide what the main driving force for forest conversion is in most of the world.

When he was doing his research in the late 1970s Norman Myers (1980) considered that for each continent, forest conversion had quite different underlying causes and reasons. In the neo-tropics the major threat was from conversion of forests to pasture lands, to raise cheap beef. In Africa the major problem was lack of firewood, local people were cutting the forests for fuel. Asia was suffering from commercial logging operations. On all these continents there is also the driving need for land to feed the people, in these situations slash and burn agriculture also plays a role - to the detriment of the forests.

The Indian sub-continent

Despite its formidable population problem India has set aside a large number of forest reserves. These are primarily for large animals such as tiger and elephant, but the orchids in them share a measure of protection too. India and the foothills to the Himalayas were long a favorite source of orchid species and enormous numbers of orchids were shipped from them. Today there are forest remnants in the Eastern and Western Ghats, the eastern Himalayas, the Khasia hills and Assam. India probably contains about 1,300 species of orchids but peninsular India only contains about 315 of them and the rest are nestled against the Himalayas and the northeastern area.

16 *Brachystegia* forest in Zimbabwe following a fire. Most of the trees survived but some of the saplings and a few of the largest trees were killed.

Nagaland is one of the Indian States on the Myanmar (Burma) border. During the 1991 census, the population of Nagaland was counted at 1.2 million, of which 85% were engaged in pastoral activities, including shifting cultivation. Although the state is relatively small in area it contains nearly 250 orchid species, more than three-quarters of the number found in the much larger peninsular India. Deorani and Naithani (1995) recently addressed the orchid conservation situation in Nagaland. Nagaland forests vary in altitude from 300 to 3,840 m and range from wet evergreen (tropical rainforests) to deciduous and even coniferous forests. The 1985–87 survey showed that about 88% of the forest-

17 Firewood for sale in the Transkei region of South Africa. Frequently these branches will have a variety of small angraecoid orchid species, still attached and awaiting the flames.

lands were in private hands. Since that time the government has purchased 19,247 ha. This forest is in addition to some 50,750 ha that were already under a variety of protected statuses.

The annual demand for wood exceeds production by 800,000 m^3, so one can expect that forest losses will continue, particularly as forestland is also lost to shifting cultivation. During the years 1991-93, 63 km^2 of forest were lost to slash and burn agriculture. However, during that same period, 90 km^2 of farmland was abandoned, making a dubious gain for nature. These numbers need to be put into perspective. The state of Nagaland covers some 16,579 square kilometers, of which about half is forested. A third of that forest is considered inaccessible because of its mountainous nature and is therefore presumably safe. During the two years from 1991–93, there was actually a net increase in forest cover for all of India. It was a net gain of 925 km^2. It should be remembered, however, that these gains are probably not equivalent in quality to other forest lost. The new forests could be either recently developed single species plantations or secondary forest, naturally reclaiming abandoned fields. In either case they would be biologically impoverished compared to mature woodland.

Pressure for deforestation in Africa

In Africa deforestation is thought to be primarily the result of a need for fuel for cooking. In a land where the per capita earnings are barely a few hundred dollars per year the costs of cooking fuel or electricity are beyond the means of the ordinary person. It has been suggested that an adult woman in Africa now spends one day in every two scavenging and searching for wood or other combustibles. Our observations in Africa suggest that forest wood is usually cleared within the radius of an easy days walk around a village, unless the woodland is part of a preserve. In many African countries epiphytic orchids receive special protection under the law and this leads to some absurd situations. In Zambia, for example trees bearing orchids may be cut down and converted to charcoal but it is illegal to take the orchids off the cut branches and sell them. In the Eastern Cape of South Africa one can find cords of firewood still festooned with small angraecoids, such as *Mysticidium*, for sale on the roadsides. Nevertheless it would be illegal to collect those exact same plants for one's private orchid collection without a special permit.

Malawi has been described as a 'mango' savanna. Most of the original trees have long since disappeared and were replaced by solitary mango trees that form the dominant tree in the lowlands. What forest remains is confined to small areas, usually situated on mountaintops and many of those forests are introduced *Eucalyptus* or pine. Outside of Blantyre in southern Malawi there is a small natural reserve on the top of a hill. An old field guide to the reserve exists that describes meadows of *Eulophia* orchids at the base of the reserve. The orchids are long since gone as the villagers have ploughed those fields, planting maize up to the very edge of the forest.

In East Africa, conditions are scarcely better. The forests, which are small islands, usually on isolated mountains, are being steadily diminished despite the fact that many are nature reserves. Here much of the open savanna has also been converted to agricultural lands.

Deforestation and the New World

At the time that the Spaniards discovered the New World, much of Central America was converted to agriculture and the forests had been reduced to patches and borders around fields. The exact extent of the forests is not known but during the centuries following the European invasion so many of the people died that agricultural fields were abandoned and forests were able to reclaim much of the land. The gains were reversed when the current population explosion forced farmers back, to open up the forests. Much of the deforestation in the central Americas has had to do with the creation of pasturelands for cattle raising. Felled forests were set on fire and then planted with pasture grasses, after several years when the soil nutrients ran out additional forest space was cleared. Costa Rica is usually held up as one of the great examples of how well a country can implement conservation strategies. Nevertheless, the progression of deforestation in this the best of situations presents a truly dismal picture (Fig. 4). During the years, 1980-85, the annual deforestation rate in Costa Rica was an astounding 4% per year (Whitmore, 1990). In 1940 67% of Costa Rica was still clad with forest but by 1983 only 17% of the land still had its primary forest cover. This is the typical picture for much of Central America. However, to a tourist visiting Costa Rica in 1983 the country would still have looked lush and tropical because about a third of the country did have tree cover of some sort. Most of that was, unfortunately either secondary or very degraded primary forest. The 17% of untouched primary forest was confined to rugged mountain areas.

The forests of modern Costa Rica were destroyed to make way for pastureland for cattle. It was often the practice to leave a few trees for shade. These trees have become havens for orchids. However, on our recent trips to both Costa Rica and southern Mexico we have noticed

18   Shifting cultivation, a small homestead in a forest clearing, Ulu Tomani, Sabah, Borneo. (Photo credit: P. Cribb).

19   Rainforest flanking a river at La Selva, Costa Rica

20   Deforestation at La Selva, Costa Rica

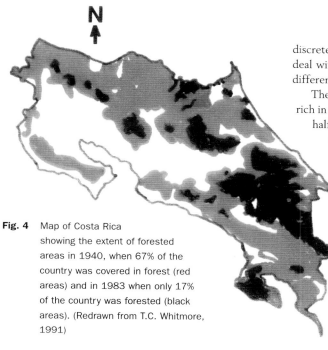

Fig. 4 Map of Costa Rica showing the extent of forested areas in 1940, when 67% of the country was covered in forest (red areas) and in 1983 when only 17% of the country was forested (black areas). (Redrawn from T.C. Whitmore, 1991)

discrete patches scattered over a wide area, but also to deal with the private property and aspirations of many different people.

The Andean countries along the Pacific Rim are also rich in orchids. Ecuador is a prime example. More than half of the forested area of Ecuador has been destroyed (FAO, 1991). First, the forests of western Ecuador gave way for agriculture and most of them have now been cut (Dodson and Gentry, 1991). Now that the eastern Andean forests have been opened up for oil exploration, there is a real concern that the eastern forests may follow the fate of those in the west. Meanwhile, the orchids of Ecuador are still being enumerated and new species are discovered all the time. The pattern in Ecuador is similar to its neighbors Columbia and Peru, which all share a similar flora.

Considering the large number of orchid species that exist in the New World, it is somewhat surprising that so few species are definitely known to be extinct. Dodson and Gentry only point to a very few. It is clear, however, that the range of many species

that many if not most of the trees left standing in the paddocks are now senile and dying and there are no replacement trees to take their place. When those trees go their orchids and other epiphytes will die as well.

Much has been written about the great Amazonian basin and its forests and it is sometimes difficult to separate the hype from the reality. This is an immense region and is one of the few places in the tropics that Myers thought would still possess significant tracts of forest well into the current century. It is likely that only 10% of Amazonia has been destroyed, but because of the grand scale of that area this 10% actually represents an enormous and significant area. The forest continues to be degraded.

In terms of orchid species, the Atlantic forests of Brazil were a center of diversity. Some of the most important plants are *Cattleya labiata*, *Laelia purpurata* and *Sophronitis grandiflora*. Less than 2% of the original rainforest cover now exists. The lowland forests are nearly all gone but patches are still found between the plantations and fields that make up most of the region. Reserves do exist but they were usually set up for animals. The Organ Mountains still have many orchid species and one can even find zygopetalums, epidendrums and maxillarias growing alongside the main highway that transverses the mountains. Additional remnants of degraded forest are scattered along the coast and many species still find refuge in those patches as well. Most of the fragments and patches are in private hands. That makes it extremely difficult to co-ordinate conservation activities as they not only have to embrace

21   Forest remnants cling to the inaccessible places on Zomba plateau, Malawi.

22   *Laeliaflava,* growing and flowering on rocks on
Serra Itabirito in Minas Gerais, Brazil in 1982.
This site was destroyed in 1986 (left).
(Photo credit: Roberto Agnes)

23   Serra Itabirito, Minas Gerais, Brazil. This former
home of rupiculous Laelieas and other plants has
been carved up in the process of iron mining. Iron
mining itself has also led to increased deforestation
with the conversion of wood to charcoal needed for
smelting (above). (Photo credit: Roberto Agnes).

24   Espirito Santo State, Brazil showing the clearing
of Atlantic forests for Agriculture (below).
(Photo credit: Roberto Agnes).

25 Remnants of forest on Serra da Bocaina, Sao Paulo State, Brazil. (Photo credit: Leandro Freitas).

26 These remnants are continuously threatened by fires in the encroaching grasslands. (Photo credit: Leandro Freitas)

has become seriously reduced. Pollinators and their ranges are virtually unknown for most orchids. Because of their innate longevity orchids may continue to exist in isolated areas of woodland and on individual trees, but they are unable to reproduce. In a way the orchids form part of what has been called the 'living dead'. They are functionally extinct and when the individuals finally die those species will disappear except for the lucky few that are maintained in cultivation.

Madagascar

Almost equal in size to Borneo, Madagascar split off from the African continent towards the end of the Cretaceous period, probably more than 65 million years ago (Preston-Mafham, 1991). There its biota continued to evolve in splendid isolation. In terms of plant species richness some people think that Madagascar rivals that of the Cape Floral Kingdom. Numerous unique and unusual plant and animal species evolved and among them, were approximately one thousand species of orchid. About 2,000 years ago, man settled the islands. They came initially from Asia and then later from the African mainland. The new colonists immediately started to exterminate the largest and most spectacular animal species, such as *Aepyornis*, a bird that laid the largest known eggs and *Megaladapis*, a gorilla-sized relative of the lemurs.

No one is quite sure what the original extent of these forests was, and there is some speculation that the entire island was covered with woodland of some sort. In the east there were extensive rainforests rich in orchid species and to the southwest unusual dry spiny forests, with very alien looking trees and succulents. Characteristic of these are some rather weird orchids, such as *Oeceoclades* species, these possess marbled leathery leaves and are adapted to dry conditions. In the northwest are drier forests with their own flora, but most of those have been degraded into a patchwork of forest fragments. The central portion of the island is a large plateau that is today almost totally denuded of vegetation, except for a few species of grass. Perhaps the most telling description of the central plateau is that of Preston-Mafham, who described the landscape as "... *a seemingly endless sea of barren grasslands forming the desiccated skin of the island, pockmarked with the livid scars of erosion gullies, the open bleeding veins of a moribund landscape.*" The plateau is thought once to have been a mosaic of savanna and patches of forest. How many orchids were there before the advent of man and how many have already become extinct? The answers are not known, the tragedy merely guessed at.

In recent years, there has been a concerted effort

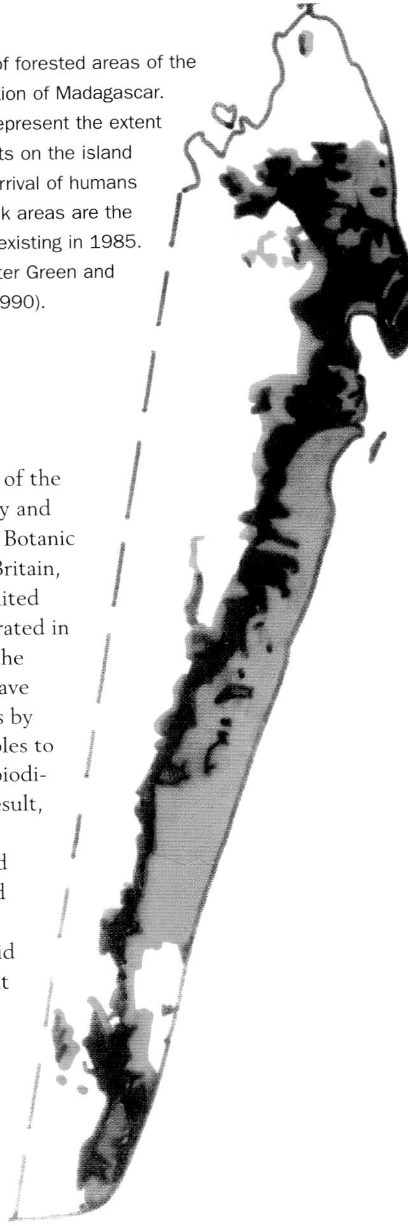

Fig. 5 *Right:* Map of forested areas of the eastern section of Madagascar. Red areas represent the extent of rain forests on the island before the arrival of humans and the black areas are the forests still existing in 1985. (Redrawn after Green and Sussman, 1990).

to catalogue much of the island's biodiversity and some of the major Botanic gardens of Great Britain, France and the United States have cooperated in this endeavor. At the same time there have also been attempts by the Malagasy peoples to profit from their biodiversity and, as a result, many of the Madagascan orchid species have found their way into the international orchid trade. It is difficult to know if the numbers of plants coming out make an appreciable dent in the orchid populations compared to the numbers being destroyed by deforestation. No doubt some of the plants emerging are very rare and growers of jungle collected Malagasy species should be aware of the responsibility in their hands. Many of these species may be on the brink of extinction.

The amount of forest that still remains in Madagascar has been difficult to determine with accuracy. Green and Sussman (1990) estimated that some 110,000 ha of eastern rainforest were lost each year between 1950 and 1985. Despite the use of aerial and satellite photography, there are many estimates of forest loss, which depend upon the author and the techniques used (Smith, 1997).

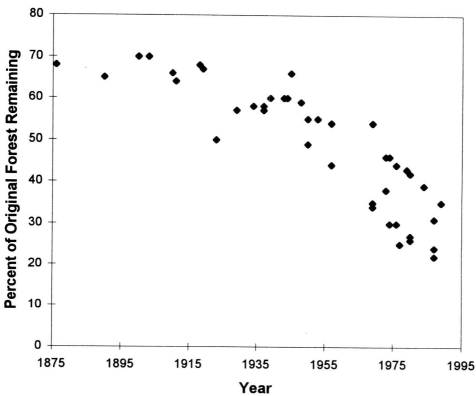

Fig. 6   Forest loss in the Philippines

How much forest actually remains? Probably as little as 3% of the original western forests and about 8% of the important eastern rain forests (Fig. 5). If the whole island was once forested, then in the year 500 AD, about 251,660 km^2 of the island had forest of some type. By contrast, by 1990 only 7,123 km^2 remained. This would be 2.8% of the whole possible original tree covered area.

The primary source of fuel for the islanders is charcoal and though there are large areas of *Eucalyptus* plantation in both the northern and eastern parts of the island for this purpose, it is insufficient and the remaining natural forests continue to be threatened. These remnant woodlands, outside of preserves, are still being cleared at a steady rate and enormous numbers of orchid species are being lost. Travelling through the eastern regions one is aware of just how much has been destroyed. The habitat not only for orchids but all sorts of plants and animals is disappearing and the world is losing a precious and unique heritage. Madagascar is one of the poorest nations in the world with barely a US$300 per capita annual income. There are medium sized cities in Africa with a larger gross annual income than the entire island. Part of the problem is that the island seems to have no natural resources for earning foreign income. Vanilla is one of the island's major sources

of foreign revenue but the total income from that spice is trifling, compared to the nation's needs. The island is rich in biodiversity but converting that into real income appears to have thwarted its people. The annual profits generated by drug companies selling anti-cancer derivatives from the Madagascar periwinkle, *Catharanthus roseus*, are probably greater than the country's gross national product but the island does not benefit significantly from the sales.

How much forest remains and how many orchids?

Today, about half of the original tropical forested area of the planet remains, but it is unevenly distributed. Many of the countries have lost 80% or more of their original stands. The very large tracts that still exist in Amazonia and the Congo bolster the amount on a global scale. Tables 3 and 4 list the amount of original forest remaining in the more important areas of the world. With so much forest gone, one should have expected that the known list of extinct orchids should be very long at this point in time yet that is not the case. But very few orchids can be said to be extinct with any certainty.

Table 3

Selected Neotropical Countries	1950 Forested Land (x 1000 ha)	1992 Forested Land (x 1000 ha)	Percentage Lost 1950–1992
Belize	1,012	1,012	0.00
Bolivia	59,176	55,261	6.61
Brazil	645,589	546,250	15.39
Colombia	62,300	49,700	20.22
Costa Rica	3,218	1,410	56.18
Ecuador	22,409	10,397	53.60
El Salvador	282	85	69.70
Fr. Guiana	7,514	7,262	3.35
Guatemala	6,843	3,609	47.26
Guyana	20,266	15,677	22.64
Honduras	6,455	3,095	52.05
Mexico	65,565	41,172	37.21
Panama	6,091	3,193	47.58
Peru	78,400	67,900	13.39
Suriname	15,024	14,839	1.23
Venezuela	41,775	29,595	29.16

Table 4

Selected Tropical Countries	1974 Forested Land (x 1000 ha)	1989 Forested Land (x 1000 ha)	Percentage Lost 1974–1989
Indonesia	122,225	113,433	7.20
Kenya	2,660	2,360	11.28
Malawi	4,850	3,740	22.89
Malaysia	22,700	19,100	15.86
Nigeria	16,700	12,200	26.95
Papua – New Guinea	38,510	38,230	0.73
Philippines	13,690	10,550	22.94
Thailand	19,260	14,240	26.07
Vietnam	13,600	9,800	27.95

Most models suggest that much of the biodiversity will continue to exist until only the last few remaining vestiges of forest are destroyed and then there will be a very rapid extinction cascade. Models predict that 2% of the forest should still harbor 50% of the species for plants whose populations are distributed like orchids (Koopowitz et al., 1994). About one tenth of the original global forested area is now in preserves of one sort or another. Many of these reserves have been placed in areas of high biodiversity and there is the chance that at least 50–60% or more of the orchid biodiversity will continue in those sanctuaries. This scenario is not as comforting as it seems. For many of the orchid species, the diversity of their gene pool has been badly eroded and in other cases, although some plants are still alive, they are merely remnants poised at the edge, awaiting extinction. There must also be cases where the plants continue to exist, although their pollinators have become extinct and without the promise of new generations of seedlings the orchids' fates are sealed.

Patchiness

What is difficult to determine is the extent of patchiness[2]. It is quite difficult to measure patchiness. Trees can be arranged in a linear fashion along watercourses or in discrete copses of different sizes. These patches are neither counted nor measured when they are less than a few hectares and are usually discounted when forested areas are measured and reported, but they can act as important refuges for orchids. Trees are often left standing near watercourses, very steep slopes, clinging to cliffs and the like. In some countries a few individual trees are left standing to provide shade for livestock. How long the patches

[2] 'Patchiness' refers to small patches of trees that remain after forest clearance

and their attendant orchids can exist after being isolated from the rest of the forest remains uncertain. Lugo (1988) was one of the first scientists to point out the importance of patches and secondary forest as refuges for species. It is only in recent years that attention has been paid to forest fragments and now their importance for conservation has been realized (Laurance and Bierregaard, 1997).

Thomas Lovejoy and his co-workers (Lovejoy *et al.*, 1984) usually get credit for our understanding of events that happen when clusters of trees are isolated from the parent forest. They set up a system of different sized forest patches in Brazil and followed the fate of various patches after they had been separated from the main body of the forest. They found that the fate of the patch was related to the size of the remnant and that smaller areas were much more fragile than larger patches. The patch appears to be most vulnerable around its perimeter and that there is increased tree mortality at the edge. At the edge, light intensities are greater than within the forest and humidity is lower, but most surprisingly the trees at the edges are exposed to increased wind velocities. Normally there is not much wind movement within a forest. The trees act as a series of baffles to cut down air movement. One of the major effects of these new physical changes is an increased mortality; expressed as tree fall. Trees are always falling down in forests, creating new gaps that can be colonized. But in small patches more trees fall down than normal and this is concentrated along the sides that have the greatest exposure to wind. As much as a third of the tree biomass is lost within a 100 meters of the patches' edge. Most of this occurs during the first four years following fragmentation. There are few studies on the fate of epiphytes in patches, but their success is linked tightly to the health of the trees on which they perch. Elevated tree mortality can only mean increased losses of epiphytes as well.

Besides the physical changes that these patches experience, there are additional but more subtle ecological problems. Patch size usually precludes the persistence of top predators, that often require vast areas and without the predators there is usually an increase in the populations of herbivores. Increased numbers of animals that feed on seeds can have a devastating affect on the species recruited to replace normal tree mortality. In fact observations on the forests left standing on small islands in Lake Gatun, created when the Panama canal was built, has shown that over the last 80 years there has been a decrease in the varieties of trees making up those remnant forest patches (Putz *et al.*, 1990). In part this is also due to a loss of the animals that either pollinated or distributed tree seeds. One should remember that not only are orchids vulnerable to pollinator losses but they may need to grow on specific tree species.

After a fragment has been produced there is increased growth in secondary vegetation that can make use of the increased light around the edges. This in turn leads to increased insect activity. What this means for the orchids is not clear and still has to be studied. There is almost no published research on the fate of orchids in small patches. Without pollinators and the right conditions for germination orchids left in the patches may not be meaningful for the ultimate survival of their species. Orchids tend to be tough and resilient plants but their persistence in a forest is no indication that they are more than biding their time, waiting for extinction. On the other hand, many orchid species are small plants and these might succeed on a single tree, hopefully, producing enough seed to colonize other surviving trees in the area.

It is now nearly twenty years since the original set of fragments were set up in Brazil, and they have been monitored at regular intervals since that time. Some specialized studies were also carried out on them. Once fragments have been formed they are not simply isolated patches of primary forest (Viana *et al.*, 1997) but acquire their own history of disturbance events and change occurs within them in ways that are not easy to predict. Those changes are often but not always an attrition of the component parts. Perhaps one of the most important tasks still facing conservation biologists at the beginning of the 21st century is to understand the ecology of forest patches and other ecosystem fragments. We need to understand how woodland fragments change and what are the important parameters we need to protect in order to extend their existence and hopefully ensure their permanence.

The scattered nature of fragments makes it especially difficult to deal with their conservation. In some areas, such as the Atlantic forests of Brazil, most of the fragments and patches are in private hands and, as one can imagine, it is well nigh impossible to co-ordinate conservation activities that embrace privately owned patches, scattered over a wide area.

It is only in some very small areas that we know what the extinction rates of orchids have been. Singapore is an island that was originally covered with forest and contained an impressive 1,674 plant species. In 1998, it was calculated that only two percent of the forests still existed, broken into little patches. Surprisingly the flora still contains 1,196 species. But the orchids were the richest component of the flora and they have suffered the highest extinction rates. An incredible 86% of the orchid species in that area are now thought to be extinct (Corlett and Turner, 1997). Fragmentation has not been kind to the persistence of the epiphytes.

CHAPTER 6

The Continuing Need for Orchid Species

When one discusses issues with people who don't collect orchids it is often necessary to explain to them why orchid breeders should still need to collect wild plants. They will often equate orchids with pansies and assert that because there are thousands of man-made hybrids available, there is no further need to go out and collect more wild species for use in flower breeding. In this chapter we will explore some of the ways that orchid species have been used during the history of orchid breeding and also why it is necessary to maintain and conserve wild plants for future uses in horticulture. The basic question is why, with all of the advances that have been made in orchid breeding over the years, there is still a need to maintain species for future incorporation into orchid breeding programs. We will examine the recurring role that orchid species have played in the history of orchid breeding and why we anticipate that they will remain important in the years to come.

While there are tens of thousands of orchid species in the wild, man has produced an even larger number of orchid hybrids. More than 100,000 orchid 'grexes' have been registered with the Royal Horticultural Society since 1856. Since this chapter concerns both hybrids and species, it is necessary to begin with a brief discussion about the naming of orchid hybrids.

The rules for naming orchid hybrids are different from those followed for most other horticultural plant groups. Orchid hybrids, if they are worthy, are actually given two different names, a grex name and a cultivar name. An orchid grex contains all of the plants that result from the mating of any two orchid plants of different origin e.g. two different species or, a species with any hybrid or, two different hybrids. If *Paphiopedilum* Noble is crossed to *Paphiopedilum* Belisair, all of the resulting offspring are given the grex name *Paphiopedilum* Paeony. In addition, self-pollinating any one clone of *Paphiopedilum* Paeony or crossing any two different clones of *Paphiopedilum* Paeony will only produce members again of the same grex. Selected clones from the group are given a second epi-

thet, a cultivar name, which is placed in single quotation marks. Famous examples of this are *Paphiopedilum* Paeony 'Regency' from the original cross and *Paphiopedilum* Paeony 'Debonaire' that resulted from a selfing of 'Regency'. Two sibling heathers or delphiniums would be given different names and the relationship would not be indicated. Grex names are not used for other plants.

The first artificial orchid hybrids were made well over a century ago, in 1863, and these gradually replaced the wild species in most hobbyist collections. The growers found that the hybrids were often more floriferous, with bigger and brighter blossoms and were easier to grow. Further hybrids were made between already extant hybrids or were produced by adding novel species into the hybrids. Before long, the hybrids bore little resemblance to their original species parents. In fact, many of the wild species appeared scruffy when compared to their hybrid progeny.

The aims of orchid breeders

Nearly all flower hybridizers, no matter what the group of flowers they work with, whether they be cattleyas, Phalaenopsis or vandas (or even daffodils, dahlias or amaryllis) all seem to have produced similar, though artificial sets of criteria, about what makes a superior flower. In each case there is a definite preference towards full, rounded, flowers with broad overlapping petals. In most cases the trend is towards creating ever-larger blossoms with petals or tepals that look as if they have been ironed flat. Clearer and brighter flowers with more intense tones and contrasts are also favored. The sought after ideal is often a precision-engineered flower that could more easily have been formed on a lathe or by using a band-saw, than bred by the patient recombination of parents containing the desired characteristics. These are clearly artificial criteria because flat, round flowers are not suited to insect eyes and, in the wild, few of these 'ideal' orchids would ever get pollinated.

There are other goals in flower breeding, but for

orchids they tend to be secondary. These include decreased time to flowering, tolerance of artificial conditions in cultivation, disease resistance, a free flowering nature, small stature, etc. However such goals are seldom articulated and hardly ever deliberately sought after, although the orchid breeders do take advantage of those properties when they occur by chance. Often if a species is added to a weak breeding line the result is hybrid vigor and one does need the occasional infusion of species blood to offset the consequences of inbreeding.

Within the major groups of orchids, we find a definite pattern. Following an initial period of hybridizing using only a few species, line-breeding inevitably occurs, utilizing the best of the hybrids which are combined and recombined again and again until the ideal shapes and color brightness are achieved. Often at this point, species genes are once again reintroduced into the hybrids, to change the looks of the flowers from the occasionally monotonous 'ideal' characteristics. There are fashions in flowers as there are in anything else. Sometimes the fashions depend upon which groups of orchids happen to be popular at the time, and sometimes they have to do with changing of forms, shapes and colors that have become boring or commonplace.

The fuel and source for changing flower fashions are the wild species. The species can be considered the spices used by the breeders for changing their hybridizing recipes. Residing in the species are the genes that will give the subtle changes or dramatic effects that will produce tomorrow's trends and fashions. No one can foretell the future, so we do not know which species will be the ones needed in the years hence. Sometimes the most unexpected combinations of species with hybrids will pay dividends, as we will illustrate shortly. Therefore, in order to hedge our bets we need to save as many species as possible. We do not know when we will need them, perhaps never. But on the other hand, we cannot take the chance of impoverishing our future by not saving as much as possible now.

There are more genes in a wild species than those that can be used for making new colors and shapes. All present day organisms are the end point or result of billions of years of evolution and natural selection – they contain the wisdom of the planet – the results of millions upon millions of trial and error experiments. For us to discard or to allow to be discarded, these precious living books, is like encouraging a blind person to throw away a series of old oil painting masterpieces, merely because, to him, they do not represent anything. A Rembrandt or Matisse is useless to a blind man who cannot comprehend the meaning within a visual masterpiece. In a similar fashion we are often blind to the potential value of a wild plant and to allow that plant to go extinct merely because one cannot see a present value in it, is not only very shortsighted but also irresponsible. Many of the potential uses of plants are not aesthetic and cannot be foreseen. A good example of this occurred when the genus *Ascocentrum* was combined with *Vanda* hybrids. The vandas, a favorite garden orchid in many tropical parts of the world, are seasonal and bloom once a year. *Ascocentrum* species are also seasonal but flower at a different time to the vandas. However, when the two genera are combined this characteristic is lost and their progeny, called ascocendas can flower at any time of the year. Some hybrids are recorded as having been in continuous bloom for more than four years at a stretch. This highly desirable reblooming trait was an unexpected bonus and could not have been foretold. In a similar vein both of the species *Cattleya luteola* and *Sophronitis coccinea* are seasonal plants. The former flowers in mid-summer, while the latter blooms in the spring. While individual clones may flower at other times each individual normally only flowers once a year. The hybrid grex between the two, *Sc.* Beaufort, flowers as each growth matures and one can get four or five flushes of bloom from a plant during the course of a single year. There are other physiological traits that may not be immediately apparent in the wild species. Some include cold or heat tolerance, an ability to withstand poor water quality (something that is becoming more important all the time), disease resistance, dwarfism, etc. Unfortunately, we don't know where to look for these genes and often have to find them by chance.

One can pinpoint a few examples where it would be useful to have some of these physiological genes. Modern hybridists, have produced some wonderful *Disa* hybrids. These large colorful flowers make exceptionally good cut flowers, lasting for weeks or even months after being harvested. Closed buds continue to develop and flower in the vase. The plants grow readily from seed and unlike most orchids do not require to be germinated under sterile conditions. They mature rapidly and will often flower the following year. Clearly the plants have the potential for being the basis of a multi-million-dollar pot plant and cut flower business. Unfortunately, there is a problem. Most *Disa* species used to make the above hybrids are prone to root infections during warm weather, especially if they are provided with poor quality water. They also have poor tolerance to salts in the water. We desperately need disease resistance genes to put into the hybrid disas. Where are the genes? Perhaps in some variant of a *Disa* species already known or maybe in some other *Disa* species, not incorporated into the hybrids yet, because of their insignificant flowers. Or perhaps, the disease resistant genes were lost yesterday when a population or plant containing the desired genes died out. One needs to preserve as many of the wild species as possible in order to keep our options open.

Some significant roles of species in hybridizing history

If one examines the history of development within the major orchid taxa one can see the ways in which species have influenced orchid breeding in the past. In the rest of this chapter we will demonstrate how the gradual incorporation of new and novel species into the hybrid gene pool has repeatedly enriched and enlivened the orchidophile's interest and appreciation of the plants. A detailed examination of the hybridizing trends within any major orchid group could encompass an entire volume. As stated before, related orchid species can hybridize readily with other species, and frequently the resultant offspring are fertile and can be used to make yet other hybrids. Thus the breeding of orchid plant species differs from animals where interspecific fertile hybrids are very rare and generally do not occur. In addition, with orchids, it is not only possible to make hybrids between different species within the same genus, but also between species of different, though related, genera. There are man-made hybrids of orchids such as *Sallyyeeara*, that have incorporated as many as nine different genera and they are working on adding even more now. The ease with which hybrids can be made is in part responsible for the enormous proliferation of new hybrids at the hands of commercial firms and hobbyists.

One of the recurrent themes in the history of orchid breeding is the incorporation of new genetic material into the breeding lines. Usually mating a wild species with a man-made hybrid brings this about. It needs to be pointed out that all members of a species are not genetically equivalent. There is considerable variation within any one species. Good hybridizers use forms of the species that contain the desired characteristics. In most cases the desired characteristics were found by chance when a group of the species flowered. The greater the pool of wild species available, the better the chance of finding a desirable selection. When you compare the descriptions of some of the superb clones that were available at the beginning of the 20th century, with those that are currently available, it suggests that the gene pool has already become considerably impoverished.

The Cattleya Alliance

Even if they don't know one orchid from another most lay people can recognize a *Cattleya* flower as an 'orchid' when they see one. This is not always true of the other major groups of orchids such as *Cymbidium*, *Paphiopedilum*, *Phalaenopsis*, *Odontoglossum* and *Vanda*. Cattleyas are synonymous with 'orchids' and since their introduction they have been the subject of intense hybridizing activity. There have been so many trends in *Cattleya* breeding that the topic could easily fill several books.

The large modern corsage cattleyas are usually the combination of species from three different genera, namely *Cattleya*, *Laelia* and *Brassavola* (syn. *Rhyncolaelia*). There were six species of *Cattleya* that were originally used in the breeding process, C. *dowiana*, C. *labiata*, C. *mossiae*, C. *trianae*, C. *warneri* and C. *warscewiczii*. Of these six, C. *trianae*, is one of the few orchids that now figures on Appendix I of CITES. It is not clear if its current threatened status is due to over collection or if it has become endangered due to habitat destruction. *Cattleya mossiae* is a spring blooming orchid, while the others flower in the autumn. The seasons when flowers are produced do not always coincide with peak demand in the cut flower market. The conditions, which cause flowering in C. *labiata*, are known in fine detail. It is possible to make this species flower at any time of the year or even twice a year by manipulating the amount of light i.e. the day length and the temperature at night. In essence, if the plants are grown in long days (16 hours, with natural light supplemented by artificial illumination) and with a night temperature of 18°C (65°F) they will not flower. In order to produce flowers on demand, the plants are exposed to a drop in night temperature down to 13°C and short days. They will flower approximately two months later. If the day length is naturally increasing during the period that one requires blooms then the plants need to have artificially shortened days. This is accomplished by covering the plants with black cloth. The point of all this is that in order to be able to control flowering to coincide with the demands of the corsage market all one needs to do is to incorporate C. *labiata* 'blood' in the hybrids. There is a continual need to keep adding that species into the hybrids, to ensure that the correct genes for flower control are still present and do not get diluted out. Other *Cattleya* species can be controlled in a similar fashion, but the details governing their flowering are not known as precisely as in C. *labiata*. During the late 1940s and 1950s, cattleyas were extensively grown and hybridized for the corsage market. There were, however, several developments that led to a decline in their popularity. The hybridizers were making flowers that were bigger and bigger and soon the flowers became so large that they could only be worn on the most ample of bosoms. In addition, magenta tones, mauves and purples lost favor as more 'modern' and brighter oranges and yellow colors were sought. White *Cattleya* hybrids, however, were always in steady demand for use in wedding bouquets. The big, white hybrid cattleyas, such as C. Bow Bells had been produced by painstaking line breeding and for the most part, with this grex the hybridizers felt that they had already achieved perfection. One would not have thought that an infusion of species genes at that point could have contributed towards the goals of the men trying to make 'perfect' white cattleyas. Man's preconceptions are frequently misconceptions. When C. Bow Bells was hybridized with the white form of the old species C. *mossiae*, a sensational grex was made. This was called C. Bob Betts, and was a flower still closer to the ideal white. In fact C. Bob Betts is so good that in the intervening years since its registration in 1950, additional improvements have been few and relatively minor. The C. Bob Betts line continues, although the market for large white cattleyas has declined.

Incorporation of two smaller flowered species into the big whites also gave a fresh breath to the industry. *Cattleya harrisoniana alba* and C. *loddigesii alba* are forms of two smaller species that produce clusters of small flowers (3–4 in (12.5–17.5 cm)), rather than the two or three large blossoms (5–7 in (7.5–10 cm) across). The first important hybrid of this type was C. Henrietta Japhet, which was bred from a large white C. Eucharis by C. *loddigesii* 'Stanley's Var.' and as a consequence these new flowers were termed 'Japhet-types' by the trade. McDade originally registered the cross in 1946, but the plants did not reach the peak of their popularity until nearly twenty years later. The Japhet-types were more economical to grow, plants were more compact and produced more flowering sprays per square foot of bench. The flowers, which were smaller and more graceful, were very popular for corsages. In addition they lasted longer. Instead of flowering only once a year these hybrids flowered twice or sometimes even three times. Furthermore instead of the two to four blooms per spike of the large cattleyas one could cut five to eight flowers from a Japhet spray. This was an ideal development but eventually, the Japhet-types themselves gave way to other sorts of orchids. Although there is still some demand for 'Japhets' from the florists, cymbidiums supplanted those flowers for corsage work.

It seems to be in the nature of man to strive after the unusual and the uncommon. The common colors in large *Cattleya* hybrids are from white through pink to mauves and purples. *Cattleya dowiana* is a yellow species and it was only natural that people should also strive for good quality large yellow cattleyas. That goal has been much harder to achieve than with most other colors. And it is only in recent years with x *Brassolaeliacattleya* (*Blc.*) Malworth 'Orchidglade' and *Blc.* Xanthette 'Chartreuse' and their offspring, that we are starting to approach the perfection found in other cattleyas. Still they frequently lack size or color intensity and often the precision of form that is now expected. In a similar manner large fire-engine red cattleyas have been slow to emerge. Here the color genes were originally derived from the miniature *Sophronitis coccinea*, a tiny Brazilian species with brilliant orange-red flowers. Some famous red flowers such as x *Sophrolaeliacattleya* (*Slc.*) Falcon and *Slc.* Anzac 'Orchidhurst' had been registered in 1920 and 1921 respectively, but fiery reds that can compete with the purples and whites for size and shape did not emerge until 60 years later and are still rare. This group has received constant attention from growers, trying to achieve better reds. It was not until the late fifties and early sixties that *Slc.* Anzac was mated to the Central American species C. *aurantiaca*. That species produces clusters of small starry flowers, the petals are narrow and normally held forward. The only desirable features are the heavy waxy substance and true clear orange coloring. Surprisingly, when mated to *Slc.* Anzac, C. *aurantiaca* produced a bevy of beautiful red cattleyas, with almost none of the species' poor qualities; the grex was named *Slc.* Jewel Box. The best clones were tissue cultured and are still widespread in cultivation today. In turn *Slc.* Jewel Box is the parent of other important red cattleyas the most notable being *Slc.* Madge Fordyce and the famous *Slc.* Hazel Boyd, which are now grown by the thousand and appear in nearly every amateur's collection. Who would have thought that the species C. *aurantiaca* could have been so useful and important?

In the 1970s there was a great increase in the cost of heating greenhouses and this had a profound effect on orchid growers. The costs of maintaining bench space were such that hobbyists started to look for smaller and more compact plants, which could also tolerate somewhat lower temperatures. A 5° drop in minimum temperature can represent a considerable saving on the fuel bill. But as far as the cattleya alliance was concerned we saw little breeding for cool temperatures but the increased popularity of small plants called 'mini-cats'. One could grow more plants in the limited space that one could afford to heat, but at the same time they could also tolerate cooler temperatures. The source for the cool genes was found in two species of *Sophronitis*. While *Sophronitis coccinea*, a tiny plant, had been used extensively in the past for red breeding, it did not relay to its progeny as much dwarfness as would be expected. The other parent's size seemed to dominate to a greater extent over the *S. coccinea*. In recent years, the very similar species, *S. brevipedunculata*, has been found to transfer much more dwarfness than its sister species and is now the preferred plant to use. While species from the genus *Laelia* have been used extensively in the past for cattleya alliance breeding, it is only recently that a subgroup, the rupicolous laelias have received much attention from the breeders. One of these, *L. milleri* had been used as an additional source for orange-red genes, in the past, but now other species have been brought into cultivation that offer a great deal of promise. One of these, *L. briegeri*, has stunning yellow flowers and from initial results will do a great deal towards producing compact plants with flowers held well above the foliage. Another dwarf species, *Cattleya luteola*, when crossed with *S. coccinea*, made the very dwarf *Sc.* Beaufort, an important breeder.

On the island of Jamaica exists *Broughtonia sanguinea*, a variable species that is also in the cattleya alliance. Another dwarf species, *B. sanguinea*, has produced a very popular series of hybrids. In this case, selected forms of the species with fuller and redder flowers than are normally found were needed to make acceptable hybrids. The species, while relatively common on the island has been the subject of a great deal of collecting pressure. Fortunately, one population still existed that had the desirable characteristics and it is from these that modern *Broughtonia* hybrids were derived. Many of the hybrids have been produced in Hawaii, so the species of one island in the Caribbean has contributed towards the economy of another island, halfway around the world in the Pacific. The *Broughtonia* hybrids illustrate a rather interesting feature about how the fashions and needs of orchid breeding occur. The first major hybrid, x *Cattleytonia* (*Ctna.*) Rosy Jewel, was made by crossing two species, namely *Br. sanguinea* and *C. bowringiana*. Goodale Moir, a prolific hybridizer in Hawaii, registered x *Cattleytonia* Rosy Jewel in 1956. Ten years later, 'Fields Orchids' registered another primary hybrid called *Ctna.* Keith Roth, made by crossing *Br. sanguinea* with the bifoliate *C. bicolor*. x *Cattleytonia* Keith Roth was, and still is, widely sold. Its flowers are a deep blood red and it looks like a larger version of the Jamaican species. The demand for *Broughtonia* hybrids did not occur, however, until the late seventies when the average grower started to ask for and buy them. This means that it frequently takes ten to

twenty years for newer types of orchids to become fashionable. When these new types reach public awareness that is the time when one tends to find a flush of hybrids being made, frequently with the species that initiated the fashion. In part, the ten year gap is caused by the time that is needed for tissue culture and to grow the plants to maturity, the selected clones will then be made available on a grand scale. The demand for the species also increases when demands for its hybrids increase.

One should not think that changing directions in cattleya alliance breeding runs along a single track. Frequently advances are being made along several fronts simultaneously. Quite some time ago an unusual variant of *C. intermedia* was discovered. Instead of the usual form, this plant had flowers that had developed pelorism, a condition where the two petals had many of the characteristics of the lip, and the flowers tended to be more regular rather than having the zygomorphic form which is found in the wild species. This variant was named *C. intermedia aquinii* after a gentleman who possessed the plant. The peloric characteristics can be passed onto the plant's offspring. Thus, during the last thirty years or so, a new horticultural race of brilliantly colored cattleyas has emerged, with petals boldly painted in contrasting lip colors. This would never have come about if the aberrant *C. intermedia* had not been found. It is worth mentioning that peloric species are not very common. One such, a specimen of *C. velutina*, was discovered but unfortunately the plant died before it could be propagated. This is a great pity because *C. velutina* has a strikingly veined lip and the peloric form had wonderfully veined and striped petals. It could have been used to breed striped cattleyas.

Cymbidiums

While *Cymbidium* species were known and grown in the last century, almost no work was done on breeding them until about 1910. Even then there was little progress. Today they rank among the top dollar earners in the orchid industry. Not only do the plants provide cut flowers, but also millions are grown as pot plants and sold in Europe and the Orient each year. The change in affairs is due partly to luck and also to the incorporation of new species into the breeding programs. Cymbidiums really got their start, when the famed British orchid breeder H.G. Alexander of Westonbirt produced a chance tetraploid hybrid, which was named *Cymbidium* Alexanderi 'Westonbirt' in his honor. There followed several decades of line breeding as hybridizers strove to produce ever-larger spikes with bigger flowers in clearer colors, influenced by the use of the tetraploid parent. When the species *C. erythrostylum* was mated to a

standard *Cymbidium* hybrid, C. Edward Marshall, another natural tetraploid resulted. This grex incorporated the early season (October through December) as opposed to the more usual January through to May season of other hybrids. In 1946, the grex was named C. Early Bird. *Cymbidium* Early Bird 'Pacific' AM/RHS was a near tetraploid and it was in turn crossed onto the older C. Alexanderi to produce C. Stanley Fouraker, which was registered in 1958. This can be considered one of the biggest breakthroughs in standard *Cymbidium* breeding and it opened the way for good early standards that were sought for the cut flower markets. Most early flowering cymbidiums, up to that time, were floppy, poor quality flowers with soft substance. The use of C. erythrostylum extended the *Cymbidium* season to two-thirds of the year and added millions of dollars to the annual earnings of the crop.

Two other species were also used in the 1950's and they also had spectacular effects - but in different breeding directions. The tried and true C. Alexanderi was mated to a miniature *Cymbidium* species, C. *pumilum* (more correctly C. *floribundum*), to produce a small plant with pinkish-beige flowers, which was registered in 1955 by Arno H. Bowers as C. Sweetheart. In turn C. Sweetheart gave rise to the now famous C. Showgirl and C. King Arthur, which are at the base of the modern *Cymbidium* pot plant industry. At about the same time another small stature species, the straw

27   *Cattleya aurantiaca* 'Tevya' HCC/AOS.
This Central American species was very important in producing a wide array of orange *Cattleya* hybrids. (Photo credit: Richard Clark and the American Orchid Society).

colored C. *ensifolium*, was mated to C. Miretta, a standard green *Cymbidium* creating the grex, C. Peter Pan, that was registered in 1957. The combination of the species and standard *Cymbidium* not only gave miniature plants but also extended the flowering period. *Cymbidium* Peter Pan and its hybrids not only flower early but also throw sprays of flowers during the summer time as well. The miniatures, however, all seemed to suffer from having rather starry flowers. A tetraploid form of C. Peter Pan was then bred onto the standard varieties and from these have come an array of intermediate sized pot plants with the more desirable rounder flowers. This breeding direction has continued with the size of the so-called miniature cymbidiums becoming larger and larger. The older varieties are now often preferred as pot plants and the newer varieties, derived from miniature breeding, appear to have far greater potential for providing sprays of cut flowers. That line of breeding has now come full circle.

A third miniature species, *Cymbidium devonianum*, introduced a totally different shape and growth habit to the group. When crossed onto the standard C. Western Rose, the resultant grex, C. Bulbarrow, had a distinctive shape with pendant spike habit and smoky tones, inherited from the species parent. Its popularity ensured that other C. *devonianum* hybrids were made. Another species, C. *madidum*, also produced distinctive pendulous hybrids but unfortunately the hybrids also inherited the enormous pseudobulbs and long leaves of the species parent.

During the last decade, there has been an emphasis on nature and conservation and this has been accompanied by a growing appreciation among gardeners for flowers and plants that 'look like wild flowers'. This concept surfaced among *Cymbidium* hobbyists, as a renewed interest in those very small species that had been grown in the Orient for centuries. Those miniature species were earlier interpreted by occidental gardeners as being rather 'weedy' in appearance, and only to be enjoyed by people with a peculiar appreciation for the curious and exotic. Once growers were exposed to traditional ancient forms they became enamored with them and it was not long before species such as C. *goeringii* and C. *sinense* were being bred into the complex hybrid lines. As was the case with *Cattleya* breeding, the aim initially was for larger and fuller flowers, but once this was achieved the breeders turned back to the species making smaller and more graceful flowers with rather different shapes and attitudes.

Phalaenopsis

From a horticultural point of view the genus *Phalaenopsis* falls into three main groups. There are standard *Phalaenopsis* that produce long arching sprays of large white or pink flowers, often called 'moth orchids'. A second group has branched sprays of smaller flowers that resemble the larger moth orchids in shape, often called multiflorals. The third group is a series of hybrids made with a variety of species with smaller starry and leathery flowers that tend to be borne on short spikes. Modern orchidists tend to call the last type, novelty *Phalaenopsis*. Currently, the large white *Phalaenopsis* are riding the peak of a popularity wave and nursery production can scarcely keep up with the demand from either hobbyists or florists. They rank among the most popular of all pot plants.

Early in their hybridizing history, there were two trends in *Phalaenopsis* breeding:

1) The line breeding of the large moth orchids towards perfection.
2) A series of primary hybrids often between the moth orchids and the novelties.

Then interest in the novelty hybrids started to

diminish as hybridizers started to improve upon the giant moth orchids and interest became focussed primarily in that direction. Most of the early novelty hybrids were lost. However, as it turned out the novelty hybrids were to play an important role in the history of *Phalaenopsis* hybridizing. But, before their usefulness could be realized they had to be remade again; fortunately though, many of the wild species were still extant.

The major species among the moth types were *Phalaenopsis amabilis*, with a pristine white flat rounded flower, and *P. sanderiana*, a closely related pink form. Line breeding led to the production of large white or pink flowers. As with other orchids, the flowers became larger and larger and closer to the hybridizers' ideal with round full forms. As the ideal was reached and progress became slower and slower, hybridizers in the United States started to look at some of the other species. The star-shaped species are so unlike the perfected moth orchids that in some parts of the world,

28 *Cymbidium* Pipeta 'Cecil Park' HCCI/AOS. This is a miniature hybrid *Cymbidium* from the diminutive C. *floribundum* (syn. *C. pumilum*). These smaller types became important horticultural pot plants. (Photo credit: Richard Clark and the American Orchid Society).

such as Britain, they continued to be ignored. The Americans, however, saw in the species a potential source for new colors. Ultimately they hoped to incorporate the colors into the cascading rounded moth types, but along the way the novelty forms gained acceptance as a new kind of hobbyist plant in its own right. The novelties bear leathery stars in brilliant yellows, waxy whites, glowing reds and even browns and are usually barred or blotched with contrasting colors. Sometimes they contain blends of colors that are difficult to describe. Several species had yellow coloring and astute breeders could see a path using those to make yellow, orange or red large moth flowers.

Attention to the species was refocused in the late fifties and early sixties when Oscar Kirch (in Hawaii) produced *Phalaenopsis* Princess Kaiulani, a primary hybrid between *P. violacea* and *P. amboinensis*. This was a great success; it is still remade and used in hybridizing more than thirty years later. In addition B.O. Bracey, at that time a California-based hybridizer, made the hybrid *P.* Samba by crossing *P. amboinensis* onto the hybrid *P.* Star of Rio. This latter hybrid also looms in the background of many modern *Phalaenopsis*. A hybrid between *P. violacea* and a spotted species *P. lueddemanniana*, saddled with the almost unmanageable name of *P.* Luedde-violacea, had been made as far back as the nineteenth century by the famous firm of Veitch and Son, in England. That hybrid was lost and had to be remade for use in modern novelty breeding, where it has proven itself to be a good parent.

The species, *P. amboinensis*, has also proven itself to be a useful parent and ancestor in modern *Phalaenopsis* breeding. Even in the present decade *P. amboinensis* is still one of the most popular parents and is combined not only with novelty but also standard hybrids. It imparts heavy substance that allows flowers to withstand adverse air pollution, definitely a plus in this modern world. It also transmits its yellow coloring to its offspring. Back in 1927, W. van Deventer had made a primary hybrid between the white moth *P. amabilis* and *P. amboinensis*. The cross was called *P.* Deventeriana but dropped into obscurity and was lost. In the late 1970s and early 1980s, *P.* Deventeriana was remade and surfaced as one of the most important parents that could straddle the gap between the novelty and moth types of flowers. It transmits soft yellow coloring from *P. amboinensis* to its offspring. Many of the yellow forms of *P. amboinensis* transmit genes for yellow coloring that tends to fade. Adding another yellow species *P. fasciata* can prevent this. In fact, the primary hybrid from *P. amboinensis* by *P. fasciata*, made and registered by Irene Dobkin in 1975 and called *P.* Golden Pride, bears flat bright and non-fading yellow stars with brown barring. So many clones of *P.* Golden Pride were awarded that the grex did much to consolidate the respectability of the novelty types.

A major breakthrough in breeding yellow *Phalaenopsis* came with the appearance of *P.* Golden Sands. One clone from the grex, called 'Canary', received a First Class Certificate from the American Orchid Society and has subsequently featured strongly in modern breeding. The grex of *P.* Golden Sands resulted when a standard large white *Phalaenopsis*, *P.* Fenton Davis Avant was crossed with the species *P. lueddemanniana*. There has been the suggestion that the registered species parent was incorrectly identified and that it may, instead, have been the species *P. fasciata* that also seems to transmit a non-fading yellow gene. Be that as it may, the combination of a species with the line-bred standard white has opened several new avenues. There is still a strong trend in *Phalaenopsis* breeding to produce large moth orchids but now the idea is to transfer the brilliant colorings from the novelty types into the more standard-shaped large flowers. Clear indications that this will succeed are already being seen in the most recent modern hybrids.

As early as 1896, Veitch registered a cross between a miniature *Phalaenopsis* species, *P. equestris* and a multifloral moth type, called *P. stuartiana*. The resulting grex was called *P.* Cassandra, but did not garner much attention. When *P.* Cassandra was remade nearly a hundred years later its potential for breeding miniature *Phalaenopsis* became apparent. *Phalaenopsis* Cassandra has given rise to a series of small floriferous pot plants. Using its genes for small plant as well as small flower size in breeding, hybridizers have been able to produce a series of small to intermediate sized plants that carry large trusses of intermediate sized flowers, ideal for dining table or desk decoration. Another miniature species, *P. lindenii*, had a different effect on *Phalaenopsis* breeding. Some clones of this species have a labellum and petals that bear longitudinal stripes. Bred to the large standard moth-shaped flowers the striping effect was transferred to the large flowers to achieve big flowers with contrasting red veins over the entire flower.

There is a tendency to try and achieve colors in flowers that are not normally extant in the wild species or even the garden varieties. Hence the successful drive to make pink daffodils, lavender-blue roses and true red *Phalaenopsis*. The latter coloring was achieved by combining genes derived from naturally occurring yellow flowered species with those of the purple species.

The current interest in *Phalaenopsis* species that can be used in hybridizing has led to the virtual extermination of a few of the wild species. Among these is *P. gigantea*, an enormously large species, which can measure as much as three or more feet (one meter) across the leaves. Fortunately, the large vegetative characteristics are usually not passed to its hybrids but the rounded symmetrical flower shape with heavy spotting is transmitted. A few plants were brought into cultivation between 20 and 25 years ago and several interesting hybrids were made that have contributed their round flower shapes to some modern novelties. In turn, these *P. gigantea* hybrids were used for further breeding. Within the past 5 years plant collectors have returned to the plant's natural habitat and have stripped out so many of the orchids that they are now endangered, if not extinct, in their natural forests.

This is another example where monetary greed has overridden the concerns of the species. *P. gigantea* has already made its genetic contribution, but the demands for the species itself (as an oddity) continues, even though most hobbyists cannot devote the room needed to grow and maintain an adult plant of the species. In addition, the species is difficult to grow well in captivity. Most of the wild collected plants have already succumbed in cultivation and unfortunately many of the others seem to have picked up viral infections. Well-grown artificially propagated seedlings are available but they just do not have the allure of a mature jungle specimen even if its chances of survival are remote. This is a case where the course of orchidology would be better served by insuring that an adequate population remained in the wild, in the event that future generations may require *P. gigantea* again.

Yet another *Phalaenopsis* species has had an even worse time of it. *P. micholitzii* was never plentiful and has not been used very much for hybridizing. Plants appeared to be confined to one small population and when they were rediscovered not so long ago, the entire population was stripped away, including even the small seedlings. Now probably extinct in the wild, *P. micholitzii* was exploited for its rarity more than anything else. This species does not have particularly showy flowers, and the plant itself is nondescript. Its potential usefulness, however, may lie in the fact that it was supposed to grow in a much cooler climate than other *Phalaenopsis* species, and hence it might have been useful in breeding cool temperature tolerance into the hybrid strains.

Another species, *Phalaenopsis javanica* is said to be extinct in the wild, although it still lingers in cultivation. It has only been used sparingly to make hybrids but has the potential for radically changing the shape of the flowers and adding a very brilliant hard gloss to the

blooms. Unfortunately unless this species can be maintained in cultivation its potential will be lost forever from the hybrizers palette.

Paphiopedilums

The paphiopedilums or slipper orchids are among the most popular in the entire orchid family and over the last century have seen the most continuous and fervent hybridizing activity. Literally thousands of hybrids have been made. In some respects the hybridizing pattern that we see in *Paphiopedilum* is reminiscent of that found with *Phalaenopsis*. Initially many species were grown and a series of primary hybrids produced. The shapes of nearly all of the tropical slipper orchid species are angular and far from the preferred flat circles found in the 'show-type' flowers in other genera. Initially, in hybridizing it appears that the breeders were merely crossing any species onto any other species just to see what would happen and to make primary hybrids for their own sake. As it is a relatively large group (more than 80 species), a great number of primary hybrids were registered. There was also an effort to collect and grow especially selected variations of the jungle species. The 'better' forms and rarer species commanded higher prices. In an effort to maintain monopolies of certain species, collectors often kept the locality secret or deliberately fabricated incorrect localities.

Over the course of the years, the hybridizers started to select for hybrids that had slightly wider petals and rounder and flatter dorsal sepals. Eventually it became apparent that a slipper orchid that conformed to the ideal 'round as saucers' shapes could be produced. At about that time, interest in species became very secondary and intense hybridizing activity towards the 'ideals' took place. Many of the fine selected species were lost, and except for a handful of primary hybrids that lingered in a few collections, most of the slipper orchids grown were what are now called standard and/or complex hybrids. Of the complex hybrid paphiopedilums, many could not be called beautiful, even though they conformed to the tight judging criteria. The flowers are frequently of harsh colors, greens, browns and somber purples. Flowers can be marked with brown, muddy flushes or even by raised black warts. The flowers have a more masculine quality and 'handsome' is a better epithet for many of them. The slippers tend to be the flowers to which hobbyists often migrate after experiencing the pretty cattleyas and spectacular cymbidiums. Perhaps they are flowers for jaded appetites.

Resurgence in appreciation of *Paphiopedilum* species started to take place in the 1960s. This was due primari-

29   *Paphiopedilum viniferum* 'JAC' (syn. *P. callosum* 'JAC') (Photo: Fred Jernigan and Francisco Baptista)

30   A flower of *P.* Holdenii, showing the dark coloring and spotted petals inherited from *P. viniferum* 'JAC' one of its grandparents (Photo credit: Kevin Porter).

ly, to the efforts of a few men in California, such as Jack Fowlie, who, as the editor of the *Orchid Digest Magazine*, began to write and publish articles on *Paphiopedilum* species. Another individual was Ray Rands, who imported jungle plants and made available large numbers of species. Ray Rands and Rex van Delden, a hybridizer at the firm of F.A. Stewart, Inc., began to make large numbers of primary and novelty hybrids. Concurrently, the complex standard hybrids were commanding very high prices for divisions of exceptional clones and had become collector's items, especially among the Japanese. In an effort to capitalize on the market, enormous numbers of complex hybrids were made. Many of the crosses were made indiscriminately and were not well thought out. Not only was there a glut on the market but the great majority of the plants gave poor quality flowers. These flowers were gawky, misshapen and sometimes downright ugly. In fact they were jocularly referred to as 'spotted toads'. Demand fell off and the market values of those plants started to plummet. Initially the demand for the seedlings declined and prices became so competitive that only the bigger wholesalers could make a profit by selling large numbers at cheap prices. Then many of the collectors' clones started to depreciate as well. The interests of the hobbyists turned elsewhere, back to the species and primary hybrids where the chances of getting an interesting and graceful flower were much better. Not only were the old primary hybrids remade but breeders also rushed to make those primaries that the early workers in the nineteenth century had neglected to make.

With attention refocused on the species, collectors went out again to bring them in. In the process many new species have been discovered and some of the older ones which had been 'lost' were rediscovered. Surprisingly, genuinely new species seemed to emerge at the rate of one every two years. Some of the newer species were so spectacular that one wonders how they could have escaped notice for so long. In recent years an even faster spate of new species have been named.

The orchid judges, first in America and then in other parts of the world, learnt to modify their concepts of what made a 'good slipper'. They seem to have realized that their concepts had been too restricted and influenced by the complex hybrids. At the current time, in Southern California, where much of this breeding continues, most of the awards given to paphiopedilums are bestowed either on species or primary and novelty type hybrids.

Along with this appreciation of species and primary hybrids there has recently emerged the concept that man can breed 'better' species. Now all of the awards given to species are not given to plants originally collected in the jungles of Asia but rather to line bred species derived from selected parents. There is also the realization that if one uses a poorly formed (in terms of judging merits) jungle species to make a novelty hybrid then the chances of producing exceptionally good offspring are remote. What one needs are good parents to get good offspring. Ultimately the source of the species is from the wild and one needs to get selected clones from there, but the current market is now becoming as receptive to seedlings from good species sibling crosses as it is to high potential hybrids. This trend is flavored with a twinge of regret. Records of earlier species clones that were in cultivation at the turn of the century indicate that many of the forms were far superior in terms of size, color and shape to anything that can be found today. If we still had those clones what wonderful hybrids we could make today. And what superior line bred species could also be produced. What a pity our ancestors had not cherished and propagated their species with more enthusiasm. Let us hope that our grandchildren do not lodge the same complaints about us.

One of the first new species to be utilized in the second wave of primary hybrid breeding in the 1960s, and which had a marked influence on hybridizing was *P. sukhakulii*. The first few plants commanded prices in excess of $1,000 each but fortunately the price soon dropped as other collections were imported. This species imparts to its offspring a set of wide and rigidly horizontal petals heavily peppered with black spots. The dominating effect of petal form and stance is expressed through several generations. These hybrids are easy to flower and make excellent 'beginner's' plants. This ancestry is in the background of modern slipper pot plant market.

At the other end of the spectrum is *Paphiopedilum rothschildianum*, which is definitely a connoisseur's plant. This species was, for a long time, only to be found in the collections of the few and the rich. The locality was lost and only a few plants persisted in collections from the original importations, which were made approximately one hundred years ago. Sheila Collinette rediscovered the plant on Mt. Kinabalu in Borneo. Perhaps the most majestic of all the *Paphiopedilum* species, it bears three to five flowers, painted with rich bitter chocolate-brown stripes over a white or ivory background. Individual flowers can measure 12 in (31 cm) from tip to tip across the horizontally held petals. Its hybrids seem to inherit both the species' size and its magnificence. Consequently there is always a demand for hybrids made with *P. rothschildianum*.

Likewise, *P. delenatii*, a soft baby-pink slipper orchid from Vietnam, was brought into cultivation in France in

the 1920s and then eventually propagated artificially. According to legend a single plant gave rise to all of the cultivated stock, until the species was rediscovered and reintroduced in the 1990s. The plant remained scarce and had a reputation for being difficult, until Lance Birk was able to produce vigorous seedlings from a selfing of one clone. During the 1970s and into the 1980s there was enormous demand for hybrid seedlings using *P. delenatii* as one parent. It was supplanted as a desirable parent when a number of closely related species, *P. armeniacum*, *P. emersonii*, *P. malipoense* and *P. micranthum*, came into cultivation during the mid 1980s. *Paphiopedilum delenatii* was rediscovered in central Vietnam about ten years ago, and although there was a flurry of black-market activity concerning this species it did not re-ignite any interest in *P. delenatii* hybrids.

Despite the fact that one can, by careful selective breeding, produce 'superior' forms of species, we still need the wild populations because within them may be variants which have arisen spontaneously, with features for which we could not line breed without much effort. The genetic variation within a wild population is usually much wider than the variation within a domesticated crop. This is even true of common garden plants such as tomatoes, where hundreds, if not thousands of different varieties have been bred, yet all of the crop tomatoes contain less variation than the few wild tomato plants that have been analyzed. It is easier to retrieve a gene from a wild population than wait for the appropriate mutation to occur in a domesticated crop. One such orchid example is *P. callosum*, where an unusually dark form (instead of the normally light lavender colored flower of *P. callosum*) was found serendipitously. This clone, 'Sparkling Burgundy' FCC/AOS, had a dorsal sepal, petals and pouch of a dark wine color and was used to make a group of hybrids called vinicolors. For nearly 20 years the vinicolors dominated slipper orchid breeding programs. In the same category are other rare mutants that make no red (anthocyanin) pigments at all. These were used in the early decades of the 20th century to produce the beautiful grass-green *P.* Maudiae-type hybrids, which are still amongst the most popular of all orchid hybrids. The mutations for albinism are not identical and seem to occur in several different forms. For example *P. bellatulum* forma *album* will give colored progeny if crossed with the closely related species *P. niveum* forma *album*.

While there have been a number of new *Paphiopedilum* species brought into general cultivation many of them are not used for hybridization. Nevertheless, there is great demand for all *Paphiopedilum* species, irrespective of their floral characteristics. This genus is probably the most popular in the entire orchid family, for amateurs making species collections, and its popularity has had consequences for the species' survival of the whole group. This is one group for which plant collection pressures may have had more impact on wild populations than habitat destruction.

Each time a desirable new species or unusual variant is discovered, or when a long lost species such as *Paphiopedilum sanderianum* is reintroduced, it creates a flurry of excitement and novel breeding opportunities. After all access to the wild species was halted when all *Paphiopedilum* species were added to Appendix I of CITES there was a marked change in both the attitude and the activity of slipper breeders. In parts of the world such as the United States, it is even illegal to sell slipper orchid hybrids made with the newly described species. Without the continuous input of new novelties, breeders have had to rely on trying to make small step improvements in their product. Much of the excitement and interest in slipper orchids started to wane and breeding appears to have gone into a decline.

Odontoglossum alliance

Said to be among the most beautiful flowers in the world, the *Odontoglossum* hybrids, bred primarily from *Odontoglossum crispum*, have always commanded attention. The species was originally obtained from the high altitude mist forests of Colombia and the best forms were collected out during the last century. This was a case where the forests were literally cut down and destroyed in order to get the orchids, rather than orchids being destroyed because the forests were being felled, as is the current situation. The best specimens had arching sprays with crystalline white floral parts. Soon hybrids were made with other species and many of these new types were noted for their intricate patterning, often as complex and schizophrenic as a fine Oriental rug. Some species with smaller, but brilliant and unusual colors were incorporated into the gene pool to widen the color spectrum. The most important of these was *Cochlioda noezliana*, a plant that produces small sprays of brilliant orange-red flowers. Other genes came from the Pansy orchids in the genus *Miltoniopsis* that are closely related to the odontoglossums. All of these were cool growing hybrids, relatively easy to cultivate in some temperate parts of the world but difficult in the continental United States and tropical countries where summer temperatures frequently rise over 90°F. In an effort to produce hybrids that could tolerate a wider temperature range, several Mexican and Central American species such as *Lemboglossum bictoniense*, *L. cervantesii* and *L. rossii*

were bred into the cool hybrids. Some *Oncidium* species such as *O. crispum*, *O. leucochilum* and *O. tigrinum* were also used for greater warmth tolerance. This process is still continuing at the present time.

Within this alliance there are several minor themes which seem to have appeared for short periods. One such short-lived phase was an interest in hybrids made from *O. lanceanum* and its allies, the mule-eared oncidiums, so-called after the shape of the large leaves. More interest was recently focused on another group of rather pretty hybrids called the equitant oncidiums. These are small colorful plants, based primarily on three species, now placed in the genus *Tolumne*. *Tolumne pulchellum* bears sprays of large pink flowers, while *T. guianense* (syn. *T. desertorum*) contributed yellow flowers. A third species, *T. triquetrum* gave red spotted or solid red flowers in its hybrids. Combinations of the three species and their hybrids produced small plants whose flowers were sprays of variably hued blossoms in a wide range of colors. For several years during the 1970s and early 1980s equitant oncidiums were quite a fad but recently their popularity appears to have slipped and plants in collections do not get replaced if they die. If the popularity of this group is 'rediscovered' a hundred years hence, will the wild germplasm still be available to refashion them?

Dendrobium

While dendrobiums have been grown almost continuously since the last century, for the most part it was the wild species that collectors sought and that the hobbyists grew. Nevertheless, there have been several hybridizing trends. One of the early trends involved *D. nobile* a beautiful Indian species. In recent years, the Yamamoto *Dendrobium* hybrids, named after the hybridist, have come to the fore as pot plants and many wonderful varieties have been developed. *Dendrobium nobile* itself is a pinkish mauve color, while a pure white form also exists. Within the Yamamoto hybrids are other colors, such as the very desirable golden-yellow hues. The yellow coloring, however, goes back to a species that was incorporated early on into the hybrids. As far back as 1874, the hybrid *Dendrobium* Ainsworthii was registered. This was a cross between the popular *D. nobile* and a yellow-flowered species *D. aureum*. About twenty years later that hybrid was bred with another *D. nobile* hybrid called *D.* Wiganiae. The resultant grex was *D.* Thwaitesiae, which nearly a hundred years later, was crossed with the white nobile-type hybrid *D.* Mont Blanc. This produced *D.* Golden Wave, which started the great advance in breeding modern yellow '*nobile*' hybrids. This was one case where the earlier hybrids were maintained and then used a century later. Usually the primary and earlier hybrids are lost, and one has to try and remake them. The point of this is that it is hard to predict when one might need a parent for breeding. One could not in the earlier days of this century have predicted that D. Thwaitesiae would have been so important, or why.

In the 1950s and 1960s much of the activity in *Dendrobium* breeding concerned *D. phalaenopsis* and its

31   *Ascocenda* Peggy Hashimoto 'Maui Gem' AM/AOS has *A. curviifolium* as a grandparent.
(Photo credit: Richard Clark and the American Orchid Society).

hybrids. As with other genera, very much larger, rounder and darker forms were produced. While these are spectacular flowers, the plants themselves are quite large. More recently, another related species – *D. biggibum* var. *compactum* – has been used to reduce the size of the *D. phalaenopsis* hybrids and make a more manageable pot plant. Unfortunately this group of hybrids, while making spectacular flowers, have relatively poor keeping qualities. Much better flower longevity is found in the *Ceratobium* group of the genus. When '*Dendrobium ceratobium*-type' hybrids or species are bred with the '*Phalaenopsis*-type' hybrids better keeping qualities are transmitted to their offspring. Many of these dendrobiums are currently grown in Asia and Hawaii for the worldwide cut flower and pot plant markets.

If one peruses the current orchid hybrid registers, one finds that perhaps the greatest current activity is taking place in the *Dendrobium* group. More hybrids are being registered and many daring crosses, using virtually unknown species, are being produced. What the major trends portend are not clear at the moment for the taxon is in an active state of flux. What is clear, however, is that many wild species are being used.

Vanda Alliance

The vandas are popular garden subjects in the Asian tropics, Florida and Hawaii. Like many other orchids they were initially line bred from only a few main species (Motes, 1997) of which only *Vanda coerulea*, one of the few blue colored orchid species, is still currently included in the genus. A most magnificent plant, *Vanda sanderiana*, with striking bunches of round flat pink and brown flowers, was transferred to the genus *Euanthe*. The other species known for many decades as *V. teres* is now called Papilionanthe. Hybrids between these three are still called vandas but they and their offspring were also combined with many other species from other genera to produce an enormous number of intergeneric hybrid names. Thailand has been a center of activity for the production of fine *Vanda* hybrids for exhibition and also a number of important intergeneric hybrids for the cut flower market.

When an opportunistic albino clone of *V. sanderiana* appeared, it became possible to breed for white and green vandas. But, it took the addition of another species, *V. deari*, to bring bright and strong yellow colors to the large *Vanda* hybrids. Now the vandas could be said to literally embrace all the colors of the rainbow.

Unfortunately vandas are large plants and they are not suited to the smaller modern greenhouses. The genus *Ascocentrum* contains quite small growing plants and when these are added to the *Vanda* mix to make asco-cendas not only was the size of the plant reduced, but brilliant flowers were produced. Two species, *Ascocentrum curvifolium* and *A. miniatum*, have large numbers of very small orange flowers, produced on miniature plants. The former species was useful for making orange, pink and red flowers; its hybrids were fertile and could be bred on. The *A. miniatum* species gave yellow to orange progeny, but it did not breed as readily. The compact plants occur in a wide range of bright colors and were very popular and fashionable. They had much more impact on the hobby grower than any of the other multitudinous intergeneric hybrids produced in the vanda alliance. For over ten years there was a flurry of breeding activity, when ascocendas were immensely popular and many orchid growers tried to grow them. Interest subsided but a certain level of ascocenda breeding continued to the present time. In Hawaii, the ascocendas were repeatedly bred back into the big *Vanda* hybrids and the brilliant orange and red colors were easily introduced into the large garden orchids. One of the unexpected by-products of the ascocentrum – *Vanda* hybrids was the production of continuously blooming plants.

Insights

We see that during the history of orchid hybridizing there has been the repeated introduction of species genes into the hybrid lines. These, in turn, have led to new directions in the production of novel kinds of flowers. It is not always the introduction of new, previously unused, species but sometimes the introduction of a special variant of an old species that can be used to introduce novelty into a group of hybrids. Wild species of orchid give hybridizers the opportunity to keep the hobby growing, allowing them to produce a vibrant, ever changing kaleidoscope of flowers. In turn, orchid growing has remained one of the largest and most intense of the gardening activities. For nearly a century and a half it has captured the interest and hearts of gardeners and will continue to do so as long as the wild species remain to fuel the hopes and aspirations of the plant breeders.

Great Britain was a dominant player in the orchid world for much of the 19th and 20th centuries, but during the last two decades of the 20th century the country lost her pre-eminence in orchid breeding. While there are no doubt many factors that contributed to the decline one cannot help but wonder if the restrictive measures concerning importation of wild orchid species, that the country enacted at that time, was not the main causal factor for the decline. Today, on a global scale, very few would consider Great Britain of any importance in modern orchid breeding. The leading countries, such as Taiwan, Japan and the USA, have had continued access to the world's wild orchids.

I believe that it is vitally important for the orchid hobby that breeders have a ready access to new germ plasm. But with this also comes the responsibility to protect our sources and that means effective conservation in the wild.

CHAPTER 6

Orchids and Ethnobotany

It is a sad commentary on our society that beauty and flowers get such a low priority when one is trying to justify the protection and conservation of plant species. Usually the needs for conservation must be couched in terms of a plant's usefulness as a source of food, timber, industrial chemicals and/or medicines. Wanting to save an orchid species merely because it is pretty or has botanical interest is unlikely to loosen the purse strings. Money talks and demonstrated economic importance will always get preference over simply wanting to save wild species. Unfortunately for orchids there is only one species within this enormous plant family that has any fiscal impact outside the flower markets and even that is not of any vital importance. The fermented seed pods of *Vanilla planifolia*, originally a Mexican species, yield the familiar flavorant that is the only serious commercial and non-floricultural claim to fame for the entire orchid family.

Are there any other orchids that have a use other than as an ornament? While orchids have in the past, been utilized from time to time as foods and medicines, this is currently a very minor role. However, this does not mean that there are no other potentially important uses for orchid species. The ethnobotanical roles of orchids are quite extensive and they have played a considerable part in the folk medicines of people around the world. In addition, they have also been featured in tribal magic and have been put to a variety of different and sometimes unusual uses. As the culture of much of the developing nations becomes homogenized and westernized we can expect to loose many of these peculiar socio-biological uses.

There is almost no authoritative documentation on the ethnobotany of orchids. Much of the information is based on hearsay and recipes are non-existent. Documentation is poor and many of the suggested uses are difficult to substantiate. In addition, the taxonomy used to label the various species is often out of date or simply incorrect. Records are scattered widely in the literature of many languages and some are very old, sometimes going back several centuries. Lawler (1984) and Miller (1978) have gathered and collated much of the

earlier information and the interested reader is encouraged to peruse their works for additional details and further references.

We will look at some of the uses that orchids have been put to in the past and this will give us a glimpse of some of the potential of the group.

Plants and chemicals

Nearly all plants, irrespective of the family to which they belong, share a common problem. Because they are the primary carbon fixers in the world, converting the energy of sunlight into organic molecules, they are also the source to which the non-carbon fixers must turn for their own energy requirements. Put simply, animals must either eat plants or other animals that have eaten plants, in order to get at the energy stores the plants have produced. Most plants cannot move very far or fast, they cannot run away from their predators and have therefore had to adopt other methods to protect themselves. The simplest method is for the plant to produce chemicals that make it distasteful, if not downright poisonous to the animals that try to eat them. These chemicals are often called secondary metabolites because they are not concerned with the everyday primary metabolic activities needed to keep the plants' cells functioning. The secondary metabolites fall into a number of distinct chemical groups including alkaloids, phenols, coumarins and terpenes. These kinds of chemicals are present in orchids as well as many other plant families. Nearly half of man's present day pharmaceuticals are derived from plant secondary metabolites, but the modern pharmacy does not currently use any medicines prepared from orchids.

It is important to realize that while we may not currently use a chemical derived from a plant species, this does not mean that that species does not contain any useful chemicals. Plants can make so many chemicals that our current and past surveys are necessarily very incomplete. It is quite possible that we have missed potentially important molecules. One cannot foresee whether a chemical may have a use in the future. It is quite common to only search for a few kinds of compounds or test the plant's chemicals against a small number of pathological situations. Considering the number of species in the family we must admit that orchids have received far less attention from the biochemists than one might have expected. This may be because there are so few cases of people being poisoned by orchids; it is often the toxic effects of plants that attract attention.

Salep

A number of orchid species have been used as a source of food, but there is only one product that has been widely used and this is called 'salep'. Salep is prepared from the underground tubers of terrestrial orchids and has been widely used in the Middle East. Many terrestrial orchids have an annual life cycle, where the plant dies down and remains underground during either the winter or dry months. When conditions improve the plants rapidly start to grow and produce new aerial shoots. In order to achieve this the plants need to provide a store of resources that can be quickly utilized. Towards the end of the growing season the plants produce an underground tuber that is filled with a variety of storage products, including starch and mucilage. The starch is built from two sugars, mannose and glucose, while the mucilage appears to be a compound related to cellulose. Together those two compounds may account for over 70% of the weight of the tubers. An additional 5% of the weight is protein. Towards the end of the last century enormous quantities of tubers were collected and dug for salep production. It has been suggested that as much as 125 tons of tubers were dug each year. It is not really known if the plants were cultivated or wild, but it seems most likely that they were the latter. This says a lot about the robustness of the orchid populations of these regions and it is surprising that any still survive.

During the course of the growing season the plant will start to build a new tuber for the following winter. Thus there are times when two tubers are present. The paired tubers were thought to resemble the testicles of familiar animals and they are therefore often assigned aphrodisiac qualities in folk medicine. The term salep is also apparently derived from the tuber's resemblance to sex organs.

When freshly collected the tubers are whitish and juicy, but after boiling for about 15 minutes they can be skinned. They are then threaded onto string, like so many beads and dried in the sun (Hansen, 1997). The tubers dry to a translucent yellowish-tan color and can be stored until needed. About 60% of the weight is lost during drying, after which they can be ground into flour, which will become jelly-like on the addition of water.

For some time, salep was considered to be among the most nutritious of foods that could be obtained and was especially recommended for convalescents. Lewis Castle wrote in 1886, that the use of salep was widespread. "It is employed, in the East particularly, as a restorative and as a powerful analeptic (stimulant), against weakness of the forces. In Poland the decoction of salep is the drink used in almost all diseases. It is highly nutritious, and may be used for the same purposes as sago, tapioca, and arrow root." It is now considered to be on a par with potatoes or corn flour, but it is less nutritious than tapioca or sago. Salep was often prepared as soup, porridge or as a sweetened beverage. It was the basis for saloop, a drink dispensed in English parlors, but it was later replaced following the advent of cheaper teas and coffees. However, in parts of Turkey it is still drunk as a hot beverage.

Fox testicle ice cream and other flavors!

Eric Hansen (1997) relates his experiences in Turkey researching a form of ice cream made from the tubers of *Orchis provincialis*. The Turkish name *salepli dondurma* translates literally into "fox testicle ice cream". The history of this dessert goes back nearly 500 years. The modern ice cream is usually fruit flavored, but Hansen describes an aftertaste "….slightly sweet with a subtle, nutty flavor similar to dried milk powder. It also had a hint of mushrooms, yak butter, or goats on a rainy day." Because of all the mucilage in the tubers, this confection has a chewy consistency and it can apparently be pulled out into long ropes. It is easier to eat with a knife and fork.

Hansen calculated that one ice cream store utilized about 2.5 tons of dried orchid tubers, which translates into nearly 5 tons of fresh tubers. With each tuber weighing only a few grams, millions of individual wild plants need to be harvested each year to supply a single ice cream producer. Yet the locals claim that the wild plants are still abundant and unaffected by the harvest.

This ice cream is reputed to have several health benefits including a salutary one on a man's sexual prowess. Hansen dodges the question on that one but points out the long lines of adult men buying *salepli dondurma*. Hopefully the newly available drugs such as Viagra® and others will finally help relieve the collecting pressures for wild orchids and rhinoceros horn.

Most of the salep was harvested from species of the genus *Orchis* and of these the best quality was found in *O. latifolia*, *O. mascula*, *O. militaris* and *O. morio*. In Turkey *O. provincialis* seems to be preferred (Hansen, 1997). Genera such as *Platanthera*, *Ophrys*, *Gymnadenia*, as well as many others were also employed. While most of the salep use was centered in Europe and East Asia, it has also been prepared as a food in other areas. In Brazil salep was made from the tubers of *Ophrys argentea*, while in North America tubers from species of *Habenaria* were used. Salep has also been extracted from the genera *Bletia* and *Eulophia*, which do not have tubers homologous with those of other terrestrial orchids, but possess underground pseudobulbs instead.

Besides being used as a food, salep has also been used for medicinal purposes and has been prescribed for such a wide array of ailments that one wonders if it could have been effective for any. Among its uses have been treatments for diarrhea, dysentery, kidney problems and even fevers, such as typhoid and enteric fever. It has also been prescribed for heart problems, arthritis, and epilepsy, to facilitate childbirth and prevent abortion. It has, on occasion, been used both to treat the "abuse of venereal pleasure" and as an aphrodisiac. It is highly unlikely that salep could have been an effective medicine for all, if any, of these ailments. Yet, 'where there is smoke there is often fire' and it is possible that certain species could have some effective medicinal properties. So many different species of orchid have been used to make salep that different species could even have some of the diverse effects for which it has been prescribed.

Vanilla

Vanilla is currently one of the most universally used of all spices and flavorings and finds its way not only into foodstuffs but also into perfumes, cosmetics and even tobacco. The flavoring is extracted from the fermented seedpods or beans (as they are called) that grow on the vanilla vine. The vines are popular plants as curiosity items for many orchid hobby growers, but few are capable of flowering them, so that their large white *Cattleya*-like flowers can be enjoyed.

Vanilla was originally cultivated in Central America in pre-Columbian times and was used primarily to flavor *chocolatl*, a drink that also contained cocoa and chili. By the early 16th century the Spanish had brought vanilla back to Europe, but it was initially used as a perfume. It was not until the second half of that century, when chocolate was being made in Spain, that the Europeans

32   *Vanilla* plantation, Ste. Marie, Madagascar. *Vanilla* beans are one of the main sources of foreign income for the Malagasy Republic.

started to use it as a spice to flavor drinks and foods. The first vanilla plants in Europe did not arrive until at least a century later. Although the plants are cultivated as oddities by hobbyists all over the world, commercial production is only economically feasible in tropical climes.

The plants themselves are unusual orchids. Many of the *Vanilla* species are climbers and hence among the few vines found in the family. Because of their climbing nature they produce the longest orchid plants in the world. Several species have lost their leaves and photosynthesize primarily through their green stems and roots, which drape themselves through the forests in a serpentine fashion. The genus *Vanilla* contains many species and is cosmopolitan, being distributed around the world nearly everywhere that there are tropical forests. Several of the species have been used to produce vanilla but not all species do produce that compound. Rather surprisingly *V. aromaticum* is scentless. Another of the more unusual orchids is *V. griffithii* from Asia, which produces large soft fruits that are sweet and edible, although here too there is no vanilla flavor. The *V. griffithii* pods are eaten as a fresh fruit in Malaysia and Indonesia. Most species produce large beautiful flowers that resemble cattleyas.

There is one species of *Vanilla* which has a most unusual use and has nothing to do with either horticulture or food preparation. Rather surprisingly, the roots of *Vanilla grandifolia* are used for the manufacture of fishing nets!

Because many orchids have very specific pollinators, it was not possible to cultivate *V. planifolia* for vanilla outside of its native country until artificial pollinating methods were devised. Much of the world's vanilla now comes from Madagascar and other islands in the Indian Ocean. While *Vanilla planifolia* is the principle species that is grown for the pods there are at least two other species, *V. pompona* and *V. tahitiensis* that are also cultivated. Several additional species are grown for local consumption and used for their flavoring. The major ingredient in vanilla is a chemical called vanillin and has long been made synthetically. However, the natural product is deemed to be superior in flavor and vanilla is still cultivated today on a large scale in a few tropical countries. The demand and consumption of natural vanilla is quite large and hundreds of tons of the beans are imported into the United States each year. Considering the worldwide use of this condiment, considerable acreage must be devoted to the crop. Vanilla can be extracted from a few other unrelated orchid genera but these are not used to produce the spice. Several other orchids do produce similar flavors. *Selenipedium chica* and *Tetramicra bicolor* yield pods that are used in Panama and Brazil, respectively, for flavoring ice cream and confections. In addition, a tea is sometimes made from *Jumellea fragrans* leaves, that also contain vanillin, but the flavoring in that beverage actually comes from coumarin, a completely different type of compound.

The primary species, *V. planifolia*, is disease prone. Earlier on in the previous century there were efforts at inducing disease resistance by hybridizing, but whether or not these efforts have been successful is not clear. We do know that as nearly all orchid species within a genus are promiscuous and can be crossed with each other, it would be wise to retain as many species and variants as possible because they could be useful at a later date.

Faham Tea

Jumellea fragrans grows on the island of Mauritius (of Dodo fame), in the Indian Ocean and has been cultivated for approximately 150 years. For many years it was known as Angraecum fragrans and is still frequently referred to under that name. The dried leaves of this plant are said to be fragrant and reminiscent of vanilla, although the taste is also said to be like bitter almonds. Tea can be made from the leaves and is known as Faham or Bourbon tea; at one time it was quite popular. People would gather to sip the fashionable drink at special teashops. The tea however, could not compete with chocolate and eventually lost favor. Although Faham tea is still available it is rarely found. The tea was also used medicinally to stimulate digestion and to treat pulmonary consumption.

Medicinal properties

Several species of orchid have been, or in some cases still are, used in folk remedies around the world. Cypripedin is one of the best known products and it still sometimes appears in western Pharmacopoeias, another is the Chinese drug 'Shih-hu' which has a very strong following in the Orient. 'Shi-Hu', as it is also sometimes written, is based upon *Dendrobium* species. Another concoction, used in Traditional Chinese Medicine, is called 'Bai ji', which is made from the pseudobulbs of *Blettila striata*. It is used to treat a number of ailments (Reid, 1995) including 'liver fire', which has symptoms like bad breath, hot-temper, unsteady heart beat, etc. External applications of *Pholidota yunnanensis* are also recommended for arthritis (Shung, 1992).

Orchids have been widely used in Africa. They provide an antimalarial agent (*Acampe pachyglossa*), a cure for skin diseases (*Eulophia dilecta*), vermifuges (*Satyrium cordifolium*) and even enemas (*Stenoglottis fimbriata*). Similar kinds of lists can be found for the other continents. In all, Lawler (1984) lists some 327 species that have been reported to be in use around the world, for their supposed medicinal effects. One expects that most of the medicines may be ineffective but that merely reflects our western bias against folk medicines. It is quite likely that some highly effective compounds do reside in certain orchids. Certainly it is currently fashionable for large drug companies to scan wild plant species, looking for anticancer or other agents. It is only during the last few decades that western science has started to examine folk remedies and herbal remedies more closely. For much of the Third World, where per capita income is very low, indigenous people are unable to afford western pharmaceuticals and must rely on herbal remedies. With the population explosion, over-harvesting of wild plants for their medicinal value is having a deleterious and telling effect on remaining wild populations.

Robert Schultes (1990) compiled a list of all those plants from northwest Amazonia thought to have either medicinal or poisonous properties. Only an insignificant fraction of the many examples he found involved orchids and only a fraction of those seem to be worth investigating. He described a wash made from *Dichea muricata* which a group of native peoples, the Kofáns, use for treating eye infections. One unidentified *Epidendrum* or perhaps *Encyclia* provides mucilage that is used to treat cold sores on lips. If this proved to be an effective herpes treatment it would be very important. Details are also known about a preparation used by the Indians of the Rio Apaporis, which is used as a remedy to treat sores on the gums and lining of other mucous membranes of the mouth. Preparations made from pseudobulbs of *Eriopsis sceptrum* are boiled in water to extract the copious mucilage that is produced. The mucilage is then applied to the area of the sore. The Indians call the preparation 'wanoomaka', which means mouth herb. Another Kofán treatment, using an orchid, involves boiling the small plants of *Psygmorchis* (syn. *Oncidium*) *pusilla* in water and then washing skin lacerations with the perfusion. In this case, one cannot be sure if the orchid does anything, for surely washing a wound with boiled water should have a beneficial cleansing effect. Schultes also describes an interesting use for a tea, made from whole plants of an unspecified species of *Masdevallia*. This tea is prescribed by Kamsá medicine men to help pregnant women urinate and also to sooth inflammation of the bladder. The effect sounds like a relaxant for smooth muscle.

A single example will suffice to show how devastating the trade in medicines can be to orchids. *Flickingeria macraei* is closely allied to *Dendrobium* and is used in Ayurvedic medicine in India. This orchid has jointed stems with swollen nodes just below the leaves and, together with its small white flowers, makes a rather unprepossessing plant. There is a report of one hundred truckloads of *F. macraei* being exported from Nepal to India for medicinal purposes. Over 500,000 plants must have been sacrificed for this purpose, although the exact nature of the illness these plants were supposed to cure was not recorded. Clearly few species can withstand those levels of harvesting.

Cypripedin

The genus *Cypripedium* contains the temperate Northern Hemisphere lady's slippers. This is a large genus with 45 species spread across the continents of North America, Europe and Asia. During the latter part of the last century tons of roots of C. *parviflorum* var. *pubescens* were collected and extracted to produce a tincture called cypripedin, which was widely used in western countries. A tincture of cypripedin was prescribed as a stimulant and to cure a variety of nervous diseases such as headaches, insomnia and depression. Most of the other *Cypripedium* species contain this drug and were also harvested, but they were generally considered to be less efficacious. There are approximately five or six common North American species, which were used by different Indian tribes for somewhat similar medicinal effects. The North American Indians chewed the roots directly as a sedative and drank a sweetened concoction for headaches.

Extracts of *Cypripedium* species have been used in folk medicine around the world. In Asia, the species C. *guttatum* was used in Siberia and eastern Russia to treat epilepsy, while in northeastern China it is used for a wide variety of other ailments, as well as epilepsy. On the Indian subcontinent, C. *elegans* was used for several disorders of the nervous system. *Cypripedium macranthos* is also used in China, but more for treatment of vascular problems than nervous ones. The medicinal uses of these plants and the preparation of cypripedin are discussed more fully in Cribb (1997).

There appear to be no records of *Paphiopedilum* species being used being used as medicinal plants. These Asian tropical species are very closely related to the temperate *Cypripedium* species and, in fact, were often included in that genus. But both genera do have similar chemical compounds, which can sometimes cause allergic reactions in people handling the plants. Neotropical relatives belong to the genera *Phragmipedium* and *Selenipedium*. Parts of the South American slipper orchid *Phragmipedium ecuadorense*, are boiled in water and the resultant tea drunk to calm stomach problems (Schultes, 1990). Some *Selenipedium* species have seedpods that provide a flavorant. It is unknown whether or not the active agents in the tropical species are similar to cypripedin.

One wonders if the Asian and American uses of cypripedin were discovered independently or if they reflect some very old and common herbal knowledge that the original human settlers brought to North America, when they migrated from Asia to the New World across the Bering Straits. Other orchids also contain compounds that are used to modify nervous activity, for example both *Ceratandra grandiflora* and *Brachycorythis ovata* were used by the Xhosa peoples to treat madness, but once again whether or not the compounds are similar to cypripedin has not been investigated. In fact, very little research has been carried out on the phytochemistry of orchids.

Coral root

There are very few orchids featured in the herbals of North America. Besides *Cypripedium*, there was one another, the coral root (*Corallorhiza odontorhiza*). This is one of those unusual saprophytic orchids that bear no chlorophyll and is completely dependent on their symbiotic mycorrhizae for nutrition. The roots are white, chunky and have the appearance, more or less, of coral. The fresh roots were said to have an odd smell but that disappeared on drying. There were several other common names given to the root, including 'Chicken Toe' and 'Turkey Claw', both portions of bird anatomy that the early settlers were probably more familiar with than coral. The main action of the medicine prepared from dried and powdered roots was that of a diaphoretic i.e. it caused sweating in the patient. Coral root was used to try to break fevers. Unlike many of the other herbs used to induce perspiration, coral root apparently did not have other side effects. About 20 to 30 grains of powdered root was suspended in very hot water and administered every 2 to 3 hours (Grieve, 1971). No doubt the temperature of the water also added its own effect. There are several different species of *Corallorhiza* and all are said to contain similar active compounds.

Coral root was often mixed with other non-orchidaceous herbs, such as cohosh and May apple for specific treatments. With blue cohosh, (*Caulophyllum thalictroides*), an Appalachian herb, it was used as an ingredient both to regulate menstruation, and to help alleviate the pain associated with childbirth (Elliott, 1995).

Three Ecuadorian orchids

D'Alessando (1987) recorded uses for three Ecuadorian species that were still being prescribed by local 'Curanderos' (witch doctors) in southern regions of that country. The first of these is *Epidendrum secundum*, which has two uses. An extract of the entire plant with the flowers is used to treat nervous disorders, while an extract with additional stems and roots is used to treat liver disorders. He claims that *Stanhopea anfracta* has been used for centuries as a remedy for coughs and lung problems. Apparently, the species contains quantities of Eucalyptol; a chemical featured in several popular western cough preparations. Children in Ecuador are also known to eat the *Stanhopea* flowers. Finally, he points out that an extract made from the roots and flowers of *Cattleya maxima* is a very effective remedy against bleeding after childbirth.

Orchids, aphrodisiacs and human fertility

Aside from the romantic notions induced by gifts of orchid flowers, a number of species have been used to promote or retard fertility. Many years ago Arditti (personal communication) tested the assertion that Australian aborigines used fruits of *Cymbidium madidum* for birth control. He fed pods and seeds to mice and although there appeared to be a slight reduction in mouse litter size it was not a clear and significant effect. One wit snidely pointed out that the *Cymbidium* fruit might be a more effective birth control device if

the whole capsule was tightly clenched between the aboriginal woman's thighs. One of the real problems in testing folk remedies is the usual absence of any recipe. Here it was not possible to find out at what stage of maturation the fruit should be picked for use and exactly how it should be prepared for ingestion.

Castle (1886) considered vanilla to be "one of the most powerful aphrodisiacs if taken in a large dose". He also pointed out that the odor could have an intoxicating effect and had such an effect on workers harvesting the ripe pods.

In Africa, the Zulu peoples employed a number of orchids as charms and treatments; they are used to induce love and fertility (McDonald and Duckworth, 1994). *Liparis remota* is said to promote affairs of the heart, as do *Acrolophia cochlearis* and *Eulophia streptopetala*. Treatment involves drinking an infusion and then vomiting by sticking a finger down the back of one's throat. This purging is said to help get rid of bile and general bad spirits making one more attractive to one's intended partner. An infusion of *Cyrtorchis arcuata* can also be used as a purge to ensure that "...your loved one will cling to you as the orchid does to the tree." A different interpretation for clinging roots is the use of *Bulbophyllum maximum* (syn. *B. oxypterum*) which is widespread in tropical Africa. Here it is used to promote the healing of broken bones "....because it holds tightly to its own support" (Biegel, 1979). This is reminiscent of the *Doctrine of Signs* in mediaeval Europe, where the use of a plant was advertised by the plant's shape. Hence many of the *Orchis* species, which have tubers that resemble testicles, were also thought to have aphrodisiac qualities. Salep made from O. *maculata* was used both as an aphrodisiac as well as a nerve tonic. Perhaps the two functions are not that different.

Making an infusion from the underground organs of *Eulophia cucullata*, *Corycium nigrescens* and/or *Disa aconitoides* and then purging with it is also thought by the Zulu to promote fertility, presumably by ridding the body of the evil that causes sterility. *Disa aconitiflora* is a widespread species in southern Africa that grows in grasslands and has small spikes of tiny flowers that vary in color from pale pink to a deep mauve-blue. It is interesting that other African people also used *D. aconitoides* to promote fertility. An infusion made from the roots of that *Disa* species was also used to induce fertility in Bantu women (Batten and Bokelmann, 1966). Considering the large number of spectacular *Disa* species available it is curious that only a rather insignificant species should have been selected. Perhaps it really works!

In many cultures, different values are placed on children of the two sexes and there can be great stress if a male heir is not forthcoming. McDonald and Duckworth report on a "procedure" to ensure the production of a son. A plant of *Bonatea speciosa*, is cut up and boiled. The concoction is then stored in a clay pot with a very small aperture. Both members of the couple sip small amounts of the liquid each morning. After sufficient time and effort a son may be produced.

Plants of *Ansellia africana* feature prominently in the Zulu herbalists' sales areas. Local orchid growers buy many of those plants but there is also a steady market for their several reputed medicinal properties. The species can be used either as an aphrodisiac or to treat diarrhea (Biegel, 1976), a rather unusual combination of effects. In other African tribes the same species is used as either an aphrodisiac or to induce abortions. There are several of these contradictory uses for orchids in ethnobotany[3], which makes one wonder if perhaps the contradictions are due to translation problems by the person collecting the folklore, rather than the actual folk usage.

On other continents orchids were also thought to promote sexual desires. Some of the *Dendrobium* species, for example, were used as aphrodisiacs. The underground portions of *Spiranthes autumnale* were used as aphrodisiacs in Europe (Handa, 1986).

Dendrobium

The genus *Dendrobium* is one of the largest in the Orchidaceae, comprising many hundreds of species. The distribution of the genus is from Asia through to Oceania. Several different types have been used for their medicinal properties. *Dendrobium crumenatum* is a fairly common orchid, used to decorate gardens and trees in Indonesia and Malaysia. It is renowned because all of the plants tend to flower at the same time. Juice from the pseudobulbs is used quite extensively throughout the Indo-Malaysian region to cure earache. Several different *Dendrobium* species are thought to have aphrodisiac effects. On the more prosaic side *Dendrobium discolor* has been used against ringworm. The drug *Shih-hu* is prepared from several different dendrobiums, of which *D. nobile* is the principle species. Dendrobiums are cultivated in eastern Asia so that *Shi-hu* can be made; it is usually a preparation from the dried stalks or pseudobulbs. Fresh *Shih-hu* can also be used. The preparation is used where a tonic or strengthening medicine is called for. It is also considered to be an aphrodisiac and a drug that can extend life.

Shih-hu is prepared from the dried canes of various dendrobiums. One herbal (Ody, 1993) gives the following recipe, 60 gm of dried *Dendrobium* is boiled in 750 ml of water. The decoction is strained and then mixed with licorice. The tea is drunk, reputedly, to restore sexual vigor. The actual chemical compounds in *Shih-hu* have only been partially analyzed. One alkaloid called dendrobine appears to cause contractions of some visceral muscles, like the uterus, but paralyses other muscles in the gut. Dendrobine also lowers blood pressure. The drug appears to be quite dangerous in concentrated form, but like many other medicines can be restorative at the correct dosage. A survey of a number of different *Dendrobium* species suggests that as many as 10 to 20% contain alkaloids (Lüning, 1964, quoted in Hegnauer, 1966).

The seeds of *Dendrobium nobile* are said to promote rapid healing when applied to freshly cut wounds (Deorani and Naithani, 1995). Whether these seeds just provide extra surfaces that help blood platelets in clotting or actually promote healing needs to be ascertained. Besides dendrobine, another alkaloid (nobiline) has been isolated from plants of *D. nobile* but the seeds do not appear to have analyzed for active agents.

A non-medicinal use for *Dendrobium* has been reported (Handa, 1986) from India, where several species of the genus are fed to dairy cows to promote milk production.

Eulophia

The genus *Eulophia* is terrestrial and usually has underground pseudobulbs that often resemble ginger-root. It is a widespread genus with a major center of diversity in

33   A variety of roots, tubers and stems displayed for sale in a Zulu herbalist market. Many different *Eulophia* species feature at these sales. Other orchids offered here were a variety of angraecoids and *Ansellia africana*.

[3] The herbal uses of plants by ethnic goups

34 This *Eulophia calanthoides* plant was originally "rescued" from a Zulu herbalist where the pseudobulbs would have been ground up and used as a purgative.

Africa and a second, smaller one, in south East Asia. One species *E. alta* is cosmopolitan and is also known from the New World, where it is currently spreading and invading Florida. It has been suggested that the plants were originally brought over as a folk medicine with the slave trade. It seems unlikely, however, that the slave traders were concerned or altruistic enough to allow the slaves to bring their own herbal remedies to America with them.

There are several different uses for various eulophias. Juice derived from pseudobulbs of *E. parvula* is put directly onto wounds by the Shona people of Zimbabwe and an infusion made from *E. petersii* pseudobulbs is drunk to combat dropsy, which usually refers to a swollen stomach (Gelfand *et al.*, 1985). I used to visit an acre plot, south of Durban in South Africa, which was a veritable herbalists' supermarket. Dozens and dozens of blankets were spread on the ground and each covered with a variety of whole plants,

strange animal parts, fossils, ground up barks, etc. Among the many orchids for sale, were several species of *Eulophia* including *E. calanthoides, E. hereroensis, E. parviflora* and others. Strings of pseudobulbs were arrayed on blankets of many of the vendors. McDonald and Duckworth (1994) list six different *Eulophia* species used by Zulu herbalists. My requests for information on the medicinal uses elicited comments that they were primarily used as emetics (agents that induce vomiting). Taking herbal concoctions to cause regurgitation is referred to as to *phalaza* and is used to get rid the body of bile. The reasons for this use were not immediately obvious until I realized that many of the Zulu people did not possess refrigerators and that eating spoiled food must therefore be a common problem. Tony Udal (1994) reported on a similar use for *E. petersii*. Here a potion is made from crushed pseudobulbs and other herbs, it is used to induce vomiting if the person had over-indulged in rich food and drink and was feeling bilious. Inducing vomiting also has other functions for the Zulu people besides making them feel better. If one *phalazas* with *E. streptopetala* one may become more attractive to the opposite sex and if one *phalazas* with an infusion of *E. cucullata*, fertility can be promoted.

Further south in Africa, *Eulophia ensata* grows. It is a grassland species with globular heads of bright yellow flowers. It is reported (Batten and Bokelmann, 1966) that the Xhosa people used this species for unspecified baby ailments. In East Africa *E. galeoloides*, is called *Dondokezi* in Swahili and the liquid from its boiled roots is administered to treat stomach problems in children (Kokwaro, 1993).

In Nagaland, India, pseudobulbs of *Eulophia dabia* are used for several different reasons. They are administered as a tonic and blood purifier but also as an aphrodisiac (Deorani and Naithani, 1995). Other *Eulophia* species that feature in Indian pharmacopoeias include *E. campestris*, which has a variety of actions. It is administered for coughs, to combat heart troubles and even as an aphrodisiac (Handa, 1986). In India, salep is also made from dried and ground pseudobulbs of *Eulophia* species and was considered to be superior to the salep made from *Orchis* tubers (Castle, 1886).

Handa (1986) also records that *E. streptopetala* (syn. *Lissochilus krebsii*) is used to treat scabies and other skin problems in Europe. The active agent is derived from the roots. There are several problems with accepting this at face value. The species is actually wide ranging in Africa and does not occur in Europe. In addition, one does wonder whether 'roots' refers to the real roots or to the underground pseudobulbs, which herbalists might merely consider to be a form of root.

Unusual uses

Polystachya ottoniana is a widespread, small epiphyte or lithophyte from South Africa. It makes modest mats of pseudobulbs bearing inflorescences, each with a small number of flowers. The flowers are about the size of pearls and are usually white with pink markings, although other color forms are known. In the eastern regions of South Africa parts of the plants were fed to babies for teething troubles and sometimes to combat diarrhea. That is not too unusual but seeds from the plant were also collected and used as snuff to induce sneezing (Batten and Bokelmann, 1966) and that is an unusual use for an orchid.

Lawler (1984) has also collected a number of unusual and surprising uses for orchids and their products. It is amazing what ideas people have come up with and how ingenious they can be. In several different parts of the world there are orchid plants that contain sticky mucilage in their pseudobulbs. These have been used to produce a variety of adhesives. The species *Aplectrum hyemale* in North America was used as an adhesive to repair glass and china crockery. Apparently the roots of *Aplectrum*, when bruised in a little water, produce a very thick and durable adhesive. Across the world in Africa, natives used gums from various *Eulophia* species' pseudobulbs to repair cracks in pots. While in China, glue from the common garden orchid *Bletilla striata* has also been used for repairing porcelain. *Bletilla* also has several different medicinal uses as well.

Two genera, *Catasetum* and *Cyrtopodium*, grow in the New World tropics and make large pseudobulbs. The sap from the pseudobulbs also makes a good and strong adhesive. In Brazil and some other countries in Latin America, the paste was used to make footwear more durable and was even used for gluing soles to shoes. In addition, glues from orchids have been used in several countries as the preferred adhesive for repairing stringed musical instruments. Some orchid glue must be quite strong indeed, because in Java, glue made from *Cymbidium lancifolium* was used for fastening knife blades to their handles. Such glue must be able to withstand considerable pressure and stress.

People who grow *Dendrobium* orchids will notice that the older pseudobulbs often take on a yellowish color. Fibers and pieces of stems from these plants have been used quite widely to give contrasting and artistic designs in basket weaving. Some species, which provide more brilliant and golden colors than others were, in the past, reserved for royalty.

One of the more unusual uses must be the use of leaves of *Plocoglottis wenzelii* to make 'G-strings' for men of the Tasaday tribe, from Mindanao in the Philippines.

The Flowers of the Dead

In Mexico the first two days of November are celebrated as two religious holidays. These are 'All Saints Day' followed by the 'Day of the Dead'. On the latter day a feast is set out for the spirits of the ancestors, who are enticed to the meal by a trail of marigold flowers. Many of the confections and cookies produced depict skulls, coffins and other morbid themes. Surprisingly, there was a confection made that featured either of two orchids, *Laelia speciosa* or *L. autumnalis*, and these became known as Flores de los Muertos or the 'Flowers of the Dead' (Miller, 1978).

Pseudobulbs of either species were trimmed of roots and leaves and ground up into a mucilaginous green paste, which was then diluted with a little water. Flour, powdered sugar, lemon juice and egg white was then added until the right texture is achieved. The covered mix was allowed to 'mature' for several days, after which the dough was rolled into a very thin sheet that could be molded into the desired shapes. These were further decorated with vegetable dyes.

Charms and magic

In many countries, particularly in Africa, the herbal uses of plants can extend beyond merely healing the sick and into the realm of the supernatural. Charms and potions are made in an effort to try and influence the behavior not only of other people but even animals as well. Many of these are love potions but other uses, less amicable, are also known.

The Zulu people traditionally made a body-wash, called an *inTelezi*, from a mixture of plants including the orchids *Eulophia petersii* and *E. streptopetala*. The lotion was applied to the body as a protective shell to ward off evil spirits and bad fortune.

The Shona peoples of Zimbabwe have an unusual use for *Ansellia africana* (syn. *A. gigantea*). Gelfand *et al.*, (1985) reported that pseudobulbs are chopped up and steeped in water. The water is then given to captive pigeons to drink. This elixir is supposed to help pigeons remember the position of the coop and helps them find their way home. Biegel (1976) reports a somewhat different story; he remarks that the orchid may be planted near the pigeon loft to ensure that the birds return to their loft. The Shona, themselves, also use *Ansellia* as an anti-emetic and make a decoction from the pseudobulbs

35 *Ansellia africana* is employed for a variety of
medicinal and magic uses, in central and southern
Africa.

that have been smeared with fat and a powder made
from dried and burnt plants of *Habenaria epipactidea*.

In a more sinister vein, the dried powder of another *Habenaria*, *H. dives*, can be used to get rid of enemies. This *Habenaria*, like many other African terrestrials, grows in an above ground annual cycle. It grows
for a while and then apparently dies away. If applied to
a person's food, the powder is similarly supposed to
induce a decline and cause the victim to die within a
year. This evil might be warded off with the correct
inTelezi. Why *H. dives* is chosen instead of any of the
many other species with similar life cycles and even
whether or not there is an actual poison in the plant, or
if the result is merely the self-induced response to a
magic curse is not clear.

East African orchids

There is still so much to learn. As we have pointed out
elsewhere, once the mode of action of a poison is understood it might have medicinal value when used correctly. Kowakaro (1993) described the uses of several
orchids for medical reasons. These include *Aerangis
thomsonii*, where plants are burnt and the ash rubbed
into small cuts made on the stomach. This is said not
only to relieve hernias but will make them disappear. It
has a similar effect on abscesses. This species also has a
magical use. If the ash is made into a paste and placed
near a clutch of eggs it will ensure their fertility and
ensure that they hatch into chickens.

Angraecum dives is used as a cure for sores. The
leaves or stem can be either chewed, or they can be
mashed and soaked in water, after which the infusion is
drunk. Crushing the large tubers of *Bonatea steudneri*
and placing the poultice over the open sore is a similar
cure. This is supposed to be effective for killing skin
maggots. A root decoction of this species can be drunk
to combat influenza and also stomach problems.

Salads and pot vegetables

Orchids have many other uses. In Western Java the
young leaves of *Ceratostylis latifolia* are eaten in salads.
In Malaysia the native jewel orchid, *Ludisia discolor*,
which is the most commonly cultivated jewel orchid by
hobbyists, is gathered by locals and cooked as a pot vegetable. The current rarity of the plant in the wild has
been ascribed to over-collecting for food (Michael Ooi,
personal communication).

Tracking down information on the uses of wild
orchids can be frustrating and contradictory. Most of it
is hearsay and often difficult to interpret. For example,

for that purpose. On the other hand the Zulus are
reported to use the plant as an emetic (Handa, 1986).
Ansellia appears to be an all-purpose remedy. An effu-
sion made from the roots is used as a cough remedy by
the Pedi peoples and Handa (1986) also reports that a
concoction made from the roots can be used as an anti-
dote to bad dreams. Perhaps it is a soporific. In East
Africa, *Ansellia* is used to treat earache. Canes are heat-
ed over a fire until soft and juice extracted from them,
this is dropped into the infected ear (Kokwaro, 1993).
That there is some difficulty in sifting the useful information from the chaff for *Ansellia* illustrates many of
the problems associated with orchids and folk medicines. Some are obviously merely 'quack' remedies but
perhaps there is a useful pharmaceutical chemical somewhere in the plant.

McDonald and Duckworth (1994) describe infu-
sions made from orchids that are used to ward off
storms and lightning. The whole plant is ground up in
water and the liquid sprinkled around the huts. Among
the orchids used for this are *Eulophia speciosa*, *E. odontoglossa*, *Disa stachyoides* and *Habenaria dregeana*. If
that does not appear to be sufficient, additional protection may be gained by driving stakes into the ground

flasks of the Taiwanese jewel orchid *Anoectochilus formosanus* were recently offered for sale in the USA. When I remarked on this, I was told by the agent that the flasks were actually made for the herbal market, for chest ailments, and flasks of plantlets are sent to Taiwanese residents all over the world. When asked exactly how it was used medicinally and for what exact symptoms I got no concrete reply. In the *Native Orchids of Taiwan*, Lin (1977) alludes to dried parts of *A. formosanus* as being components of expensive Chinese medicines, but no additional details are offered. Yong (1990) remarked that *Anoectochilus geniculatus*, was used in the past when it was more readily available as a pot herb, i.e. for food, in Malaysia, but *Ludisia discolor* was used by the Chinese to treat a variety of chest ailments. Which is correct? Perhaps both assertions are valid? 'Gold Coin Grass' is the common name used for *A. formosanus* although that species does not appear to have gold veining like some of the other *Anectochilus* species. Through a series of intermediaries I was finally able to make contact with a herbalist in Taipei. He offered the following: 'Golden Coin Grass' is a cure for 'stagnant chi', which has symptoms like lethargy, slight difficulty in breathing (chest area) and it also has a calming effect. Furthermore, some people, in order to make a better sale, make exaggerated claims of its magical power. Fresh 'Gold Coin Grass' is boiled in water with some Rock-sugar or Rock-candy. The decoction is then drunk. In North America the related *Goodyera pubescens* was used to treat scrofula, which is swelling of neck lymph nodes (Miller, 1978).

Dendrobium chicken legs

Sometimes in China there is a very fine line between herbal remedies and eating food that is good for one. Thus in some Chinese cuisine, herbs and drugs are combined into foods. What follows is a recipe for Tung-Chung Soy Chicken or what I call *"Dendrobium Chicken-Legs"*. Barbara Hansen published the recipe, in the Los Angeles Times on May 13, 1998 on page H6. This dish is supposed to improve a weakened body condition. However, one of the other ingredients might psychologically damage the more conservative westerner. This ingredient is 'Cordyceps', which is derived from a caterpillar or similar worm that has been invaded and consumed by a fungus (of the genus *Cordyceps*), during its winter hibernation. The fungus and worm remains are then dried and used as an ingredient. For those stalwart orchidists who want to try the recipe is given below:

This is an expensive dish to make, as both the *Cordyceps* and dried *Dendrobium* are highly priced. The herbs can be obtained from Chinese herbal shops in larger cities that have 'Chinatowns'. The flavor is said to be well worth the expense and the meal is also supposed to project a feeling of well being.

> 10 grams *Cordyceps*
> 5 grams dried chopped *Dendrobium* canes
> 2 chicken legs
> 5 cups water
> ½ cup soy sauce
> 3 tbsp. Rice wine
> 2 tbsp. Chinese rock sugar
> 5 large scallions (shallots), halved, white part only
> 5 slices ginger root
> 1 red jalapeño pepper.

The *Cordyceps* and *Dendrobium* are rinsed and then all of the ingredients, excluding the chicken legs, are brought to a boil. The chicken is then added and returned to a boil. The mix is simmered for twenty minutes and allowed to stand for an additional 10 minutes. The chicken is set aside and the rest of the liquid brought to a boil again and reduced in volume to about half a cup. The liquid is strained and used as a sauce for dipping the chicken. *Bon appetite!*

Conservation and ethnobotany

Ethnobotanical uses of orchids impinge on their conservation in two different ways. On the one hand population pressures increase the direct demand for herbal products, and thus results in the over-collection of species for herbal usage. On the other hand, land conversion and deforestation lead to the extinction of species before they can be assessed for additional potential uses or products for the western pharmacopoeia.

McDonald and Duckworth (1994) point out that in Southern Africa small quantities of product were traditionally gathered and the amounts were then sought by the herbalist in direct proportion to the need. These days the plants are harvested and brought to the cities where they might be needed. In addition, the plants are not being collected by the herbalists but by plant gatherers who sell plants for a living. They therefore over-collect. The example of wholesale trade in *Flickingeria* between Nepal and India indicates that there is a similar problem in Asia. There is concern about this problem in Africa and some small attempts are being made to farm wild species but, unfortunately, orchids do not lend themselves readily to this type of farming practice.

It used to be the case in Third World countries, where per capita annual income is less than a few hundred dollars a year, that people could not afford to buy modern pharmaceuticals. They had no choice but to turn to herbal remedies, but there is now a growing market for herbal products in the more developed countries of the world and many of these products, effective or not, mean big business and more importantly place demands on wild populations of orchids. Potions containing cypripedin and illustrated with lady slipper orchids on the boxes are currently available in the popular 'Health Food' stores in the United States. These are made from wild collected orchids. One can only hope that demand will not increase. Also, one can only hope that the developed world will not want wild *Eulophia* species with which to '*phalaza*' in the future. Such prophecies might be deemed far-fetched but who, thirty years ago, could have predicted the current popularity of acupuncture in western society.

Future uses?

Quite clearly, many native peoples have been clever about how they utilize their orchids. One suspects that there must be literally hundreds of other potential things that could be done with the various species. This chapter is by no means complete. There are many other species that have a variety of uses, some of which could well be important. As we survey the current states of endangerment of these plants, remember that not only flowers are lost when a species goes extinct. The entire plant is lost too and with it go other potential uses. There may be ways of using orchids that we have not dreamt of before but we will not discover them in the future, if they no longer exist. This is true of all species, orchid or otherwise. The human race potentially impoverishes itself with every species it allows to go or forces towards extinction.

The argument is made that modern and future technologies can and will be able to tailor make chemicals for specific needs and that we no longer need to keep the various species around for medicinal purposes. This is a strong argument and difficult to counter. But, all of the orchid species that currently exist in the world's forests, are the current endpoints of perhaps three and a half billion years of evolutionary experiments that nature has carried out. Many, if not most of the chemicals they contain, could be unique solutions to problems that we can scarcely imagine today. Species could contain chemicals and compounds that we may not need today, but which could be vital tomorrow. The chemicals usually referred to as secondary metabolites are thought by many to be protective devices that plants have evolved to deter or protect themselves against predators. For example, *Orchis militaris*, a familiar European species produces a chemical compound (orchinol) that has phytoalexin activity, which protects the orchid against fungal infections (Harborne, 1972). Many of the secondary metabolites are poisons that could have their effect at any one of a variety of levels ranging from cellular metabolism to organ functions. Slightly modified or used at the correct dosage many of the toxins can be used to heal instead of impair. The current AIDS epidemic sent scientists scurrying back to the forests to look for compounds that might have antiviral properties and they did find some (but not in orchids, if indeed they looked at orchids). No doubt the future holds similar challenges and we will need all the resources we can lay our hands on to fight back. Many of those resources are in the natural compounds made by plants and when those species are gone we cannot make them reappear.

Plant products can have other uses besides medicinal ones. Plants can produce compounds that are needed in industry and manufacturing. There is a burgeoning need for 'organic' or natural products such as dyes and inks that can be obtained from flowers and other plant parts. We are impeded only by the limits of our imagination and the biodiversity losses we allow to take place. Nevertheless I have the uneasy feeling that perhaps the orchids may have very little to contribute to the world's wellbeing beyond their wonderful flowers and interesting biology. For many of us, however, that is more than enough.

CHAPTER 7

In Situ Conservation

There is no doubt that the best way to conserve orchid species is to ensure that they continue to exist as an integral part of intact ecosystems. If this is to be the case then they either must live in untouched forests or managed forest preserves. We will ignore for the time being those species that occur in grasslands, near hot springs and other non-forested ecosystems. There has been a steady push by both developing and developed countries to set aside natural forested areas. In particular, organizations in the richer countries have tried to purchase lands to put under various kinds of protection. Developing world countries have been encouraged to swap land for foreign debt and this can be used to create additional protected areas. Exactly how that protection is defined is variable and in many cases there is no more protection than words on paper. In addition, these are not reserves designed *per se* for orchids but are areas in which orchids can be afforded some protection, provided that they already exist within the designated preserve.

The goals for preserves

There are several quite different goals for preserves. Some are human orientated, while others are not. The goal most often articulated is to maintain species in a state that will prevent their untimely extinction, so that future generations of people can enjoy and study them. Some people see the goal as maintaining species in case people might want to use them in the future. Others would preserve them merely for their own sake and with disregard to human activities and uses. But there is another possible goal and this has nothing to do with economic or other uses, for botanists this goal overrides the other reasons.

Until relatively recently in human history, orchids lived in the wild and they were under the influence of a variety of natural factors; some species flourished and others declined. Orchids currently appear to be in the midst of an active evolutionary radiation, with the production of large numbers of new species. We can see this in the populations of several species, where each population is somewhat different from others of the same species, but they are not really sufficiently distinct to be called a separate species. Taxonomists deal with this by making subspecies or variety designations to describe some of these differences. Given enough time some of the new incipient species would succeed and form new species, others would dwindle towards extinction and disappear, while yet others might be submerged back into the parent stock and never evolve a unique and distinct identity. One of the goals of a preserve should be to allow these processes to continue naturally. As soon as man starts to interfere with the natural evolutionary processes, they lose their integrity and are tainted by aspects of artificial selection.

The more active management that a preserve requires, the greater the likelihood that the effects of artificial selection will become prominent and ultimately the reserve's species will change away from their normal state. On the other hand, for some species, active interference and management may be the only way that the plants can be saved from extinction. Preserve managers often have to walk a tight line between too little and too much management. Unfortunately guidelines for the management of orchid populations in the wild have never been clearly formulated and managers must often make life and death decisions in the absence of good information. Fortunately, this has not deterred people from devising action plans to save endangered species. How successful their efforts will be in the long run still remains to be determined.

Reserve design

There are very few nature reserves in the world that were created specifically for their orchid denizens. Reserves are usually set aside for the protection of animal species or as examples of kinds of communities or entire ecosystems, little thought is given to the populations of orchids contained in them. This is especially true of the tropics where orchids abound.

It is not enough to have a reserve where orchid plants remain alive and are protected against various depredations. The orchids are part of an interacting community and may be dependent on components in the ecosystem for their continuance across generations. Some of the other essential participants in the community such as pollinators and mycorrhizal fungi are clear, but other species may also be essential for successful reproduction. Among these less obvious interacting species are the correct species of trees which will accept the epiphytes, species of mosses and lichens that help create micro-environments in which seed can be lodged, so it can interact with the correct mycorrhizal fungi and the ants that might patrol and protect them. Not only must one protect the trees on which the orchids perch but also those organisms that protect and interact with the trees. Therefore, one needs to worry not only about the orchids' pollinators but also the trees' pollinators as well. But unless a reserve is to be designed specifically for only a certain few orchid species, it is impractical to expect that all the necessary knowledge about various species' interactions can be gathered together.

We do have a few general rules for reserve design. The first and probably the most important has to do with its size. The number of species that a reserve can hold is directly related to the size of the reserve. Many of the reserves in the world are actually too small to be able to sustain themselves without active management. Ecologists have found that there is a simple mathematical relationship between the size of an area and the number of different kinds of species that it can contain. This assertion comes from studying the numbers of species found on oceanic islands. On a larger island there should be not only a greater average number of each species but also greater numbers of different species. When biologists actually looked that assertion was confirmed. There is a very clear relationship between the area of the island and the number of different species accommodated on that island. Because patches of forests are islands in a sea of human activity, it is thought that they should react similarly and lose or gain species in accordance with their size. If one carves out a piece of a rainforest as a reserve the number of species in the new reserve would tend to be much greater than in an isolated piece of forest of the same size. Our hypothetical new reserve, will, if isolated from the rest of its surrounding forest, start to lose species until it returns to a new equilibrium. The number of species will depend to a large extent on its area. The extinction of species under these conditions is usually termed 'species relaxation' and it has been both documented and modeled for several reserves. Many tropical countries have built giant lakes and in the process made real islands. It is only in recent years that some of these islands have been used as models to document species relaxation and to begin studying those processes. Rates of species relaxation depend directly on size and a small reserve will have greater species relaxation than a large one. In a large reserve species relaxation may be very slow, but nevertheless still occurs.

For quite a long time now there has been a debate between conservation biologists as to whether or not it is better to have one single large reserve or several smaller ones. Given that there are very limited resources to purchase new reserves should all the money be pooled to buy one large area or should it be spread around to purchase several smaller ones? Larger reserves will be more stable and smaller reserves will need much more active management to ensure the protection of their inhabitants and prevent eventual extinction. A series of small reserves that are scattered across the landscape can actually encompass more species than a single large one, but their prospects for long-term survival will be more fragile. Opting for a single large reserve means saving fewer species but in the long run those species have better survival prospects. To that end the suggestion has been made that we should be saving examples of different kinds of ecosystems, rather than focusing on their component species.

A second important need is for a buffer zone between the reserve and the surrounding landscape. Scientists have found that the physical environment at the edge of a forest patch changes drastically when the patch is formed and some of these effects can occur hundreds of meters from the edge towards the center of the patch. A buffer zone will help ameliorate edge effects. In some places where native peoples must rely on the forest for their livelihoods they can be allowed use of the buffer zone.

Corridors are strips of natural area that could be used to join reserves. These allow passageways for the migration of and interaction between members of a species in different reserves. Obviously the corridors are of more and immediate importance to animals than plants but plants are secondarily affected because of their dependence on animals. Like nearly all other factors there are both good and bad features to corridors. Critics point out that these strips of joining land can allow diseases to migrate between preserves. Also because corridors are narrow strips, organisms in the strips are particularly vulnerable to hunting, pilfering and poaching.

The management of preserves

Management Plans: Under the most ideal of conditions a reserve will be self-sustaining and require a minimum of management, but the smaller the reserve is the more active management it will require. Reserves should have good, written, management plans. This is particularly important because conservation is a long-term effort and a good management plan encourages continuity in effort and also avoids having to 'reinvent the wheel' each time new management or administrative personnel come on board. There will always be changes in personnel, some of these can be anticipated and one can plan for a smooth transition, but stochastic changes also occur and unless there are specific guidelines and previous reports, such transitions can spell disaster. Specific, concrete guidelines and goals need to be spelt out. Goals can vary from maintaining the *status quo* to the re-establishment of self-perpetuating populations of designated species. Built into the plan should be methods of self-examination so that progress in achieving goals can be regularly evaluated. From past experience one can usually also predict future problems and it is worthwhile building that information into the master plan. Only long-term experience can allow one to anticipate and prepare to deal with cyclical problems, but the system must have some form of memory in order to guarantee this. The ultimate achievement of a great management plan would be the ability to withdraw management at some future time without jeopardizing the continuance of the species.

The way that one evaluates, at any point in time, the success of a preserve is to compare both biodiversity and population size of the component species with their initial conditions. In many if not most preserves, however, checklists of species are only compiled some time after the preserve is set aside. There are rarely censuses of plants. Birds and large mammals are usually counted but plants are often just taken for granted or totally ignored. It is important that a census should be completed as soon as the preserve is set up as this will form the base line against which future success or failure will be measured. At a minimum, a checklist should be prepared and in the absence of an accurate count vague category designations such as rare or common for each species would be helpful for future evaluations. One aspect of plant censuses that is useful is the age composition of the species' populations. What proportion are seedlings, young adults, mature plants or senescent individuals? Changes in composition in time, weighting the population towards the senescent side, would be of concern but might not be noticed unless specifically measured.

Manipulating Populations. Management implies manipulating the size and structure of the populations under concern. One assumes that it would rarely be the case that orchid populations might need to be culled. It is more likely that new individuals will need to be added to supplement the population. With temperate orchids several *Action Plans* have been developed but even their long-term success has yet to be tested. There are so few cases of tropical orchid management that no clear guidelines have been developed specifically for those kinds of orchids. There have been some ill-fated attempts to reintroduce some species in the wild. One of these, concerning *Paphiopedilum rothschildianum*, will be discussed at length in the appropriate chapter. Introducing and re-establishing any plant, orchid or otherwise, is no easy matter. Part of the problem is that few individual specimens are well adapted to their natural environment and die out in the seedling stage. If seedlings are raised under nursery conditions, where such selection is very reduced, many plants can often be grown to a large enough size to try and establish them in the wild. At that stage natural selection comes into play again and many of the plants will succumb. Intensive management, with watering and pest control may be needed to ensure continued survival. That is merely a form of gardening. It should be remembered that it is as important to ensure the survival of the pollinator as the orchid species. Without the pollinator the orchid populations will require continuous management and never become self-sufficient. At present there are few attempts to manage the pollinator species and management assumes that they will appear 'spontaneously' which is hardly ever the case.

If a population falls below a certain level, and 500 plants is often taken to be that level, inbreeding depression is liable to become a problem. Theoretically, the introduction of foreign genes at low frequencies can help to alleviate that problem. This may mean the re-establishment of a few plants from an outside source but it may merely be easier to achieve the same result by artificially pollinating a few specimens with pollen from another population. This is one of the very few times when artificial pollination should be practiced. It would be better to try and build up the population using local materials.

There is the possibility that many orchid populations prefer disturbed sites and are transitory in nature. They may be established and after a few generations dwindle and disappear only to be replaced by other populations emerging elsewhere. We only suspect this and have relatively little evidence that this may indeed be the case, however if this is true management may be quite difficult. Alves (1998) recounts how *Dactylorhiza* and *Orchis* species had stable populations in grazed meadowlands in Czechoslovakia until the mid 1980s, when conservationists pressured the government to protect the orchid plants. Subsequently grazing was forbidden at some of the sites. As usually happens in these cases, the absence of cattle allowed fast-growing weeds to invade, and these choked out most of the orchids. This is not an unusual incident and has been recorded many times for other plants. It is another example of where our efforts, although well meant, have jeopardized instead of benefiting those species we aim to protect. It is important to understand the ecology of the species in question.

Reintroductions. Richard Warren and David Miller carried out one of the few successful establishments of tropical orchids in a private reserve of coastal forest in the Serra do Mar of Brazil. In that case they tried to re-establish salvaged plants of *Laelia crispa* in regenerating forest. They found that plants tied to living trees tended to produce little growth and subsequently died while plants tied to dead trees, not very high above ground level, produced abundant root growth and consequently flowered (Warren and Miller, 1992). The reasons for this difference are not clear and it was unexpected. Plants had originally been salvaged from the upper forks of felled trees. When the re-established *Laelia crispa* flowered they were pollinated both artificially and naturally, and eventually seedlings were found in surrounding trees. After an initial spurt of seedling development many died off (Warren and Miller, 1994). This is what one might expect, because in most other species of either animals or plants very few of the progeny survive to reach sexual maturity.

Artificial Pollination. There was a time some ten to twenty years ago, when it was fashionable to go out and 'assist' orchids in the wild by pollinating their flowers. On the surface this seemed to be a good idea. Increasing the seed yield might in turn increase the number of plants in the following generation and these increases in number would help drive the species away from extinction. This approach was very popular and orchid hobby groups as far apart as Mexico and South Africa would take field trips to go out and pollinate the wild orchids. Special 'how to' manuals were published. There are several reasons why this was a particularly bad idea. Artificial pollination by humans is unnatural. Two members of the same species are not genetically identical and humans don't perceive the cues that insects use. Artificial crosses introduce, either consciously or otherwise, the normal human bias into the evolutionary process with the concomitant changes in gene pool frequency in the next generation. Let us take an example.

If we have an individual of Species A, which has a faulty gene and does not produce the correct scent to stimulate its pollinator, that plant would normally be selected against and not used for seed production. Along comes a 'do-gooder' who uses that faulty individual to pollinate a wide number of other individuals. The gene pool in the next generation would contain a larger percentage of individuals with the faulty gene. Humans deliberately or unconsciously are attracted to larger flowers and brighter colors and preferentially tend to use those for pollination but, the resultant new flowers might not be the best fit for the particular environment in which they live. Artificial pollination in the wild is tampering with natural processes and the normal course of evolution. No biologist, ecologist or taxonomist studying a plant in the wild that was the result of artificial pollination has any assurance that he is studying the real thing and unfortunately would not know that the plant is question was an 'artificial construct'.

There are other problems too. Different orchid species hybridize promiscuously and mistaken or deliberate pollination between two different species can happen. There is a possibility that this operation has been performed deliberately in the wild with regards to some of the European terrestrial orchids and it has merely served to confuse and obfuscate our understanding of nature.

The production of seed capsules in the wild, as in cultivation, places an energy drain on the individual plant. Usually in nature, orchids are pollinator limited and fewer than one in ten flowers makes a seed capsule. If one artificially pollinates many of the flowers on a plant the resultant energy drain may weaken the plant to the point where its survival becomes threatened or it may take many years to recover. Excessive artificial pollination may end up threatening the very plants one is attempting to save.

Two populations in different areas, even of the same species, may show local adaptations to the area in which they live. Natural selection will either have or be in the process of determining the optimum genes for each population. If one deliberately introduces genes from a distant population, as has been done with some of the wild populations of North American cypripediums, one can drive the evolution of that group away from its optimum. This is known as outbreeding depression and can make populations less fit for their environment.

Artificial pollination should only be resorted to in the last extremes where it is apparent that heroic efforts will be needed to save a species. But one should remember that the resultant manipulation could produce a plant that is neither genetically normal or a natural example of its species.

Recovery plans

The United States Fish and Wildlife Service has produced recovery plans for some of the North American endangered species. These plans often have to be built on insufficient data and in this way often resemble the situation of other tropical species. We will consider the North American terrestrial orchid *Platanthera praeclara*, the 'western prairie fringed orchid', as a model (USFW, 1994). The plan has a one page executive summary, which we will condense even more here.

- It starts with a summary of the species current status. In 1994, the species was known to occur in 74 populations. Only 5 were on federal property and 29 on state-owned lands. Other populations were scattered under a variety of different ownership categories.
- This was followed by a short description of the orchid's habitat, the North American native tall grass prairie. The destruction of these grasslands and their conversion for agricultural croplands is the major threat to the species.
- The objective of the recovery plan was the eventual de-listing of the species.
- The criteria for recovery were to protect and produce self-sustaining populations in 90% of the species' historical range in each state.
- The recovery plan identified six specific actions that were needed:
  a. Potential habitats needed to be identified and searched for.
  b. The habitat of known populations needed to be maintained.
  c. Appropriate research and monitoring was needed.
  d. Develop and implementation of habitat management plans.
  e. Dissemination of information about the species.
  f. Provision of legal protection for all populations.

Costs were calculated for each of the six specific actions for each year for 10 years. The costs for the first year were $992,000 and diminished each year with a final total projected at $4,429,000. The major component of the actions was appropriate research and monitoring which started off costing about half a million dollars in the first year.

The plan suggested that if all the recommendations were followed, then perhaps the species might have recovered enough the orchids might be de-listed by the year 2030. It was thought that the best management strategy would be to maintain the quality of the habitats and as such required relatively little manipulation of the orchids themselves. The project did not receive significant funding but the project has continued on a shoe-string, with some volunteer help.

Pros and cons for reserves

Like anything else, there are both good points and bad points for nature reserves. On the plus side, one finds that if preserves are large enough, they allow for reasonably good prospects for the continued survival of a particular species, provided that other components of the community and ecosystem are also intact. In a healthy community there may be little need for species manipulation and consequently management may merely need to concern itself with protective police action, requiring wardens to control human activities. A deep understanding of the ecosystem as such may not be required, and the cost savings in those respects can be considerable. Species 'hands-off' policies minimize interference and they will allow nature and evolution to takes its proper course.

On the other hand, there are several problems with using reserves as the sole source of protection for orchids. Frequently preserves are only set up on behalf of charismatic animal species and these will always receive preferential consideration over plants. Usually the wardens focus on the animals to the exclusion of the plants. There have been many instances in the past where preserves have been so successful in promoting their animal denizens that the animal populations proliferated to such an extent that they destroyed much of the vegetation in those preserves. This was particularly true of the Kaibab deer in the Southwestern USA, which destroyed so much vegetation that many of the deer died of starvation. I have seen similar situations in Africa where the vegetation was so degraded by the 'successful' antelope populations that animals were forced to eat bitter aloes, normally avoided, in order to survive. While plant species may not have gone extinct their populations were certainly depleted. There will always be considerable resistance to diverting financial resources away from the animals and towards plants.

Perhaps one of the greatest difficulties with reserves is with the inability to police them effectively. Poaching appears to be a way of life and few desirable species are safe merely because they are in preserves. This has been noticeable in the case of *Paphiopedilum rothschildianum* and *P. sanderianum*, to name but two of many orchids that have been stolen out of nature preserves. The former is only found in the park on Mount Kinabalu and the latter was originally found in the area that is now Gunung Mulu National Park. Both parks are in Sarawak in Malaysian Borneo. I have seen recently collected jungle plants of *P. rothschildianum* in both Malaysia and in Japan, which must have been poached from the park. Very few plants of *P. sanderianum* still exist in Mulu, they were stripped away by unscrupulous poachers, but fortunately there are still some untouched populations outside the park.

Preserves are meant to be havens that protect biodiversity from human activities but with increasing human pressures it has become difficult to isolate preserves from all human activity. Not only do human populations often abut directly onto the boundaries of most reserves but unless they are strictly policed, squatters will usually settle within them. Human activities include conducting slash and burn agriculture, or grazing herds of goats or cattle within the reserves. These activities lead directly to degradation of the area and the loss of its prime function, the preservation of the plants and animals inside the reserve.

Preserves are not inviolate. Merely because a preserve has been set up, does not mean that it will continue to exist forever. For a variety of reasons parts of a reserve may be cashiered and protection entirely or partially revoked. Mineral ores or oil can be discovered and the pressures to exploit them may be immense. Preserves in different parts of the world can be run by very different sets of rules and variable levels of harvesting may be permitted within those areas. There is sufficient graft, greed and influence buying, even within the most 'honorable' governments, that special interests can end up jeopardizing decades of conservation work.

The three essentials

There are three types of activities that are important for the running of a nature reserve.

The first of these is inventory. This needs to be done early on in the history of the reserve, as it will be the base line against which future success or lack thereof, will be measured. One needs to do more than merely make a list of those species found in the reserve. One needs a census as well.

The second activity is timely monitoring. Only by comparing a census of the species at regular intervals against the initial inventory, can one determine if the species populations within the area are increasing in numbers, holding their own or decreasing and in peril.

The third is active management. One must know where and when management must interfere with natural processes. This is usually difficult because there are so few rules or guidelines and not enough background information about most species that occur in reserves. This is particularly true of tropical situations.

Under ideal conditions, management also includes a research component. Only by understanding the ecology of a species can one devise effective management policies and guidelines.

The importance of other organisms

We have stressed in other places in this book that orchids are merely one component of a complex ecosystem and that fact cannot be ignored in preserves. The health of the orchid populations will depend directly on the health of their pollinators, as well as those host trees and the micro-organisms that provide the specialized environments that the orchids require. *In situ* management dictates a thorough understanding of the interplay between all of the organisms but sadly this is usually lacking.

Climate change and preserves

We need to place as much territory under protection and as soon as possible, to save the optimum number of orchid species. To that end conservationists should not allow themselves to be distracted from the task at hand. Nevertheless, the specter of global warming will inevitably raise its ugly head and may impact negatively on reserve success and may even affect acquisition.

The major problem induced by global warming is that despite a modest increase in average global temperatures, e.g. of only half to one degree Celsius, the increases will not be evenly spread across the globe. Temperatures are projected to fluctuate more widely at the poles than the equator and with larger changes at greater latitudes. In the tropics the real threat will come from changes in rainfall patterns, rather than changes in temperature. No matter how large it is or how well a tropical reserve is policed, changing rainfall patterns can jeopardize it as effectively as any other threat. If there is no drying then we can expect an increase in area where orchids will grow, provided there are still forests and sufficient water. Unfortunately most of the models suggest there may well be a generally drying of those regions.

The threat that global warming poses for the temperate orchid reserves are more real. At higher latitudes we expect considerable fluctuations in annual temperatures with much more drastic changes in local climates. These changes will have a profound negative impact on species within reserves. In the past the smaller natural temperature oscillations that signaled the end of the ice age had a profound impact on the extent and species composition of the temperate forests and their attendant floras. Orchids that are often associated with bogs and damp forests will be adversely affected, and many of the local preserves erected to protect orchids will become ineffective as refuges.

In situ legislation

These days many countries have legislation, which protects plants regardless of whether they are found in reserves, other areas, and sometimes even on private property. For example in parts of South Africa it is illegal to pick any wild flower within two hundred yards of the center of the road. This unfortunately does not affect private landholders, but it does ensure that at least a strip of natural vegetation remains along the verges of the roads. In some parts of the country it is along these road edges that one finds extensive populations of *Eulophia* species, such as *E. speciosa* or the brilliant scarlet *Satyrium princeps*.

Individual countries often formulate lists of species that are afforded special protection. In Zimbabwe, all epiphytic orchids are protected anywhere but terrestrial orchids are not. In Malawi, epiphytic orchids only seem to be protected in forestry reserves and as most natural forest is now in reserves that means that most epiphytes do receive a certain amount of protection. Similarly, Zambia also protects flora within forestry reserves. Orchids in KwaZulu, Natal, may be collected by Zulu peoples, to use in medicines but the same plant species may not be collected by non-Bantu people. While it is legal for a Zulu person to buy an orchid to grind up for medicine it is illegal for the same plant to be bought by white enthusiasts to grow in an orchid collection. The rationale is that it would deter collecting plants for sale to hobbyists. Should one really look for logic? Despite the variations in the laws of different countries there are some laws that generally afford a certain amount of protection to orchids even outside of reserves.

However, very few countries afford protection to those orchid species or other endangered plants that occur on private property, even though they offer protection to endangered mammals and birds in the same situation. Even within a single country, laws are often not uniformly applied, but vary according to the component states or provinces. Since orchids were listed on Appendix II of CITES they have received more atten-

tion from various governments, generally under the assumption that since the entire family is listed that they must all be *endangered*. Permits can usually be obtained to collect plants, but they tend to involve considerable red tape and sometimes 'special contacts' within the responsible bureau.

The fragility of wild areas

The world continues to shrink and the truly wild regions, little perturbed by man, continue to dwindle away in ever decreasing areas. Some of these regions are still rich in orchids but the probability of their persistence diminishes under the continuous threat of human encroachment. Mexico has one of the most diverse floras of any country and this is particularly true of orchids. Geographically that country narrows to an isthmus before it broadens again to form the Yucatan Peninsula. Known as the Isthmus of Tehuantepec, this narrow landbridge was once considered as a possible site for building a canal between the Caribbean and the Pacific Ocean. The land, one of modest mountains and valleys, is one of the last truly wild refuges in Mexico and it contains many different kinds of forest. These are the Chimalapas mountains, which cover nearly 800,000 ha, on the Caribbean side and contains rainforests, montane cloud forest and above those elfin forests. It becomes drier as one goes towards the Pacific and extensive pine forests appear. These in turn give way to drier deciduous forests. Each has its own kinds of orchids, but it is the montane cloud forests that are so rich in epiphytes.

The area is sparsely settled, but there is human occupancy and slash & burn agriculture is practiced. Land is owned communally and occupancy predates the Spanish invasion. Trees are felled and set on fire. After the fire has died down the ash is dug into the soil as fertilizer and can be cropped for about 5 years. After that the land remains fallow until it has had some time to regenerate.

The year 1998, was an *el niño* year and it produced one of the worst droughts in southern Mexican history. The forests of the Chimalapas caught fire and unfortunately even the normally dripping cloud forests were tinder dry. Nearly one third, some 243,000 ha of the forests burned, including the various rainforests that some ecologists had thought might be immune to fire. Smoke from the fires, created hazardous health conditions as far away as Houston in Texas. Similar fires were devastating the forests of Indonesia. How did the fires start? It was, in part, slash and burn agriculture that had burned out of control because of the drought, but White (1998) also suggests that the fires may have been deliberately set. He points out that satellite photographs showed two lines of fires running directly across the Chimalapas, many in areas far from human habitation. He thinks that incendiary bombs, dropped from an airplane, may have started the fires. Why this should have been done is not clear.

After the conflagration White inspected the area and reported that while much of the area was charred there were small islands of greenery that might help to re-colonize the forests, but that he thought it would take centuries to return the woods to their original condition. Almost definitely, some species became extinct in that fire and others may still follow. But now that the fires are out new threats have raised their heads. Five major rivers run through the isthmus and proposals have been made to dam all five. Among the costs of dam building is the flooding of valleys and the drowning of forests. Then there is a project to a build a new petrochemical plant on the Pacific coast. If that were not enough, there are also proposals to build both a four lane highway and a railway line across the isthmus to ferry cargo containers from ships on the Atlantic side to other ships on the Pacific side. White is also concerned that opening up the Chimalapas would encourage the 'harvesting' of tropical timber with the subsequent opening of the land to additional agriculture.

The threats that the Chimalapas faces are not unusual, this is merely one example of the constant erosion of tropical wild lands that is happening in all parts of the globe. Unless the wild places are actively and legally preserved they will all eventually undergo conversion and become degraded.

Reserves

During the last 15 years or so there has been increasing encouragement and pressure for tropical countries to create additional reserves of their forested areas. On a global level about 10% of the tropical forested lands have been set aside as reserves in one form or another. This may be sufficient to safeguard as much as half of the world's wild orchids. The total amount of area set aside may in fact be somewhat higher, if one also includes high security facilities such as microwave and other communications towers and military reserves, set in forested areas. Small municipal parks and inaccessible natural terrain outside of preserves are an additional set of refuges, although the long-term value of the former is questionable. By 1991 there were over 3,000 national parks or their equivalents in tropical forested areas and this covered over 400 million hectares (Whitmore, 1991). The quality of these parks and their management, however, is very uneven.

UNESCO has been involved with promoting two different kinds of reserves that have importance for tropical forests. One type is called a Biosphere Reserve, which contains a core area of forest that is supposed to remain intact and untouched. The core is surrounded by a buffer zone of forest where human activity is permitted. Theoretically the activity allowed is one of sustainable utilization. A second kind of UNESCO reserve covers natural areas that are considered to be so uniquely valuable that the whole world recognizes their importance. This consists of a mixture of 630 cultural and natural sites. About 128 are important natural sites and those in the tropics contain rainforest. In terms of importance for orchids one could assert that these areas will offer protection for some resident orchid species, but few of the World Heritage Sites are really important centers of orchid biodiversity.

Important orchid preserves

Although wildlife parks are rarely erected specifically for orchids, there are several reserves both large and small that have some importance for the survival of a variety of orchid species. Parks like the Mt. Kinabalu State Park in Borneo are large enough that they can protect hundreds of species, many of which have great horticultural importance. Other forest reserves, like the Marloth Nature Reserve overlooking the small town of Swellendam in South Africa, only contains a few orchid species but among them is *Disa aurata*, a very important yellow species, that is only known from this one area. Thus the little reserves are important in their own right. Around the world there are many other hundreds of these parks and reserves, and in this section we briefly review a few of them to give a feel for some of their triumphs and problems. Most, but not all, of these of these are areas that the author has visited and with which he has some familiarity. Once again one must reiterate that there are very few reserves that are specifically managed to optimize orchid survival. But, either by perseverance or blind luck, many orchid species are able to persist and sometimes even flourish safely in these parks

Mt. Kinabalu

The Mount Kinabalu State Park is arguably one of the most important wildlife parks in the world and within its boundaries is contained an appreciable fraction of the world's plant biodiversity. The park is a giant granite mountain that rises above 4,000 m in the northeast corner of Borneo and is part of Bornean Malaysia. Wood,

Beaman and Beaman (1993) enumerate close to 600 different orchid taxa in the park, but with further exploration many more species are likely to be added. Approximately 11% of the known species are endemic and found only within the park boundaries. Others consider the total numbers of species to be nearly twice as much (Lamb, 1989).

The park covers an area of 75,350 ha and has many different forest types and disparate soils and rocks. No doubt this accounts for the much of the biodiversity. The lowest forests start at about 400 m and the mountain peaks extend above the forest levels to alpine vegetation. As in many other regions of the world the greatest orchid diversity is contained in the montane forests between 1,000 and 2,000 m. There have been several monographs devoted to the orchids of Mt. Kinabalu, with the best being that of Wood, Beaman and Beaman, 1993.

Among the better known and most famous species in the park are *Coelogyne pandurata*, *Paphiopedilum rothschildianum*, *Renanthera bella*, nine different species of *Cymbidium* and four species of *Phalaenopsis*, including the large white *P. amabilis*. Other species-rich genera in the park include *Bulbophyllum*, *Dendrochilum* and *Dendrobium*.

The boundaries of the park are not inviolate and it has suffered a variety of changes and insults in recent years. On the Pinosuk Plateau most of the lowland forest was logged. A copper mine was permitted above the Lohan River and its tailings have poisoned much of that river, including the trees along its banks. In 1990, much of the forest near the Lohan River was lost to fire. Other economic projects that have impinged negatively in the Pinosuk region include the construction of a golf course, which is said to have obliterated a population of *Paphiopedilum javanicum* var. *virens*. Both dairy and vegetable farms have been set up. Illegal squatters also threaten parts of the park. Population pressures are particularly intense in some regions of Malaysian Borneo. In Sarawak, the state where Mt. Kinabalu is situated, by 1985 over 3 million ha were under shifting agriculture. Much of that area was within 'permanent' forested preserves.

It is typical of these kinds of parks to have limited resources available for wardens and rangers. Poaching has been a problem within the park. There is still a market both in Malaysia and other parts of south east Asia for jungle collected *Paphiopedilum* species, particularly *P. rothschildianum*, and populations in the park are said to have been devastated.

Ecotourism has been a mixed blessing. While this brings money to the region and provides an easily under-stood incentive for the maintenance of the park by local inhabitants it also has adverse influences. Most of the *Phalaenopsis amabilis*, which used to be quite common, have long since been stripped out for sale to tourists. Thousands of tourists also have a measurable effect on the wear and tear of paths and the adjacent forests. But the park is very large and these problems may be a very small price to pay for the conservation of the rest of the region's diversity.

Gunung Jerai

Gunung Jerai is a long mountain in northwestern peninsular Malaysia. It stands as an island with a flat, low altitude plain, flanking its northern side, which has been converted to a monotonous sea of rice paddies. To the east and south are the even more monotonous plantations of oil palm and rubber trees that now seem to make up the majority of the Malaysian countryside. To the west is the ocean, the Strait of Malacca. Gunung Jerai rises above this, still clad in forest that changes to scrub at its summit.

Only part of the mountain is accessible. There is a narrow paved road that goes up to transmitting towers on the summit. As one ascends the mountains the trees get shorter and shorter until, near the summit, there is only shrubbery a few meters tall. The mountain is rich in plant species of many kinds, besides orchids, including the pitcher plant, *Nepenthes*, begonias and other rare herbs including an unusual *Burmannia* species growing as a small rosette of grassy leaves with little blue flowers. Once considered a sister group to the orchids, the *Burmanniaceae* is mainly a weird assortment of saprophytic plants, lacking chlorophyll and dependent on fungi feeding on decaying vegetation for their sustenance. The species here is a rare free-living green plant still able to photosynthesize.

The orchids of Gunnung Jerai are rich and varied, giving a taste of how splendid the orchid flora of the Malaysian peninsula must have been before the land became converted to palm and rubber plantations. Along seepage rivulets between the trees in the upper parts of the mountain are the remnants of *Paphiopedilum callosum* var. *sublaeve* populations, that were heavily collected before the area was placed under protection. Two to three meters above the ground perches *Cymbidium dayanum*, sharing tree branches with a variety of dendrobiums and erias. On the ground, nestled among the decaying leaves of the forest floor litter, can be found a variety of jewel orchid species with bronzed leaves reticulated with gold and copper veins. Near the transmitting towers are huge mounds of a white flowered *Coelogyne* species, on the ground beneath white flowered *Rhododendron* shrubs and probably sharing similar pollinators.

The lower reaches of the mountain are a popular picnic and recreation area for townspeople and schoolchildren from nearby towns and villages, but few of them venture into the higher regions where the orchids abound. Most of the visitors are not interested in the orchids, although some of the larger flowers will be picked. Motor cars have been banned from the upper reaches where the road gets steeper, thus forcing explorers to walk. This has drastically reduced the number of visitors to the fragile upper forests and that in turn helps the orchids escape both the attention and traffic of the tourists.

Much of the rest of mountain is not easily accessible without several days of arduous hiking but even in the accessible parts one can find orchid seedlings. Seedlings of the slipper orchids occur showing the recovery of the population, now that collecting has been curtailed.

Swellendam

Swellendam is a sleepy agricultural town almost 200 miles due east of the City of Cape Town, in the Western Cape province of South Africa. The Cape contains many mountain ranges, which are tall and often have precipitous slopes. The settlement, although small, has a long history and for a few months even had the status of an independent republic. The town is nestled at the base of a very long mountain called Langeberg (which means long mountain). It is a lengthy ridge that reaches up and forms a bulwark to the north of the town. It contains a number of rocky spires that tower over the town below. The lower slopes are covered with plantations of pine trees. At the level of the first shoulder, pine forest gives way to natural vegetation. Here there are some small patches of natural forest, surrounded by the typical 'fynbos' vegetation of the western Cape. There are several small streams that run down the flanks of the mountain, forming a series of small pools on shoulders and wider ledges. This flank of the mountain forms the Marloth Nature Reserve, named for an early botanist and covers some 11,000 ha.

The small patches of natural forest contain a few epiphytic species, none of which are particularly rare or spectacular. Nevertheless there is uniqueness here because this is the most southern patch of forest on the African continent that has epiphytic orchid species and, as such, merits consideration. There are other orchids in this reserve, along the streams and rocky crags that are terrestrial and one of those species has been of considerable horticultural importance. That species is *Disa aurata* and it is not known to occur naturally anywhere else on the planet. This species has spikes of bright yellow but rather small flowers. Nevertheless, this species has been very important in the development of spectacular large yellow *Disa* hybrids such as *D.* Auratkew and *D.* California Gold. It is purely coincidental that *D. aurata* occurs at Swellendam and receives the added protection of the reserve.

Several years ago, we were able to get a permit, to collect a few plants of the golden *Disa* from the Swellendam reserve for molecular analysis. The species was known to form fair sized colonies at the edges of pools and streams, experts gave us exact directions to find the plants. Like good citizens we reported at the forestry office to sign in and speak to the white ranger who was on duty. He was not interested in our project (which was understandable) and totally disinterested in the fact that his reserve contained small numbers of a unique plant found nowhere else (which was not understandable). In fact when asked about the whereabouts of *D. aurata* he was totally unfamiliar with that species. These rare species were neither animals nor the pine trees and hence not worthy of his attention. Unfortunately this attitude has been a common occurrence through much of the world.

There were no plants around the pools that had been described to us. It took us two days of clambering about the mountain before we found a rivulet lined with *D. aurata*. Other streams where the plants were said to be common and in quantity were bare. It looked as if both vegetation overgrowth and illegal collecting had combined to wipe out most of the well-known population sites. In this case, the species had received no more protection than if it had existed outside the forest reserve.

Espirito Santo

Espirito Santo is a small state north of Rio de Janeiro, situated along the Atlantic coastline of Brazil. The state covers some 45,600 km^2 and has diverse topography that holds a number of different vegetation types and forest ecosystems. This was an area rich in tropical biodiversity. Most of the state was originally forested but probably less than two percent of the primary forest cover remains today. It is a major area of concern in terms of conservation and considerable attention has been focussed on the future prospects of the Atlantic forest systems. This is now generally recognized to be among the most endangered of all tropical forest ecosystems.

Augusto Ruschi was born in the city of Santa Teresa, in Espirito Sancto, in June 1913. He became an agronomist engineer and eventually titular Professor, at the National Museum of the Federal University of the State of Rio de Janeiro. Ruschi had a special affinity for Espirito Santo and spent most of his life studying its plants and animals. He was especially drawn to the orchids. He had witnessed the continuous loss of natural areas and encouraged the formation of safe areas for the region's biota. He died in 1986, shortly before the publication of his book on the orchids of the region (Ruschi, 1986). The country recognized his work and, in his honor, the Brazilian President renamed the Santa Lúcia Reserve as the Augusto Ruschi Reservation.

Brazil itself holds approximately 2,350 orchid species and over one quarter of these, some 600 species in 125 genera, are known from Espirito Santo. Ruschi (1986) estimated that 150 orchid species were endemic to the state and most of those had ornamental value. Included among them are the most important showy orchid genera such as *Cattleya*, *Laelia*, *Oncidium*, *Rodriguezia* and *Epidendrum*. Ruschi listed 107 orchid species that he considered to be among the most endangered and that register includes many species that are familiar to the world's orchid growers. Among the eight *Cattleya* species that he considered to be endangered, are the well-known C. *guttata* and C. *labiata*. Thirteen species of *Laelia*, including the popular dwarf purple L. *pumila*, are threatened in this area and Ruschi also listed 23 threatened species of *Oncidium* with O. *forbesii*, perhaps the best known. Ruschi thought that perhaps as many as 200 species of orchid had become extinct by 1986, but unfortunately he did not list them.

The population of Espirito Santo in 1987 was only about 2.3 million, compared to the 13 million in the slightly smaller neighboring State of Rio de Janeiro (Brawer, 1991). The threat to natural areas had come more from the expansion of agriculture over several centuries, than population growth. Much of the remaining forest is now preserved in a series of parks and conservation areas, administered by a variety of agencies. In 1986 there were 15 main protected sites covering about 118,690 ha. Of these the largest is the Caparaó National Park at 25,000 ha, it includes some higher altitude regions. The smallest park is Caixa d'Água at only 22 ha. There are four medium sized reserves ranging from 2,300 to 4,000 ha, each administered by the agriculture State Department management. Not only do Municipal governments also manage parks but there is also the substantial Linhares Forest, administered by the Vale do Rio Doce Company. The National Museum controls at least one park and the Brazilian Institute of Forest Development has responsibility for four separate areas.

Control therefore, is spread through a number of different governmental, educational and private organizations. In some respects this spread of responsibility is good, because it buffers the whole set of reserves against extreme changes in policy by any one agency. There is active management of the reserve areas in that they are supervised, admission tends to be restricted and there is some attempt to minimize theft of wood and ornamental plants, but the focus is not specifically on orchids.

Monteverde Cloud Forest Reserve

Costa Rica is the home of the Organization for Tropical Studies (OTS), a consortium of USA universities which, together with the University of Costa Rica, has trained several generations of tropical biologists. The success of OTS has also been translated into direct effects on the country itself. Eco-tourism has become big business and the country has built up a reputation for being at the forefront of tropical nature conservation. Costa Rica has been a model country with regards to conservation and has set up a number of reserves in a variety of different localities, covering a range of tropical ecosystems. An enormous amount of the country's natural vegetation has been lost. Much of the remaining forest has been set aside as reserves and many of these reserves are associated with research stations and have made important contributions to our current understandings of tropical ecology.

The montane cloud forests of Costa Rica are particularly rich in epiphytes and the Monteverde Cloud Forest Reserve is a good example of one of these protected sites. The epiphytes within the reserve have been enumerated (Ingram *et al*, undated) and include 140 epiphytic species and no doubt there are additional terrestrials as well. With 31 species, *Pleurothallis* is the largest genus and *Maxillaria* follows with 20 species. Other orchids include eight species of *Masdevallia* and 15 of *Epidendrum*. The orchid with the largest individual flowers is *Lycaste leucantha*, while that with the smallest is most likely *Platystele microtatantha*.Because of the ecological, educational and research focus on Costa Rica, the orchids in Monteverde and most of the other reserves in the country are relatively safe. Major problems that they face are indirect and involve the effects of pesticides on the orchid's pollinators. There has been widespread use of a variety of insecticides in Central America and these gradually work their way into the ecosystem, placing many of the pollinators at risk.

Two Malawi forest reserves

Blantyre is a very large city in the south of the small African nation of Malawi, which occupies the southernmost part of the rift valley in the south central part of the continent. Close to the city are several forest reserves. One, at Mount Soche, is quite small but the other Mount Mulange, is substantial. Both hold large numbers of orchid species, many of which are poorly known to the world's orchid growers.

Mount Soche is a nature reserve that occupies one of the three main mountains outside of Blantyre. It is close to the city, scarcely 6 km away. The mountain is quite rich in orchids, both epiphytic and terrestrial. The city is expanding and the need for space and land is so intense that a village now lies adjacent to the reserve and all the land up to the boundary of the forest has been ploughed for crops. Much of that land is strewn with large boulders but nearly every square inch of land that can be dug, has been turned over.

Although the people are not allowed to chop trees down in the reserve, any branches or trees that fall are fair game. This leads to one of the 'cleanest' forests on the continent as all broken branches and even twigs tend to be scavenged. In addition, the dominant trees in the forest, species of *Brachystegia*, have woody seedpods that can be used as fuel. Children scrounge through the reserve filling gunnysacks with dried seedpods. The forest is gradually being leeched of its organic matter. The forest is quite species rich, with a large variety of orchid species and many branches are thickly strewn with epiphytes of the genera *Bulbophyllum*, *Polystachya* and *Jumellia*. Terrestrial orchids include a *Stenoglottis* species, probably *S. zambesiaca*, and the curious saprophytic *Eulophia longisepala*, which contains no chlorophyll and must be dependent on symbiotic fungi for its nutrients.

A nature guide to Mt. Soche, published in 1989, described the surrounding fields as being rich in terrestrial orchids, particularly the beautiful pink *Eulophia cucullata* and the related yellow *E. zeyheri*, forming swathes of yellow and pink flowers. Five years later, only one plant of *E. cucullata* could be found growing within the forest boundary – there were no plants of *E. zeyheri*. The area previously described was all under the plough.

The long-term prognosis for Mt. Soche is poor. One can expect a gradual impoverishment with the slow loss of species. Being small and having a village on its boundary makes it particularly susceptible to both accidental and deliberate fires. Many of the species only have small populations and the numbers may not be self-sustaining. This reserve has all the vulnerability that one can expect from small areas under constant human pressures.

36   Mt. Soche reserve, outside of Blantyre, Malawi. Note the new spring foliage is red to protect the developing leaves from the harsh sunlight.

37   Mt. Soche. The preserve starts on the right side of the footpath. All the land that used to be rich in terrestrial orchids – such as *Eulophia cuculata* – has been ploughed.

Further away from the city is the Mulanje Massif, with a plateau reaching over 3,000 m above sea level; it has been considered the highest mountain in Central Africa. It is not a trivial undertaking to explore the entire mountain and several days are required to climb it. Although there is a considerable forested area of introduced trees on the lower flanks of the mountain there are also native forests as well. It is known for its African Cedar forests (a species of *Widdringtonia*). Mulanje is rich in orchids, among others, the Mulanje district contains 4 species of *Aerangis*; 14 of the country's 17 *Bulbophyllum* species; 17 species out of a total of 56 *Eulophias* and 18 of the 32 species of *Polystachya*. Many other orchid species also find refuge on the mountain.

Mulanje is a large area, much of which is a secure preserve, and many of the species in it are probably relatively safe. They are as protected by the strenuous climb needed to reach the orchid rich areas, as much as Mulanje's preserve status. However, some of the lower elevation species around the base of the mountain are probably at risk. Nevertheless, the long-term prospects for the orchids here are far more optimistic than orchids in other smaller and more accessible refuges.

Perinet and Mantadia – Malagasy

The rapid deterioration of the Madagascan natural environment and its biodiversity has received focused attention and the island now contains some 30 reserves. Nearly 2% of the island's area is under some sort of preserve status (Preston-Mafham, 1991).

Near the small town of Perinet, which lies in the mountains between the capital city of Antannarive and the coast of Madagascar, is a nature reserve for the Indri. Indri are the largest of the extant lemur species, and the preserve is known as the 'Analamazaotra Special Reserve', although it is more commonly just called the Indri Special Reserve. This is a small preserve of only 810 ha that contains eastern montane forest. It ranges in altitude between 930 and 1,040 m and the canopy is some 25–30 m above the ground. The forest is not pristine, but has been selectively logged and many of the big trees have long been removed. The Special Preserve has been protected since 1927 but was only officially established in 1970. It is home to 34 species of mammal, including nine different species of lemur (including the Indri), and ten species of 'Tenrec'. The latter are curious insectivores that resemble small shaggy hedgehogs. There are over 100 bird species in the sanctuary, 28 reptile and 76 amphibian species. The reserve is obviously administered for its animals, despite the approximately 600 plant species that include numerous orchids. Being the largest of the lemurs, the Indri attract attention and as they are usually easily seen in the special reserve, Perinet is on the itinerary of most eco-tourists visiting the island. The special reserve is surrounded for the most part by *Eucalyptus* plantations, so it does have some buffering, but the small size of the reserve is of concern.

Near the special reserve, but not quite adjacent to it, is another patch of natural forest that also contains Indri. This is the Mantadia National Park, which covers 9,875 ha and has only been opened to the public since 1998. Mantadia is rich in orchids, ranging from *Eulophiella roempleriana*, which flaunts its large pink flowers from the spiral crowns of *Pandanus* trees to the

very desirable *Angraecum vigueri*, *A. equitans*, *A. teretifolium* and others. *Aerangis citrata* appears to be common but other aerangises such as *Aerangis platyphylla*, *A. fuscata* and *A. stylosa* festoon the trees. At least 35 different species of *Bulbophyllum* abound. In addition there are several species each of *Aeranthes*, *Jumellia*, *Polystachya*, and *Liparis*. Both an *Oenia* species and *Oeniella polystachya* share the forest with the unusual epiphytic *Calanthe repens* and the rare *Beclardia macrostachys*. We counted three different species of epiphytic *Cynorchis* but there are probably more. At present the national park in Mantadia is relatively pristine, but how it will fare as it becomes more widely known and suffers from a greater tourist influx remains to be ascertained.

Across the road from Analamazaotra is a small two-hectare plot of forest, around a small lake. This is the 'Orchid Park', which is discussed under the chapter on *ex situ* conservation.

All of these parks are jointly administered by ANGAP (Assoc. Nationale de la Gestion des Aires Protogées), which is under state control. Only half of the entrance fees to the parks are returned by the State to ANGAP. How much of that gets back to the park that originated the income is not clear. There is additional foreign income from USAID, SAF/FJKM, the Japan Wildlife Research Center and VITA (Volunteers in Technical Assistance) for the parks in the Perinet area. The WWF and other institutions are also very active. There are 49 guards/conservation officers who work these parks but they only get paid when they take tourists through the parks. Income for these people is therefore sometimes quite unpredictable. Only one of these workers knows the orchids really well, although other guides are thirsty for information. In fact, there is probably only one native Malagasy in ANGAP who is really well versed in the orchid flora.

Amber Mountain – Malagasy

At the very north of Madagascar lies the small city, still known as Diégo-Suarez, but described on modern maps as Antsiranana. Some 40 kilometers from here is a large extinct volcanic massif, with several small crater lakes that form the Amber Mountain National Park and Reserve. It ranges in altitude from 850 to 1475 meters and covers some 18,200 ha. Most of the park is covered with rainforest and like other rain forests on the island it is rich in epiphytes, particularly orchids. ANGAP and the WWF jointly administer the park. Amber Mountain was established as a forestry station in 1920 and became the country's first National Park in 1958.

38   Mont Ambre Forest reserve in Northern
Madagascar. This forest is still in near pristine
condition.

Geographically the park is isolated and attracts relatively few tourists, which has added a measure of protection
to its biota. It only has seven species of lemur, but over
1,020 plant species have been noted and many of these,
of course, are orchids. As in other Madagascan rainforests, *Aerangis citrata* is common but at least five
other *Aerangis* species are also known, ranging from the
spectacular *A. stylosa* to the diminutive *A. hyaloides*.
Many of the *Angraecum* species that live in the park are
also well known in cultivation, including *A. obesum*, *A.
germanianum*, *A. equitans* and *A. compactum*.
Ubiquitous bulbophyllums abound in many species, as
do various jumellias, aeranthes, oberonias and others.
Non-orchid epiphytes such as medinella, begonia and
kalanchoe are also common.

Besides epiphytes there are several common species
of terrestrial orchid among the decaying leaves of the
forest litter. *Eulophia puchra*, arguably one of the most
common orchid species in the world, is prevalent and so
is the spectacular *Phajus schlechteri*, which shares the
forest floor with a variety of *Liparis* species, including
the unusual purple-leafed *L. purpurescens*. Many of
these orchids are in abundance and situated close to
paths and roads, which suggests that there is very little
pilfering within this park.

The park appears to be effective in its *in situ* orchid
conservation and most of the species within its boundaries have a fair measure of protection. This should continue, provided visitor numbers remain at a low level.

Barro Colorado Island

When the Panama Canal was built an artificial lake was
formed. This is Gatun Lake and one of the hills in the
flooded valley ended up as an island in the lake. Named
Barro Colorado Island, it is now a biological preserve
administered, since 1923, by the Smithsonian Tropical
Research Institution, headquartered in Washington, DC.
The lake was created in 1914 and thus the island can be
taken as a representative of what can happen to a preserve over nearly a century. The island covers some 1,500
ha and is about five and a half kilometers at its widest
diameter. The island is covered with tropical forest and
for many years has been one of the major tropical
research stations of the world. Its forests have been as
well studied as any other and over a period of many years
an enormous backlog of information has been built up
(Leigh et al., 1996). The island itself is part of the Barro
Colorado Nature Monument of Panama, which includes
five peninsulas of mainland that approach the island.
There is also an adjoining national park to the north.

The forests on Barro Colorado are best described as
semi-deciduous, meaning that there is a dry period during the year when some of the trees loose their leaves,
thus it is a monsoon forest. Some of the forest appears
to be undisturbed but there are also areas of secondary
forest. Much of the attention has been focused on the
forest trees and less on the epiphytes that can be found
there. There is great plant diversity. In 1976 a flora was
published listing 1,407 species and in part this was
based on a 1933 list (Foster and Hubbell, 1990). More
recent listings suggest only 1,207 plant species (Foster
and Hubbell, 1990). It is not clear if the difference
points to extinctions, changes in taxonomy or mistakes
in the original listings. But in fact one might expect to
see a certain number of extinctions within the preserve.
If the entire difference is due to extinction since the formation of the island then 14% of the total plant species
will have been lost. How many of those are orchids is
unclear. The orchids are the second largest plant family
on the island with about 75 different species and are
generally representative of the kinds of orchids known
from Panama. Because of the renown of the island all
species within its boundaries are relatively safe, except
for those being driven towards extinction by natural
processes and the 'island effect'. Because this is a
research institute and it is necessary to keep conditions
as natural as possible one cannot expect the types of
management and manipulation that one could get in a
preserve designed specifically for the protection of its
orchid populations. Nevertheless, this island is a haven
for its wild plants.

CHAPTER 8

Ex Situ Conservation

There are several very different ways that orchids can be conserved but first we need to define exactly what we mean by conservation. Conservation is the effort used to maintain a species in such a manner that it avoids extinction. In other words it is keeping a species alive in the face of pressures that might otherwise cause the death of all members of that group or taxon. Others could argue that this is merely a definition of preservation and that successful conservation goes beyond this. It could also include providing an environment in which the species can continue to survive, reproduce and, if necessary, change and undergo normal evolution in response to natural changing environmental conditions.

Species maintained in the wild or in preserves, under more or less natural conditions, are examples of *in situ* conservation. Species that are maintained under artificial conditions i.e. in cultivation or in gene banks, could be considered as examples of *ex situ* conservation. In this chapter I examine and suggest ways that orchids can be conserved using *ex situ* methodologies.

Artificial methods of keeping species alive include seed, gene and tissue culture banks. These last methods, while well worked out for other plants, have been poorly developed for orchids. However, in the long run, they could be the most important methods for maintaining the largest numbers of species. Neither *in situ* nor *ex situ* conservation methods are fail-safe and ideally all of these techniques need to be used in order to maximize the possibility of maintaining the largest numbers of species for the use and enjoyment of future generations.

While there is an enormous need to conserve species, we should not lose sight of the fact that hybrids should also be preserved. When one considers the conservation of orchids there is a tendency to think only about wild species, but during the last 150 years we have seen the appearance of numerous important parent plants from myriad hybrids. Most of those were due to the chance combination of diverse parental genes. Repeating the same cross, using identical parents may not necessarily result in similar offspring. For example, it is highly unlikely that the clone *Cymbidium* Alexanderi 'Westonbirt' (a chance tetraploid) would reappear if its diploid parents, C. Eburneo-lowianum and C. *insigne* were mated again. It would be even less probable if an important hybrid many generations removed from its parental species, such as x *Sophrolaeliacattleya* Hazel Boyd, were remade starting from the original species.

Collection problems

Conservation of any type is beset with problems, but those posed by *ex situ* methods are probably the most intense and difficult to deal with. Living collections of plants require constant attention and resources and these must be provided for in perpetuity. Forever is a very long time. Nevertheless for the many species where the normal habitat no longer exists *ex situ* conservation may be the only viable alternative to extinction. The author was intimately involved with the building, maintenance and funding of an ex situ plant collection at the University of California at Irvine, Arboretum for 20 years. While that collection focussed on African geophytes and contained only a few orchids, it did engender an appreciation for the problems that successful ex situ conservation must be able to overcome.

The ideal goal of an *ex situ* living collection of plants would be to not only keep the species alive, but also to maintain some semblance of the original gene pool of that species. This means that very large numbers of plants need to be maintained. One rule of thumb, which many plant conservationists use, is that 50 randomly selected individuals contain 95% of the genetic variation of the population (Given, 1994). The probability of collecting a species with a rare and desirable gene is very small, probably less than one in several thousand, and unfortunately, the rare genes are usually the ones that are important in horticulture.

Fifty plants, is therefore considered to be the lowest number to be maintained and presupposes that no individuals will die. A greater number is a far better alternative, both as a hedge against mortality and also for collecting and maintaining the rarer genes. Consequently many conservationists consider that 500 different randomly selected individuals is a far better alternative. While 500 different plants of a small *Leptotes* species might be manageable, maintaining 500 specimens of a large *Cattleya* or *Cymbidium* species is a totally different matter. In addition, the gene pool of one population could differ considerably from that in another isolated population of the same species. Several collections might be needed to cover the species properly.

There are many things that can go wrong in maintaining an *ex situ* collection. All growers know that their plants eventually die. Death can come from disease, neglect, and unpredictable catastrophes such as earthquakes, hurricanes, tornadoes or power failures and then sometimes the plant itself naturally senesces and dies. There are records of keeping plants for a long time (over 100 years) in cultivation but these are surely the exceptions.

For perpetual *ex situ* collections the material may need to be rejuvenated from time to time and fresh juvenile material produced. Here we meet another problem. When one makes an orchid seed capsule several thousand seeds result. In nature the majority of the seed never find a suitable germination site and, of those that do, most die. Under artificial conditions most would survive. Natural selection is relaxed in cultivation and most of the captive population will contain individual plants that nature would have weeded out. In addition, there is a tendency because of the large numbers of seedlings that are produced not to use the entire population for breeding the next generation. Only two parents would provide most of the offspring. Within a small number of generations most of the natural variation will disappear. This is known as inbreeding and the major harmful effect of it is the appearance of homozygosity. Homozygosity allows deleterious genes to be expressed and the results are weak, non-vigorous offspring often bearing malformed flowers or leaves. This is often called inbreeding depression and leads ultimately to extinction. Inbreeding depression is particularly obvious when one starts off with populations containing small numbers of individuals. In fact 50 plants is thought to be sufficient to induce inbreeding depression although, theoretically, one needs about 500 randomly breeding individuals to avoid it (Given, 1994). This is another reason why it is desirable to keep captive populations as large as possible. When one deals with endangered species, however, one might not be able to get 50 let alone 500 different individuals. One might be lucky to get only 5 different plants and in

extreme cases there may only be one surviving individual, as is the case with *Cypripedium calceolus* in the United Kingdom.

Artificial selection

At the same time that natural selection is relaxed there is also the possibility of artificial selection occurring. There are many qualities in flowers than man appreciates, such as large round and flat blossoms, which would be selected against in nature because they reduce the possibility of pollination. Likewise, we prefer short dumpy plants, as they are easier to manage. Selection of parents must be independent of those preferences. The most vigorous seedling produced will also have been artificially selected for because it has a physiology that does well in an unnatural greenhouse regime. This is also a form of artificial selection. After several generations of artificial selection the end product can be quite different from the wild plants that we originally sought to save. Recent line breeding of species towards human ideals shows just how altered the plants can become. In the genus *Paphiopedilum* importation of jungle collected species has been forbidden by international treaty (see Chapter 10). During that time there have been many successful attempts at breeding all of the available species. Several generations of breeding have been accomplished for several species such as *P. bellatulum* and *P. sukhakulii*. These plants have either been line bred for rounder flowers or wider petals, to the point that the average plant in cultivation is now quite different from the average plant that was originally collected from the wild. These *ex situ* populations are bred for horticultural reasons and are not equivalent to the wild populations from which they were derived.

The problem of artificial selection is exasperated by some of the unique properties of orchids. Because so many seeds are produced by one fruit a single pollination is usually more than sufficient to provide more plants than can be handled. Because of the expense of germinating and growing on orchid plantlets, collection managers are usually reluctant to process more than a few fruits. Because there is less chance of contamination green pod embryo rescue is preferred to dealing with dry seed. Growing a small proportion of a generation of plants from a single pod promotes gene pool uniformity and the loss of rare alleles from the population. Because of the way that orchid pollen is packaged, it is often the case that the pollen that fertilizes the eggs in the ovules of a single fruit is also derived from one individual plant. Only a few plants' genes have a proportionately large effect in the resulting generation. This can promote drift of the characteristics of the *ex situ* species away from their original form within a relatively few generations.

Pooling seed from several pods and planting some of the resultant mixture can only partially help to overcome this problem. In addition, crossing unrelated plants can help circumvent inbreeding. Gene pool variation in the captive population can be promoted by producing large blocks of seedlings and selecting the most diverse of the resultant seedlings from the original parental stocks. Additional breeding across generations is also desirable provided the seedlings are not backcrossed to their original parents.

Perhaps the most pernicious of the problems is virus control. After relatively short periods and despite the best intentions and precautions nearly all orchids in cultivation become infected by any one of a variety of viruses. These usually sap the strength of the plant. While methods of cleaning virus out of stock are known, for plants that can be tissue cultured, the procedure is expensive and impractical for large collections. Virus is usually excluded from seed but pollen from an infected plant can in turn infect another clean mother plant. This becomes a greater problem with hybrids because seed grown stock will not resemble the parent stock.

Labeling plants and keeping the labels correct can be a real problem too. Not only do labels get switched accidentally but also, when labels are renewed transcription mistakes often occur and after the name or number has been written three or four times by different hands, it may be totally unrecognizable and bear little resemblance to the original name or number. Of course with modern computerized databases such problems should be minimal but the mistakes are made on the potting bench rather than at the office desk.

Ideally *ex situ* collections should be grown and maintained in their country of origin and near the site where they normally occur. Many developing world countries do not have the interest, the resources or the skills to carry out those activities. This means that effective *ex situ* attempts usually involves developed countries, most of which have temperate to frigid climates. Freezes and electricity failures can cause catastrophic losses for cultivated orchids. Such events are commonplace in temperate climates and many amateur orchid growers can attest to devastating plant losses under those unfortunate conditions.

Collections

During the Second World War, the major herbarium in Berlin containing priceless orchid type specimens was bombed and destroyed. At the same time England could not afford to heat all the greenhouses at Kew. Selected plants from the Royal Botanic Garden's collections were sent to the New York Botanical Gardens, among others, for safe keeping. But only a few selected plants could be saved. Moving large *ex situ* collections would have been impossible. Unfortunately, war, civil unrest and destructive riots seem to be peculiarities of the human condition and nowhere on the planet is immune from those disturbances. What this bodes for long-term conservation is not clear but it needs to be taken into account if one is to have a clear perspective on the fragility of long term ex situ conservation. In this section I will examine the fate of several major orchid collections to look for patterns in the problems that might arise.

Masdevallias at the Golden Gate Park

Theft and greed as well as seemingly innocuous attitudes such as apathy and disdain, unfortunately, can have severe consequences for plant collections. Here is one example from many.

The Conservatory at the Golden Gate Park in San Francisco had a wonderful and renowned conservation collection of masdevallias and draculas. At its peak there were 400 different species of *Masdevallia* alone, many of which were very rare. George Marcopulos assembled the collection and the San Francisco Orchid Society provided a generous stipend to him for the initial purchase of plants, San Francisco being an ideal climate for those genera. Both the collection and the plants grew beautifully and at its peak contained about 1,500 different cultivars, although there were seldom more than three or four clones of any particular species. Masdevallias need to be divided regularly and volunteers helped with those activities and they were rewarded with divisions of the plants that they had divided. The rarest plants were divided the most often and some started to diminish in size as people started to help themselves to excess divisions. Some plants disappeared completely from the collection while parts of other plants were also sometimes stolen. In an effort to save the most important rare plants George removed their labels from the pots. He, of course, could recognize the individual plants, though who knows what would have happened if an accident befell him. George was then promoted in charge of the entire conservatory and he had to hire a replacement for himself. As this was a civil service position funded by the municipality of the City there were strict guidelines about who was eligible and could be hired. The person he had to bring on board actively disliked masdevallias and those species suffered through benign neglect. The collection dropped from 400 species down to 200. Apparently draculas were acceptable and those plants did not suffer. Eventually that person was replaced with another who had empathy for masdevallias but the damage was done. George's concern now is the realization that whenever there is a change in staff, even if the person is committed to the plants, there is a training period during which time plants will be lost.

The Ball State University Collection

Enthusiastic amateur collectors and horticulturists build many important orchid collections. What happens to the collections after they leave the collectors' hands can be instructive. Bill and Goldie Wheeler were fascinated with cattleyas and had built an unusually fine collection of important hybrids and selected species. After Bill's death his wife Goldie looked for a new home for the collection. She found a willing recipient in Ball State University in Muncie, Indiana. She was prepared to give the University her greenhouse to hold the collection but the University opted for building a larger and more modern facility. In the interim the collection was moved into a greenhouse, leased for a year from a commercial grower. Goldie red-tagged those plants she considered to be the most select and precious. Towards the end of this period the head orchid grower left. In 1970 the collection was moved to Ball State University and at that time contained about 1,500 mature orchid plants. Eighty percent were selected *Cattleya* hybrids and the other 20% were primarily *Cattleya*, *Oncidium* with some *Dendrobium* species. Sometime between the move into the leased greenhouse and the Ball State Greenhouse many of the red-tagged plants disappeared. Once at Ball State, the collection started to deteriorate and in 1973 Russ Vernon was hired to resuscitate and look after the collection. He worked with the collection until 1987. During this time the collection was saved and grew in size to 3,000 specimens. It now also contained an important species collection with 95% of the known *Cattleya* and *Laelia* species. If one included the named varieties of those species the collection approached 85% of all types. The collection gained the reputation of an important conservation collection. Vernon organized and motivated a group of volunteers to look after and help with the collection. Towards the end of his tenure with the collection Mr. Vernon grew disillusioned. He needed to start a fundraising drive to enlarge and maintain the collection. But the University administration dithered about and could not come to a decision whether or not to permit this. In the end, rather disillusioned, he left.

Following the loss of Vernon, the collection rapidly deteriorated until only 800 specimens remained alive. Half of the rare species were lost. All of a collection of New Guinea and Australian dendrobiums died, as did an entire *Paphiopedilum* collection. During the last ten years the state of the collection has oscillated. It has improved somewhat in recent years and is maintained at about 1,200 specimens. But it is now quite different from what the Wheelers had anticipated.

Looking back at his experiences, Vernon lists three parameters whereby matters went wrong and predisposed the collection to potential failure. In the first and most important case, the collection was not endowed. The university should not have accepted it without an endowment and it should not have been bequeathed under those conditions. Administrators can not foresee the state of their resources at future times and accepting a living collection under such uncertain circumstances is an unacceptable gamble for a living conservation collection. The second problem was that the administration at the University changed, as it was likely to do. New policy makers may feel that they have no obligation to maintain a collection, even if they are aware of their predecessors' promises. The third obstacle was the fact that the administration did not realize either the nature or the value of the collection for which they had assumed responsibility.

The Kennedy and Fowlie Collections

Dr. George Kennedy was a Professor in Geophysics at the University of California at UCLA, who was intensely interested in orchid species. He personally visited many regions of the world and amassed a large and important personal collection of species. He was fascinated by the genus *Lycaste* and he interacted with Dr. Jack Fowlie, who, during the mid-1960s, was examining that genus and writing a monograph about it. They shared observations. At one stage Kennedy needed to make room in his greenhouse and he made space by sending an interesting collection of orchid species down to Prof. Joseph Arditti at the nearby University of California at Irvine, who was at that time gathering a study collection. Jack Fowlie, in the meantime, was housing his collection at the Los Angeles County Arboretum, where Earl Ross worked and was the curator of Jack's plants. George Kennedy died unexpectedly and his wife sold off much of collection piecemeal. The remainder, that was difficult to sell, was donated to the Botanic Garden in the San Francisco Golden Gate Park. What still remains of that, is uncertain. Jack Fowlie also died prematurely, although it was about 20 years after Kennedy. Then Earl Ross lost his champion and funding priorities at the LA County Arboretum changed. He had a difficult time maintaining the Fowlie collection and had to rely on volunteer help. The collection at the LA County Arboretum held many unique plants, including a number of unusual *Lycaste* species. Among them was the type plant of *L. mathiasae*, the only specimen of that species that had ever been collected. That plant and pieces of several others were later donated to the National *Lycaste* Collection maintained by Dr. Henry Oakley, a famous *Lycaste* grower, in the United Kingdom. Meanwhile Earl Ross has retired and the fate of the collection is uncertain. For a variety of financial and political reasons the resources allotted to Prof. Arditti were also removed. Many of original Kennedy species had died from enforced neglect and a few survivors were taken into his private collection where they also now face an uncertain future.

The collection at Piracicaba, Sao Paulo

The neotropics possess many of the most important orchid species. One of the most significant collections of South American orchids is housed in Piracicaba, at the University of Sao Paulo. As related by Cassio van den Berg the collection was started in the 1930s before the Second World War. Dr. F.G. Brieger expanded it during the years 1951–70, with funding from the Rockefeller Foundation. Brieger's name is commemorated in the name of a popular yellow orchid, *Laelia briegeri*.

From the early years up until the present about 32,000 plants have been collected and brought into the collection. About 13,300 species are, or were, represented in the collection, which includes South American plants from the Colombian Andes down to Uruguay, with the majority of the specimens drawn from Brazil. It is strongest in the Laeliinae and has at times had extensive representations of most *Cattleya* and *Laelia* species. Van der Berg recounts that the *Cattleya* collection contained 1,400 clones drawn from 80 populations and representing 23 species. These are the sort of numbers that approach those one would like to see in good conservation collections. Other extensive collections cover *Laelia*, *Encyclia*, *Maxillaria*, *Bifrenaria*, and *Cataesetum*. Among the collections many new species were recognized and described, including the now familiar *Cattleya kerrii*, *Laelia alaorii*, *L. esalqueana*, *L. milleri* and many more that are less well known.

Because of the hot climate, few cloud forest or upper montane Andean species can be grown. At one time there was also a large collection of terrestrial orchids belonging to the Spiranthoid and Orchidoid subfamilies. That collection was lost due to a combination of staffing problems and the

39 *Laelia milleri*, once thought extinct, this species is still known from a very few small and protected populations. There are probably more artificially propagated plants of *L. milleri*, in orchid collections, than exist in the wild.

more exacting requirements of terrestrial orchid culture. Of the 32,000 accessions collected over the years, van den Berg reckons that 10,000 are still alive at the present time. This is barely 31% of the total number of plants brought into the collection since the beginning of the project.

This collection was not originally conceived as a special conservation collection but it has started to take on those aspects. When van den Berg was working with the *Cattleya* species he noted that some of the localities from which they had been collected had been destroyed. He visited other localities expecting to find plants still growing but in many of them the sites had been completely cleared. Some had been lost through logging operations and others through urban expansion. The plants in the collection are now the sole existing representatives of those populations. How seriously the caretakers hold their responsibility is uncertain?

Orchids at the Royal Botanic Gardens, Kew

The Royal Botanic Gardens at Kew, is synonymous with orchid expertise and many of the most famous orchid taxonomists over the last two centuries have been associated with that institution. Orchids have also been a prime component of their living plant collections for much of the past 215 years, making it probably the oldest surviving living collection of orchids anywhere. The collection contains about 5,000 species and about 20,000 plants, figures that have not changed much this century. However, the species composition has changed to reflect research interests and because of mortality of plants. Most orchid species could, potentially, be very long lived. Thirty- to fifty-year life spans are not unusual. While there are some plants in the Kew collection in excess of a century these are very few. It is probably fair to assume that of the tens of thousands of living orchids that have made their way to the Royal Botanic Garden over the last 215 years, the percentage of long term survivors is considerably less than 10%. In all fairness it should be pointed out that for most of the collection's life, research and amenity rather than conservation have been its primarily goals. Nevertheless the percentage of surviving plants demonstrates very clearly the difficulties that can be faced by even one of the world's greatest institutions.

The Eric Young Orchid Foundation, Jersey

Eric Young was one of the world's leading orchid growers, famed for producing exciting new hybrids, particularly in the genera *Cymbidium*, *Paphiopedilum* and *Odontoglossum*. He set up a trust to run his collection after his death and built a new complex of glasshouses, library and laboratory at Victoria Village on Jersey in the Channel Islands. The collection was moved to the new premises just before his sudden death in 1978. Since then it has been under the management of Alan Moon, Eric Young's able orchid grower; the collection has thrived and continued to produce world-beating hybrids.

The collection, although dominated by hybrids, contains a good selection of the most attractive species, using them for display and for breeding purposes. Amongst their successes, the production of tetraploid clones of many orchids has been pioneered and the resulting plants have been used to produce some outstanding clones e.g. in *Phragmipedium*.

The Trust is well endowed financially and its future success depends largely upon attracting a talented manager, outstanding growers and hybridists.

Paphiopedilums at Palmengarten

The Palmengarten in Frankfurt, Germany is under city control and built a respectable reputation under the Directorship of Gustaf Schoser. The garden was renowned for its collection of *Paphiopedilum* species. The collection originated at the Tübingen University Botanic Gardens and donations of species came from a variety of sources. The collection was an important one from a comparative point of view. People could compare their plants with those in the collection. In this way it was determined that *P. sukhakulii* was a new species. The collection was also the source of *P. callosum* 'Sparkling Burgundy', which played a very important role in the creation of vinicolored slipper orchids and helped to initiate and sustain the worldwide interest in the genus.

When Schoser became director of Palmengarten the main portion of the Tübingen collection was transferred to Frankfurt. The collection continued to be built up and new species were added. (Schoser, 1987). A program was set up to propagate rare slipper orchid species from seed. The emphasis then shifted towards interaction with the local people and their education. In recent years, however, there has been a decline in international interest and awareness about the Palmengarten collection.

The Czechoslovak Academy of Sciences Gene Bank Collection

The Czechoslovak Academy of Sciences maintained a large collection of tropical plants in their greenhouses. Among the various species were more than 600 different orchid species, many of them from Cuba and Vietnam. At the transition from a communist to free market economy the government no longer wanted the expense of maintaining the plants in the greenhouses. Ownership of the greenhouses reverted back to the original proprietor and funds for the heating of the greenhouses was withdrawn. Alves (1998) calculates that all but 5% of the plant collection then died. Horticulturists and other private orchid enthusiasts rescued the few surviving plants.

Orchid Gardens in Jamaica

In most parts of the world where there are orchid collections they are maintained in cultivation under very artificial conditions. In Jamaica there are two collections of native orchids that are held in unique conditions. These are semi-natural plantings of Jamaican orchid species. These are the Martin Hill Orchid Sanctuary and the Schwallenberg Orchid Sanctuary (Gloudon and Tobisch, 1995). There is an intensive aluminum mining operation on the island, which has resulted in the destruction of a considerable number of orchid habitats. Mr. Ancille Gloudon, a local commercial orchid nurseryman, was able to persuade the company Alcan Jamaica's agricultural division to set aside two small areas where salvaged plants could be re-established in orchid gardens. He was instrumental in the design and completion of the gardens.

The Martin Hill Orchid Sanctuary is the smallest, covering only 0.4 ha, but it still contains approximately 30,000 orchid plants in 101 species from 72 genera. This is slightly less than half of all the Jamaican orchid species and includes 24 of the island's 66 endemic species. One of these, *Epidendrum scalpelligerum*, is considered extinct in the wild. Survival of the orchids has been tracked and only two and a half percent have been lost. This is a very good survival rate. The Schwallenberg Sanctuary is larger but still only covers 1.6 ha. Here there are some 15,000 plants in 58 species from 30 genera, including Jamaica's famed *Broughtonia sanguinea* and *Encyclia cochleata*.

Both sanctuaries are controlled and maintained by the Alcan Jamaica Company and while they may be doing a good job currently there does not seem to be any assurance that the gardens can or will be maintained in perpetuity. With all these species in such close proximity and under semi natural conditions one wonders how much hybridization between species occurs and whether or not this is a source of 'contamination' for the island. Such concentrations of plants are very fragile, not only in terms of their continuity but also because potential weather hazards, such as hurricanes, which might easily wipe them out. On the other hand, collections like these are true sanctuaries in that their constituents would have long since been destroyed. In addition, they act as powerful education devices. Finally, they are *ex situ* refuges where rare species can continue to exist, albeit not under perfect conditions.

The Barbara Everard Trust for Orchid Conservation

This trust was set up by the late Barbara Everard, with the help of the Orchid Society of Great Britain, The Royal Horticultural Society and the Royal Botanic Gardens at Kew. Its aim is to preserve collections whose owners have fallen ill or died. A reserve greenhouse stands ready to receive plants at a day's notice from anywhere in the UK. The Trust has widely distributed its red warning triangles, which give full details of how to contact the Trust in case of emergency. The warning triangles have a sticky surface and can be affixed to the orchid greenhouse door to alert people. To date the Trust has saved thousands of plants that would otherwise have perished. Rare plants are offered to the Royal Horticultural Society and Kew, while the rest are auctioned. The money raised is shared by the estate and helps to support the Trust and its work.

The Australian Orchid Foundation's Seed Bank

This enterprise which has now been underway for over 20 years has been one of the success stories of conservation. The term 'Seed Bank' is possibly a misnomer because the storage facilities are short term, one to three years only. However, orchid growers around the world send surplus seed to the bank, which then acts as a clearing house, distributing seed to growers not only in Australia, but elsewhere as well. Growers can thus gain access to fresh or nearly fresh seed of a great variety of species, including many that are naturally rare, all for the cost of only the handling charges.

The Seed bank is funded by the Australian Orchid Foundation, set up to foster orchid science and horticulture in Australia. It has also supported much original research on a wide variety of orchid topics.

The Orchid Park near Perenet

Similar to the orchid gardens in Jamaica is a semi-natural collection of orchid species across the road from the Special Indri Reserve near Perenet, Madagascar. This is a small two-hectare plot of forest surrounding a small man-made lake, filled with blue waterlilies. Along one side is a wooden lath structure that houses some of the larger and more spectacular orchids, such as *Grammangis ellisii*, *Angraecum eburneum* and *Cymbidiella rhodocheila*. There is a path around the lake that brings the visitor to the forest edge and here many different orchids have been fastened to the trees. Beds of orchids are also planted in the forest litter. Although many of the orchids are originally from the Special Indri park and the nearby D'Andasibe-Mantadia Preserve, the aim is to grow a collection of approximately 250 different orchid species, about a quarter of the entire Madagascan orchid flora. The initial set-up funds for this project were provided by VITA (Volunteers in Technical Assistance) and it was an American financed project. The garden is essentially an educational project and most plants are labeled.

Much of the labor and all of the current expertise is derived from a single park employee from the nearby wildlife preserves. His name is Joseph (he only has one name) and he is unique in being the only ANGAP employee with a deep interest in the native orchids. He works under tremendous handicaps. If he needs to identify a species he must travel, at his own expense, to Antannarive, to consult the one available book on Malagasy orchids. Like other ranger's working for the park, he is only paid by the number of tour groups that he conducts through the park. Joseph has been able to supplement his expenses by pollinating some of the orchids in the park and providing seeds for some foreign growers. A major threat to the garden is theft by local people, who find it easier to steal plants off the trees than go into the forests after them. Stolen plants are resold to local visitors.

Because both natural and artificial pollination occurs

in the park there is a possibility that some of the introduced species or even some accidental hybrids might invade the adjacent parks and preserves. This needs to be balanced against the educational aspects of the park that informs visitors that, besides lemurs and birds, there are special plant species whose conservation is also worthy.

Collection concerns

At institutions there are fluctuating interests as administrators change. Interests and focus can easily shift away from the *ex situ* collections. Expertise can be lost when gardeners retire or are hired away and 'secrets' for cultivating difficult plants will often leave with those personnel. Financial problems are very intense. Unless the collection is endowed with sufficient income there will be times when resources are limited. This seems to occur every time there is a financial recession or depression. At those times it is usually the collection that suffers as staff are retrenched. This was noticeable at the UCI Arboretum where plant loss rates went hand in hand with financial cutbacks. Administrators and governments hardly ever take the long view but are content to survive from day to day or year to year – these are not attitudes that are conducive to good conservation practice. While it is relatively easy to get grants to carry out research on conservation it is very difficult to get the money needed to practice *ex situ* conservation.

There are so many species of orchids, (with estimates ranging from 20,000 to 30,000), that no *ex situ* collection could handle more than a small fraction of them. It would take enormous resources on a worldwide basis to preserve even a portion of all those species. In addition, there are real problems in ensuring the correct identification of the species involved. This is especially crucial when plants must be bred. Many orchids, although morphologically very similar, may in fact be sister species and if bred together will result in hybrids. This has already happened several times in recent history. As an example consider *Phalaenopsis violacea* from peninsular Malaysia and Sumatra and *P. bellina* from Borneo. Sibling crosses between the two forms were distributed as *P. violacea* but nowadays would be considered hybrids.

Minimizing the *ex situ* problems

The concerns expressed above may seem overwhelming and depressing but, as I have already pointed out, *ex situ* conservation will be the only choice for many orchid species as their habitats are destroyed. It is of no use to merely sit back and wring ones hands at the situation. We are going to have to deal with the situation and optimize

our efforts to conserve these endangered plants. There are many ways to minimize and overcome problems that exist as long as the commitment is also there to carry on with the work. In this section I will discuss the ways one can deal with some of the issues.

Encouraging genetic diversity

Among the recommendations for setting up a collection is one for a minimum of 50 randomly selected plants of each species. However, if one were to deliberately select plants that appeared to differ drastically from each other e.g. dwarf plants versus tall and early versus late flowering, etc., one could maximize genetic diversity. The proportions of genes would differ from those found in wild populations but one could assemble the rarer genes that might not surface in a randomly selected sample. There may be reduced fecundity associated with these wide crosses. This is sometimes called out-breeding depression.

Handling large numbers of plants

Not all of the 500 plants need to be grown in the same institution. In fact, it is better for the protection of the group, if the plants are parceled out between a number of institutions which each have shared responsibility for part of the group. This requires collaboration, coordination and some bookkeeping.

Starting with small numbers of plants

Most wild plants are relatively heterozygous, meaning that there are usually two different genes for each character. In inbred plants the members of each gene pair tend to be identical. One way of ensuring that many of the genes from the initial parents are saved in the captive population is to grow up a large population in the first generation bred from the founding generation. The more plants produced the better the chance of retrieving most of the genes. If only a few plants are selected from each generation one will lose genetic variation quite rapidly and within a relatively few generations most of the plants will be genetically uniform.

Dealing with inbreeding depression

Hybridizing one inbred clone with another unrelated inbred clone can retard inbreeding depression. This will often result in heterosis (hybrid vigor) but unless the two parents have quite different genetic backgrounds the reprieve will only be temporary. This is because inbred species tend to have two copies of certain recessive deleterious genes, which are expressed. Inbred clones from different origins will have other, but different, pairs of deleterious genes and when they are bred together the recessives will get masked again, resulting in vigor. Pollen banks are possible for some groups of plants and these can be used to ensure against inbreeding depression. Pieces of pollinia from several different parents can be placed into the same stigma.

Focused collections

When collections are set up it is a good idea to focus attention on a well-circumscribed group. This is a good idea for several reasons. With a well-defined group it is easy to know what species are missing and still need to be added to the group. It is easier to develop a reputation for being a conservator of for example, *Laelia* species, rather than merely a collection of miscellaneous orchids. Often similar related species will have similar cultural needs and this simplifies culture and the few species with special needs are easily identified.

Replication

A conservation collection is particularly susceptible to catastrophic losses from a wide variety of circumstances. An entire collection could be destroyed by an electrical failure in January in Canada, or by a hurricane during November in Florida or perhaps a terrorist bomb in England. It is essential therefore to spread the responsibility by having several duplicate collections in widely separated geographical areas. Replication has another use. It allows one to maintain a larger captive population than any one institution would normally prefer to manage on its own. In such reciprocal arrangements between collections, one should be considered the prime or alpha collection and others as back-ups and all interactive activities concerning that taxon should be the major responsibility of the alpha collection. Cooperation between the prime and back-up collection institutions is essential and attempts need to be made to avoid rivalries developing between *ex situ* collections. Growing institutional rivalry can be side stepped if each institution has responsibility for its own major taxon.

Good hygiene

Good hygiene can go a long way towards retarding the spread of viral and other diseases. Animal vectors usually spread viruses. However, spread is accelerated if there is direct contact with the cytoplasm or sap of an infected plant, with that of a clean plant. Cutting tools used for trimming and/or dividing plants are common ways of

moving the disease between plants. Disinfecting cutting tools is helpful for retarding spread but it will not stop it completely. It is almost inevitable that, given enough time, the disease will infect the entire ex situ population.

Seed and gene banks

There are several alternatives to maintaining collections of living plants and these avoid some of the problems posed by living collections. One could also maintain species in the kinds of seed, gene and tissue culture banks that are used for many other kinds of agriculturally important crops or wildflower banks, but these techniques have not been well worked out for orchids. There are seed collections for nearly all agriculturally important crops ranging from beans to rice. Traditionally the seed was kept for several to many years before it was planted out and a new crop of seed harvested to be returned to the seed bank. This system will not work with orchids because their seed normally only stays viable for a few weeks or at most a few months. The life span of a seed is dependent on both the temperature it is stored at and also the amount of moisture in the seed. The cooler the ambient air and the drier the seed, the longer it will survive. There is a rule of thumb that says that the life span of the seed will double for each 5°C drop in temperature or 1% decrease in moisture content (Harrington, 1972; Hondelmann, 1976; Plunknett *et al.*, 1987). As the effects are multiplicative, longevity in excess of hundreds of years can be achieved. Whether or not longevity continues to double with each 5°C drop below freezing has not conclusively been demonstrated, but is thought to occur. Workers have demonstrated that many seeds can be frozen and thawed without loosing viability, provided that moisture content can be reduced to a level where damaging ice crystals are unable to form. However, if moisture levels drop below 4%, seed can be irretrievably damaged. Currently the recommended international standards for non-orchid seed storage are −18°C and a 5% moisture content.

As early as 1972, Bowling and Thompson reported that they had successfully frozen and retrieved seeds of 30 different tropical orchid species. The seeds were held at −10°C and after being thawed could be germinated. Together with Robert Ward, a graduate student at UCI, we froze, thawed and germinated seeds of the Mexican orchid *Encyclia vitellina* (Ward and Koopowitz, 1984). There were some other investigations on freezing and thawing orchids, using liquid nitrogen, but those involved terrestrial and mainly temperate species (Pritchard, 1984).

Orchid seeds are so small that one could store literally hundreds of thousands in a few cubic inches. These large numbers and the potential longevity of frozen seed should help one to get around all of the problems that are associated with the living *ex situ* plant collections. So why don't orchid seed cryogenic banks exist? Starting in the late 1970s and early 1980s people started to establish a variety of wild flower seed banks and there was some talk of orchid banks. At UCI we were getting ready to start one such bank and had even advertised our program in the Bulletin of the American Orchid Society. But soon after that a bombshell was dropped (Pritchard, 1986), which brought a halt to all thought of conventional subfreezing orchid seed banking. Pritchard reported that some of the orchid seed which was originally frozen by Thompson and Bowlin, was retrieved after 3 years at –10°C and had shown some viability but, after 8 years, there was no viability. All of the seeds were dead. This report was devastating and dealt a near fatal blow to those who saw orchid seed banking as an economical, if not the only rational way of saving the large numbers of orchid species that appeared to be endangered.

Some workers wondered if the results Pritchard reported were just due to poor storage techniques, i.e. storage of seed at too high a temperature maybe –10°C was not cold enough or in refrigerators with temperatures that oscillated. Perhaps the seals on the containers leaked and the seed lost too much moisture as it dried out in the cold air. Other experiments (Seaton and Hailes, 1989) with *Cattleya aurantiaca* seed in liquid nitrogen gave results that sometimes suggested seed storage was possible but at other times the results suggested the opposite. There seemed to be no point in freezing orchid seed if the results were unreliable. Perhaps the microscopic nature of orchid seed, itself, worked against the possibility of long-term seed banks.

In 1993 Pritchard and Seaton summarized their thinking on long-term orchid seed banking. Their prognosis was somewhat gloomy. They pointed out that the long-term conservation of seeds under normal seed-banking conditions (i.e. –18°C and 5% moisture content) was problematical. They suggested that there was a change in the nature of lipids and fats in the cells of the seed that accounted for the problems seen in dried seeds under subfreezing regimes. They suggested that humidification of the thawed seed prior to sowing might be useful. They found that seed stored at above freezing (5°C) and at a relatively high humidity of 30% could extend viability. But it seemed unlikely that those conditions could extend viability long enough to make orchid seed banking a viable option for orchid conservation.

Nevertheless the notion of long-term orchid seed banking was important enough to keep some of us thinking about possible solutions. When agricultural seed bank-

ing techniques were originally developed researchers used above freezing temperatures to look at the effect of temperature on seed longevity. Seed life span is directly dependent on temperature and the warmer conditions would shorten the seeds' life spans to manageable times. It is difficult to conduct experiments that run for decades much less centuries. With orchids there is also the additional problem that much of the world's forests might be logged and their orchids lost before the experiments had been completed. Together with Alan Thornhill, we decided to repeat some of the earlier types of experiments that had been conducted with conventional seeds. We wanted to store orchid seed at temperatures above freezing point, so that we could investigate how this would affect viability during storage, using short-term experiments.

Disa uniflora is a beautiful South African orchid with large scarlet flowers. We thought this might be an ideal candidate to investigate seed aging and the relationship between temperature and seed longevity. We had several plants to produce seed that were line bred and derived from the same seedpod. The experiment could therefore be run with genetically similar seeds. The seed of this species is somewhat larger than most other orchids, all of 600 micrograms, but this makes it easier to weigh and handle. Most importantly, like nearly all orchids, the seed normally loses nearly all of its viability when stored at room temperature for two or three months. Most other orchid seed requires special tissue culture techniques to make it germinate, but during that process many things can go wrong, which may jeopardize germination. *Disa* seed is, by contrast, easily grown in a conventional greenhouse by sowing it directly on top of moist, peat-based potting mix. If the seed pots are covered to prevent drying, until they germinate no watering is needed until they germinate. The seeds germinate and grow faster than most other orchids, so that the percentage of germinated seed could be counted within a few weeks of planting.

When the seed is held at a single temperature for different lengths of time one can plot the rate at which viability is lost on a graph and calculate the time needed to lose half of its viability at a particular storage temperature. We repeated the experiment at six different temperatures and obtained the 50% viability time for each temperature. This data was then used to extrapolate down to temperatures below freezing (Thornhill and Koopowitz, 1992). Depending on the mathematical assumptions made, there were two possible outcomes. In one scenario, the half-life of *D. uniflora* seed at –10°C, was about 4.5 years, similar to that reported by Pritchard. But there was another possible curve (from the same results) where the life of the seed stored at –25°C would be greater than several hundred years. But which is the real situation? If the second case was true then orchid seed banking should be feasible. But who would perform the long-term experiments?

At the bottom of one of the UCI gene bank freezers, Robert Ward had placed several vials of *Encyclia vitellinum* seed for his experiments, but he had not used all of the samples. We found the unused ones 10 years later when seed was being transferred to a new freezer. One sample was defrosted and held in moist air for several days, before being sterilized and planted. Within a short time protocorms swelled and greened up. Good seedlings were obtained and currently many have flowered. Viability was in excess of 95%. At that time the results were very encouraging that sub-freezing seed storage in conventional freezers might be possible. But our optimism was crushed when a second sample was withdrawn after 16 years. Now there was less than 1% germination. It might be pointed out that the second older sample had not been sealed in glass, as was the case with the 10 year-old sample. The seeds could gradually have become dehydrated over the 16 years, to the point where viability was compromised. Setting up carefully controlled, long-term, subfreezing experiments should be a top priority of the orchid conservation community. This aim should be the top priority of all orchid researchers, concerned with conservation.

It is imperative that methods be worked out for an easy and economical method of long-term banking for orchid seeds. We cannot set up and maintain sufficient *in situ* reserves to preserve all of the world's orchid species. We would very lucky to preserve 50% of all species and in reality we are likely to be able to conserve only a small fraction of all orchid biodiversity. Living *ex situ* collections are fragile and it is therefore of critical importance for orchid species conservation that we carry out adequate research on methods of long-term seed storage. Yet there has been very little action in that direction. If the usual long-term methods turn out not to work then we should be searching for alternatives. One can not overstate how important this is for orchid conservation and our ability to produce living examples of species for future generations. It is of the highest priority, but almost no one acknowledges it and very little is being done to ameliorate the situation.

Once methodologies have been worked out several problems will rear their heads but these are all solvable.

Past experience suggest that it is desirable to set up duplicate seed collections. No one collection of seeds is immune from catastrophes, be they induced by acts of man or of God. It is preferable that duplicate seed collections be maintained some distance from each other, perhaps even in different countries.

a   Seed should ideally be tested for viability using biochemical tests. Germination tests if demanded should be carried out after the main sample has been processed and frozen. Seed can often take months to germinate *in vitro* and samples held at room temperature would deteriorate while trying to determine their viability.

b   The exact taxonomic nature of the seed may be difficult to determine. Wild collected seed is always preferable, but it can also be produced by controlled artificial pollination. However it is not always possible to determine the exact species when one comes across a seed capsule in the forest. But because samples take up so little space it would not be a problem to store the occasional seed aliquot, even if these species' exact identity is unknown.

c   Producing seed samples for storage from *ex situ* plant collections is important, but they are also subject to the same problems encountered in those collections. There is the potential for accidental hybrids, reduced genetic diversity, inbreeding problems, etc. Voucher specimens or pictures should be taken when the seed is collected to ensure the sample's identity.

d   Records should be kept of the seed samples in the bank in both electronic and written form. Electronic databases can become obsolete, others may be corrupted and, of course, computers crash and become infected with viruses.

e   A clearly stated policy about the conditions under which samples can be withdrawn is desirable. One needs to know what conditions justify the thawing and growing out of a sample. Who has the power to withdraw a sample? The disposition of the resulting seedlings and adult plants should also conform to the seed bank's policy. Should seed be made available to commercial firms for exploitation? How should one decide? In discussions with potential support groups we have found that these policy statements can be more troublesome than any other aspect of gene banking.

The current situation is similar to the apathy shown by professional biologists in the face of all biodiversity losses. They pretend it is not their concern and that someone else will take care of the problem. At a minimum they should be raising their voices in unison and demanding action. The few orchid biologists themselves merely wring their hands or make lists of species that might or might not be endangered. Nobody is making the right moves to save significant numbers of species. How will we answer to our grandchildren?

CHAPTER 9

CITES and Orchids

The Convention on International Trade in Endangered Species (CITES) looms large in the life of most orchid growers. The treaty was originally designed by biologists and ecologists in an attempt to regulate international trade in endangered species. It was originally embraced by most members of the international community, who were concerned about the obvious decline in biodiversity around the world. CITES concerns trade across international borders, it was not designed to protect a species within its native land except by regulating the export trade of that species. Signatories must implement the convention at a minimum level, but they may also impose more stringent controls if they so wish. Since its adoption, more than a quarter of a century ago, control and implementation has moved from conservation biologists to lawyers versed in international law. Implementation is now carried out by enforcement officers who are often unfamiliar with much of the reasoning behind the original listing of several plant groups. The species listed in the appendices are considered to be endangered, but this is not always the case. The convention also regulates trade in many species that are not endangered.

A Short history of CITES and the IUCN

During the years of 1990 to 1995 more than a half million wild orchid plants were in international commerce each year. This, however, was only a small fraction of the more than twenty million man-made orchid hybrids also circulating in international trade. The movement of all of these plants is regulated by CITES. It is the responsibility of the individual governments who are signatories to the convention to regulate and report on the import, export and even re-export of species listed by the Convention. This data eventually ends up being collated by a body known as the World Conservation Monitoring Centre (WCMC). But different governments have different regulations for these controls. How did this state of affairs come about?

Conservationists have been interested in the problem of diminishing plant and animal biodiversity for the last half-century, although initial concerns had primarily to do with the loss of animals. At that time a society, the International Union for the Protection of Nature was formed, which held annual meetings to discuss conservation issues. In 1956, the name was changed to the International Union for the Conservation of Nature and Natural Resources, first abbreviated to IUCNN and later to IUCN. The organization soon received official recognition from the United Nations and before long the main world governments started to send representatives to its meetings. During these initial years the group turned its attention to major conservation issues such as the state and number of National Parks, the plight of African ungulates, the wetlands of Europe, etc.

The IUCN was formulating policies needed to reverse species and habitat losses but had little clout in actually getting anything carried out. Its recommendations depended on the goodwill of the concerned nations and governments where there was actually relatively little interest. Many of the Third World or less developed countries were then battling with their own political agendas and conservation had low priority. To move from an advisory to an activism stance required substantial amounts of money and towards this end the World Wildlife Fund (WWF) was created. Its role was not only to acquire the necessary funds but also to promote education and research in conservation issues. Several members of Europe's royal families became prominent fundraisers or lent their names to WWF activities.

These organizations have the bad habit of changing names and/or acronyms as soon as the public gets educated about them. Recently the organization changed its name to the 'The World Conservation Union' because the early name was considered to be too long. But IUCN was too familiar to be dropped by the general public and the official title is now even longer 'IUCN – The World Conservation Union'. In a similar, poorly thought out scheme, 'The World Wildlife Fund' (WWF) was converted to 'The World Wide Fund for Nature'.

The old, familiar name was gone and people found this very disconcerting. The general public never seems to have sorted out that change!

The TPC

In 1974 the IUCN turned its attention to plants and asked Professor Hesslop-Harrison to set up a 'Threatened Plant Committee', abbreviated to TPC. At that time Hesslop-Harrison was Director of the Royal Botanic Gardens at Kew in London, England and since that time it has maintained an active and center-stage role concerning plant conservation issues. Among the first tasks of the TPC was to try to identify threatened plant species. As a result regional TPCs were set up to make lists and publish Red Data books of threatened species. In some cases there were no regional TPCs but local experts were asked to compile lists of rare and threatened species. The TPCs eventually became concerned with the role of botanical gardens in conservation.

There are now several independent groups that seem to impinge on CITES. Much of the work involved with collating information and promoting plant related activities is run by a unit associated with the RBG Kew, called Conventions and Policy (CAPS), which covers Kew's CITES Scientific Authority role and its CBD implementation. The Convention on Biodiversity (CBD) is independent of CITES, but may in the future have a profound influence on the use and movement of orchid species. CAPS has coordinated the publication of lists of names and synonyms of orchids and other plants whose trade is regulated by CITES. IUCN has an office in Gland, Switzerland with a Plants Officer, while CITES itself is headquartered in Geneva. As an important NGO (non-governmental organization) IUCN's views are taken seriously by the CITES people. IUCN is advised by a committee of the SSC (Species Survival Commission) called the OSG (Orchid Specialist Group). The OSG is composed of a mixed group of orchid scientists, enthusiasts and commercial growers from around the world. CITES itself has its own committee of 'experts', with an office in Geneva, Switzerland and a Plants Officer, who, together with the Secretariat, reports and responds to the Convention of the Parties.

Red Data Books

The first plant 'Red Book' lists were real eye openers. It seemed that for nearly all regions of the world at least 15% (but usually more) of the area's flora, fell into the threatened categories. This was particularly the case in Eastern Europe where enormous numbers of species were declared as threatened. Oceanic islands all over the world appeared to be in danger of losing most of their native plants. In tropical countries orchids often featured prominently on the lists. In actual fact, the major components of the mainland lists were species that were naturally rare. Rare, unfortunately, does not have a precise definition and is usually interpreted as meaning not common. Most of the rare species were not actually threatened with extinction or endangered at the time that the lists were compiled, but it was felt that these small populations could be vulnerable and easily wiped out and thus needed the 'protection' of being listed. The lists of species for which there was hard data to suggest that they were really threatened was actually quite small and rare plants helped to bulk up the Red Data Books. In the neotropics about one quarter of all plant species have only been recorded from a single locality or place (Koopowitz et al., 1994) and more than half the species are only known from three or fewer areas. Other tropical regions, such as the Philippines, have similar high levels of rarity (Koopowitz, et al., 1998).

With orchids the numbers of rare species is greater, 35% are recorded from single localities and more than 75% are only known from three or less localities (Koopowitz, 1992). Thus most tropical orchids can be considered 'rare'. But inclusion of rare species biases lists and actually gives a false impression of the real situation, making it difficult to know which species are actually currently under active threat and which species merely have the potential to become threatened at some future date. As even very common species can be reduced to threatened status by over exploitation or land conversion it is not really very helpful to have rare species combined into threatened species lists and it distracts from species that do need active help. In addition, the listing of rare species inflates the Red Data lists and promotes false ideas about the true rate of biodiversity losses. Overestimation of species loss can cause credibility problems when discussing or arguing about the urgent needs for good conservation policies. For the last 30 years, inflated rates of biodiversity loss have been publicized and various pundits have been taken to task for crying wolf (Mann, 1991). They are in danger of losing credibility, but at the same time biodiversity losses are happening and it is important not to be distracted from the task at hand. But we need to fight with real statistics.

For more than a 150 years there has been active trade in wild orchid plants, with the majority of the traffic going from the less developed countries to the more affluent countries in North America, Europe and Asia. This one way traffic came under scrutiny in the 1970's. In an effort to stem the trade in endangered animals and birds the IUCN lobbied for international trade controls. It was thought at the time that individual, less developed countries, were either unable or unwilling to police or protect their own endangered species and that blocking the entrance of the organisms or their parts to the countries with buying power would stem the trade in endangered species. Conservationists hoped that restrictions on the importing side might be sufficient to protect those species. It has been suggested that organizations such as the European Union introduced import permits because they thought that too many endangered species were slipping through. Others have interpreted this action as a form of trade protection. In 1973 IUCN engineered the Convention on International Trade in Endangered Species of Wild Flora and Fauna (CITES), which was to come into effect after it had been ratified by 10 countries. Two years later the requisite number of countries had signed and the signatories were obliged to start enforcing it. By 1997 a total of 142 countries around the world had signed the convention.

CITES was initially designed for larger animals and it was put together by people who understood mammals and birds. Those creatures have slow reproduction rates. But other smaller animals such as amphibians and tropical fish can produce enormous numbers of offspring. Plants which can produce hundreds of seeds at a time and orchids, which produce tens of thousands or more seed in a single seed capsule, should be regarded differently. However CITES does not take this basic difference into account. The basic reproductive differences between rapid reproducers and slow reproducers should have indicated the need for different conservation strategies. It is quite noticeable at the major meetings, called 'Conventions of the Parties', which are held every three years, that the so-called 'charismatic' mammals are the still the main force and the rapid reproducers are merely poor second cousins.

One might also question whether or not those pushing for the inclusion of plants also had a strong understanding of the Pandora's Box they were setting into motion. For example, there was considerable trade in animal parts, heads, pelts, tusks, etc., so the convention not only regulated trade in live animals but also their parts. Parts of plants also became regulated. Vanilla essence is part of a farmed orchid plant and leaves of *Aloe vera* (a common plant) are an important component of many cosmetics and shampoos. Suddenly CITES was regulating trade in those products. This embarrassment was quickly corrected and in far shorter time than is usually taken to correct problems, demonstrating that money counts. However, *the bits and pieces* regulations still are effective in regulating movement of Appendix I plants. Hundred-year-old herbarium specimens still need CITES permits. This absurdity should be revoked.

Appendices

The species that are afforded protection by CITES are enumerated on three lists, known as the Appendices. Appendix I contains the most threatened species, supposedly those animals and plants that will definitely go extinct unless Herculean efforts are made to save them. Appendix II lists species or groups of organisms where trade is being monitored. These species are not necessarily threatened but might become so if excessive trade in wild individuals occurs. Appendix III is for species threatened within particular countries but are not threatened globally or over their entire range. Appendix III organisms receive relatively little attention.

Because CITES is a legal document, the various definitions have had to be carefully and precisely defined. These have become modified and refined over the years. At first the definitions were qualitative but recent changes have attempted to add a quantitative aspect as well. The Convention and all of its modifications have become quite complex and sometimes only a trained legal mind can puzzle through it. Willem Wijnstekers (1994) has reviewed the various changes to the Convention; his book is recommended reading for anyone who wishes to understand the force and limitations of the treaty.

Categories of threat

There have been many changes to CITES over the years and this also applies to the descriptions of the various categories of threat that a species may face. For 25 years the definitions were relatively vague, but while these have become more precise they have failed to take into account the nature of normal plant distribution. The following list of terms is derived from Mace and Stuart (1993-94) as well as the final version of the document that was adopted by the IUCN Council in 1994, to which the reader is referred for additional details.

Threatened: Any species where the population has been reduced to a level where it's long term ability to survive is in jeopardy. This is an all embracing term without a clear definition but takes in all of the following terms. It is often used when the exact category of threat cannot be defined.

Extinct (EX): A species, which no longer has living members.

Extinct in the wild (EW): This is self-explanatory and covers those species that only remain alive in captivity or horticulture and can no longer be found in the wild.

Critically Endangered (CR): A taxon or group of organisms, which face an extreme risk of imminent extinction.

Endangered (EN): Not in the CR category but nevertheless facing a very high risk of extinction in the wild in the near future.

Vulnerable (VU): Neither CR nor EN, but facing a high risk in the medium term future.

Lower Risk (LR): This category is at lower risk if it was evaluated and did not fit into the CR, EN or VU groupings. Organisms in this category can be subdivided into three subcategories:

Conservation Dependent (cd): These are groups that depend on conservation management to keep them out of any of the above categories. If management ceased one would expect the population to fall into one of the above categories within a 5-year period.

Near Threatened (nt): A number of taxa are placed here which are not conservation dependent, but might be close to or approaching vulnerable status.

Least Concern (lc): Groups that do not fall into either *cd* or *nt* categories.

Data Deficient (DD): Here sufficient data on population sizes or distribution is either unavailable or unknown. It alerts one to the fact that the taxon is possibly, but not necessarily, faced with threat. For orchids, if the system was truly honest, this is where most of the threatened species would be placed.

Not Evaluated (NE): Organisms are NE when they have not been assessed against criteria (see below).

There are lists of criteria that help one to decide into which of the threatened categories above that a taxon should be placed. Here I will only examine one example. In order to qualify for endangered status (EN) a species or taxon needs to fit into any one of the following criteria. Criteria will vary for other categories of threat.

A. The population has suffered an observed, estimated, inferred or suspected severe decline of at least 50% during the previous 10 years, or 3 generations, whichever is longer. The reduction could be assessed by any of the following: (a) direct observation; (b) index of abundance appropriate for the taxon; (c) a decline in area of occupancy, extent of occurrence and/or quality of habitat; (d) actual or potential levels of exploitation; or (e) the effects of introduced taxa, hybridization, pathogens, pollutants, etc. The taxon could also have a suspected or projected 50% reduction in population numbers in either the following 10 years or within the next 10 years or 3 generations based upon **B**, **C**, **D** or **E**.

B. The extent of occurrence is estimated to be less than 5,000 km^2 or the area of occupancy is less than 500 km^2 and any two of the following. (1) Occurrence at less than five localities or severely fragmented localities; (2) continuing decline, inferred, observed or projected for area of occupancy and number of mature individuals; and (3) extreme fluctuations in area occupied, extent of occurrence, number of subpopulations, number of mature individuals.

C. Population is less than 2,500 mature individuals and either. (1) An estimated continuing population decline of 20% within 5 years or 2 generations or, (2) a continuing decline, observed or projected, in numbers of mature individuals and the population structure is such that no sub-population contains more than 250 individuals or else all populations are in a single sub-population.

D. Population is estimated to be less than 250 mature individuals.

E. Quantitative analysis showing the probability of extinction in the wild is at least 20% within 20 years or 5 generations, which ever is longer.

These criteria may work well for animals, but there is very little reliable data for plants, especially tropical orchids. The criteria are easily abused because they can be inferred, suspected or projected, rather than critically demonstrated. Because most tropical plants, as well as orchid species, appear to occur in fewer than three populations and occupy less than 5,000 km^2 and are usually in severely fragmented habitats, one could place an enormous number of naturally rare species into the Endangered category. And here is the problem. Once one places tens of thousands of plants into these categories the problem becomes both Herculean and realistically unmanageable. We simply cannot control and protect all of the populations that are merely *potentially* endangered. We must save our energies to focus on those populations that are truly endangered. Otherwise, one may as well throw both hands in the air and concede the battle to save those species that need help.

How Orchids got onto Appendix II

Some years ago, I had a conversation with Gren Lucas (then the Deputy Director of the RBG Kew) who had participated in the process of formulating the lists of plants to be included in the appendices. He recounted some of the thinking that went into the initial listing of the entire Orchidaceae. Major concerns at the time were which plants might be endangered due to unrestricted trade in wild species. But there was scant information on international trade in wild plants. At that time there was no information on many of the wild orchids that contributed to the global commerce in these plants. A list was made of all the plants, as well as orchids, which were known to be grown by hobbyists. Some of the names on the list were entire families (e.g. the Orchidaceae, Euphorbiaceae and Cactaceae); others were genera (eg. *Aloe*) and some were species. The participants realized that if the names on the list were added to Appendix II of CITES there might be a mechanism for determining how large the trade in those taxa might be. And so the mischief was wrought. There was no hard data that most of the taxa actually contained significant numbers of threatened or endangered species or that international trade was a significant component in the decline of any group. There was no compelling evidence that trade was causing endangerment for the Orchidaceae, but once the lists were published it was automatically assumed that all or most of the members of the lists were threatened species. As orchids make up between 8% and 10% of all plant species this meant that CITES was to monitor an appreciable fraction of the world's biodiversity. In fact CITES only tracks about 4,000 of the world's 25,000 orchid species. So it should not be surprising that it has trouble doing its job.

It seemed important at that time that some individual plant species should be listed in Appendix I. Representatives at the meeting were asked for nominations and a series of orchid species were put forward. These were *Cattleya skinneri*, *C. trianiae*, *Didicica cunninghamii*, *Laelia jongheana*, *L. lobata*, *Lycaste virginalis* var. *alba*, *Paphiopedilum druryi*, *Peristeria elata*, *Renanthera imschootiana* and *Vanda coerulea*. The list was a farce. *Cattleya skinneri* was threatened by internal collecting for garden plants in Costa Rica, where it is the national flower. Internationally this species had been propagated artificially and in a way that did not threaten the wild populations. *Didicicea cunninghamii* is an obscure narrow endemic from Nepal that was never in the trade. *Lycaste virginalis* var. *alba* (the national flower of Guatemala) is not a variety in the botanical sense but rather a white form that occurs scat-

40 *Peristeria elata*. The 'Holy Ghost Orchid' occurs in Panama and Colombia. Used to decorate churches at Easter this species became threatened from over-picking. It was one of the original orchids placed on Appendix I.

tered in the normally pink populations. *Peristeria elata*, the national flower of Panama had been over-collected to decorate churches in Panama, but was still abundant in neighboring Colombia. *Paphiopedilum druryi* did warrant listing in Appendix I. But whether or not any of the other species did is arguable, although several still remain on the list.

41. Line bred *Vanda coerulea* 'Truford' AM/AOS received its quality award in 1988. But even larger, flatter and rounder flowers have been bred. (Photo credit: Richard Clark and the American Orchid Society).

42. *Vanda coerulea* was the first orchid to be protected by law in Asia. This species was over collected for the European hobby market. More widespread than originally supposed, this is one species that has been artificially propagated and "improved".

Current Appendix I orchids

The following orchids are currently listed on Appendix I, a feature that they share with endangered animals such as snow leopards and panda bears. The species include *Cattleya trianaei, Dendrobium cruentum, Laelia jongheana, Laelia lobata, Peristeria elata, Renanthera*

imschootiana, Vanda coerulea and all species of the genera *Paphiopedilum* and *Phragmipedium*. The criticism heaped on CITES by its detractors since the listing of the two genera *Paphiopedilum* and *Phragmipedium*, plus the growing savvy of people with orchid interests in working within the system, makes it unlikely that wholesale listing will be easily achieved again. The most recent addition is *Dendrobium cruentum*. I was an observer when *Dendrobium cruentum* was up-listed at the 9th COP in Fort Lauderdale in 1994. Several 'orchid authorities' had recommended up-listing this species, despite the plea from Professor Rapee Sagarik, a well-known and highly respected Thai orchid conservationist that up-listing was unnecessary. In addition that species was being artificially propagated in Hawaii. While the plant was being collected in Thailand it was not certain that there was great international trade or concern in that species. At that meeting an attempt to up-list the entire genus *Cypripedium* had been brought up as well and much effort went into blocking it. Once this was achieved the proposal brought about by Thailand was passed, it was considered a small price to pay for having the *Cypripedium* up-listing rejected. Most of the countries voting merely followed the recommendations of the plants committee.

There are probably many species of orchids that warrant listing because their populations have become so reduced as to threaten their continued existence. But the probability of many of them ever being listed is unlikely. The chance that listing would even help in their rescue from extinction is uncertain and the lists become difficult to regulate if they become too cumbersome. Many of the species referred to here are not threatened by trade but by land conversion and deforestation. In addition, other species will become extinct without our ever being aware that they were threatened, while others will become extinct without us even being aware of their existence. One can predict that, as the ineffectiveness of CITES to save species becomes ever more widely appreciated, the reluctance to support the convention will become more evident.

The lists are not static. Organisms can be up-listed (i.e. moved from Appendix II to Appendix I) or even down-listed if conditions improve. At the present time getting species or taxa placed in or removed from the Appendices is a difficult and time-consuming process. Down-listing the original Appendix I species took many years. Proposals have to be initiated by a country, the trade must be analyzed and the proposal passed for review. The final recommendation is made to the 'Plants Committee', after which it is brought to the General Assembly during a COP, where it is voted upon. The COP is like a mini United Nations; there is intense lobbying behind the scenes, both at the individual and country level. Political agendas often gain more prominence than biological ones. It takes an astute person to pilot a listing proposal through the system. Yet because the Parties only meet every three years there is often a rush to consider things and towards the end of the sessions proposals may not be treated fairly. Many of the plant issues seem to be dealt with towards the ends of the meetings when the participants are exhausted or fatigued.

Over the years there have been several attempts to ease some of the initial restrictions on the movement of orchids, but several pernicious controls remain. The movement of dried herbarium specimens falls under the 'bits and pieces' paragraphs. The way around this is to use a scientific CITES permit, which allows the movement of accessioned specimens between registered institutions. Unfortunately many orchid specialists are amateurs, without an association with a scientific institution. This means that they are unlikely to have access to a scientific permit. To complicate the matter further, relatively few institutions have registered for the permits.

One successful change was the removal of *in vitro* flasked seedlings or meristems from the CITES requirements and the consideration of artificially produced Appendix I species as Appendix II plants. CITES now appears to be run by lawyers rather than conservation biologists, and this has greatly complicated the operation of the convention. One example of this has been the convoluted procedure that was necessary to define the word 'flask'.

Appendix I orchid seed is not exempt from CITES control and while seed that is still in a green capsule may require a CITES certificate, a cut flower does not. It is not clear what is needed to transport pollen or DNA across international borders. CITES is becoming so convoluted that one has to ask government agencies to interpret its regulations and, of course, different countries can have different interpretations for the same CITES regulations. Officials within a single country may also come up with contrary interpretations. In the United States, seeds, flasked seedlings and pollen of Appendix I orchids, need a paper trail to show their legitimacy. This is not true in Europe.

McMahan and Walter (1988) have analyzed the trade in orchids during the period from 1976 (when records were first kept) to 1985. The authors came to the conclusion that the "CITES tool has been a poor one to date", which was due to the incomplete nature of recording. While the recording was inadequate during the first few years, the complete set of records over the whole decade is very interesting. The trade in orchids had increased until 1985. During that year a total of 3,345,000 orchid plants were reported, most of which were artificially propagated hybrids. During the next ten-year period the annual reported world trade rose to over 20 million plants. The great majority of these were artificially propagated plants. However, unless one is familiar with the species in question and the country involved with its export, it is difficult to determine how many of these plants were wild collected rather than being artificially propagated. The source if often undeclared. In 1985 only 13 species had more than 10,000 plants reported in the trade. McMahan and Walter noted that the species with the highest numbers in commerce was *Pleione formosana*, with 213,486 plants being exported from Taiwan. The source of these orchids was declared as 'unknown', however it is likely that they were artificially propagated.

I have seen extensive ranges where enormous numbers of pleiones are grown in Taiwan. One species that was undoubtedly wild collected was *Paphiopedilum callosum*, where 35,502 plants from Thailand were sent to Europe. Even those numbers are inflated however, because clumps of *Paphiopedilum* were traditionally broken apart into fragments containing one to three fans of leaves. These were then sold and recorded as individual plants. In *P. callosum* it is not unusual to find individual plants containing 20 or more fans of leaves. Also recorded among the highest volume species were two species of *Bletilla* from China, *B. ochracea* and *B. yunanensis* with 23,000 and 55,000 plants respectively. Many of these are likely to have been collected from the wild. Bletillas are traditionally sold as single pseudobulbs, but in the wild they often grow in chains or clumps containing numbers of pseudobulbs. Because of this it is very difficult to judge the true numbers that are involved.

McMahan and Walter also list some 71 species, where quantities of between 1,000 and 10,000 plants are traded. While many of these have been wild collected, others were artificially propagated. Unfortunately 'artificially propagated' can also mean that a wild collected plant was later divided in a nursery. This seems to be the case with many of the *Phragmipedium* species, which are currently coming into the USA from South America.

Major orchid exporting countries during this time (1990–94) included Belize, China, Ecuador, Japan, Madagascar, Nicaragua, The Philippines, Paraguay, Surinam and Thailand. Among the major importing countries were the United States, Germany and Japan. In 1992 (when there were 115 signatories to the Convention) 51 countries reported that they were exporting plants, while 34 countries were importers.

Export permits list not only the number of plants being exported, but also the country to which the shipment is directed. One can therefore compare the numbers arriving at their destination. For example, in 1991 Austria reported that 60,044 orchids had been imported from Germany, but Germany did not report exporting any orchid plants to Austria. It is interesting to note that while Austria imported over 100,000 orchid plants during the years 1990–92 it does not have a reputation as an orchid growing country, unlike Switzerland, Germany or the United Kingdom. Similar disparities crop up when other countries' reports are analyzed.

There are several other interesting points in McMahan and Walter's review. During the period from 1990 to 1994, 1,400 different orchid species were reported to be in international trade. Of these only eight species had an annual average trade of over 10,000 plants and another 14 species had annual average trade numbers greater than 3,000 but less than 10,000 individuals.

At the time of writing the situation has hardly changed. Although the reporting of orchids in the trade appears to have improved slightly we still have relatively little information about what is actually collected in the wild and what is artificially propagated. Of greater importance is the almost total lack of information about population size and demography of individual wild orchid species. This is absolutely crucial, because in its absence the data on trade is totally meaningless. For example, if the wild population contains over a million individual plants, which is not an unreasonable number for many species, then an annual trade of 10,000 wild collected plants could be sustainable. On the other hand, collecting 50 plants from a population of only 500 could put the entire species in jeopardy. Other kinds of information are also needed. It is not sufficient to just undertake a survey of wild populations. One also needs to know the longevity of the plants and the rate by which new reproductive adult plants are produced and recruited into the population before one can assess the impact of collection on any wild population. These important estimates are routinely made for endangered

animals, but they have not been addressed in the case of orchids. We have very few statistics for any of the tropical orchid species. IUCN is currently trying to obtain reliable data from Madagascar and China about the state of their orchid populations. These countries contain so many orchid species, which are spread over vast distances, that any data collected about a few of the individual species would not be useful for making generalizations about the other orchid species in those countries.

The Eleventh Convention of the Parties was held in Zimbabwe during June 1997. The Secretariat and Plant's Committee Coordinator reviewed the international trade in orchids and other plants for the five-year period from 1990 to 1994. A comparison of this with the earlier study is interesting. The composition of the list with the major species in the trade (averaging more than 10,000 specimens per year) has changed. Only *Habenaria rhodocheila* appeared on both lists and that species was the major plant in the trade, with an annual average count of 48,834 tubers. This species was exported from Thailand and was primarily destined for Japan and Europe. In the report, Thailand was considered to be the major species exporter. The trade in wild Thai species has been declining for several years and the country has now suspended all exports of wild plants. It reputedly only issues CITES permits for artificially propagated plants.

Over the years, CITES has evolved in directions that were never foreseen by its original proponents.

43. *Habenaria militaris* (syn. *H. rhodocheila*). Thousands of tubers of this plant were collected and sold annually in Thailand.

CITES was designed to control international commercial trade in listed wild species, but it now does more than that. It also affects the international movement of plants that are not in commerce; these include species that are being used for scientific investigations and plants that are in the possession of an individual which are being transported across international boundaries as private and personal possessions. The legality of these restraints is open to question, but challenging them in the courts is too expensive and time consuming for most individuals. There are other areas of interaction and control of non-commercial movement as well.

Until recently, the scientific names of organisms such as orchids had been decided by consensus among plant taxonomists. While there are definite rules that govern the 'correctness' of a name, these are easily challenged. Scientists often disagree on the exact boundary between species and as a consequence the names may be in dispute. Approved lists of species' names are now being published by the IUCN, ostensibly so that trade can be monitored more effectively and efficiently. Lists of cacti were the first to be produced, but orchid lists are now being published. The first orchid list (Roberts *et al.*, 1995) covered a few of the important genera such as *Paphiopedilum* and *Phalaeonopsis*. A few 'experts' opinions were solicited (I was one of them) and a list of the best names was decided upon, other names were relegated to synonymy. If there was a name in contention, another expert's opinion was solicited. This seems a perfectly reasonable way of achieving the end result, but some recognized taxonomists were not consulted. Such catalogs might be useful for species that are listed in commerce. One could argue, however, that the production of lists for genera that are rarely traded, such as *Disa* (Roberts *et al.*, 1997), is not only a waste of resources but totally inappropriate

In an effort to streamline and make CITES less burdensome for the legitimate orchid growers several countries now have a program of nursery licensing. These firms are able to issue their own CITES documents. This has worked well in small countries such as the United Kingdom, where most of the trade is in hybrids. However the concept has met considerable resistance in larger countries, such as the United States, where the distances between nurseries and federal officials can be quite considerable. The cost of policing the regulations for the United States has not been determined, but the record keeping that has been proposed has taken on nightmarish proportions. It was obviously written by people who had little understanding of plants and the fact they can die or multiply at unpredictable rates. Maintaining proof of the legiti-

mate nature of parent stock is difficult to provide because the majority of the plants entered the country before CITES controls were initiated. The concept of nursery regulation is therefore universally mistrusted in the United States. This unanticipated offshoot of CITES is forcing countries to consider regulating their nursery industries, even though it has no direct effect on the maintenance of wild populations.

Despite all of this, is it possible that CITES has actually had a beneficial effect on orchid and other plant conservation? The answer is a qualified yes, but not in the way originally envisaged. While it is likely that few species have benefited directly in the field from being listed, CITES has succeeded in bringing the plight of plant species to the attention of governments around the world. Because some entire plant families, such as orchids, are listed in Appendix II it has been assumed therefore that all orchids are endangered species and as such merit some type of consideration. One result has been to ban the export of all orchid species from certain countries or to make it exceptionally difficult to get the correct documentation for legal export. This sort of concern, although it is usually based on no data whatsoever, is better than total disinterest. Certainly with *Paphiopedilum* and *Phragmipedium*, the listing of all species in Appendix I has led to wholesale captive breeding of most of those species in the more affluent countries, with the result that many of the once rare species are now quite common in horticulture. Artificial propagation, however, does not necessarily mean that the plants are seed or tissue culture grown. A wild, field collected plant merely needs to be maintained in a nursery and divided, to be considered artificially propagated. In several countries, which shall be nameless, wild collected plants are not even accorded this modicum of culture but are directly collected in the wild and then proclaimed artificially propagated on their way to the nursery.

The reasoning behind maintaining all orchids, even hybrids, on CITES Appendix II is that one cannot expect customs inspectors to be able to differentiate between the 25,000 wild species and 100,000 plus man-made hybrids. Unfortunately, this is a specious argument, because one cannot expect the same customs inspectors to be able to differentiate between Appendix I species and their Appendix II hybrids. In reality customs inspectors have difficulty differentiating orchids from other plant families, let alone distinguish between different species of orchid. As a consequence they have to assume that the names stated on the declaration are correct.

The CITES Secretariat has prepared a manual to help custom officials to distinguish between nursery grown and wild collected materials. It has also been suggested that they could be supplied with guides to help them to distinguish the endangered species from the common species or hybrids, but this has proved to be a difficult task. Identification in the absence of flowers is almost impossible and even highly trained botanists often have trouble using floral keys to identify species. Expecting custom officials to devote the time to do this for entire shipments of plants is unreasonable. However, there are simple ways to tell whether orchid plants were nursery grown or jungle collected and these have been disseminated to customs officials in most countries. Plants that have been collected in the jungle often have diseased or damaged leaves, while the roots are often cut short. Roots on plants that were grown in flower-pots, on the other hand, are normally entire and show the curvature that has been enforced on them by the confinement of the pot.

CITES experiences

There are many ways in which CITES impinges on orchid growers. If the Convention was actually conserving orchids one could have some sympathy and patience with it. But the common perception is that the Convention merely erects an unnecessary barrier of bureaucracy that has nothing to do with conservation. The following are a number of personal experiences and observations on how the system works and the ways in which it impedes the aspirations of legitimate orchid activities.

Imagine that you are a tourist visiting Rio de Janeiro and you visit one of the well-known orchid nurseries outside the city. You see a really nice hybrid *Cattleya* plant in flower at the nursery and it is available for sale. You have your plant import permit number so that you could take a few plants back to your home country. However, you also need something called a CITES permit. In Brazil it takes between twenty and thirty days to process that paperwork.

Alternatively let us pretend that you are visiting Japan. You visit a friend who has an orchid collection and see an exceptionally fine specimen of a complex hybrid *Paphiopedilum*. This orchid is the result of nearly 100 years of careful breeding and it is now some 6, 7 or more generations removed from the original species. Your friend is happy to present you with a division of this fine plant. However in Japan they will not issue you with a CITES permit, because all of the species of *Paphiopedilum* are listed in Appendix I (see below). But the plant offered to you is a hybrid. What is the problem? A large number of different Japanese nurs-

eries have tried to get permits to export man-made *Paphiopedilum* hybrids and all report that the bureaucratic problems and uncertainties have caused them to abandon efforts after six to nine months of trying. Such problems do not exist for other orchids and naturally they blame this problem on the Japanese government's confusion about wild species and man-made hybrids, after all the Asiatic slippers were up-listed to Appendix I.

Consider that you are a commercial orchid plant producer in the United States who has received an order of plants from Australia. Australia will not issue an import permit without proof that a CITES permit will also be issued. In order to get a CITES permit in the United States the plants first need to get a phytosanitary certificate, showing that they are probably pest free. You live in Orange County, next to Los Angeles County, where the CITES permits are issued. That is convenient but it involves driving over 100 miles. You could get a phytosantiary certificate from the closest plant inspection unit in Orange County and mail that to Los Angeles to get the CITES, but if you are in a hurry it is best to make an appointment with the appropriate official and drive the distance. It may mean taking a day off work. Once you have obtained the CITES permit, it must be sent to Australia. Fortunately Australia will accept a fax and then, after a variable amount of time, that country will then eventually issue the import permit. By the time that you have been informed that the import permit has been received by your customer, the date on the phytosanitary permit will probably have expired and you will need to go through the expense and time of having a new inspection and getting a new certificate issued. Finally, the plants can be shipped.

In a few countries CITES certificates are actually issued by the nurseries themselves, which cuts out part of the bureaucracy, but they have to be registered to do that. Many nurseries do not have a large export component and they are therefore unwilling to bear the brunt of the necessary nursery registration and inspections. So, in most of the world, one must spend days trying to overcome the almost insurmountable bureaucratic red tape.

Consider another scenario. You are a professor at a major university and one of your doctoral students calls from Costa Rica. He has picked up some orchid plants from broken branches on the forest floor. The usual fate of orchids that fall is premature death. This is a young man who is intensely committed to conservation and hates to see anything die. You have to tell him to abandon the plants because it would be too difficult for him to get CITES papers. Or perhaps you are an honored orchid taxonomist in Denmark to whom people keep sending pickled orchid flowers to identify. However, because the flowers arrive without CITES documents you get into trouble with the authorities. Never mind that you were one of the people responsible for placing the entire orchid family under CITES protection in the first place. On the other hand you could be a boisterous orchid scientist in Germany, who is denied access to 100-year-old dried herbarium specimens because they do not have the correct CITES documentation. All of the above examples are true. Is it any wonder that orchidophiles are generally disenchanted with CITES?

Salvage and rescue

There are also those who see CITES as negatively affecting prospects for salvaging orchids whose habitat has been destroyed and this impedes effective conservation. This has developed into a major bone of contention and has been used by CITES detractors. Without a doubt the main threat to most plants is not from trade but from forest clearance or the plowing-up of savanna for crops. In this process countless millions of orchids are being destroyed. Most of the signatories to the Convention will not issue CITES for salvaged plants and without that the plants are usually doomed in their native lands. In reality, only a few of the orchids could be rescued, because the numbers being destroyed are so large that it would be impractical to find homes for more than the merest fraction. In a few exceptional cases, salvaged orchids can be brought into registered native nurseries, as is the case in Mexico. These eventually find their way into commerce. The usual pattern, however, is more like that of Zambia where it is legal to turn a branch bearing live orchids into charcoal but it is illegal to take the orchids off the branch to export before burning the wood.

How CITES needs to be changed

No matter how much 'gnashing of teeth' takes place, CITES is not going to go away. It has become a force within itself and those who are disenchanted with the Convention must either change it from within or change the ways that their governments enforce the Convention. It is unlikely that the Convention itself will be abolished. The treaty should be focussed on species that are actually threatened. It will do useful work but those species need to be recognized by name and their listing based on real data.

Plant groups, which are not truly threatened, should be down listed. Merely listing a plant family, to monitor trade, is unreasonable and detracts from organisms that truly need help. There should be recognition that the lists need to be cleaned up to restore credibility.

Plants should only be listed (even on Appendix II) on the basis of hard evidence and not on the 'educated guess' of some expert. Many of the major groups on the list were placed on it to determine if there was substantial trade in them. Twenty-five years is more than long enough to determine if that is indeed the case. The treaty has had a history of needing to down-list many of the plants from the original lists. Many of the lists were based on guesswork because hard data was unavailable. The wording in the convention should be changed to reflect that only hard data is appropriate evidence.

All restrictions on the movement of dried herbarium specimens should be abolished. The unenforceable aspects of Appendix I species, such as the maintenance of dead parts, should be dropped. We are not dealing with the skins of critically endangered animals.

The artificial propagation of all plants should be encouraged and expedited. To that end, the prohibition against the movement of dry seed, green pods, pollen or tissue-cultured plantlets (even of Appendix I plants) should be deregulated. In orchids, where a single seed capsule can contain tens of thousands or even millions of seed, there is no evidence that the trade in these propagules would jeopardize the existence of any species.

Could the money have been better spent?

The amount of money spent annually to enforce CITES must be enormous. To this must be added the cost of travelling to the various meetings of committees and conventions. If only part of the money spent on CITES over the last 25 years had been made available to actual and real conservation activities, such as buying up forested lands or policing preserves, the world would now be a better place and conservation would have been far better served.

CHAPTER 10

Paphiopedilums and CITES

The protection accorded to the slipper orchids is one of the most contentious aspects of CITES (the Convention on International Trade in Endangered Species). In 1992, two of the genera of slipper orchids, were transferred from Appendix II to Appendix I of the Convention. This, in effect, precluded all legitimate trade in jungle and wild collected plants of all *Paphiopedilum* and *Phragmipedium* species and it brought the issue of CITES into sharp focus for the orchid growing community.

The slipper orchids are a small group of plants that are widespread over the world and have been favorites of orchid hobbyists for nearly 150 years. The genera include *Cypripedium*, the north temperate lady slippers, which range across both Old and New World areas. A few species of this taxon descend into Central America and Tropical Asia. The genus is not covered by CITES, although there have been recent attempts to include it. Another important genus is *Paphiopedilum*, which ranges from Southern India into the Himalayas and then Indochina, through Malesia and as far south as the Solomon Islands. It is the most important genus in terms of horticulture and trade. The genus *Phragmipedium* is found in Central and South America and resembles its Asian counterparts quite closely, but these were not widely grown until they were placed in Appendix I, whereupon they became very popular. Two other genera are *Selenipedium*, which is not cultivated, though potentially it has some economic importance as an ice-cream flavorant, and the newly erected *Mexipedium* which contains one obscure species native to Mexico and was described originally as a *Phragmipedium*.

Historically, both *Paphiopedilum* and *Phragmipedium* species were cultivated in the last century and when orchid hybridizing became possible in the mid-1800s both genera were used equally to make primary hybrids. Later on, as new and diverse forms of *Paphiopedilum* species came into cultivation, attention became more focused on the Asian slipper orchids – almost to the exclusion of their South American cousins. Literally thousands of *Paphiopedilum* hybrids were created, while relatively few *Phragmipedium* continued to be grown. During this period, which lasted until about 1985, there were few significant importations of wild plants of the Latin American slippers. Nurseries did not stock those species as they were difficult to sell and there was no interest in them. Many of the *Phragmipedium* species have dull coloring, being mainly mixtures of browns and greens. A few of the older hybrids, based on the one pink species *Phragmipedium schlimii*, were available but there was relatively little demand for those. In reality there was little demand for many of the less showy species of *Paphiopedilum*, until the early 1960s. Many of the collecting sites were either lost or forgotten. Dealers in wild orchids listed many of the species in their catalogs, but the demand was modest. However, in Europe, species such *Paphiopedilum callosum* and *P. ciliolare* were used as pot plants. In those days, jungle plants were comparatively cheap to import, when compared with the cost of raising seedlings.

In the 1960s there was a marked change in the attitude of the collectors and growers. Dr. Jack Fowlie assumed the editorship of the *Orchid Digest* magazine and he started to publish a number of articles about *Paphiopedilum* species. Many new species were described and articles about other slipper orchid species appeared regularly in the pages of that journal. Importers on the West Coast of America simultaneously started to offer increasing numbers of jungle slipper species. One of these importers was Ray Rands. He was not only a source for inexpensive wild 'paphios' (as they were known at that time) but he also offered a few of the much rarer species at exorbitantly expensive prices. A plant of *Paphiopedilum hookerae* was offered at $10,000. These prices attracted attention to the more unusual species in the genus. Rands also started to make and sell primary hybrids between the various *Paphiopedilum* species. Within a decade both the species and their hybrids became quite popular and soon there arose a group of orchid growers who specialized primarily in the Asiatic slipper orchids. At the same time Ray also imported small quantities of *Phragmipedium* species, but they did not prove to be as popular as their Old World counterparts.

A few unusual clones of slipper orchid species surfaced and these focused interest on the slippers beyond those growers who were already devoted to them. The plants in question were *P. callosum* 'Sparkling Burgundy' and *P. callosum* 'JAC'. The first appeared at Palmengarten, the famous Botanic garden in Germany and the second in a batch of imports in Holland. Divisions of both plants made their way to the United States and into the hands of breeders at two famous orchid nurseries. These were Rex van Delden at F.A. Stewart Orchids in Southern California and Norris Powell at the Orchid House in Central California. Both of these plants bore very intensely colored purple-burgundy flowers. They were approaching the mythical black orchid in color. An enormous demand for the hybrid progeny of these two parents (called vinicolors) was created. As stud parents they were almost priceless. Divisions of the plant *P. callosum* 'JAC', now called *P. viniferum* 'JAC' (Koopowitz and Hasegawa, 2000) were advertised for sale at $10,000 and several pieces were actually sold at that price. At least one unflowered seedling hybrid derived from the other parent exchanged hands for $1,000 and selected hybrids that had flowered claimed prices several times in excess of that. Nearly everyone who grew slipper orchids wanted at least one of these new black slippers. The high prices that were being paid only whetted appetites and many speculated on seedlings that had the potential to produce these new and desirable colors. One of the consequences of this was a renewed interest in all types of slipper orchids.

Nevertheless, an independent observer might question the excitement and interest in this group of plants. Most of the tropical slipper orchid species are not beautiful and novice orchid growers are not usually attracted to them at the outset. New orchid enthusiasts tend to appreciate the large and flamboyant colorful flowers of the cattleyas and *Phalaenopsis*. They see the slippers as being dingy and weird, often bearing colors similar to those of half-cooked liver and petals covered with black spots and hairy warts. The appreciation for slipper orchid species grows with time and experience; it is a group of plants to which orchid growers graduate.

Because of two additional events, the 1980s turned out to be a golden decade for slipper orchid fanciers. There was the discovery of a series of Chinese slipper orchid species with stunning flowers that even beginners appreciated and these were rapidly and widely, though illegally, distributed. Many of the Chinese

species were closely related and distinct from other known slipper orchid species. They were mainly related to *P. delenatii*, a species from Vietnam that had been known about for a long time. It was one of the few species that could be called pretty, being a demure pale pink flower with a darker lip and pink and yellow staminode.

Paphiopedilum armeniacum was the first of the Chinese species to create a sensation. The name itself had created a stir after the Chinese botanists, Chen and Liu described the flower, in 1982. The epithet *armeniacum* referred to the color of the flower and means apricot. Generally one expects apricot to be a yellow color, containing overtones of orange and pink. This was a desirable color that did not occur in any other slipper species and in very few hybrids. Plants were eagerly sought and when they appeared in the trade they were eagerly purchased. The blossoms turned out not to be apricot but a rich intense bright yellow, itself a brilliant shade not seen previously. All over the world the first flowers to be exhibited brought accolades, 'First Class Certificates', Gold Medals or equivalent awards. Rarely had a species ever achieved such instantaneous recognition and fame. At the same time another species was imported. This was *P. micranthum*. The species had been described in 1952 from a pressed plant and a dissected flower bud. The epithet is also a misnomer. It means tiny flower but these flowers actually have the largest pouches of any of the species. A well-grown plant in flower is a real eye-opener and plants appeared to be of high potential for hybridizing. This was born out when the first hybrids were brought into flower. Within a short time two other species became available, *P. malipoense* and *P. emersonii*. Each was very different from the other and all four were highly desirable plants. Literally thousands upon thousands of plants of *P. armeniacum* and *P. micranthum* were exported and brought into the trade. There were never as many plants of *P. emersonii* or *P. malipoense*. Those were more expensive and importers never seemed to have large quantities, but altogether substantial numbers were collected and appeared in orchid collections around the world.

The second event was the reintroduction of two spectacular species that had been lost since the turn of the century. These were *Paphiopedilum rothschildianum* and *P. sanderianum*. The former is a magnificent brown striped flower that can reach over 30 cm (11 in) in width while the latter has the distinction of having the longest petals of any flower in the plant kingdom. Petals over one meter (39 in) long have been measured. Both species had been introduced towards the end of the 19th century in England and had created a sensation at that time. Several hybrids were made with each species. The species, *P. rothschildianum* was used to make a variety of distinctive and large flowered hybrids. Unfortunately, *P. sanderianum* was lost to cultivation and nearly all of its hybrids died out. The original collectors had not divulged their collecting sites and had in fact falsified those sites in the reports to their employers. At the RBG Kew, there was specimen from the 1890s with the exact locality on the sheet, but this was not publicized. It seems that much of the original collecting and interest in nearly all slipper orchid species faded with the coming of the First World War.

When interest later re-emerged there were a few plants of *P. rothschildianum* surviving in collections, but no *P. sanderianum*. It was not until the mid 1970s that *P. rothschildianum* was rediscovered by Sheila Collenettte in Mount Kinabalu National Park in Borneo. Shortly afterwards *P. sanderianum* was found in nearby Sarawak, during the late 1970s. Mulu National Park was created in part to protect the *P. sanderianum* population. The demand for these two species was enormous. By the middle of the 1980s *P. rothschildianum* had been artificially propagated from survivors of the original collections, made nearly 100 years previously and when those new plants flowered they proved to be superior to the original parents. The seedlings were relatively expensive but much cheaper than divisions of the parent stock that had previously exchanged hands for thousands of dollars. The asking price for a seedling was $10 an inch measured up and down the longest two leaves. *Paphiopedilum rothschildianum* was slow to mature from seed often taking as long as 12 years to yield their first spikes of flowers. Field collected specimens were smuggled out of Mt. Kinabalu National Park and one was advertised in the American Orchid Society Bulletin as a jungle plant and offered for sale at over $4,000. That advertisement was merely placed as a hook to create interest, but it backfired.

Conservationists pointed to the enormous amounts of money that hobbyists were prepared to spend in order to possess a jungle plant although very few plants would actually change hands at those prices. The advertisement provided potent ammunition for those determined to cut off trade in wild collected slipper orchids. The first plants of *P. sanderianum* were also offered at high prices but only a few were sold at those inflated prices. However, prices of $1,000 to $1,500 were not uncommon. Even today a well-grown specimen of either species still fetches a comparable price, even if artificially propagated.

Both of these groups of plants excited the imagination of orchid growers and also built upon the excite-

ment that the vinicolors had achieved. The new plants were wanted not only for their own sakes, but also for the potential they might add to new garden hybrids. There were races among slipper orchid breeders, across the world, to see who would be the first to offer seedlings made with these newly available species and who would be first to flower them. Seedlings made with the new parents often sold for $100, for single small, unflowered plants. But the species themselves were also very desirable in their own right and many growers were eager for a chance to posses them.

Trade routes

Trade in wild species was quite complex and plants often changed through many hands before ending up in private collections. The plants were dug up in the wild or stripped off trees or rocks by local people, who then sold them at fairly cheap prices to individuals who might or might not try to establish the plants. With the Chinese species they were usually planted in gardens until sufficient had been assembled for sale (J. Fowlie, personal communication). Philippine or Indonesian slippers were merely piled together, often in baskets. Dealers were people in the original country that assembled the plants from several collectors, they either found exporters or exported the plants themselves. At this stage many of the clumps were sub-divided into single or at most three connected fans of leaves. Some dealers employed specific collectors who could search out required species while others just went to local street markets and bought what was offered there. There were famous wild plant markets near Bangkok and Hanoi that have recently been disbanded under pressure from IUCN. Plants that survived were eventually sold at wholesale prices to commercial nurseries in Europe, Japan or the United States. Here they often passed from nursery to nursery before being offered to the public. Each time they passed hands along the route the prices would double or treble, in part this was due to financial losses that occurred while plants were being established in cultivation. The percentage of plants that died along the route is not known. Some species were tougher than others and most of these survived, but other more tender species such as *P. adductum*, *P. randsii*, *P. bougainvillianum*, and *P. wentworthianum* succumbed.

When collectors and dealers realized that there was a market for unusual and new species of slipper orchid, attempts were made to find many of the rarer species that had never been common in cultivation or in the field. These included plants such as *P. hookeri* var. *vol-*

unteanum and *P. wentworthianum*, to name two. There was some concern that the populations of those species could not support the harvest of plants. When tens of thousands of plants of the Chinese parvisepalums appeared on the market concerns were heightened. Efforts were initiated, primarily in England and Europe, to find a way to restrict trade.

The allure of jungle Paphiopedilums

Despite the great successes in artificial propagation of most *Paphiopedilum* species, which results in plants that are more amenable to cultivation, there is still a demand for wild jungle material, despite its contraband nature and fragility. The reasons for this are not always apparent, especially to the conservation biologists trying to stem the trade in wild plants. Wild populations of species have great variability, whereas those in cultivation usually tend to be genetically quite uniform. The lure of the jungle plant resides in the possibility that one will produce an unusually colored morph or have exceptionally fine flowers. Albinistic slipper orchids (i.e. those that are unable to make anthocyanins, the red to purple coloured pigment in the flowers) are much sought after and command exceptionally high prices. Only one or two albinistic clones are usually found in any one species and are still unknown for many slipper orchid species. The possibility of finding one of these desirable flowers is quite small, but the chance does still exist. Few jungle plants can equal the quality of a modern domesticated species and at the same time be as easy to grow and flower. Apart from new species, there is relatively little need to bring more stock into cultivation. Growing wild collected plants has an aura akin to gambling, because the final outcome is unpredictable and the grower could hit the jackpot by producing an exceptional blossom. However, for the sake of the orchids, it would be better to confine one's gambling to state lotteries.

Historic trade

Enormous numbers of *Paphiopedilum* species have been harvested from the wild since the last century. Kumar and Manilal (1994) record that Fosterman sent the firm of Sanders 40,000 plants of *P. spicerianum* in 1884. Similarly large numbers of *P. insigne* and *P. villosum* must also have been sent in the early years. The letters of Sander's collectors frequently reported shipments of slipper orchids running into hundreds or thousands during the 1880s and 1890s.

The size of Paphiopedilum trade

What were the actual numbers of slipper orchid plants reported in the trade during the time when it was still possible to collect and sell species on the international market? Because trade was more-or-less monitored by some, figures are available.

The arguments for restricting trade were based on the idea that the wild populations of slipper orchids could not support the numbers of plants being collected indefinitely, and unless collection could be stopped many of the species would be faced with imminent extinction. It was argued that one could not expect customs officials to be able to distinguish between the various species of *Paphiopedilum*, especially when they were not in flower. And that the only way to protect the threatened species was to ban all trade in jungle slipper orchids, even if some of the plants might be common in their natural habitats. The sentiments were noble but the issue soon became controversial. Many of the growers, who were sympathetic towards trying to protect endangered slipper orchids in their native habitats, felt that the issue was clouded by personal animosity between some of the plant traders and conservationists. It was unfortunately also perceived that conservation was not the prime motive behind the movement to ban the trade but rather the result of personal vendettas between these prime players. Although this perception may have been totally inaccurate it did color the attitudes of those who were against the up-listing.

The way that trade in wild plants could be halted was by moving the species thought to be threatened from Appendix II to Appendix I, a complicated and politically involved procedure. CITES is designed so that hasty actions cannot be made. If a request is made to add or remove a species from the appendices the proposal must be championed by one of the member countries. Convincing documentation demonstrating that trade is indeed adversely affecting the persistence of those particular species in the wild must be presented. The documentation is brought before a working committee, in this case the Plants Committee, for discussion and they will make a recommendation that may then brought before the General Assembly for action or otherwise. The major concerns in the General Assembly are with the charismatic animals. Plants tend to get short shrift and resolutions concerning plants tend to be hurriedly discussed and considered in an often-cursory fashion. This usually occurs towards the end of long sessions, which can run for many days. Unless a country is vitally concerned about a particular species they tend to rely on recommendations of the specialist committees and vote without due consideration.

What happened with the slipper orchids? An analysis was made of the numbers of plants for each species reported in the trade for both of the *Paphiopedilum* and *Phragmipedium* genera. Indeed the reported trade levels were very high for some species. While these reported figures were probably true they did not reflect the situation accurately. The traders sold their plants by the number of growths. Each growth is a fan of leaves produced during a single season. The plants usually flower from a bud produced at the center of each growth. A new growth is produced from the base at one side of the previous seasons. Plants were priced according to the number of growths that they possessed. Both collectors and exporters soon realized that they could make more money from selling plants of only 1, 2 or 3 growths than the large clumps that many species naturally formed. Only a few of the dark forest-floor species seemed to produce plants with just a few growths, most other species make hefty plants with 10 to 20 or even more growths. What this meant for the trade numbers was simply that they were inflated. A thousand plants recorded in the trade may have represented only 100 plants taken from the wild. Efforts to point this out were ignored.

Perhaps the most valid criticism of the trade evaluation was that it contained no hard data about the extant population sizes of any of the species in the wild that were to be up-listed. It is not unusual for a species of plant to have several million plants in the wild. Others, of course, may only number a few thousand and in extreme cases only a few hundred. It is the latter that can truly be considered endangered. At best, much of the knowledge of slipper orchids in the wild was made up of informed guesses and hearsay. It is only in recent years that attempts to get accurate information have been made. This, however, appeared to be sufficient to sway the Plants Committee in its recommendations. One species, *Paphiopedium delenatii*, that everyone was convinced was probably was extinct in the wild was found nearly 20 years later, occurring in enormous quantities in the wild. This species will be discussed again later on in this chapter. Numbers in the trade are meaningless unless the situation in the wild is reliably known. Removing 100 plants from a population of only 500 can be devastating but removing 50,000 from a population of 5 million would only have a trivial effect.

How many species of both *Paphiopedilum* and *Phragmipedium* were really threatened with extinction to the point that they needed to be placed in the most protected category? Two of the species were at that time thought to be extinct in the wild. *Paphiopedilum druryi* was known from the south of India and the site was rumored to have been destroyed by fire by an unscrupulous collector who had wanted to raise the value of the plants that he had collected for resale. A second species, from central Vietnam was known from a single collection of two plants. Fortunately, a plant ended up in a Paris Botanic Garden where it was propagated and later introduced into the trade. This species was usually quoted as an example of how a species had been preserved in cultivation by orchid growers and as a justification for the continued trade in slipper orchid species. Both of the supposedly extinct species have since been rediscovered. Mammen and Mammen (1974) first described *Paphiopedilum druryi*'s rediscovery in 1974, and it is reputed that 3000 plants were collected at that time. Kumar and Manilal (1994) report that dealers out of the area enticed local collectors to gather plants. Eventually over 600 plants of *P. druryii* were found by the State Forestry Department of Kerala at a local nursery and were presumably confiscated. One wonders what happened to them? As *P. druryi* grows and spreads by long underground rhizomes and can make sizable patches of genets (single clones), the numbers of plants reported are actually those of individual growths rather than discrete plants. Recently, at least two populations of *P. druryi*, have been rediscovered and are being studied (Kumar, personal communication). It is estimated that at least 3,500 plants of this species still exist. Vast quantities of the other species, *P. delenatii* were found to exist in central Vietnam. There were other species that were also considered to occur in very limited numbers, these included important and spectacular plants such as *P. rothschildianum*, and *P. sanderianum*. These were growing in preserves but had nevertheless been almost collected out by poachers. Some species grew far off the beaten track in difficult to reach places, up vertical cliffs or on seldom visited islands. It was too difficult or hazardous to make a census of their populations. Rumors of additional populations of those species outside the reserve were originally dismissed, but at least some appear to be true.

During the last few years of legitimate jungle trade, I was concerned about the natural disposition of *Paphiopedilum* populations in the wild and asked scientists who worked there and importers which species they considered truly rare. One scientist, Dr. James Ascher, convinced me that *Paphiopedilum victoria-mariae* was extinct in the wild and had been collected out. About two years later I saw an importation of several hundred plants of that species which had all the earmarks of recently collected jungle plants. Shortly before the imposition of trade restraints, in a conversation with Ray Rands, a well-known orchid dealer and importer, he

44. *Paphiopedilum victoria regina*

suggested that the only extinct species was *P. randsii*, the slipper named for himself. He said that people at the site had assured him that no more of that species existed. A few years later, on a visit to an orchid nursery in Japan, I saw several hundred contraband jungle plants

45. *Paphiopedilum armeniacum*, the first of the Chinese parvisepalums, was brought into cultivation in the mid-1980s and caused intense breeding activity. Probably hundreds of thousands of these were exported before the genus was moved to Appendix I of CITES.

of *P. randsii*. This pattern seemed to be repeated.

There was another way of gauging the rarity of the various slipper orchids and that was simply by examining the asking price for wholesale plants. Many of the species were being sold at prices of less than one dollar per plant, whereas a few rarer species were being offered at much higher prices. Clearly the cheaper plants such as *P. bellatulum, P. concolor, P. hirsutissimum* or *P. venustum* were neither rare nor endangered. Actually *P. venustum* had been in cultivation for over 100 years without its price escalating beyond normal inflationary rates, suggesting that vast numbers of the plants must have existed or that trade was at sustainable levels. This appeared true of many other species as well. Even plants that were thought to be rarer, such as *P. godefroyae* and *P. niveum* (they were supposed to be situated on only a few islands off the Malaysian Peninsula) never achieved high prices. According to the trade levels those species should have been collected out decades previously, if they only occurred at the publicized localities. But they were still available at cheap prices, suggesting that there were either other large populations, unknown to the western conservationists, or that the plants were being harvested at sustainable levels.

Newly discovered species used to be brought onto the market at outrageous prices. But this was a ploy devised by the dealers who only initially released a few

46. *Paphiopedilum micranthum*, a spectacular slipper orchid from China.

specimens of a new 'rare' species to the most avid collectors or breeders and then prices plummeted after a few years. Initially the retail price for *P. armeniacum* was $100 for a single growth and the first plants of *P. micranthum* were considered to be so valuable that they were not sold. They were traded for divisions of very valuable and desirable plants, such as the most highly awarded hybrids, that often sold for thousands of dollars a division. Within less than a decade wild collected *P. micranthum* was selling at less than $1 a plant, when bought in bulk. Similarly, the few originally collected plants of *Phragmipedium besseae*, a brilliant red Andean slipper orchid, were sold in a sealed bid auction fetching thousands of dollars per plant. Later jungle plants of *P. besseae* were being sold on the black market at less than $5 a plant. Obviously none of these plants were really rare.

It is true that some populations must have been totally wiped out by the plant collectors, but the arguments are often made that many of the plants would have been destroyed anyway by the land conversion that was, and still is, sweeping through South East Asia. Professor Leonid Averyanov from St. Petersburg, studies the vegetation of Vietnam and has an interest in orchids, especially the lady slippers. He has recounted seeing a patch of *Paphiopedilum hirsutissimum* var. *esquirolei* a kilometer long and 500 meters wide, with thousands of plants in flower. Two years later a road had been built near that site and the forest trees cleared. Although the paphiopedilums were left following deforestation, in the absence of protection from the surrounding trees, the entire population was destroyed. This is not an isolated incident. Deforestation, accidental and deliberate fires, together with the conversion of land for agriculture, take their toll on wild populations.

Within the IUCN, now known as the World Conservation Union, there are a series of committees set up to advise the body on specific groups of endangered species. These are collectively called the 'Species Survival Commission'. Each committee is called a 'Specialist Group' and hence there is an 'Elephant Specialist Group', a 'Cycad Specialist Group' and an 'Orchid Specialist Group' (OSG), among others. Each Specialist Group has an international membership of appointed experts; in the case of orchids it is very large and consists of 129 members. I have been a member of the OSG for many years. Theoretically this group should have the expertise to comment on up-listing proposals and should have a strong voice in the success or failure of such proposals. The OSG meets in conjunction with the World Orchid Conferences, which are held every three years. It is at that time that the maximum number of committee members seems to get together. Other meetings are held in conjunction with orchid events in various parts of the world and at irregular intervals. One would have expected that all or most members of the OSG should have been asked to comment on the up-listing proposal. In fact one might have expected such a proposal to originate with the Specialist Group in the first place, if it had been necessary. This was not the case. Purely coincidentally, when travelling through England, a member of the group asked me if I had responded to the proposal. In fact I had not even seen it, which was surprising as it was well known that I was very familiar with the slipper orchids and kept a close eye on the trade. After up-listing, the matter was discussed. It was the general opinion of the OSG that such an up-listing was neither desirable nor recommended. Many members of the committee thought that it had been bypassed because 'some powers' realized that up-listing would not be supported.

CITES change

After the two genera had been up-listed to Appendix I there was a set time before the new 'protections' came into effect – approximately 6 months. Enormous quantities of plants were collected and exported to the major markets in Japan, Europe and the United States. I remember visiting nurseries during this time when thousands upon thousands of wild jungle collected plants came in. One particular incidence impressed me greatly. I walked into the nursery of a renowned importer and the entire floor was set up with piles of bare rooted paphiopedilums. Each pile contained hundreds and hundreds of plants. One heap in particular fascinated me as it was made up of jungle plants of *P. mastersianum*. This had never been a very plentiful species and was rather rare in collections. Although it was potentially a very important plant for slipper orchid breeders it had only been brought in previously in small numbers. Here, in this one heap, were more individual plants of *P. mastersianum* than I had seen altogether in my previous 20 years of orchid growing. I remember wondering at that time if any plants had been left at all in the wild during this last legal orgy of wild slipper collection. The plants were only collected in those quantities because it was the last time that they could be collected legally. As I left the nursery I discovered a second, equally large mass of *P. mastersianum*. This scene was repeated for most of the species and in each of the nurseries that I visited. I had the distinct feeling at that time that CITES up-listing, instead of protecting the species, had 'forced' a frenzy of over-collecting and if many of the species were not really endangered at the time they were being considered for up-listing, they were now truly be threatened. Any remaining respect that I had for CITES and its professed goals evaporated at that point.

Along with the Asian slipper orchids, the neo-tropical slippers in the genus *Phragmipedium* were also up-listed. They rode in on the *Paphiopedilum* coat tails. At that time there was negligible trade in *Phragmipedium*. There are approximately 17 *Phragmipedium* species (Gruss, O. 1996), but only 2 of these were really considered desirable for the trade. One species, *P. caudatum* and its varieties, vied with *Paphiopedilum sanderianum* for petal length, but there was not the drive to import these in vast numbers. The other was *Phragmipedium besseae*, the scarlet slipper, first found in Peru but later in Ecuador. Once again, the range of the species was not well understood and it was thought to occur in very small numbers and with a limited distribution. The demand for this species was very high. Jungle plants brought in about $100 to $200 for a modest division. As far as the other known species were concerned their flowers were either small or undistinguished and imported jungle plants simply did not sell.

Little was known about the conservation status of any phragmipediums, besides *P. besseae*, which was thought to be very rare (probably a mistake, considering the volume of plant material that subsequently came into the trade). The only other really rare species known at that time was *P. exstaminodium*, a Mexican form of *P. caudatum* with an unusual third stamen. Whether or not *P. exstaminodium* is a real species or merely a population carrying a peculiar mutation is still in contention. Most of the other species have flowers that, at best, can be described as scrawny and with muddy colors in shades of green to beige. Importers were reluctant to handle them.

This all changed with the up-listing. Suddenly even the least exciting of these unexciting species became highly desirable and prices rose. It was, and still is, not unusual to find phragmipediums for sale among recently imported plants items brought into the USA from various neo-tropical countries. Some of these plants have resided in local nurseries for a short time before being declared 'artificially propagated' and are thus legally imported. The red slipper, *P. besseae*, turned out to be easy to raise and flower from seed and the price of jungle imports dropped drastically. Even though the seed raised plants are easier to grow under the artificial conditions of greenhouses and windowsills compared to wild plants, some demand for jungle plants continues. A jungle plant has a special aura about it. It is not only that

it is forbidden fruit, but also, with a wild plant one never knows what quality and kind of flower nature may have produced. There is always the small chance that the new plant could produce flowers in novel and unexpected colors or have other exceptional qualities. These plants appeal to the gambling instinct that many of the orchid growers and breeders possess as they look for better and more unusual flowers.

Forcing artificial propagation

If one looks back on the effect of CITES up-listing on the slipper orchid growers, it has in some respects actually been of considerable benefit to both the hobbyist and commercial growers. With the end of mass importation, it was clear that demand for species would have to be filled by artificial propagation. Immediately, slipper orchid growers started to propagate species. At first it was only *Paphiopedilum* species and of course *Phragmipedium besseae*, but as the demand for all *Phragmipedium* species rose, attention turned to these other Latin American slipper orchids as well. Many of the species that heretofore were only brought into cultivation as jungle plants such as *Paphiopedilum callosum*, *P. philippinense*, *P. purpuratum*, etc., were now being produced from seed and artificially propagated. Some species such as *P. randsii*, which were very difficult to reestablish from jungle collections, were offered as the much easier to grow seedlings. Not all species have been easy to grow or produced in sufficient numbers of seedlings to meet the demands. Routine sibling crosses between *P. micranthum* or *P. armeniacum* have been difficult to produce reliably and the resultant progeny have been slow to grow. Only a few scattered breeders have had limited success with the parvisepalum species, but it has not been sufficient to fill the needs of all hobbyists that wish to grow those species. Much of the current demand is filled by the vegetative asexual reproduction from the original wild imports. Other plants such as *P. bouganvilleanum* and *P. wentworthianum* have been easier to germinate from seed but tend to be very difficult to establish and are usually lost outside of the flask and these have not been mass produced.

Despite the limited success with the propagation of some of the species there has been good success with the majority. One such success story concerns *P. lawrenceanum*. This was a very important species in the early breeding of the Maudiae-type slipper orchids that have become the mainstay of the commercial slipper pot plant industry. It is a pretty flower with a large sail-like striped dorsal sepal borne on a plant with attractive mottled leaves. The species is endemic to Sarawak on the island of Borneo, but its precise locality is unknown. In recent times it was never been very abundant and is now considered to be among the most endangered of the Bornean Slipper Orchids (Chan *et al.*, 1994, Cribb, 1997). Prior to CITES, divisions of the few plants available fetched prices in excess of $75 a division. The plant has been so easy to produce in cultivation that a nearly flowering sized seedling in the United States can be purchased for $10, which is close to the price of a hybrid slipper pot plant. Many other species such as *P. niveum* and *P. sukhakulii* have also been mass-produced and good, easy to grow, plants are available at very reasonable prices. With artificial propagation comes artificial selection for plants, with better flowers and more amenable growing habits. The end result is a better product for the hobbyist, affordable plants with good flowers and an easy disposition. Thus, in some respects, gardeners have really profited from the CITES up-listing.

The Chinese trade

The Chinese slipper orchids, in particular those belonging to the parvisepalum alliance, *Paphiopedilum armeniacum*, *P. emersonii*, *P. malipoense* and *P. micranthum*, feature heavily in the events that led to the up-listing of the genus. Trade in these plants was probably in the tens of thousands for each species, each year, prior to up-listing. The two species most commonly encountered in the trade were *P. armeniacum* and *P. micranthum*. Because these plants proliferate asexually by means of underground stolons many of the trade records, while probably accurate, also grossly exaggerated the situation. Exported plants were usually only single or at most, double growth plants. In cultivation, plants can easily produce many runners so that in a few seasons individual plants often produce 10 or more growths. It is likely that the trade figures were probably quite inflated, compared to the number of plants actually removed from the wild to provide the 'number of plants' in the trade. Reports and pictures of plants in the wild suggest that both *P. malipoense* and *P. micranthum* actually form clumps with considerably more than 10 growths. Once again, without knowing the actual number of plants in wild populations and their demography, it is impossible to know if the trade was actually harming the wild species.

The CITES embargo on the trade in the Chinese species did cause a loss of market in those countries that conscientiously adhered to the CITES covenant. But that did not end either the trade or collection of those species. Visitors to China reported and took pictures of pots of both *P. armeniacum* and *P. micranthum* being hawked on the streets of several cities, including Beijing.

This is a considerable distance from the Yunnan province where the species occur naturally. The domestic market seems to have taken up some of the slack caused by the loss of export markets. Indeed there are also flourishing wild flower markets in southern China at Kunming, Wenshan, and Baosha, among others. By 1997 there were reports of tens of thousands of plants arriving in Taiwan. The Taiwanese nurseryman who discussed this with me pointed out that as Taiwan is considered an internal part of China, they did not have to worry about CITES documentation. Some black market trade still continues. I walked through an orchid nursery in Japan a few years ago and noted over a thousand each of *P. armeniacum* and *P. micranthum* that looked to me to be recent imports. In two other nurseries in Japan in 1997 I saw many recently imported plants of *P. malipoense* and *P. jackii*. Later on in South Africa in 1999, I saw many hundred of each species in a nursery. They had been imported from Taiwan. There are also hearsay reports that many *Paphiopedilum* species are smuggled into Western Europe through the back door, i.e. via the Eastern European countries.

Contraband trade

How large the current black market trade is in jungle *Paphiopedilum* species is difficult to estimate, but it must be substantial. This is obvious from the way that newly described species or varieties find their way into private collections all over the world.

In Geneva, in 1997, at the large European Orchid Congress where there was a meeting of the Species Specialist Committee on Orchids for the IUCN, plants of *P. sangii* were being openly displayed for sale. It is most unlikely that they could have been obtained legitimately. Only a very few specimens had been brought into cultivation before the embargo. At the 2000 European Orchid Congress in Denmark, a flowering plant of *P. vietnamense* was on display. These are not rare instances. I have seen many of the new species in private collections in many different parts of the world.

The acid test

As I suggested above, the acid test for CITES occurs when new and desirable species are discovered, or 'lost' species are rediscovered in the wild. Does CITES actually help to protect these new and desirable plants in their native habitats? There have been many such exciting discoveries in recent years that seem to indicate that, despite CITES legislation, the plants continue to be collected.

During the war in Vietnam and for the 20 or so years

of its isolation following the American withdrawal, little was known about the orchids of Vietnam. The pretty pink slipper orchid, *P. delenatii* had originally been described in 1924 but had been discovered about 10 years earlier. Most of the plants currently in cultivation have been bred from the original plants taken to Paris. Because the status of the species in the wild was unknown to western gardeners for the next 65 years it was assumed that the species was either extinct or very rare. Cribb (1987) in his monograph, *The Genus Paphiopedilum*, noted that the plant "....certainly must be rare and of restricted natural distribution". In the early 1990s the Vietnamese government was looking for sources of foreign income and approached several Japanese orchidists to advise them on the marketing of their native orchids. It soon became apparent that the species had been found again, in the area around Nha Trang, where it had been discovered for the first time in 1922. It was in fact relatively common, with a wide altitudinal distribution. Just how common can be gauged by some of the numbers of plants that ended up in the trade. There was a report of a government nursery with 40,000 plants of *P. delenatii* in pots. Of course the CITES ban on international trade of wild *Paphiopedilum* plants had already been instituted and so jungle collected plants of *P. delenatii* could not be sold openly. At that time the Vietnamese government was not a signatory to CITES.

Because Taiwan has an uncertain political status (in some situations the island is considered an internal part of China and at other times a sovereign nation) it was not a CITES signatory either and CITES documentation was not demanded for the entrance of orchid plants. At least one Taiwanese nursery imported 10,000 plants of *P. delenatii*. In all it is thought that eight metric tons of *Paphiopedilum delenatii* were exported (Averyanov, personal communication). A well grown, three-growth plant of *P. delenatii* weighs between 50 and 100 grams. One ton could contain between 10,000 and 20,000 plants. If Averyanov is correct, then between 80,000 and 160,000 plants were collected in the wild and exported from the country. Many of those plants then reappeared in Japan and small numbers filtered from there to other parts of the world. Actually, many of the *Paphiopedilum* species breeders were able to beg pollen, which was then used to make seedlings of *P. delenatii*, using the inbred cultivated plants as pod parents. This was a sensible thing to do in terms of conservation strategies, but visits by Averyanov showed that most of the wild *P. delenatii* had been stripped out. By 2000, another good population of *P. delenatii* had been found and these have appeared in Europe. The point here is that up-listing of *Paphiopedilum* to Appendix I was

47.   *Paphiopedilum delenatii*, a line-bred form of this Vietnamese species.

almost totally ineffective as a conservation strategy for this species and it also indicates how imprecise was our understanding of *P. delenatii* distribution during the hysteria that led to up-listing.

Towards the end of the 1990s a significant series of new species were described. Some of these were very desirable, others were insignificant, but all ended up in the illegal trade. *Paphiopedilum jackii* looks like a lesser *P. malipoense*, but varies in details of its fragrance and staminodes. This plant was known from only two populations in Vietnam. Despite the fact that the plant was neither pretty nor particularly desirable, the species started to appear in collections scattered through Europe, the United States and Japan. One Japanese enthusiast boasted to me that a large shipment of *P. jackii*, he had tried to import, had been confiscated by the authorities. The first flower that I saw of this variety was a plant I was asked to identify at the Missouri Botanic Garden, it had come in with a shipment of plants exchanged between the gardens and a sister institution in Vietnam.

Another Vietnamese species was *P. helenae*,

48. *Paphiopedilum jackii*, the first of the Vietnamese "new" species to enter the Black-market trade in quantity

described as recently as 1996. A diminutive plant with small yellow flowers the plant was collected from a steep rocky habitat and did not appear to be widespread. Within a month of the description being published plants were being offered on the black market at about $700 per plant. In 1998 at least one nursery in the United States was offering *P. helenae* openly for sale at $250 and plants could be bought at $50 each in lots of ten from foreign dealers, suggesting that many plants were in the market. Dr. Averyanov, who named the species, could identify lichens growing on the leaves of plants at the nursery that are similar to those found growing on the plants in the wild. These could not have been artificially propagated. The original locality of *P. helenae* was described as containing a handful of plants. The second time that Averyanov visited the site nearly all the plants were gone. In fact hundreds of plants had made their way to Taiwan and then to the rest of the world. Other sites had been discovered and were raided immediately. CITES did nothing to promote the conservation of this species.

Paphiopedilum gigantifolium, described at the end

of 1997, was offered on the black market in Germany before the species was officially published. I saw plants in American collections soon afterwards. By 1998 one eyewitness described tens of thousands of *Paphiopedilum* species derived from jungle plants in Dutch nurseries. Such plants are probably appearing with CITES documentation and described as artificially propagated. The latter usually means that the jungle plants were cut apart in a nursery somewhere, or grown on for a year or six months. Artificial propagation is not always conservation friendly.

In a rather amazing fashion a series of very desirable new slipper orchid species (*P. vietnamense*, *P. hangianum* and *P. anitum*, among others) were found in Vietnam and the Philippines towards the end of 1998. By the middle of 1999, plants of these species were common in cultivation in Europe, Japan, North America and South Africa. An effort to stem the tide in Europe made it more cumbersome and difficult, as well as costly to obtain the appropriate CITES permits for slipper orchids. As the black market trade is able to work around that, the only effect has been to penalize legitimate growers of truly artificially propagated species.

Vietnam has been a treasure trove of new *Paphiopedilum* species and of these the most exciting was a large, deep pink flower, named *P. vietnamense*. Two populations were discovered originally. Within a short time all the plants at those sites were collected and dispatched to various parts of the world. It is not known if other localities exist for this species. This was the critical test for CITES. It demonstrated very clear-

49. *Paphiopedilum vietnamense*, the most spectacular of the new species, both of the original populations appear to have been completely collected out. (Photo credit: O. Gruss).

ly that once a very desirable species was discovered the most stringent regulations were totally useless for protecting the species, without the active management of the plants in their native habitats. This species is now being used all over the world for breeding new kinds of slipper orchids. Those law-abiding companies that refused to buy the plants are the ones that are penalized. This is perhaps the clearest demonstration yet of the total ineffectiveness of CITES in regulating the international trade in slipper orchids.

Japan and CITES

One of the problems with CITES is that it is administered according the whims of the individual signatories. Some countries deal with it effectively but others do not. Japan is one of the largest sinks for orchid material in the world. There are reputed to be over 100,000 orchid growers in that country and they demand the best, the most innovative and most fashionable orchids. This enormous market has led to a one way stream of plants into that country through both legitimate and illegitimate means. *Paphiopedilum* hybrids go into the country legitimately with CITES permits, but most slipper orchid species enter through the black market. Nurseries that operate legitimately in Japan say that their government will not issue CITES permits for the export of *Paphiopedilum* hybrid plants. Presumably they think that the plant officials are unable to differentiate between wild species, *ex situ* raised species, and man-made hybrids. Actually, the largest component would be slipper orchid hybrids. All the trade with Japan is therefore one way, and what would in any other part of the world be considered legitimate, i.e. export of man-made hybrids, is forced into illegal channels. This is somewhat ironic since Japan is also probably one of the world's largest sinks for illegal trade in wild collected species.

The major arguments – *pro* vs. *anti*

The major arguments for up-listing *Paphiopedilum* and *Phragmipedium* were essentially as follows. We know that there is still a substantial trade in wild, tropical slipper orchid species. We are not sure that the trade is sufficient to jeopardize the wild populations, because in most cases we have no ideas about the natural demography and population size of the wild species. However we do suspect, looking at the numbers in the trade, that many if not most of the species are in jeopardy. In addition, because it is unreasonable to expect a customs official to be able to differentiate between endangered and non-threatened species, particularly if they are not in flower, it is better to err on the safe side and give blanket protection to the entire group. This can be best achieved by up-listing both genera. As one benefit of the change in status they might point to the increased *ex situ* propagation of species and the production of plants that are more amenable to cultivation. This might even be pointed to as a success story. Many of the species that were unavailable in the trade before up-listing are now relatively common.

Those who are against the regulation of 'the trade' might argue that up-listing was not necessary. For the greater majority of species the numbers in the trade were sustainable. While not having hard data to back themselves up they could point to the stabilized unit prices of many of the species as an indication that resources were not dwindling. They might argue that actual numbers of populations in the wild were more numerous than anticipated because many tropical areas are poorly explored and there is a long history of the discovery of additional sites for many species.

Another reason for the up-listing of both entire genera could be that customs officials would be unable to discern the really threatened species from those that were not threatened. This is a frequent argument, used for listing many common but non-threatened species, which are difficult to discern from their rarer relatives. The argument is not strictly logical because customs officials cannot differentiate between hybrids and species either, and hybrid slippers were not up-listed. But, in fact there are a few countries, such as Malaysia, where it is extremely difficult if not totally impossible to get CITES permits to export *Paphiopedilum* hybrids.

Of course, one could point out that those impediments to trade in legitimate garden plants reported above for Malaysia, Japan and other countries, are not the fault of CITES, but rather in the way that individual countries interpret and enforce the treaty. Nevertheless, the problems have arisen because of the existence of CITES and the treaty itself is both at the root and core of the problem. As I mentioned earlier CITES does exist and it is not going to go away. It is extremely cumbersome to change the treaty and doing that requires both determination and political finesse at the international level, while working within the system. This is beyond the reach of most individuals. The treaty's ineffectiveness and ultimate impotency are also a fact. The rarest of the rare, such as *P. rothschildianum*, are still being poached from within reserves and transported across international boundaries. New species reach the black market in Europe and Asia as soon as they are described and sometimes even before that event. And in the face of unstoppable human expansion, we will see the continual whittling away of wild slipper orchid populations that has nothing to do with trade.

For the handful of *Paphiopedilum* species for which there was justifiable concern, there is no question that up-listing was an appropriate action but for most of the other slipper orchid species there was little justification for the extreme step of up-listing the entire contents of both genera. In retrospect this was an unfortunate over-reaction.

There is no argument that, prior to up-listing, that enormous numbers of wild plants were being uprooted in the wild, perhaps not as many as claimed by TRAFFIC, but there were substantial numbers that had been taken. In August 1997, I was able to visit several localities in Malaysia that had been known as earlier collecting sites for slipper species, these included Penang Hill, Gunung Jerai and the Langkawi Islands. I found slipper orchids at each of the three sites mentioned. The Langkawi islands have *Paphiopedilum niveum* on nearly inaccessible cliffs and those did not look as if they had been over collected and there were many of these plants. At the former two sites, there were relatively few mature flowering sized plants but there were many new seedlings and the populations appeared to be growing. In particular, *Paphiopedilum callosum* var *sublaeve* appeared to be well on the way to recovery. In part the recovery is actually a response to CITES, because demand for those species is very low and export permits are not available. The *P. callosum* population's recovery was also assisted by restricting automobile access to that part of Gungung Jerai, where they grow. Were the plants still there because international demand for cheap wild plants of those species had been halted or was it the fact that they were in preserves which was the effective factor?

Halting international trade sometimes merely diverts plants into the domestic market and then, because they do not command high prices domestically, more plants will need to be collected to bring in the same monetary returns. This appears to be the case with regards the Chinese parvisepalum slipper orchids. The proper way to protect slipper orchid species is with enforced legislation at the national and not the international level. Without that no amount of international goodwill is going to impede illegal trade. The idea that because markets are in the developed countries that those developed countries need to regulate the trade (because one can not rely on the poorer countries to do it) smacks of both paternalism and condescension. I

have seen poorer countries such as Malawi and Zimbabwe and richer countries such as Malaysia and Costa Rica, effectively regulate their nature reserves. In addition, all governments are now aware of the potential fortunes locked away in the DNA of their native species and we will see increased efforts to protect those national treasures. And, if they were to choose not too save their native species, that would be unfortunate, but that is their choice. To think otherwise, harks back to the paternalism of colonial days, when European countries felt that they knew which were the important and correct ways of doing things. Fortunately, most of us have now evolved beyond those attitudes and have left them behind us. But there are still people in the conservation movement who believe that they, and only they, know what is best for the world.

Changing CITES

CITES is a fact of life and it will not go away. There have been several conferences and symposia by orchid growers and hobbyists to discuss the treaty and there is strong sentiment against it. At this point, all but the most naïve understand that CITES is here to stay. It has been possible, however, to change several of the provisions but one needs to work within the system and that requires acute political savvy. At this point the treaty has been changed to allow artificially propagated plants as Appendix II plants. Interpretation of this varies from country to country. Dry seed, pollen, seedlings in flask, or cut flowers are not subject to regulation in some countries. On the scientific side one needs to be able to exclude herbarium specimens from CITES regulation. If studies are ever done that demonstrate individual slipper orchid populations are large enough to support sustainable harvest then perhaps those individual species should be down listed. Certainly retaining them on Appendix I because Customs officials cannot determine the validity of the species is a fallacious argument. To be consistent with that argument, it should be noted that all *Paphiopedilum* and *Phragmipedium* hybrids, out of flower, cannot be differentiated from wild species and those are not tightly regulated. Slipper hybrids that are mass-produced in commercial trade, as cheap florist's pot plants, should be totally deregulated. This latter aim may be the easiest to accomplish, as there are now trials to deregulate some cacti as 'supermarket' pot plants. Any deregulation or lessening of restrictions, however, can only be accomplished by playing within the system and with finesse.

CHAPTER 11

The Amateur's Role in Orchid Conservation

Perhaps the most frequently asked question when I lecture on orchid conservation comes from the amateur hobbyist without resources. People approach me and ask "…but what can I do to help?" Obviously, they cannot go out and buy a tract of land to set up a preserve, nor can they go and change the laws of some foreign country, let alone their own, to slow down development of a particular region. Many people want to be able to do something significant about the problem, but feel impotent because they do not see how they can effect any major change.

There are several things one should remember if one contemplates joining the conservation fight. Hardly anything happens spontaneously. It takes an individual to set things in motion. Every grand achievement had to start with an idea. Some person had to sit down and at some place think "We need a dam", or "a giant suspension bridge!", "a city theater" or even "we need to conserve *Encyclia vitellina*". It takes more than one person to construct a dam or a theater, in fact, it takes a legion of people just to handle the bureaucracy, before one can even think about raising the money to start the project. Yet, individual people all over the world are conceiving and initiating projects right now. The worldwide movements to save whales and baby seals were started by concerned individuals, many of whom had no formal training in conservation. But, they had the ideas and the motivation. Ideas are cheap, but to be effective an idea has to be coupled to drive, motivation and leadership. Unfortunately, the last three commodities appear to be in short supply.

What can one small person, who lacks drive, motivation and leadership achieve, when all that he or she has going for them is a good heart? Few people single-handedly achieve anything. Most human activities involve many people, each doing a few small tasks. An ant cannot carry much more than a few grains of sand at a time but enough ants cooperating can build an ant city capable of housing millions of their species. The same is true with people. One needs to find an organization or group of people already at work on conservation projects. It is the combined strength of hundreds or thousands of people that has given the various conservation movements the ability to achieve their effectiveness. Join a big group like the North American *Nature Conservancy, Sierra Club* or the British *Fauna and Flora Preservation Society* – nearly every country of the world, whether an advanced superpower or a small developing country now has organizations that are interested in preserving and promoting their natural resources.

You say, "I want to save orchids", but all of the big societies that have been mentioned are only interested in saving habitats or marsh marigolds. No matter, orchids live in a variety of habitats and you can assume the role of the watchdog looking out for the local orchids. If the people in your group respect you, then there will come a time when they will listen, when YOU put forward the plan to save a *Sphagnum* bog filled with lady slipper orchids.

One of the major needs of all conservation groups is fundraising. There is never enough money to purchase a piece of land or fund some special project, all groups need people to go out and find money to cover the costs of their operations and projects. This requires little expertise and it is easy to get involved and be active in this aspect of conservation. It may be possible to earmark funds you raise or donate specifically for orchid conservation. While societies generally do not care to have strings attached to the gifts they receive few will turn down money. By requesting specific projects, you also alert the society to the fact that there are people who are interested, primarily, in saving orchids.

If you prefer to work within the narrow focus of orchid conservation, then confine your efforts to an orchid society. These plant-orientated groups occur at many levels from local societies, up to the national and international orchid societies. Write to their conservation committees and ask what they are doing and if you can help. In addition, you can play an important role at the grass roots level by helping to spread the word and to educate your orchid-growing friends. There is still an enormous amount of room for raising the consciousness of the lay public, about the plight of endangered species. This applies not only to orchids, but to other plants as well.

Local societies can play a very active part in promoting orchid conservation. They can do this in several different ways. The society can formally request that members do not trade with dealers who are suspected of smuggling and selling illegally obtained plants. They should request that members who go on orchid collecting trips minimize the numbers of wild plants that they collect. In the past, members of some Southern California Orchid Societies have partially financed expeditions to observe tropical orchids in the field, by bringing back large quantities of wild species and selling them. We feel that this is an inappropriate activity in this day and age and should be discouraged. However, there would be nothing wrong in sending an expedition funded by other activities of the society such as banquets, dances or auctions to collect orchid species specifically for nursery propagation and then selling propagated plants to the membership (you do, of course, need the correct permits before doing this).

As a group activity, a society can propagate and distribute rare species. But they may have to raise funds to support those activities. Sometimes it is possible to 'kill two birds with one stone'. For example, if some members have very rare species they might donate seedpods to the society. Young plants could be raised and sold to the membership, either to cover the costs or, if it produced a reasonable profit, to help pay for future endeavors. In this way, the rare species become disseminated and the process not only pays for itself but also makes a modest profit. The general society membership gains by having access to these rare materials.

Societies are a good forum for raising money for conservation. In the United States many societies have plant raffles at their monthly meetings. Frequently there are profits from sales booths at local flower shows, while admission ticket sales to orchid shows can leave a society with a handsome nest egg. In America, at least, most orchid societies are non-profit making, educational organizations that should not be sitting on too much accumulated wealth in the form of large bank accounts. The money can be put to good use promoting conservation. Donations clearly earmarked for conservation projects make both sides happy. The society feels that it is doing something worthwhile for posterity and the recipient organization obtains funds with which it can work.

However, it does take individuals to motivate and drive local societies. Somebody has to be prepared to take the initiative, do the work and monitor the progress. As long as one or two people in a group have the energy and the will to organize and make the rest of the society feel that they are participating in a worthwhile project, then others will usually pitch in and do their share as well. Most people would rather be led, than lead. It takes less energy. They still do their share of work but don't have to accept the responsibility. This is easy to understand and there is nothing wrong with that provided competent leaders exist and projects do not get lost in squabbles or petty politics.

I mentioned earlier that one might boycott unscrupulous dealers. In the opposite vein one should support those nurseries that are actively concerned with the propagation of rare and endangered orchid species. Most of these nurseries perform this service because of their love for the plants, rather than merely as a way to make a living. Actually it is far easier to make money in many other professions. Few people get rich from orchids. In fact families that make their real livings from other sources fund many of the renowned and famous large orchid firms. Most small orchid companies are the result of hobbies and avocations that have grown out of control. They are usually run by people who adore the plants and have devoted their lives to them. It takes more money to grow a species from a protocorm than to buy jungle-collected plants; thus the incentive to deal in jungle plants. However, jungle specimens are usually weaker than nursery raised stock; they often suffer from considerable root damage from which they must recover, and the plants are frequently subdivided into such small portions that it may take several years before they reach flowering size again. In addition, the quality of most flowers from jungle collected species is quite poor, only the exceptional clone is of 'award' quality.

Siblings that have been raised from the deliberate hybridization of two selected species parents tend to yield more and much higher quality offspring, than one would find in jungle collections. This has now been realized that to a certain extent in the United States, where more and more sibling crosses are being produced, that the resultant offspring receive more awards. Obviously, buying a greenhouse-raised plant also provides much more chance of cultural success for the hobbyist, because the plant is already surviving and growing in captivity. It is easier than trying to adjust and domesticate a wild plant. Also, from a conservation point of view, inhouse breeding of orchids must be encouraged. The best way to do this is to buy seedlings that have been raised in this manner, preferentially over jungle collected plants. Encourage your orchid-growing friends to do likewise.

Obviously there will be some times when one wants or needs jungle materials, especially if it is a rare, new or previously unknown species. Someone has to start somewhere and with jungle plants. But, there is no excuse for raping the forests to bring in these endangered species. Most orchid genera can now be mass-produced in captivity without much trouble. Let us look an example. *Encyclia vitellina*, is now endangered in its natural habitat in Mexico. It could easily be raised by the hundreds of thousands, either from seed or by the tissue culture of selected clones. I recently visited a well-known greenhouse and saw a bench holding about 5,000 recently collected jungle plants of *E. vitellina*. The proprietor, in one breath, bragged that this was probably the last collection that would be allowed of that species. And then he added that the plants were so inexpensive, only 50 cents a piece, that it did not matter if more than half died while he was adjusting them to his greenhouse conditions. That kind of attitude belongs in the Dark Ages, not at the beginning of the 21st century. Despite the fact that Mexico has laws banning exploitation of its native orchids, wild collected *E. vitellina* still appears in the nurseries in the United States.

Advertising jungle plants

We must de-glamorize the concept that there is something desirable about growing a plant which itself once grew in an exotic forest. This is where the everyday orchid grower can take a stand and influence events concerning orchid conservation. Most local societies have periodic newsletters to keep the membership abreast of events, lectures, shows, workshops, etc. Many of the newsletters carry advertisements for local orchid importers and nurseries. If the advertisers promote jungle-collected materials in their advertisements, get the society to request that those firms do not use the words 'jungle' or 'wild' collected in their advertising copy.

In addition, write to the editors of the big international and national orchid journals requesting that they reduce the emphasis on wild collected plants in their advertisements. If you do not get satisfaction then organize a 'write-in campaign' to get the editorial policy concerning advertisements changed. Explain to your friends what you hope to do and request that they also write a brief note of disapproval to the editors. We are not suggesting that journals should not advertise species, instead we are suggesting that they not advertise *Jungle Collected* plants. We would also encourage advertisements to contain the wording 'nursery propagated' if that is true. Nursery propagated implies an increase in the number of plants from an original stock and not merely the conversion of a jungle into a greenhouse plant by dividing the plant in half after it has reached the nursery. There are many reputable firms and very nice people who make a livelihood from selling jungle

collected plants. They see the above proposals, understandably, as a threat to their means of making a living. Unfortunately nature is not an infinite resource, if the wild populations are not harvested responsibly and sustainably, they will come to an end and we will all be the poorer. It is possible to switch over from selling jungle plants to artificially propagated as long as the buying public will be supportive. People no longer buy jungle-collected animals - it is just not done. The same attitude must develop about jungle collected plants.

The value of private collections

There is another very important role that the amateur orchid grower can play in the general conservation of orchid species. In the private collections of the world, both large and small, there resides a formidable resource in terms of the numbers and kinds of species that are grown. There is a tendency, especially in institutions, to discount the value of the plants that exist in private hands. A similar condition exists for plants about which no collection data are available. There is a trend for scientists to dismiss these plants, to consider them worthless. We believe that in the future such plants will become an extremely valuable resource and in many cases may represent the only surviving members of their species.

One of the most important things an individual can do is to set aside some space in their collection for species. Grow one less gaudy *Cattleya* hybrid or give away a large *Cymbidium* hybrid and replace it with a few pots containing species. Try not to choose the very colorful species but instead give a home to those plants that have less to offer. The humble ugly ducklings are the ones that need homes, the very spectacular species, are usually widespread in cultivation already. We find that even the small plants with 'insignificant' flowers tend to have special charms of their own. Friends brag about bringing to flower bulbophyllums, which sweet pea and chrysanthemum growers would consider as having little or no obvious "socially redeeming value".

Novices will exclaim ... "You mean that is an orchid?" As they gaze in wonder at some small brown flowered *Maxillaria*. This gives the grower a chance to enlighten the novice about the fine coconut pie scent of *M. tenuifolia* and display his or her erudition about finer points of the orchid family. It is curious that the orchid greenhorn is usually more impressed that very small plants with even tinier flowers can be orchids, than when presented with a ten inch *Cattleya* blossom that could only be worn by an exceptionally well endowed lady. While giant hybrids can generate awe, the smaller species can generate wonder and that is as fine a response.

The vast majority of orchid enthusiasts do prefer to grow hybrids. This is understandable; after all, hybrids are designed to flourish under artificial greenhouse or indoor conditions. They frequently have more spectacular flowers, greater vigor, ease of flowering, and often flower more than once a year. On the other hand, many hybrids will frequently have lost the grace and delicacy found in the 'wildlings'. Despite the growing popularity of species orchids, there is still a real need to incorporate more species into collections. For example, the little pleurothallids, of which there seem to be a zillion species, are not widely grown and their American forests are disappearing very rapidly. In Asia many of the small species of the *Sarcanthinae* (relatives of the genus *Vanda*), are almost unknown in cultivation. In contrast, there are a few genera where species, no matter how ugly or unattractive, are avidly sought. The Asian slipper orchids, the paphiopedilums, are a prime example where every species, no matter how unattractive, is in demand and plants are stripped out of the forests as rapidly as they are discovered. It was not unusual for a new slipper orchid species to appear in the market place in the tens of thousands.

Protecting your own species

Species in private hands must be afforded the same consideration that is given to an expensive treasure or a potentially valuable antique. Nature has lavished nearly a half of a billion years of evolution on the terrestrial plants and the wild species are the end product of an extremely rigorous selection procedure. They merit not only care and love but also respect for what they represent. Living collections of orchid plants that are maintained in temperate climates are very vulnerable, especially, in the winter. We suggest that all rare species should be tagged with a brightly colored label that is easy to see and a notice pinned on the greenhouse door such as "Rescue all *yellow* tagged plants first". The special plants need to be sign-posted and easily distinguishable. One cannot expect a stranger to hunt through an entire orchid collection on a gray winter's day, peering at faded labels while trying to decide which of some 500 plants are worth trying to rescue. Some societies in the U.K. already have rescue networks that come into operation if the owner meets with some unfortunate accident. (See Chapter 10, on 'The Barbara Everard Trust'.) However, if one goes on vacation and merely has a friend or neighbor looking after the collection for a few days, it would be worthwhile to alert them to particularly rare species. Make contingency plans about what should be done with plants in the case of a prolonged heating failure or similar disaster.

Demands for wild plants

While one encourages people to grow as many species as possible, it is important at the same time that the demand for jungle plants should not be excessive. A very large market for wild species will merely encourage illegal collecting and the resale of vulnerable species. This leads to a common dilemma. Illegally obtained plants are not going to be returned to the wild from whence they came. They will either end up in someone else's collection or linger on the shelf until they die. Why not buy them, give them the best of care and try to ensure their survival? However, if one purchases the plant, then one, in effect, rewards not only the importer and retailer but, in addition, all of the middle men down to the collector who originally may have illegally stripped them out of the forests.

Purchasing large numbers of species leads to a greater demand and eventually the total demise of the wild population. While some orchids are widespread, others are confined to local populations where every last plant can be collected. This has happened before in the past with *Paphiopedilum druryi* and *Phalaenopsis micholitzii*, to name only two from a vast legion.

There are many orchid dealers in the trade, who do not take seriously the notion that some orchid species are endangered, or if they believe it, they do not recognize that there is any need to conserve species in the wild. Perhaps to them all that is important is making a quick profit. Others see that the forests are going and the orchids will go too, so they may as well try and make a profit while the plants are still available. Most orchid species are not endangered. If one goes to a dealer, how does one know which were legally and which were illegally collected species? How does one decide that it is all right to purchase jungle plants of *Cattleya aurantiaca* but not *C. skinneri*? Can one be expected to know that *C. skinneri* is definitely an endangered species in the wilds of Central America, even if it is also one of the commonest *Cattleya* species in cultivation. The species itself has been bred in cultivation for some time and is readily available in several different forms and variants. It does not make sense to boycott that species unless the plants have been wild collected, but how is one to know? Ask the dealer about the origin of the plants. If they have been propagated in a nursery then by all means buy them. Species that are on CITES Appendix I should not be purchased unless they are nursery propagated. Others are fair game, but at all times buy nursery materials rather than jungle plants, if you can. Patronize firms that specialize in nursery grown and propagated stock. Make a point of deliberately asking dealers, if they carry nursery-grown materials. Say clearly that you prefer to buy that kind of plant. Dealers will not import large quantities of plants for which they feel there may only be a limited market. Can one believe the dealer? Maybe or maybe not, use your own judgement.

A pragmatic approach

What if you have been searching for a certain very rare species for years, either for your breeding program or to enhance your own collection and the only source is some orchid dealer with a relatively unsavory reputation? Furthermore, you suspect that the plants were obtained illegally. Should you buy the plant? In an ideal world one would say no! That would be rewarding the dealer and maybe further jeopardizing the survival of the plants left in the wild. On the other hand, the plants on the dealer's bench have already been collected. But if there is a market for the species then one might expect further forays to collect it again. However, the world is not ideal and the temptation can be very great.

If you feel that you absolutely have to have the species then buy it, better yet, buy *two*. Make a deal with yourself. Get the plant, but do something to help promote the survival of that species. Now you have a responsibility, you must grow the plant well, allow the orchid to flower and propagate it. I suggest you grow at least two different clones, because cross-pollinating them will usually produce more vigorous offspring than self-pollination will (see below). Furthermore, you should endeavor to distribute the seedlings widely. In effect I suggest that you salve your conscience by actively taking a hand in propagating that species. This is a pragmatic rather than an idealistic approach, but one that I believe can work, ultimately towards the good of the species. Most orchid people are not saints and it is hard to resist those rare beauties. At least, if the purchase is tied to the idea of propagation there is the assurance that the plant will be put to some good use.

Propagating species

The idea that widespread propagation and cultivation are a good way to ensure the conservation of plant species has been widely endorsed by many conservation leaders. However, the effort to build and assemble a large collection in cultivation is certainly no excuse to go out and plunder or otherwise destroy the wild populations.

People who want to propagate their orchid species sometimes have the mistaken idea that the best thing to do is to self-pollinate that species when it comes into flower and then grow on the seedlings. Unfortunately, seed from self-pollinated plants usually results in seedlings that tend to be weaker and show more aberrations than are normally found. In most species, nature has gone to great lengths to ensure that out crossing, between two different individuals, takes place. These species sibling crosses (mating between two different individuals of the same species) tend to produce offspring that are more vigorous than the results of self-pollination. Self-pollination should always be a last resort. Only self a plant if there is no other hope of getting pollen from another individual. It is relatively easy to create a small pollen bank and, in some species, pollen can be stored for extended periods. If you have a rare species that you want to propagate and you come across that species in bloom in another collection. Beg some pollen and store it until your plant comes into flower. Place some silica gel in a screw top jar and make a simple pollen bank. The pollen can be maintained in a twist of paper or gelatine capsule and the entire unit stored in a refrigerator (but not the freezer section). If you are scared that the pollen is no longer viable, then make a selfing as well as an out-crossing. Both pollens can be placed on a single stigma if necessary.

Support orchid societies in Third World countries

One indirect way of fostering orchid conservation is to support and subscribe to orchid society journals produced by developing world countries such as the India, Malaysia, Thailand, etc. If those journals and societies can be supported it can encourage local interest in their own native orchids. Those journals are ideal places to submit short articles on conservation that encourage the locals to get involved with saving, not exploiting, their local indigenous species. In some countries, such as South Africa, this is already evident. Aspiring orchid judges, who are usually primarily interested in hybrids, are expected to have a modicum of knowledge about their native African species. It would be ideal if developed as well as undeveloped countries followed suit.

Rescue operations

In tropical countries and even in some of the more temperate areas, amateurs can play a very important role in rescue operations. If they know which areas are to be destroyed, logged, burnt, cleared or flooded, then they can go into those areas and retrieve plants. These rescue operations are more effective when epiphytes need to be rescued, as many of the terrestrial species seem to be very difficult to transplant. In several countries like

Brazil and South Africa, rescue operations have become routine practice. Their local groups are well organized and will sometimes even be contacted by the authorities before the area is cleared. In other countries, where rescue operations have not been attempted before, the bureaucratic hassles and red tape can be very arduous, but if one perseveres each operation will become easier and easier. The local press, which is usually very sympathetic towards rescue operations, tends also to give rescue operations prominence in the news. It is usually easier for societies, rather than individuals to get permission to carry out rescue operations. Sometimes it will be mandated that plants should be given to Botanic Gardens, although rescued plants are not always welcomed by institutions. These organizations may feel that they want to select the plants and species to which they have to devote scarce resources.

There is almost no data on the effectiveness of rescue operations. This, however, should not deter one. A single surviving plant from a rescue operation is better than the loss of every plant. We certainly know of cases in South Africa, where there have been successful rescues of species like *Bonatea cassidea*, but unsuccessful rescues of various *Satyrium* species.

One should mention that the rates of deforestation are so great that rescue attempts in the tropics could only save the smallest fraction of the plants that are doomed.

Orchid societies have had some heartwarming successes. In Brazil, an orchid-rich area (especially *Laelia purpurata*) near Persepolis was slated for clearance to make way for a multimillion-dollar hotel complex. Members of the local orchid society banded together and fought to save the forests from the developers. After a fierce battle the members of the society were successful and an alternate site for the hotel was found. We applaud the society's initial efforts. Concerned people can make a difference. Unfortunately, conservation takes eternal vigilance, because, following their success, the *L. purpurata* site was neglected for a while and a subsequent visit to the site disclosed that it had been turned into a garbage dump (R. Agnes, personal communication).

Real examples of conservation activities

Below are some actual activities that have been initiated by amateur orchid societies or small groups of concerned individuals that are directly related to orchid conservation. They show the range of options that are available and what can be achieved with a little initiative. This is only a small sample. Your potential achievements are only limited by your imagination.

The Greater New York Orchid Society

This is one of the major orchid societies in the United States and is responsible for staging a wonderful annual orchid show, just before Easter in the World Trade Center. The society has a formal meeting each month. In 1997, the society set up a Conservation Committee, which administers its conservation fund. So far the projects have been primarily of an educational nature and the committee looks for groups that already have a proven track record. The money is earmarked for uses that might have a long lasting effect. One project that they funded was the 'Children's Rainforest Alliance', which educates schoolchildren in Costa Rica about the environment. In this case the money was allotted to help with the purchase of computers that could be use in their educational programs. The Society raises money in several different ways. They solicit donations at their show and at the time of membership renewal. In addition they sell reproductions of a poster (commissioned especially for fundraising) and gift cards, illustrated with photographs of orchids. The profits from these sales go towards the fund. Society members donate plants, which are auctioned. The committee also creates an educational display about orchid conservation for the main show. It attracts a good deal of attention and helps to educate the visiting public.

San Diego County Orchid Society

One of the strongest orchid societies in the United States, the San Diego County Orchid Society has been involved with a large variety of conservation projects over the last 15 years. During this time they have raised over $64,000 for a wide variety of conservation projects in countries ranging from Australia to Peru.

The *Paphiopedilum sanderianum* study

Paphiopedilum sanderianum is a fabled orchid with the longest petals of any flowering plant. It grows on the island of Borneo and was thought to be very rare. There is a great demand for this species and despite being listed on CITES Appendix I (see chapters 9 and 10) there is still illegal trade in jungle collected plants. In addition farming and deforestation threaten plants outside of the Mulu National Park, in Sabah. The actual state of the species in the wild is not very well understood. There could be millions of plants left in the wild or only a few hundred. Two young people, Terre Rogers and Greer Bohan, decided that they wanted to study the plants in the wild. They found an eco-tour group that was going to Borneo to visit at least one of the *P. sanderianum* sites. But what could they do that might be meaningful during their short visit to the site? Realizing their lack of expertise they approached an ecologist from a nearby university and asked for some ideas. A simple exercise was set up for them to do a demographic survey of the populations they might visit and also assess how successful plants were at setting seed capsules. They did this and discovered that the populations they visited only contained relatively few plants that were of mature flowering size, but that over 30% of the orchids produced seedpods. This was interesting because so little data exist for wild paphiopedilums and the success rate was surprisingly high. During their trip they made friends with some of the guides and decided that they needed to return for a follow-up study. Now there was a problem, because they had used up their funds.

They talked about their trip to friends, other orchid growers and a few societies. One society made a donation towards the expenses for a second trip, which could be carried out on their own and without the encumbrance of a tour group. But the donation was not enough. One friend decided to donate flasks of seedlings that could be sold and part of the proceeds donated for the study. That friend persuaded a firm that sold flasks of seedlings, to list her flasks and advertise them as supporting the *P. sanderianum* study. This raised nearly half of the funds needed. A small group of friends in Detroit decided to help out. They made divisions of many of their orchid plants and held an orchid plant 'garage sale'. The proceeds were given to the pair for their study. Thus several people independently ended up contributing to the success of the study. On their second trip Terre and Greer revisited the old sites from the first trip and found several new sites. More importantly they were able to interest local people in their project and found that they were open to ideas about protecting their own plants and embraced the principles of biodiversity conservation.

Verloren Vallei

Not all of the orchid reserves must be forested lands. There is a high valley system in the northeastern part of South Africa, which is the nesting site for the rare and endangered wattled crane. This is a large elegant bird with only a few nesting sites. A preserve called Verloren Vallei (which means Lost Valley) was set up for the crane and other birds. Verloren Vallei is an area of higher altitude rolling hills (over 2000 m) and shallow valleys. The area is dominated by a grassy landscape, traversed by bogs and small rivulets. The hills are rocky.

50.   Verloren Vallei, a high altitude grassland preserve in South Africa. This preserve is a Crane sanctuary but also serves to protect a large number of terrestrial orchid species.

Among the grasses is a rich flora of unusual flowers including over 50 taxa of species, subspecies and varieties. Among these are some fine species, such as *Disa cooperi*, which can carry up to 50 creamy-white flowers and *D. chrysostachya* which flaunts its 30 cm spikes of brilliant orange flowers, standing above the grass like so many orange popsicles. Over the years a group of amateur orchid enthusiasts have visited the reserve on a regular basis, making notes on when populations of various orchid species are in flower, as well as the approximate number of plants that are in flower. One aspect of their work is incidental, but of vital importance to the well being of the orchids. When visits were started to the reserve the major emphasis was on the birds and mammals that lived under its protection. The Ranger and his staff were not interested in the plants. But the continuous and regular visits by the orchidists have imbued the ranger with awareness for those plants and their importance as organisms to be conserved has been recognized. They are no longer merely part of the greenery.

51. *Eulophia foliosa*, growing in Verloren Vallei.

52. *Disa chrysostachya*, growing in Verloren Vallei.

Sikkim Slipper Orchids

Nearly 40 years ago, Keshab C. Pradhan rediscovered a delightful slipper orchid called *Paphiopedilum fairrieanum*, growing in southern Sikkim. This is one of the most graceful of all of the slipper orchids and one that always captures the attention of enthusiasts. The species, which used to grow in some quantity, is now reduced to remnants that persist in rocky areas that local orchid collectors find difficult to reach. Plants were dug up and sold to residents of Namchi, as garden plants. The remaining orchids are now on government forested lands, while other plants persist on adjacent private lands (usually cardamon farms).

Mr. Pradhan, is the Chairman of the Sikkim Development Foundation, which is involved in an ecotourism project at the village level. They aim to use local people at a project to promote both tourism and help save the slipper orchid. Under Pradhan's direction a survey of the remaining plants is being made. But they are not satisfied with that, they also plan to artificially propagate the species and reintroduce it back into areas where it once flourished. This will involve a number of organizations and individuals. For example they propose to use local rock climbers, from the nearby Institute of Mountaineering at Darjeeling, to replant the species in nearly 'inaccessible' rock crevices. Once plants are re-established he proposes to form a 'protection force' from local village people to oversee the plantings. Some of the plantings would be available as tour sites for visitors. Finally he champions the formation of an orchid interpretative center, whose aim will be to educate both the local population and visitors.

This is an ambitious scheme but there is no reason why it should not work, especially as it involves the local people. It is an excellent example of orchid conservation activity at the grassroots level and is a template that can be followed by others in many different parts of the world.

Getting involved

In this chapter we have discussed several ways and given examples of how individuals can get involved with orchid conservation activities. Perhaps the easiest of these is to put together an educational poster for display at your local society's next orchid show. If you live in the United States, things have been made easier for you because the Conservation Committee of the American Orchid Society has already prepared such a poster that can be individualized for particular regions of the country. All you need to do is contact them to borrow the display. But there is no reason why you should stop at that. Start a study group, help raise funds for projects, educate yourself and get involved.

CHAPTER 12

Conservation and Commercialism

There is a tendency to blame much of the current threat to species on overexploitation by commercial orchid hunters. In part, this is still a carryover from the last century, when European orchid collectors and their firms publicized the size of the shipments being imported.

The great firm of Sanders had an enormous number of collectors scattered through the tropics. Their primary responsibility was not only to find exceptional new orchid species, but also to procure them in sufficient

quantities that enough could survive the long trip back to Europe, where they would be profitably sold. At one stage the famous nursery actually had a railway siding built to bring trainloads of plants directly to its greenhouses. There are several reports of consignments with thousands of plants being lost on route to the ports or at sea. Intense rivalry between firms led to competition for plants, not only by keeping localities secret but also by deliberately misleading competitors. Thousands of trees were cut down to provide orchids for individual shipments. Advertisements in the *Gardeners' Chronicle* in the late 1800s clearly demonstrate the extent and excesses of wild orchid collecting, to satisfy the English market. In the first three-quarters of the 20th century orchid collectors were seen as colorful, brave and heroic characters and the stories of how important orchids

53.   The warehouse at the MacRorie McLaren Co., in San Francisco. This was a single shipment of *Phalaenopsis sp.*, probably *P. schilleriana* from the Philippines, being unpacked. (Photo credit: Los Angeles Times).

54. Two clones of *Paphiopedilum helenae*, flowering in Taiwan. This species was described from North Vietnam. Since then many of the localities have been stripped and plants were sold on the black market around the world. This species has since been artificially propagated.

were discovered became legends (Richter, 1965). However, in the light of current thought, most of the commercial collectors are seen as fortune hunters, 'eco-pirates', who pillaged the forests. While they may have been brave explorers, in one sense, these men probably gave little thought to the effects of their depredations on the ecosystems that they were ravaging. The forests may have seemed limitless then, but they did complain about the efforts to find new sources once an area was plundered. They were also aware of how small a percentage of their spoils made it back alive to the auction houses and nurseries.

Jungle vs. established plants

Initially in the history of the orchid trade, enormous numbers of wild collected plants were shipped to orchid growing countries. In the effort to establish the plants in cultivation many died either en route or during the initial stages of establishment. The situation was not helped by the fact that prices were usually based on quantity, not quality of the imported plants and large plants were usually fragmented into smaller pieces. Even today it is not uncommon to see newly imported South American species broken into one or two pseudobulbs. Unfortunately, growers will buy these remnants, especially if they are rare and desirable, even though they know that most of them are destined to die. Even when large jungle plants are imported a large percentage of the imported plants will still fail to sur-

vive. When one considers the shock of uprooting, desiccation, time in transit and attempted re-establishment under conditions far different from where the plant originally grew it is not surprising that there is a high mortality rate. In the old days there were often delays caused by slow sea travel. That has been corrected now with the advent of rapid air travel, nevertheless, other conditions still shock the plant. Major problems with re-establishing the plants are caused by root damage, particularly when the plants are torn off trees during their active growth cycles, or if they are moved when the season's growth is only partially matured.

In an effort to ameliorate the high mortality, major efforts have been made to discourage the importation of plants directly from the jungle. Plants that are re-established prior to importation should stand a better chance of surviving the journey to their new homes. This resulted in bans on the sale of obvious jungle collected orchids at orchid shows, where traditionally orchid sellers gather. In addition, most orchid growing countries also ban the display of flowering pieces of jungle plants. In addition, a few countries have total bans on the importation of jungle collected species. The idea has been to promote the artificial propagation of species with the hope of achieving two goals. In the first, one would obtain plants that were well established and secondly, artificial propagation should relieve pressures on the wild stock. This would be true if artificial propagation really meant growing plants from seed or tissue culture, but it can also be legally interpreted to mean increasing the number of plants by asexual methods, such as by means of cuttings or division. Once jungle plants have been brought into the nursery they can be grown for several months and then marketed as artificially propagated. I have seen jungle plants languishing in nurseries in Southeast Asia waiting for the initial die off while they are being established and before they can be sold. It is not unusual to see South American phragmipediums, recently imported from the jungle, declared 'artificially propagated', where they have merely been chopped into small pieces.

Promotion of established plants may be great for gardeners but in reality it does nothing for conservation. It does not reduce the pressures on the wild populations – it merely changes the locality where many of the plants will die. An acceptable exception to this are the rare cases where salvage is allowed and the survivors can then be admitted into commerce. But this, like the situation above, greatly depends on the honesty of the grower. Countries are scared that licensed salvagers will turn to illegal pillage and, for this reason, it is often difficult to get nursery licenses.

CATTLEYA TRIANÆ.—CATTLEYA TRIANÆ.

THE TRUE IBAQUE VARIETY.

HUGH LOW & CO.

Have pleasure in notifying arrival, per R.M.S. *Don*, of a further importation of the above in simply PERFECTION of condition. The plants are of good size, and especially well-leaved. In fact, they could not have reached us in better order. Also

ODONTOGLOSSUM CRISPUM ALEXANDRÆ,

FROM THE BEST PACHO DISTRICTS.

This importation is, without doubt, the GRANDEST we have ever received—bulbs being perfectly sound, and truly THE PLANTS COULD NOT BE FINER. NOT FIVE PER CENT. DEAD!

CLAPTON NURSERY, LONDON, N.E.

ENORMOUS SALE, BY ORDER OF

Fred. HORSMAN & CO., Colchester & Marks Tey.

ABOUT 1000 GRAND MASSES OF ODONTOGLOSSUM CRISPUM,

Collected by the famous Odontoglossum hunter, Mr. CARDER, and guaranteed by us to be of the true PACHO TYPE. Among them will be found masses with upwards of FORTY LARGE BULBS.

FOR FURTHER PARTICULARS SEE CATALOGUE.

THE ABOVE will be SOLD at PROTHEROE AND MORRIS'S SALE ROOMS, 67 and 68, Cheapside, London, E.C., on TUESDAY, FEBRUARY 19, 1895. (*Please note date*).

ENORMOUS SALE — WITHOUT RESERVE,

BY ORDER OF

Fred. HORSMAN & CO., COLCHESTER.

OVER 1000 GRAND MASSES OF LÆLIA PURPURATA

FROM A NEW DISTRICT.

Among them will be found huge masses with upwards of 200 well-leaved bulbs, measuring from the tip of the leaf to the base of bulb 34 inches. Also grand masses of

The rare DENDROBIUM ALBUM (AQUEUM),

CATTLEYA LEOPOLDII,	CATTLEYA AMETHYSTINA,
CATTLEYA HARRISONIÆ,	ONCIDIUM CRISPUM, &c., &c.

CASES of LÆLIA HARPOPHYLLA, LÆLIA PURPURATA, CATTLEYA HARRISONIÆ VIOLACEA, LÆLIA DORMANIANA, CATTLEYA LEOPOLDII, MILTONIA CUNEATA MAJUS, &c.,

Will be Sold without the Slightest Reserve.

FOR FURTHER PARTICULARS SEE CATALOGUE.

The whole Consignment is offered WITHOUT RESERVE, at

PROTHEROE & MORRIS'S SALE ROOMS

67 & 68, CHEAPSIDE, LONDON, E.C., on FRIDAY, FEB. 1, 1895.

(PLEASE NOTE DATE.)

55 Advertisements from the *Gardeners' Chronicle*, 1895, advertising new shipments of jungle-collected orchids.

56   *Laelia purpurata*, once widespread, this popular
      species' populations have been decimated by over-
      collecting, deforestation and development along the
      Atlantic coast of Brazil (photo: Roberto Agnes).

57   *Laelia purpurata* 'Twin Peaks' HCC/AOS shows the
      allure of this species that made it so desirable in
      the late 19th century.

Modern orchid growers

The great majority of orchid plants in the trade today are hybrids. These often trace their pedigree back through many generations and are very far removed from the jungle species. Hybrids are usually easier to grow than the species and usually have larger and more colorful flowers; it is easy to understand their popularity over species. There are, however, many people who are attracted to the species and this creates a market, albeit relatively small, for species. The majority of orchid nurseries offer artificially bred species orchids from time to time, and there are also some nurseries where propagated species are their mainstay. These account, however, for a small part of the general orchid market.

Native growers

One recurring theme that appears to surface from time to time is the idea of using native people to grow and sell the orchids from their own region. At first glance this seems to be quite sensible. The native orchids of a region are already pre-adapted to the local growing conditions and they should therefore be easy to grow. This sort of cottage industry allows the local people to directly profit from their natural resources and should also instill a protective appreciation for their own native biodiversity. The main source of the plants could be from salvage and thus the project would be a way of both saving and profiting from plants that would otherwise simply be fated to die.

Very few, if any of these plans have succeeded. Why that should be is fairly simple. It is very difficult to produce plants that are equal in quality to the nursery plants to which customers in major consumer countries have become accustomed. The areas where plants occur are also the sites where their natural enemies are at home. The phyto-chemicals needed to protect plants are often too expensive for the local people to afford. In addition, there is little demand for the majority of orchid species that are obscure and have small or indifferent flowers. Because of the bureaucratic requirements of obtaining CITES and general nursery permits it is difficult to move the 'cottage industry' plants to markets in other countries. There is usually insufficient demand for their products in their own home countries. This is not strictly true of some of the more spectacular orchids such as *Cattleya skinneri* in Costa Rica, *Cattleya maxima* in Ecuador, *Paphiopedilum armeniacum* or *Paphiopedilum micranthum* in China. Those species do find local markets in their home countries at modest prices but this does not hold for the smaller species with more subdued flowers.

In major orchid countries such as Brazil, there is a steady market for the better forms of their own large flowered species, such as *Laelia purpurata* or *Cattleya labiata*. These can command very high prices and attract the attention of wealthy hobbyists.

In a few other countries, small export nurseries have been set up, but these usually cater for the North American hobbyist markets. These nurseries tend to move relatively small quantities of choice and often relatively obscure species, which command higher prices, than they would have earned in their native countries.

The Chiapas Plan

More than 25 years ago an ambitious scheme was initiated in southern Mexico to try and halt both logging and promote the conservation of local orchids (Withner, 1977). 'The Plan Chiapas' originated with Walter Hartman, who was then the Technical Coordinator for the Council for the Protection of Nature in the State of Chiapas. The plan included an extensive education program for the local schools and, in cooperation with local government, all logging was to cease. Alternative methods of agriculture to the traditional slash and burn techniques were publicized. Local people were encouraged to grow their local orchids for sale to individuals, institutions and nurseries, thus obtaining some financial incentive as a reward for promulgating their concerns about conservation.

Unfortunately, after the initial burst of enthusiasm the plan appears to have faded away and little has been heard about it in subsequent years. The initial optimism has been replaced by indifference. While there are some orchid nurseries in the Chiapas area, the cottage industry that was so hoped for never amounted to much and land conversion has continued (Withner, personal communication).

Orchid species and current trade

The United Kingdom prohibits the importation of jungle or wild collected orchid plants and most of the amateur and commercial orchid growers must rely on artificially propagated stock, if they wish to grow species instead of hybrids. This is not true for most of the rest of the world and there is still substantial trade in wild species. Europe and in particular, Holland and Germany, provide ready markets for orchids extracted from the wild. North America is another major sinkhole for jungle material and there are numerous importers. Recent publicity about the plight of wild species seems to have made them even more attractive and there is a

58   Wild collected plants of *Angaecum magdalenae* – offered for sale in a Malagasy market.

growing North American appetite for wild species. Increasing sophistication of the orchid growing public has also produced a more ready acceptance of small plants with tiny insignificant flowers. Such plants are now being deemed cute or "precious".

Conservationists have brought pressure to bear on countries such as Thailand and India, (which were major sources of jungle orchids) and this has had some affect on curtailing trade. Other poorer countries, such as Madagascar, Ecuador and Indonesia, see trade in their wild species (both animals and plants) as important sources of foreign revenue and appear reluctant to restrict it.

Following recent developments among conservation bodies concerning 'sustainable harvests' there appears now to be more of a readiness to trade in wild species. Major concerns are that so-called sustainable levels in fact may not be sustainable after all and are no more than an excuse to go out and over collect to the point of endangerment. But then, these arguments must be balanced against the cold facts that forests and other areas outside of preserves are still being destroyed at steady rates and will continue to be converted to other uses whether or not the orchids on them eventually end up in commerce.

Artificial propagation?

The relative ease of artificial propagation of many orchid species has encouraged some countries to permit the export of their orchid species, provided they have been artificially propagated. This is particularly true of some South American countries, as well as India and Thailand. When most orchid growers think about artificial propagation they envisage a laboratory where orchids are propagated from seeds, embryos or meristems, using sterile tissue culture procedures. Artificial propagation, however, also refers to vegetative division of, or taking cuttings from, large mature plants. Thus, in reality, a jungle plant that has been divided into three or four pieces with a pocketknife is considered to have been artificially propagated.

For a few years India banned the export of wild orchid species, but then trade reopened (although this was supposedly only for artificially propagated species). Examination of offerings in catalogs shortly after the resumption of export trade once again listed many obscure as well as famous species. One list included *Paphiopedilum fairrieanum*, with plants being priced in quantities of one thousand. It is feasible that those could have been artificially produced. However, a blatant accompanying paragraph informed the customer that if that species was bought it would be shipped under a false name to avoid problems with CITES. This definitely calls their propriety into question.

During the summer of 1998, an acquaintance visited orchid nurseries in a northern district of India. This part of the country is renowned for its orchid nurseries. My friend carefully arranged to visit the nurseries on weekends when the proprietors were away and only maintenance staff present. He then ingratiated himself with the staff. At every nursery the staff admitted that the plants for sale were jungle collected and that their 'artificial propagation' was merely a sham. This situation is likely to be repeated in almost every tropical country that sells 'artificially propagated' orchid species.

Government exploitation

Small Third World, developing countries sometimes look at their orchids as a source of foreign revenue. This was the situation in Vietnam during the early 1990s. The Vietnamese government approached certain Japanese plantsmen for advice on how their native orchids could be turned into hard cash. The major orchid species for which Vietnam was renowned was the pink slipper orchid, *Paphiopedilum delenatii*. At that time the species was thought to be extinct, but, if it still existed, it might be a considerable source of income. The plant was rediscovered and found growing in enormous numbers. A special government nursery was set up to hold and establish the plants. At one stage it held at least 40,000 potted individuals. But the species was on Appendix I of CITES and most of the potential market countries were signatories of CITES, which forbade trade in any jungle collected plants of

any *Paphiopedilum* species. In the end, enormous numbers of the plants were sold cheaply to Taiwan whose international status precluded it from being a CITES signatory. Even at the cut price rates the dollars earned by Vietnam were probably useful.

In recent years Dominica has also looked to its native orchids as a potential source of income. Here trade is straightforward as Dominican orchid species are only listed in CITES Appendix II and thus perfectly acceptable for international commerce.

Ecotourism

One of the ways that governments cash in on their native orchids is through ecotourism. Seeing orchids in the wild brings with it a thrill that all plant lovers, irrespective of their biases, seem to enjoy. It is surprising how many photographs of orchid flowers feature on travel brochures and in advertisements.

Many countries now earn substantial income from tourists arriving to enjoy their natural wonders. This has, in turn, made many other governments sensitive to issues of biodiversity and conservation. They have become aware of the foreign revenue that can be earned from maintaining intact forest ecosystems. Still, unless there is spectacular scenery or there are exceptionally charismatic animals it can be difficult to attract sufficient interest to an area. An interesting example is Mt. Kinabalu, which is home to the orangutan. These large apes tend to be solitary and shy animals and tourists do not usually see them in the wild areas of the park. After a day or two stalking through the forests the tourists are usually ready to move on to greener pastures. At Kinabalu, an effort was made to retain the visitors by building a golf course on Pinosuk Plateau, within the boundaries of the park. Unfortunately in doing so they destroyed the habitat of one of the parks rare slipper orchid species; so much for orchid conservation in national parks.

The countries that appear to have been quite successful in attracting ecotourists are Costa Rica, Brazil, Madagascar, Malaysian Borneo, Kenya and South Africa. While many of these countries have a fine range of orchid species, the orchid flowers are merely incidental. The major attractions are still the birds and animals. Most tourists are unaware of the orchids, other than as pretty flowers decorating the brochures. They will, however, respond positively if such plants are pointed out to them.

Ecotourism can be a double-edged sword. If it is too successful there may be sufficient traffic to damage or disrupt fragile ecosystems. Even if the visitors are confined to special paths or walkways, one often notices that wild orchid plants are rarer close to those areas that are used by the tourists. This suggests that the plants are gradually stripped and that populations are eroded in those areas where access is easy.

Species saved by commercialization

Up until this point most of the commentary has been on the negative aspects of commercialism but in fact there are also many examples of how orchid businesses have played a major role in alleviating collecting pressures on wild plants. There have also been several instances where species have been saved from extinction. There are some famous cases of species where commercial propagation has been very effective.

Epidendrum ilense: This is an unusual reed-stemmed species from Ecuador, which has a pendant terminal truss of ivory colored flowers. The lip of the flower bears long pale filaments. Only a few plants were ever found and the species was thought to be extinct in the wild. Initially the species was propagated at Selby Botanical Gardens in Sarasota, Florida. This is a small Botanic Garden, but it is world renowned for its focus on tropical plants. At one stage the garden had a micro-propagation laboratory and it was here that the species was taken. Small plantlets were sold to the orchid growing public and from there it spread into general cultivation. It has persisted in cultivation and the trade, despite not being very showy, and most growers realize the threatened status of the species. This was one of the first species successfully marketed as artificially propagated while being thought to be extinct in the wild. More individual plants now exist in collections than those few that still struggle to exist in the wild.

Phragmipedium besseae: A brilliant scarlet slipper orchid, this species created an enormous fuss when first discovered. It was thought to be exceptionally rare and the Selby Gardens auctioned off the first few plants brought into cultivation, under sealed bid. Only one of the original plants is known to have survived and it did not play an important role in subsequent events. Originally the species was recorded from Tarapoto, Peru. Later on reasonable quantities of additional plants were found in Ecuador. Some of the latter were brought to Europe and also offered in the United States. Plants were sold for about US$600 for small divisions. A few plants ended up at the 'Orchid Zone Nursery', a large wholesale orchid-propagating nursery near Salinas, California. Using their few initial stock plants they were

able to develop propagation techniques into a fine art and could flower the species in 18 months from seed. Within a few years they were able to mass produce the species by the thousand and flowering plants could be offered wholesale at a mere $15 each. The vigorous, nursery-bred stock was more desirable than the jungle plants and they therefore reduced collecting pressure on the remaining wild populations.

Paphiopedilum rothschildianum: This magnificent species only occurs in a small population on Mt. Kinabalu in Borneo, and its story has been discussed in other chapters of this book. This was always one of the higher priced orchids, easily fetching prices in the thousands of dollars for the few divisions available, and there were many attempts to propagate the species from seed. Most of the early attempts appeared to involve self-pollinating whichever clone was in flower and the resultant seedlings were weak and slow to mature. In the early 1980s cross-pollination resulted in more vigorously growing seedlings. Robert Jones of 'Hanes and Madonna Orchids' in California first marketed these. Jack Tonkin and his wife, running a small slipper orchid nursery, also made a similar cross but they grew all of their seedlings to flowering size. When they first flowered it was an amazing sight as the bench in their greenhouse contained several thousand flowering plants. This was probably more than grew wild on Mt. Kinabalu. Plants from 'Tonkin's Orchids' made their way into collections all over the world. Suddenly there were large numbers of this species available. Priced at $10 an inch across the longest two leaves, while cheaper than before, were still expensive. However, they were strongly growing, did not suffer from transplantation shock following division and now available to anyone who could get sufficient money together. Most of the plants went to other commercial growers who in turn made crosses between their plants of P. rothschildianum. Since then, culture methods have improved considerably and the long wait between seed and flowering has been reduced from nearly ten years down to five. In 1998 'Tokyo Orchids' were selling hundreds of artificially produced flowering plants of P. rothschildianum at a couple of hundred dollars each. One expects the price to drop even further. There are over 80 other species of *Paphiopedilum* and nearly all of them are actively and artificially propagated.

Mexipedium xerophyticum: This is a most unusual slipper orchid that was discovered as recently as 1988 in a secret location in Mexico (Ledoux, 1996). Only seven plants were originally found and small pieces of some of them taken back to Mexico City where they were described in 1990. Pieces of two clones were sent to the United States under a special dispensation called a Scientific CITES (this is used for exchanging accessioned specimens between institutions). The plants in the United States prospered. Seed was made available to commercial businesses and, following selfings and crossings between the two original clones; thousands of the plants now exist all over the world. Even the two original clones, themselves, have been divided many times and distributed to orchid growers and commercial companies. The continuance of the species seems to be assured. This is one of the clearest success stories of *ex situ* conservation.

Commercial companies

There are many commercial ventures in the world, that are responsible, have concerns for the future of orchids and do their bit to legitimately propagate species. Some of these firms will be highlighted here but the reader should be aware that this is merely a small sample and based upon the author's own experiences.

J & L Orchids

In Connecticut, there is a small orchid nursery run by three ladies, Cordelia Head, Margaret Webb and Lucinda Winn. The firm specializes in rare species and sells artificially propagated orchids. Although small, it has a worldwide reputation for the propagation of unusual species, particularly those of the pleurothallid alliance. Cordelia is active on many of the conservation committees and bodies involved with conservation around the world. We will focus on this nursery here and examine the role it has played in the propagation of some rare species. What follows is a small selection from the many plants that they have mass-produced and introduced.

a. Masdevallia datura: Rather an unusual *Masdevallia* species, this plant bears enormous white trumpets that superficially resemble the flowers of jimsonweed. Carlyle Leuer, a famous pleurothallid taxonomist, discovered it on a single tree in Bolivia. He named the species in 1983 and brought a very few plants back with him to the United States, distributing them among a small number of commercial nurseries. Among the nurseries was the firm of 'J & L Orchids', which specializes in small botanicals. Here and at the other nurseries, plants were selfed and seedlings produced. The species has never been plentiful in cultivation but gradually people have been able to acquire divisions or seedlings and,

by now, several generations of the seedlings have been produced. The species is thought to be extinct in the wild because a second expedition to the site found that the original forest habitat had been destroyed. The single tree was gone and, despite several attempts to locate it again, the species has never been refound. The species persists in cultivation.

b. Masdevallia exquisita: Much smaller than *M. datura*, *M. exquisita* bears small white flowers with a contrasting purple throat and long golden tails at the tips of the sepals. This species is also from Bolivia and was also named by Dr. Leuer. On this occasion he returned with three plants of the new species. One was pressed to make the 'type' herbarium specimen. Of the remaining two plants, one was given to the commercial firm of J & L Orchids and the other to Phil and Ann Jesup, well known amateur enthusiasts. As the story goes, both plants flowered for the first time at the same time. A meeting was set halfway between the two growing ranges. There on the back seat of an automobile a fruitful union between the two plants was consummated. J & L grew the resulting seedlings and many hundreds of plants were produced. The situation of this species in the wild is unknown but it appears to be safe primarily because of the trade.

c. Epidendrum melanoporphyreum: Cordelia Head, of J & L Orchids, discovered this species in Peru and returned with a single individual that appears to be self-sterile and does not make seed pods when self-pollinated. It is an unusual species with reddish leaves and intense reddish-black flowers. A second trip to Peru to find a mate failed to produce any other plants of the species, but a piece of the original plant was sold to 'H & R Nurseries' in Hawaii who put it into tissue culture and were able to mass-produce it. For the moment the species appears to have been pushed away from the brink but it is not really safe. Plants produced by tissue culture are normally genetically identical. Unless plants still exist in the wild the evolutionary history of this species has come to an end. Yet the species continues in a fashion thanks to its commercial value.

d. Oncidium viperinum: *Oncidium viperinum* is another plant that has been preserved by tissue culture. Despite many attempts this *Oncidium* species refuses to set seed after self-pollination, and there appear to be no other clones in cultivation. Like *Epidendrum melanophporphyreum* this species is maintained in cultivation by using the rapid multiplication techniques of tissue culture.

e. Dendrobium cuthbertsonii: J & L Orchids were also the first to propagate *Dendrobium cuthbertsonii* from seed. This is a highly desirable species with brilliantly colored long lasting flowers (up to 10 months) on dwarf plants. For years no one seemed able to germinate the seed and divisions of the original importations were much sought after and quite expensive. Now everyone seems to be able to grow these gems from seed and prices have dropped substantially. The species has become quite common in cultivation. In the United States this was almost solely due to captive propagation, although wild plants are said to have been imported into Holland.

Cal Orchids

This nursery is situated in Santa Barbara, Southern California and carries a mixed range of hybrids and species. James Rose and his wife Lauris have a special commitment to species and have propagated a variety of them, including many of the more obscure African orchids, such as *Aerangis* and *Polystachya* species. The firm has been joined by Ned Nash, who has a great understanding of CITES and conservation problems and represents the American Orchid Society in that regard.

Hoosier Orchid Company

The Hoosier Orchid Company works out of Indianapolis, Indiana. They have a unique program where anyone is encouraged to send orchid species seed to them. The seed is cultured and the original provider receives either a flask or community pot of seedlings depending of their preference. The president of the company is William A. Rhodehamel who chaired the Conservation Committee of the American Orchid Society for many years. He and his staff are committed to the conservation of wild orchid species, but they also appreciate the role that *ex situ* commercial production can play. They see *ex situ* propagation as not only alleviating the demand for wild species but also as a way to conserve those species whose habitat has been destroyed and where *in situ* conservation is no longer a viable alternative. Among the species that they have artificially produced are *Cattleya rex*, *Laelia grandis*, *Gongora aceras alba*, *Angraecum vigueri*, *Trichocentrum haagii*, *Grammangis ellisii*, *Lycomormium fiskei* (a rare *Peristeria* relative), *Mormodes tuxtlensis*, and *Polystachya piersii*.

Erich Mikels, one of the workers at Hoosier, is a talented micropropagation technician. He has perfected aseptic media for germinating terrestrial orchids and grows such diverse species as *Disa cornuta*, *Bonatea speciosa*, *Habenaria militaris*, *Sacolia speciosa* and *Stenorrhynchus speciosa* from seed. This frees one from the more cumbersome techniques of needing to culture the mycorrhizal fungal for terrestrial orchids that were developed in European laboratories.

Hoosier Orchids have encountered some problems in their seed program. Often seed from foreign countries is damaged in shipping and the taxonomy of hobbyists may not be accurate. Many people tend to self pollinate their plants instead of out-crossing them to other members of the same species and this usually results in weak populations of seedlings. Nevertheless, companies like Hoosier's show that artificial propagation is a viable alternative.

Aranda

This is a plant nursery near Rio de Janeiro in Brazil run by Roberto Agnes. In common with most orchid nurseries in that country only artificially propagated native species are offered. Aranda offers a good selection of *Cattleya* species, among other genera, but the nursery also offers a diverse selection of hybrids in many different genera. This nursery has its own modern laboratory facilities that are used to propagate its plants.

L & R Orchids

In many respects the orchid industry is global in its scope. It is customary for major orchid shows to have sales booths, where various orchid nurseries also sell plants. Merchants may be selling their plants in Tokyo one weekend and in New York the following week, as sellers follow the major flower shows around the world. L and R Orchids are based in New Zealand, but sell their plants all over the world. They produce and sell hundreds of different species, all artificially propagated. Their success is marked by the bustle of activity that usually surrounds their sales benches and the rapidity with which those benches empty of plants.

Easy Orchids

Murray Shergold is the proprietor of Easy Orchids, an Australian operation that offers orchid seedlings in flasks. They offer a wide variety of species from many parts of the world. He has been able to produce not only epiphytic orchids but terrestrials such as the South African *Satyrium* species as well. The main outlet for Murray's flasks is the large Australian hobbyist market. Murray has made contacts with indigenous people in Madagascar, who have provided or sold seed of many of the rarer and more unusual Madagascan orchids. The lists of species that he has offered are impressive.

Sunswept Laboratories

Dr. Robert Hull is a psychiatrist by training and an orchid grower by avocation. He runs a small orchid production company called Sunswept Laboratories in Southern California, which concentrates on producing and selling rare species. The species propagated come from a wide variety of geographical areas. Plants are sold in flasks or as individual plants. Hull sees his efforts as a positive force in helping to maintain orchid species, not only in cultivation but also in existence.

Equatorial Plant Company

Working out of the United Kingdom, Dr. Richard Warren provides artificially propagated species in flasks for British hobbyists and other growers in other parts of the world. He has been particularly effective in propagating New Guinea species of *Dendrobium*, but his list also includes a wide range of species from around the world.

The Orchid Zone

This wholesale orchid nursery, near Salinas in central California, has been very effective in mass producing many of the rarer species of both *Paphiopedilum* and *Phragmipedium*. Under the guidance of Terry Root, the 'Orchid Zone' has been able to propagate large quantities of the Asiatic species such as *Paphiopedilum hookerae, P. rothschildianum, P. fairrieanum, P. malipoense* and many others from seed. At the Orchid Zone they have also mass-produced very rare forms of the species such as *P. bellatulum album* and *P. philippinense album*. Success at this nursery in producing *Phragmipedium besseae* and *P. schlimii* is almost legendary, they have grown enormous numbers of seedlings, probably well in excess of wild

population numbers. Their success has made these plants available to any slipper orchid enthusiast who wishes to grow them. The plants, all artificially propagated, are extremely well grown and vigorous and well adjusted to greenhouse and home environments, making them a much more satisfying purchase for the grower than any jungle imported plant. This one nursery alone convincingly demonstrates the role that commercial firms can play in the propagation of rare species.

Legitimate propagation?

Not all artificially propagated orchids have the same legal status in the world. Seed of species on Appendix I of CITES can be exported if they have a CITES Appendix II permit, issued by the country of origin of the particular species. Although artificially propagated orchids are usually handled as a global commodity, with plants produced in Holland ending up as far afield as South Africa or Canada, their legitimacy can vary depending on how each destination country interprets the CITES regulations. Shortly after the rediscovery of *Paphiopedilum delenatii* in Vietnam, Holland was mass-producing large numbers of seed grown plants derived from the new wild plants. With typical Dutch efficiency very vigorous, robust seedlings (which were close to flowering) were being offered on the wholesale market. These were sold at a fraction of the price asked on the black market for jungle plants of the same species. Instead of welcoming this as a diversion on collecting pressures on the wild plants the legitimacy of these plants was brought into question. In some parts of the world (such as Europe) the plants are considered as legitimate, being artificially propagated, while at the same time in the United States they are considered to be illegal. As artificially propagated CITES Appendix I plants, the United States demands a paper trail back to the Vietnamese government before it will consider any of the artificially propagated *P. delenatii* as 'clean'. Conservation has taken a back seat and the spirit of the law has been superceded by the word of the law.

CHAPTER 13

Orchids in Peril

There are many species of orchid in the wild parts of the world that are now reduced by human activities to the point where their future has become questionable. But what exact proportion of the large orchid family now faces dwindling population size is not known. Attempts have been made to estimate the problem. IUCN recently calculated that 5.6% of the 30,000 orchid species were in some category of threatened status (Walter and Gillett, 1998). That worked out at 1,680 species. They also calculated that some 12.5% of all flowering plant species are threatened which, if their numbers are correct, places the orchids in a favorable position compared to the rest of the plant kingdom with orchids only having about half of the proportion of threatened species found in other families. But the numbers are probably both wrong and misleading. In the first place very few countries have complete data sets. The best information available is for the western European countries, as well as Australia, South Africa and the USA. But the important countries for orchid growers are tropical ones such as Mexico, Ecuador, Columbia, India, Malaysia and the Philippines, to name only a few. These nations possess very incomplete floristic inventories.

There are also many, many, species that are naturally rare. IUCN lists 646 species as being rare but my analyses (Koopowitz, 1992; Koopowitz *et al.*, 1994, 1998) suggest that more than ten times that number of species are only found in one locality. If one includes species reported from three or fewer sites as being rare, then over half of the orchid species should be considered as rare. This would suggest that perhaps 15,000 orchid species, 5% of the entire plant kingdom are naturally rare. But naturally rare species while easy to destroy, do not face the same perils as those whose numbers have already been reduced by human activity.

In this chapter we will discuss several important and a few rather obscure species that are now or were once thought to be in jeopardy in the wild. Whether or not they can persist in their native habitats is not clear. Some of the examples selected are well known names to the orchid gardening public, but one should remember that there are also large numbers of lesser species that are also being threatened. In fact it is almost certain that some species, now on the verge of extinction, may never have been scientifically described.

In this chapter there is only space to deal with a few 'flagship' species that can illustrate the range of hazards that orchid populations face. Some of these will end up surviving but others will almost surely be lost. It is difficult to predict which will be the lucky species. During the last half-century, many orchids were proposed as being extinct or facing a particular hazard. However obtaining hard data on any of them is extremely difficult and what data is available should always be treated with a degree of caution.

Paphiopedilum rothschildianum

Rothschild's slipper orchid has always enjoyed a special position in the lists of exceptional orchids. It is a magnificent plant that bears spikes of enormous stately flowers. The flowers are not really beautiful rather they are majestic. The sepals are large and heavily striped with a deep brown-purple over a contrasting ivory background. The narrow strap-shaped petals are held horizontally and flowers can achieve a spread of over 30 cm. With three, four or even five flowers on a meter tall spike these plants can assume a grandeur that is hard to match in the orchid world.

This species was introduced into cultivation in 1887 and was described the following year. The original habitat appears to have been deliberately falsified and plants were reported to have been collected in New Guinea. A synonym was also described in 1988 as having originated in the Philippines. In 1889 Whitehead reported seeing *P. rothschildianum* growing among piles of loose rock on the tops of hills of Mt. Kinabalu (Wood *et al.*, 1993) but that report appears to have been lost or forgotten. For nearly half a century the exact locality was a subject for conjecture and there was even uncertainty on which island the species grew. In 1959 plants were rediscovered growing on the lower slopes of Mt. Kinabalu in the northeastern part of Malaysian Borneo. After more exploration, another population was found. The first population must have contained a fair number of plants because specimens (all in flower) were taken and used to decorate a bower to welcome Prince Philip to Kota Kinabalu, in 1959. The fate of those plants is important. They were distributed to David Sander of the historically important orchid firm of Messrs. Sanders & Sons of St. Albans, England, and hence made their way into important orchid collections in various parts of the world. They are the progenitors of most of the *P. rothschildianum* now in cultivation.

In 1979, Tony Lamb discovered another wild population along the border of Mt. Kinabalu Park, in a region called Bukit Hampuan. This portion of the park had its protected status removed in the early 1980s. The original population, however, was some 12 miles away within the boundaries of the park. There is no information about other populations that might exist outside the park and several authorities have assumed that there are none. Several years ago a few plants of a smaller dwarf form of the species was offered on the international black market. Those plants were said to have come from a population outside the preserve. Whether or not there truly was a third population and whether or not it ever existed or has now been collected out remains to be determined. It is clear, however, that plants have been poached from within the park and that practice still continues despite sanctions against it. Wood *et al* (1993) suggested that *P. rothschildianum* must now be one of the rarest *Paphiopedilum* species in nature. Not only is the species in jeopardy from over-collecting but the original known populations are also under pressure from "unauthorized logging, shifting agriculture and forest fires" (Wood *et al*, 1993). This is despite being under the protected status of a nature reserve.

There was a disastrous undertaking to reintroduce the species back into the park. But initial attempts were actually quite hopeful and there was optimism that it might actually succeed. Two seed capsules had been collected in 1982 from within the southern population and a large number of seedlings reared in Germany. Plants were quite vigorous and grew considerably faster than plants resulting from previous attempts. When these were considered large enough (i.e. with leaf spans of 10–28 cm) 100 plants were returned to Borneo (in 1987). Two positions had been selected that appeared to be physically similar to the sites where the original two populations had been found. These were in Bukit Hampuan, a portion of the park that had been removed from protected status, but it was hoped that the promi-

nence of the project would help get that part reincorporated. In one area 50 seedlings were planted and in the other 40. The other 10 seedlings were given to Botanic Gardens in Sabah. The following year, the majority of the seedlings had not only survived but had grown appreciably larger. A report on the project was published in the *American Orchid Society Bulletin* in the same year (Grell *et al.*, 1988). Nothing further was reported and most of the orchid public who remembered reading the piece assumed that the reintroduction had succeeded.

Initially there was support for the project from the WWF and the outlook appeared to be very promising in early 1990. There appeared to be political support for the project and it even seemed as if Bukit Hampuan was to be reincorporated into the park. At that point WWF began to withdraw from the project. A conference on Borneo's Forests was held at the University of Malaysia. This was opened by the Chief Minister, who in his opening remarks declared that Bukit Hampuan would be reincorporated into the park. This was given wide play in the local press. The project itself was discussed and unfortunately exact locality data was publicized, which was seized upon by the local population in Ranau (who had always had anti-park sentiments). In an attempt to halt reincorporating the section back into the park Bukit Hampuan was set on fire. If they were not to be allowed to benefit from logging of the area then no one else would either. This was one of the worst 'dog in the manger' scenarios. Among the casualties of the fires was the one *P. rothschildianum* site where the two reintroduced plantings had been made. All was lost.

Odontoglossum crispum

This is a magnificent species that bears long arching sprays of 3–4 in white flowers. The individual blooms may have yellow, brown or magenta spots and markings. The species gets its name from the sepal and petal edges that are crisped rather like the pinked rim of a carnation petal. The species was originally found in the cloud forests near Bogota in Columbia. When they were introduced to Europe in the middle of the nineteenth century it created a furor. The flowers were immensely desirable and there was enormous demand for the plants especially the finer clones. Plants were auctioned off and the best forms fetched extremely high prices. A member of the Rothschild family is known to have bid a thousand guineas for a single plant of the finer clones. In those days that sum represented a fortune, much more than the average yearly salary. But this only served to whet the appetite for more plants. Additional plants were demanded and the collectors chopped down the forests tearing off the plants. They were easy plunder. One shipment was recorded as containing 40,000 plants and there were many shipments. The way the plants were collected was to cut down the trees and then strip the plants off the branches. Plants were carried in baskets on the back of mules or by canoe to the coastal cities and from there on sailing ships to England. Many of the plants either succumbed along the way or reached England in such weakened condition that they died soon after or dwindled away after a few seasons. Others did survive and their glorious flowers initiated further demand for the plants.

Odontoglossum crispum was one of the dominant life forms of those cloud forests, where they grew in the cool damp forests at altitudes of 7,500 to 8000 ft (2,286 to 2,438 m). Here the temperatures were relatively constant hovering around 60°F (14°C). It must have been a magnificent sight to see the sprays of large pristine flowers arching off the tree branches. Early collectors recorded that the species was quite common. The best forms, with the whitest and flattest flowers, carrying well-overlapped petals were known to come from the forest near a village called Pacho.

The demand for not only this species but all large flowered wild orchid species was so great that the famous orchid firm of Sanders in St. Albans, England actually had a railroad siding built to deliver shipments of wild orchids directly to the nursery. Literally boxcars of wild orchids arrived from all parts of the world. The better specimens were auctioned off to the highest bidder, and were carefully tended in private collections. The percentage that survived in the long run was miniscule compared to the numbers destroyed to feed the appetites of the orchid-growing gentry. The foundations of the modern orchid hobby are built on the excesses of the past.

If one were to return to the mountaintops today one could not find the forests, let alone O. *crispum*. Most of the forests have been destroyed and the orchid is now difficult to find in the few copses that have managed to persist. Those plants of this species that still exist in the wild (Bokemühl, 1989) are rather poor specimens lacking the flower shapes and colorings that had made them so desirable 150 years ago. Certainly the gene pool of the survivors must be depauperate, when compared with what existed at the time when the species was originally discovered.

However, O. *crispum*, does exist in hundreds of private and commercial collections around the world. The plants still bear arching sprays of the idealized white flowers with crisped edges and appear to be safe in cul-

tivation. But these orchid plants are not equivalent to the wild populations either. Nearly all of the cultivated plants are line-bred from the initial imports that started nearly over 150 years ago. They have gone through a bottleneck where plants were selected for ease of cultivation and flowers approaching the human perception of perfection. Plants of O. *crispum* in cultivation are also tetraploids. They have evolved away from the wild forms and are no longer equivalent to the species that once graced the hills above Bogota.

Vanda coerulea

In 1837 Dr. William Griffiths described an orchid with big blue flowers from the Khasia Hills of Assam. Blue is not a common color in orchids and it is exceptionally rare in orchids with large flowers. While there is some variation in flower color, true blue flowers could be found among the wild plants. He named the plant *Vanda coerulea*, for this rare color, and from the outset the orchid achieved enormous popularity. *V. coerulea* proved to be easier to grow and flower under European greenhouse and conservatory conditions than its spectacular Filipino cousin, *Vanda sanderiana*. It originated from the temperate forests, rather than the hot humid lowlands.

V. coerulea was a more compact plant than *V. sanderianum*, it could even tolerate drier conditions and light frosts. Besides this they flowered several times a year and it was no wonder that demand for the plants was high. Plants were stripped out of their natural habitat and thousands packed off for Europe. As was the case with so many of the wild-collected species, a lot of the plants died in transit and others were so weak that they died soon after reaching their destination. But many others did survive in cultivation and descriptions of superior clones are preserved in early issues of the British journal *The Orchid Review*. Some of those earlier ones were magnificent and no doubt contributed towards the development of modern *Vanda* hybrids.

As early as 1875, Samuel Jennings a vice-president of the Agri-horticultural Society of India wrote that the species, "…is becoming very rare." He thought that the species was only found in the Khassia and Jynteah hills, in the south of Assam. By the beginning of the twentieth century so many plants had been removed from their habitat that concerns were being raised. The blue vanda found itself with the distinction of being the first tropical orchid to be afforded official legislative protection from over collecting in its native habitat. It became illegal to collect the species for trade reasons. This did not seem to have stopped the trade in the plant, although it was diminished. The species continued to be offered in the wild species trade for over another half century. Actually the legislation, while it stopped the wholesale plunder of the species, did not really protect them. The small forest trees (primarily oak), which the orchid lived on, were ideally suited for making charcoal. While the orchid trade was now negligible, the host trees continued to be destroyed and the populations of the plant continued to decline. Their habitat was being destroyed to provide cheap fuel for cooking fires.

When CITES came into being in the 1970s *Vanda coerulea* was listed on Appendix I as one of the few 'truly' threatened orchid species. By this time several things had occurred. The range of the species was no longer thought to be confined to the Assam Hills, in fact *V. coerulea* has turned out to be quite a widespread species and is much more common than was originally realized. It is found in the Himalayan mountains at altitudes from 2500 to 4000 ft (760 to 1220 m) (Motes, 1997) and ranges across an enormous stretch of territory, from India through to Thailand and even into Southern China. While it has been severely depleted in one area its wide distribution really did not warrant its inclusion among the most highly endangered of the endangered.

Thailand was the center of the wild orchid trade for many years and it is known as a center for the breeding and production of orchids for the cut flower market. Also originating in Thailand, *V. coerulea* naturally came to the attention of the Thai breeders who proceeded to line breed and 'perfect' this species. The result was a race of spectacular, if not stunning flowers. The depth of blue was intensified and the flowers became larger and larger. The original wild flowers of the blue vanda have their petals twisted through 180° so that, as one looked at the face of the flower, one was actually seeing the reverse side of the petals. This would not do! Orchid fanciers like their flowers large, round and flat with disciplined overlapping petals. The flower breeders succeeded and now the majority of artificially bred *V. coerulea* conform to the ideal. They often do not even resemble the original wild flowers, which with their gracefully twisted flowers, looked like a cloud of blue butterflies.

This is a common predicament. Man-bred orchid species are in fact artificially selected. Not only are they selected for plants that grow and flower easily under artificial greenhouse conditions, but the form and shape of both the plant and flower can be changed to conform to man's idea of what makes a desirable shape. It turns out that with a little artificial selection plants are so malleable that after just a few generations they no longer resemble the wild forms that nature had selected over

hundreds of thousands of years. Are species that have been line bred in this fashion still equivalent to the wild species? If not, what is the value of maintaining species after this fashion? Perhaps it is a case of half a loaf is better than none; an artificially selected species is still preferable to an extinct species.

Laelia milleri

The rupicolous laelias are orchids that live on exposed rocks, on ledges and mountains of the Atlantic Coasts of Brazil. *Laelia milleri* created a sensation when it was first described and brought into cultivation in 1960, because some clones had flowers that were blood red in color. Withner (1990) described two forms of the species. One form has larger spidery flowers was an orange-red color, while the more desirable deep red clones had smaller flowers with wider tepals. The two color forms appeared to be distinctively different. The plants were relatively dwarf, with pseudobulbs about 6 in tall, bearing succulent leathery leaves. Thin flower stems carried an inflorescence of half a dozen 2 in diameter (5 cm) flowers with a narrow frilly labellum that had a contrasting yellow blotch at its base. There has always been a premium on producing hybrid flowers in the cattleya alliance and here was a promising avenue to pursue. Among the first hybrids made were x *Laeliocattleya* Rojo and x *Sophrolaelia* Jinn that were quite famous in their day. These in turn were used to produce other hybrids. x *Sophrolaelia* Jinn was the parent of x *Sophrolaeliocattleya* Wendy's Valentine, a very popular red flower that was tissue propagated and is still widely grown.

While there was considerable demand, especially for the redder forms of the species, it proved relatively difficult to grow and never became as popular as many other species of this genus. The species itself was never plentiful but was imported and offered to the orchid growing public many times.

Laelia milleri grew on rocks on the rich iron bearing mountains, the Serra dos Ingleses, near Itabira in Minas Gerais. These mountains were strip-mined for their iron ore and for many years the species was considered to be extinct. In this case their habitat had been destroyed as the mountains were literally consumed to feed the foundries of the country. While some plants were maintained in cultivation, Withner (1990) decried the fact that there seemed little interest in actively propagating the species. Here we had an orchid, thought to be extinct in the wild and for some reason, despite its many desirable characteristics, seemed to evoke nothing other than indifference.

In recent years, a couple of small populations have been re-discovered at other sites. These localities are being kept secret. The species is now available in Brazil from several nurseries and those plants appear to be artificially propagated stock. Why this was not done earlier still remains a mystery.

Acrolophia ustulata

There are many different ways that species can be forced to the brink of extinction. One of the more unlikely is at the hands of botanists who describe and collect species for herbarium specimens. Stories have circulated that collectors have jeopardized some species of orchid. Harry Bolus is a famous name in African orchid taxonomy. He had been born in England in 1834 but as a teenager went to live in South Africa, eventually he became a very successful broker and was able to retire in 1894. Much of his life was spent investigating the flora of the region. His interests spanned other plant families as well as orchids (Reinikka, 1995). At his own expense, Bolus produced two sets of books, one on the *Orchids of the Cape Peninsula* and a second, more famous set of volumes, on the *Orchids of South Africa*. The books contained drawings and descriptions of plants that he had collected and studied himself. The first species to be featured in the *Orchids of South Africa* was *Acrolophia ustulata*.

Harry Bolus had described this species as *Cymbidium ustulatum* in the *Journal of the Linnean Society* in 1884. Four years later he had changed the name to *Eulophia ustulata* in his *Orchids of the Cape Peninsula* and finally in 1894 to *Acrolophia ustulata*, by which it is still known. This is really a nondescript little orchid. The plant produces a slender rhizome, from which spring short but fleshy, almost tuberous roots. There is a tuft of some six to ten slender grassy leaves usually less than 2 in (5 cm) long and only about $^1/_{12}$ in (2 mm) wide. The inflorescence bears 3 to 6 small flowers that were described as deep chocolate approaching purple or black. The species epithet, itself means burnt, and describes the burnt toast color of the little flowers. For much of the twentieth century the plant was considered extinct.

The species never appears to have been very plentiful. Originally only one locality was known. In the summer of 1882–3 a patch of the species was found in a sandy valley across from an old hotel in Muizenberg, then a small village outside of Cape Town. There in one spot less than 100 yards wide grew between 60 and 80 plants. Harry Bolus collected his type specimens and made his descriptions from these plants. Just how many

plants did he collect to make his specimens? The type sheet in the herbarium at the Royal Botanic Gardens, Kew contains the remains of eleven separate and individual plants. Another sheet in the Bolus Herbarium at the University of Capetown has the remains of ten plants. We know that Bolus also made duplicate herbarium sheets that were deposited at other herbaria and that he had his own private collection as well. It is quite likely that he wiped out half of that Muizenberg population of the new species he had just found.

In all, the species was only known from three sites, two localities on the Cape Peninsula, including the Muizenberg site, and a third in the Robinson's Pass near Outshoorn. There is no indication of how many plants were growing at the other sites. Schelpe (1966) wrote that the species had not been collected since November 1921. The species was rediscovered about 10 years ago. It turned out that when they are not in flower they are extremely difficult to discern among the grasses and other vegetation where they grow. Surprisingly, this species seems to flower the second year after veldt fires and at that time the flowers could still blend in with the charred remains of surrounding vegetation. They would be easily overlooked unless one was specifically searching for them. Kurzweil found a locality in 1987 with at least 252 plants (Kurzweil, personal communication) and other areas with *O. ustulata* have also since been found. It is one of those species that is just hard to distinguish in the field.

While Bolus must have decimated that one population of *O. ustulata*, he really did not jeopardize the whole species with his collecting zeal. There are, however, cases of very rare, *Disa* species from southern Africa whose herbarium sheets bear as many as 30 to 50 individual plants. In those cases severe damage must have been done to the populations (Kurzweil, pers. Communication).

Lycaste skinneri

Some countries are inordinately fond of their flowers and will raise them to special status. Such is the case for Guatemala and the orchid *Lycaste skinneri*, with its even more beautiful white form that was singled out to become that country's national flower. Among the many beautiful orchid species of the world *L. skinneri alba* (syn. *L. virginalis*) must rank close to the top. The large triangular white sepals were likened to a nun's cap and for that reason it is sometimes called the nun's orchid.

This is a species that is much loved and very common in cultivation and for that reason the species cannot be considered endangered. But, the story for plants

59   *Lycaste skinneri* occurs in several color phases. The more usual pink form of *L. skinneri* – 'Royale Promise' AM/AOS – possesses more intense coloration on the petals and lip than most clones.

Fig. 6   Map of upper and lower Verapas, Guatemala. The red area was the extent of cloud forest where *Lycaste skinneri* could be found. The black areas were the remaining habitats of *L. skinneri* in the 1990s. Note that there is still substantial cloud forest, but it is now devoid of this particular orchid. (Otto Mittlestaedt Villela, personal collection).

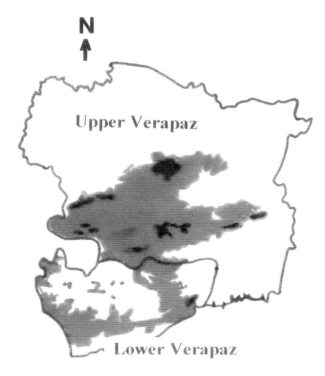

in the wild is a different matter and goes to show that, even a National flower can not persist in the face of economic development. The species was formerly widely distributed in Central America, ranging from Chiapas in Mexico through Honduras, Guatemala and into El Salvador. The Mexican variety tends to have smaller blossoms and come into flower at a different season. For that reason it has been suggested that they may be another separate species. It seemed to have been most common in Guatemala and particularly in the vicinity of the town of Cobán, in the region of Alta Verapaz. This was in a region of highland forests in the north central District of Guatemala.

The flowers of the species are very variable in color, ranging from pure white through blush to pink and lavender. Fowlie (1970) enumerated nearly 50 distinct varieties that had been described or mentioned in print and estimated that probably only one in 2000 plants bore the pure white flowers. The species must have originally been quite common, for the white form of the nun's orchid was singled out to be the national flower, which presupposes that enough of the white forms were known and hence there must have been enormous numbers of the colored forms as well.

Fowlie (1970) relates how he found *L. skinneri* growing at about 5,000 ft (1,524 m), in seasonal cloud forests on the branches of fairly large trees, where it was both cool and light intensity was relatively low. But he also adds how difficult it was to find plants, they occurred in isolated and hard to reach areas.

Otto Mittelstaedt Villela was the son of a German immigrant and a Guatemalan mother. Both his mother and grandmother lived in Cobán and grew orchids, including the nun's orchid. Otto learned how to care and tend for these flowers and grew to love them. When he grew up he farmed coffee, cardamon, cocoa and various tropical spices. Forests had to be cleared for new plantations as agriculture spread in the area. Villela was aware that forests had to make way for new plantings and he collected as many of the displaced orchids as he could and tried to re-establish them on his farms. But one man could not save all the plants that were being dispossessed.

Villella calculated that there were approximately 3,250 km² of cloud forest in Upper and Lower Verapaz in 1930 that were suited to *Lycaste skinneri*. They consulted with old Indian orchid collectors and mapped out the range for the nun's orchid. This was forest that ranged in altitude from 3,000 to 12,000 ft (914 m to 3,657 m), but excluded forest containing coniferous trees that *Lycaste* appeared to avoid.

By the year 1970 only 1,000 km² remained and populations of the large *Lycaste* had become scarce. As Fowlie recounted, the orchids were only to be found in remote and difficult to reach places. By 1990 the most optimistic estimates had reduced the habitat to only 165 km² and the few remaining localities had become closely guarded secrets. If one visits the area today you will still find large tracts of cloud forest but the orchids are not there. What happened to them?

The plants succumbed, not only to the clearing of forests for plantations but also to the over collection of plants for both domestic and foreign markets. Local orchid lovers amassed extensive collections of the plant. But the indigenous peoples who did the strenuous work of collecting did not really profit, for they received a mere pittance for their efforts, each plant brought in only pennies. Although special varieties were quite valuable their desirability was only ascertained after they flowered in captivity. There was high demand for the species in England and Australia and they became renowned centers of *Lycaste* hybridization. Other countries such as Japan also focussed attention on *Lycaste* hybrids.

What does the future hold for the species? There is now concern for the continuation of the plant in its native land and it is unlikely that it will become extinct. The species is easy to mass-produce and there has been talk of trying to re-introduce it back into the wild. However, experience with other species has shown that re-introduction is quite difficult, expensive and the resultant plants, while of the same species, belong to an altered gene pool. One can never return to the conditions of Eden. The plants resulting from re-introduction are not strictly comparable to those of the same species that existed in the beginning. The wild populations had been extremely variable but any re-introductions would, by necessity, be markedly less so.

When the initial Appendix I orchids were selected *Lycaste skinneri* was listed. The white form was considered a separate species and it was known to be very rare in the wild because it naturally occurred in such small numbers. Of course, it was merely a variant of the pink species and despite its decimation in the wild the species itself did not deserve such status. Listing created several debacles. *Lycaste skinneri alba* was quite easy to propagate artificially. It had become quite common in the United States and well-intentioned efforts to return flasks of the white form back to Guatemala for reintroduction were stymied. As an Appendix I species, international movement of any plants, even artificially reproduced, was forbidden. It was only later that these restrictions on flasks of Appendix I species became somewhat eased and eventually the Guatemalan national flower was de-listed.

There is a rider to this account. Over the last few decades there has been increased use of insecticides in Central America to control the spread of various fruit flies and in particular to stop them from getting to the United States border. There was due to a program by the USDA to blanket spray all of Central America with Malathion. This had been carried out with little publicity until certain Central American scientists brought it to the attention of US conservation groups. The major concern was that the natural pollinators would be severely depleted, and in fact populations of the important bee pollinator species did seem to have suffered. In response to concerns by US scientists, promises were made that spraying would be limited, especially in nature reserves. There has been no follow up to see if the new recommendations were followed. In the meantime scientists in Guatemala continue to report that there have been steady decreases in fruit set in wild orchids in recent years (M. Dix, personal communications) culminating in an absence of seed pods for the year 1998. One cannot help but speculate that *L. skinneri* might have lost its pollinator too.

Phalaenopsis gigantea

Phalaenopsis gigantea is a monster. Why would any one want to grow a plant that had several enormous oval-shaped leaves, each measuring nearly a meter in length? The answer appears to be just that. Because it is so big! Humankind has always reacted and been impressed by very large animals or plants and the response to this, the largest of the *Phalaenopsis* species, is no different. Its owners point out large specimens with considerable pride.

It is an impractical plant to grow. Besides being too big for the conventional hobbyist's greenhouse, the species prefers to be mounted or at least have its container tilted to one side so that the leaves can hang down. On top of that, its cultural requirements are not easy to reproduce and it is a difficult plant to keep alive. Growth is slow and unpredictable and few specimens really look very good in cultivation. It does bear impressive pendant spikes of large rounded and waxy flowers, of either translucent white or yellow, covered with rich brown 'polka dots'. About 20-30 years ago the species was used in hybridizing and produced desirable novelty flowers, but the leaves were often just too big and the plants tended to be unmanageable. Nevertheless the species was the direct ancestor of several *Phalaenopsis* hybrids that went on to become important and famous breeding plants Among those plants were *P.* Liu Tuenshen, *P. Reichentea*, *P. Natasha*, and *P. Eye Dee*, which in turn produced equally important breeding stock. However, fashion has led to smaller and more compact hybrids and, while *P. gigantea* genes still exist in the background of many modern hybrids, the continued need for the direct use of the species in breeding has declined.

Phalaenopsis gigantea hails from Borneo and was first collected in 1897. Herman Sweet (1980) has recounted the history of the species since then. Forty years after its initial introduction a large population of the species was rediscovered during the development of a rubber plantation in eastern Borneo. Those plants were collected and offered for sale. Another forty years went by, when it was reported again, but this time from Sabah (northern Borneo). Since that time it was been in and out of cultivation. It would seem that every time a new population of plants is discovered it is decimated and jungle plants find their way onto the market. There is little need for this, unless those localities are slated for deforestation, because artificially produced seedlings are readily available. As with many other wild collected plants, this species does not readily adapt to greenhouse conditions after it is extracted from the jungle. The seedlings are more accommodating, although both seedlings and jungle materials are slow growing and take considerable patience to reach flowering size.

The extent of the species in the wild is not known, but it is generally thought to be quite rare. Every time that it is rediscovered and collected out from the new site the species is declared extinct in the wild. At least, until a new population is found. The size of the individual orchids makes the species unmistakable and because jungle plants still command high prices it places this species in special jeopardy. It needs effective legislation to protect it in its natural habitat. We also need an education program to counteract the prestige that amateurs attach to growing this unwieldy species. Prestige has its place but not at the expense of wild populations.

Cattleya trianaei

This species is the classic orchid, the flower that first comes to mind when the public thinks of the word 'orchid'. These are the flowers that the well to do gave to their dates to wear on those special occasions, during the first half of the twentieth century.

The species was formally named in 1860 after a Dr. Triana from Colombia. At one time it was a widespread species and common along all three major mountain ranges in that country. Countless numbers of plants were collected and shipped to Europe and North America. Withner (1988) reports that the Burrage collection in Massachusetts, alone contained over 2,800 plants. *Cattleya trianaei* bloomed in the winter and had the common name of the 'Christmas *Cattleya*'. The demand was great and orchid collectors were often asked to supply individual orders of 5,000 or more plants at a time.

Just before the Second World War a book was published (MacDonald, 1939) that glamorized commercial orchid collecting and recounted efforts to find and collect *C. trianaei*. It is worth reading, for it portrays the naivete of those times and an era when the wild places were there for exploitation and the need for conservation had hardly surfaced. It is basically a real life adventure story that gives a feel for the difficulties that people encountered while collecting species that would eventually form the foundations for the modern orchid era. It also demonstrates the excesses of those collectors, although the heroes of this particular book do recount that they persuaded their native collectors only to bring in plants that had at least eight leaves - as a conservation measure. Actually by 1939 the supply of the orchids was starting to become scarce and MacDonald recalls the difficulties he encountered trying to find fresh sites to plunder.

There must have been hundreds of thousands, if not millions of plants originally. Not only were they collected for overseas nurseries but the forests were ransacked for plants for local consumption as well. Withner describes a church roof and the surrounding yard wall, near Medellin, which was decorated with *C. trianae* plants. By the time that CITES Appendix I plants were being selected for inclusion on the list Dr. Triana's *Cattleya* seemed to be a perfect candidate and, as yet, is one of the original nominations that has not been subsequently down-listed. But what is the true situation? Is this species close enough to the brink of extinction to warrant the attention? No one would argue that *C. trianaei* populations have not suffered at the hands of orchid collectors, but have the populations been reduced to the point that further trade would force the species into the oblivion of extinction? The loss of half a million plants from a total population of a million plants will not put that species in jeopardy, and wild populations of other kinds of plants often do reach into the millions. On the other hand, the loss of 500,000 plants from a population of 600,000, should be a matter of grave concern. We have census numbers for almost no orchid species and one needs true census numbers to know the reality of a situation. In the case of *C. trianaei* the true position is obscure.

60   *Paphiopedium druryi* growing in its habitat,
in the Travancore Hills, Southern India.
(Photo credit: S. Kumar)

Paphiopedilum druryi

Here is another species that was considered extinct until fairly recently. An unusual slipper orchid, *P. druryi* comes from the Travancore Hills in Southern India, some hundreds of miles distant from the Himalayan species that are its close relatives. This *Paphiopedilum* has some unusual vegetative characters, which distinguish it from its closest cousins. The plants produce long rhizomes, rather like strawberry runners, between the individual fans. Plants that appear to be individuals may actually be connected together and represent a single clone. Runners are known from the *Parvisepalum* sub-genus and are also known from the sister genera *Mexipedium* and *Phragmipedium*, but are quite rare in *Paphiopedilum*. The flowers of *P. druryi* are usually in shades of yellow to green, each petal and the dorsal sepal bear a dark brown strip running down the midline. Many hobbyists consider it to be quite pretty. The plant was brought into cultivation in 1875 and featured modestly in hybridization programs, until 1937 when it seemed to have been lost or forgotten.

There followed a long hiatus, until the species was reintroduced about 25 years ago. Kumar and Manilal (1994) recount that the story of its rediscovery (Mammen and Mammen, 1974) was displayed opposite an advertisement in the *Orchid Digest*, where the person who had discovered it was offering divisions of the plant for sale at US$50 per growth. Over 3,000 plants were taken from the wild at that time and this, in turn, prompted local nurseries to collect additional plants. Authorities confiscated over 600 plants from one local nurseryman.

A story circulated at the time that the locality was deliberately burnt to destroy any possible survivors of the species. One must assume that this helped to inflate the price of the collected plants, so that the customers paid more for the last survivors of the species. People assumed that the species was probably extinct in the wild. This led to concerted efforts to artificially propagate the plant and growers routinely self-pollinated their specimens hoping to produce more. Cribb (1987) wrote: "Regrettably, *P. druryi* is now either extinct in the wild or on the verge of extinction." Other authors echoed these sentiments.

In recent years, the species has been rediscovered, and is now undergoing the kind of demographic analysis that we actually need for most endangered species, if we are to have an accurate assessment of their conservation status. A number of discrete populations are known and several thousand plants have been counted (S. Kumar, personal communication). We do not know, however, how many discrete clones actually exist. This species propagates itself asexually by means of long rhizomes and what may appear to be a large number of plants could in fact merely represent genets of the same clone. The number of potentially interbreeding genets is important for the long-range prognosis of a species.

If we take the best case scenario and assume that each plant is indeed a unique genet then there is probably enough genetic diversity still within the surviving population for its continuance. But the total numbers are small and the species is vulnerable to the kinds of stochastic events that could easily wipe it out. This slipper orchid must therefore be considered endangered.

Herschelianthe barbata

The genus *Herschelianthe* is a first cousin of *Disa* and according to the whim of the time, may or may not be included in the latter genus. They differ from *Disa* in having grassy foliage and a large labellum. This can be elaborately fringed and fluffed in some of the species. However, their main claim to fame rests with the gentian-blue coloring that certain species display.

Few species of this genus are common and in recent decades one of them, *Herschelianthe barbata* has become increasingly scarce. This is a South Africa orchid from the Western Cape, originally found in the vicinity of Cape Town. The plant is now extinct in the areas by the city, but there is a single population of no more than a few hundred individuals, growing some distance out of town.

The plants grow among restios (grass-like plants) and shrubs and often blend in with the background, which makes them hard to see. *Herschelianthe barbata* grows to a height of between 30 and 60 cm. It bears three to seven radical leaves that can be over a foot long (30 cm). The scape can reach 60 cm in height and bears several flowers. They tend to be white with a faint blue tinge and somewhat darker blue lines on the hooded dorsal sepal. The petals and lip can be a pale yellow. The lip is modesty fringed and lacinated, hence the trivial epithet, which means 'bearded'.

It is not clear why the species has declined. In part the reason is that some of the habitat was either overgrazed or turned into urban landscape, but the plant was also found in a number of mountains such as Baviaan's Kloof near Genadendaal and the Houw Hoek Mountains, which have been protected for a long time.

Over ten years ago, I was lucky to join an outing of the Cape Orchid Society, which had organized a tractor-drawn hayride, on a private farm, to picnic and go out looking for *H. barbata*. It was the wisdom of the day that wild orchids should be pollinated and this was to be done in order to encourage seed production and hopefully increase the 'wild' population. We spent much of the morning eating and drinking wine and enjoying the wild flowers, of which there were many rare varieties. These were primarily bulbous plants. There were a few other orchid species but no specimens of *Herschelianthe*. It was getting late in the afternoon when we decided to abandon attempts to find the orchid, but we did decide to have one last try. The tractor stopped and every one headed into the bushes. Suddenly there was a clamor of "I found it, I found it." and with a noise like a charging bull elephant one of the men emerged through the bushes waving a handful of the rare orchid that he had picked.

So much for conservation!

Soon after that incident the farm was declared a preserve and the bearded *Herschelianthe* still exists there. There has been talk of artificially propagating the species and trying to reintroduce it, but other species of this genus are notoriously difficult to establish outside of the flask and the probability of success is slim. Nevertheless, these attempts need to be made because this is a species that is difficult to maintain in cultivation and its best chance lies in being left to grow in the wild

Mexipedium xerophyticum

One of the most unusual slipper orchid discoveries in recent years was a small flowered species from Mexico. It was originally described as *Phragmipedium xerophyticum*, but was subsequently placed in its own genus. The move was somewhat controversial and has yet to be settled, although the new generic name of *Mexipedium* appears to be gaining more acceptance.

The tiny white flowers of this species have been compared with lily-of-the-valley for size and color, although the arrangement of the scape is rather different and this slipper orchid has no obvious fragrance. This plant has, like *Phragmipedium*, a branched inflorescence and can bear three or more blooms simultaneously.

The species was found rather unexpectedly in a dry region of Mexico and only seven different plants were initially discovered. The site was kept secret to protect the orchids from commercial collectors. The species reproduces asexually, by means of long stolons and individual plants can have many genets. It proved possible to collect parts of the original specimens and grow them on, without jeopardizing the remainder. Attempts to grow the plant in Mexico City failed, but fortunately the botanists who found the species had the wisdom to try and get them into the hands of knowledgeable growers in the United States. Two clones were sent to a *Phragmipedium* taxonomist and another different clone to a well-known *Phragmipedium* grower and enthusiast. In their hands, the species seemed very easy to grow and soon pieces of the plants were being exchanged among many orchid growers in the United States.

Initially, attempts to grow seedlings artificially in flask were met with little success, but eventually reasonable techniques were worked out and now seedlings bred from two of the original clones have been widely distributed. The seedlings themselves have flowered and today hundreds if not thousands of plants exist in private collections all over North America. Some plants have also been disbursed to other parts of the world as well. Clearly this is a victory for *ex situ* conservation.

While the species lingers on in the wild it has an expanding population in cultivation.

Formerly placed in the genus *Phragmipedium*, it has been argued that *Mexipedium xerophyticum* still qualifies as an Appendix I CITES species, because all wild *Phragmipedium* species were placed in Appendix I, even though this was before the species was discovered. Merely changing its name cannot cause the down-listing of a species. In fact, *M. xerophyticum* is probably one of only two species that deserved to be put onto Appendix I. The other plant is *Phragmipedium exstaminodium*. The prognosis for the continued existence of the former species is assured, not because it was listed in Appendix I, but despite it. The distribution of the species across the globe has occurred by ignoring the bureaucratic hassles and red tape that would have to be endured if they were to be moved legally. All of the specimens were merely smuggled to their final destinations. It is one of the inconsistencies of the modern world that a species can be saved from extinction by indulging in illegal activities. Hopefully the few wild plants still continue, undisturbed in their natural habitat.

Isotria medeoloides

Many species of orchid are rare and are known from a single locality. However there is another category of rareness, which includes species that are widespread, but occur nowhere in large numbers. The small whorled pogonia (*Isotria medeoloides*) is an excellent example of such a North American orchid. Despite the fact that the species is widespread, ranging from North Carolina up into Maine and even into Canada, it is also quite rare and occurs in very small and widely separated local patches. *Isotria medeoloides*, was, at one time, the only officially federally listed terrestrial orchid, rare enough to be classed as an endangered species by the US government.

This is a small terrestrial orchid that has a short stem at the top of a rosette of some five to six drooping dusty-green leaves. The flowers are rarely more than one in number and are of a dull olive-green. Originally the species was placed in the genus *Arethusa* and then transferred to *Isotria* in 1838. It was then placed in *Pogonia* in 1867 and then back into *Isotria* in 1901, but Schlecter placed it into *Odonectis* in 1911. It is now considered *Isostria* again but the pogonia name has been maintained through all the changes and is still used as its common name. This can hardly be called a spectacular plant, but together with its one sister species *I. verticillata*, has a unique arrangement of leaves compared to all other orchids. A woodland orchid, at home on the forest floor, it is dependent on the continuance and integrity of the forests that it inhabits.

The species was described as long ago as 1814 but never seems to have been observed in large numbers at any one place. However some colonies were observed and studied for several decades (Leuer, 1975). One colony was first seen in 1920, near Williamsburg, Virginia. It was observed at intervals for the next 50 years, until the 1970s, when it became threatened by encroaching housing development in the mid 1970s.

Isostria medeoloides has the luxury of growing in a first world country that has both the money and interest in maintaining some of its threatened plant species, even if it does not have stunning flowers. More detailed information has been collected about this orchid's demography than is known for most comparable tropical species. The small whorled pogonia has been recorded from 20 different states, in addition to Washington, DC and the province of Ontario, Canada. Populations have been monitored for some time and each state has analyzed the condition of it's own *I. meleoloides* populations. The species is known to be extinct in Washington, DC and Missouri. It is probably extinct, or, if not, extremely endangered, in Maryland, New York and Vermont. In 13 other states, the plant is considered to be endangered and it is vulnerable (the least threatened category) in the other four states. On the other hand the plant is difficult to identify (Case, 1987) when it is not in flower because it resembles its sister species *I. verticillata*, as well as the herb *Medeola virginiana*, for which it is both named and often associated.

As a federally listed endangered species, *I. medeoloides*, attracted considerable attention from the federal government, as well as many non-governmental organizations interested in either wild flowers or conservation problems. Consequently a reasonably complete census was carried out during the 1980s and 1990s. As many as 54 sites were known in 1985 and additional exploration had taken that number to 142 localities by 1991. In 1996 we knew of 201 living populations of the plant, an additional 88 sites were known, where the species had once grown but where it was no longer to be found. While some of the extant populations only had a handful of individual plants in them, there were clearly many more plants than were recognized when the species was listed. It seemed inappropriate to continue listing the lesser pogonia, as an endangered species and it was down-listed in 1994 to 'threatened status'.

As with many other terrestrial orchid species attempts at rescuing this species from developers have not been very successful. Bill and Carol Fyler transplanted 150 plants of *I. medeoloides*, which were in the path of a development and followed the transplants for ten years. They found that 98% of the transplants failed to re-establish themselves (Falk *et al.*, 1996). While there do not seem to been any attempts to grow and reintroduce plants from seed, there are indications that it may be possible to manipulate the populations. Selective logging of trees to admit more light appears to result in increased growth and flowering. At this point, and despite the large number of historic sites where the species is extinct, the situation for the small whorled pogonia does not appear to be as dire as was once thought.

Sobralia xantholeuca

This is a superb, showy orchid from Central America, with tall and leafy thin reedy stems that bear enormous yellow *Cattleya*-like flowers at the tips of the canes. The species was showcased in the first IUCN Plant Red Data book in 1978. This *Sobralia* is only known from one site in El Salvador. It has also been recorded from two localities in Guatemala, near San Cristobal and Huehuetenango. There is also the possibility that the species may occur in Honduras as well, but it never seems to have been very plentiful.

The yellow *Sobralia* grows as a terrestrial or lithophyte orchid in El Salvador, but the Guatemalan members of the species can also been found as epiphytes. In both regions they prefer temperatures between 18-23°C and inhabit the moist montane forests that were also prime areas for coffee plantations. Much of the land where they grew in Guatemala has now been converted to coffee and other kinds of plantations. The pressures facing this species are identical to those that have caused problems for *Lycaste skinneri*.

Fairly easy to grow, the plant makes big clumps with leafy foliage and can even be use as an outdoor plant in shady conditions in suitable subtropical climates. It has the potential for use as a landscape plant in the coastal regions of southern California and may be useful for hybridizing.

The locality of *S. xantholeuca*, in El Salvador, was given protective status before the Red Data Book was compiled. While it was suggested at that time that the localities in Guatemala also deserved to be in nature preserves, the current standing of the species in either country has not been discussed in recent years. One of the problems that we face is the absence of long term records of endangered orchid species. Many orchids were identified as being endangered over 20 years ago but most of them have never been properly studied and their current status is now unknown. Rather curiously the yellow *Sobralia* was not included in the extensive

list of orchids featured in the 1997 IUCN Red List of Threatened Plants (Walter and Gillett, 1998), although the editors do admit that the list is not inclusive.

Danhatchia australis

Few people think about New Zealand when they consider wild orchids and this is especially the case with regard to orchid conservation. But almost no place on the planet is immune from man's interference and even here, in this isolated set of islands, the few orchids that naturally occur face the same set of problems we have seen in more tropical climates. Forests are cut to provide pasturelands or for building timber and the plants associated with those woods are in trouble. *Yoania australis* was chosen as an example of an endangered orchid in the *IUCN Plant Red Data Book* (1978), since when its name has been changed to *Danhatchia australis*. Because it belongs to a group of orchids that are probably among the most difficult to grow, it makes an interesting example. The plant is a saprophyte, unable to photosynthesize and thus it must rely on a fungus to provide its nutritional needs and is dependent on a complex ecosystem. The orchid plant possesses an underground mass of branching white rhizomes, each about 4mm in diameter. From this system arise aerial branches that grow up to 20 cm tall. The stems do not branch and each carries approximately seven scale-like leaves. There are up to five small white and brownish-pink flowers.

New Zealand used to possess rich forests of kauri (*Agathis spp.*) trees. These are gymnosperms of large size and desirable fine-grained white wood. The trees were exploited by the early white settlers and tracts logged to provide high quality timber. Within these forests were other tree species including a tree called taraire (*Beilschmeidia tarairi*), a member of the Lauraceae. The taraire formed an association with *Lycoperdon perlatum*, a puffball fungus that was also associated with the *Danhatchia* orchid. Logging the forests for kauri wood also meant that the taraire was damaged or killed and this, in turn, destroyed the delicate relationship between the orchid and the fungus. It is possible that the fungi were intermediates, relaying nutrients produced by the trees to the orchids. There are many localities with taraire trees, but relatively few contained the orchid at the time that it was listed.

Fortunately, many sites where the orchid occurs are now in preserves and the species has been removed from its endangered status (D. Given, personal communication) and it continues to exist within the confines of those protected areas. The reasons for its removal from the list are not clear. Perhaps, as with many suspected endangered species, there was insufficient evidence and excessive zeal, which led to a premature listing.

As one might expect this would have been a case where *ex situ* conservation methods just could not work. Although one might be able to culture both the fungus and the orchid it would simply be too expensive to provide the correct conditions to grow sufficient plants in perpetuity to save the species. Fortunately the need to do that no longer exists.

Dendrobium cruentum

Many of the *Dendrobium* species have been over collected. This is, in part, because a number of them can be used for medicinal purposes, but there are also species that have suffered because of their ornamental uses. *Dendrobium cruentum* belongs to the section Formosae, and is one of the least pretentious or ornamental of the group. It has only been used moderately in hybridizing programs. It is thought to be endemic to Thailand, although Schelpe and Stewart (1990) remark that a collection was thought to have been made in Burma. Plants grow to about 30cm high; canes bear pale green to cream flowers either singly or pairs. The whitish labellum has a contrasting red callus and red side lobes. Horticulturally speaking, its most important feature is its willingness to flower throughout the year.

Dendrobium cruentum was up-listed from Appendix II to Appendix I of CITES in 1996. This follows a period when many of the original Appendix I species, that had been listed after inadequate study, were subsequently removed from the list. Several of those were national flowers and one suspects that politics had originally played a part in their nomination. I was an observer, present at the Convention of the Parties in Fort Lauderdale, Florida when *D. cruentum* was up-lifted. Here a different kind of politics was involved.

While no one disagreed that *D. cruentum* populations were probably depleted, there was some hesitancy about advocating up-listing. Jungle collected plants were in commerce but the species was also actively being artificially propagated. In fact it is quite easy to mass-produce *D. cruentum* from seed. At least one well-known Thai orchid academic also disagreed that the species needed to be moved to Appendix I. But at

that time Thailand was one of the world's largest exporters of wild orchid species and up-listing might drive home a lesson that all species needed more protection. Up-listing might emphasize the international interest and concern about the exploitation of Thai orchid species. During the sessions several other nominations for up-listing were also presented, the most contentious of which was the entire genus *Cypripedium*. There was much work behind the scenes to prevent this, because a similar ban on *Phragmipedium* had merely increased interest and black market activity in that genus. Besides which, the *Cypripedium* data presented in the case was not really compelling. Actually the data for *D. cruentum* were not that compelling either, but it seemed a reasonable compromise to allow the listing of *D. cruentum* in exchange for dropping the case for *Cypripedium*.

What is the real situation with *D. cruentum*? It is still not clear. In the 1997 Red Data list of orchids the status of this *Dendrobium* was listed as 'Indeterminate', which meant it was thought to belong to one or other threatened categories, such as Endangered, Vulnerable or Rare. But not enough information was available to allow one to make a clear determination.

Protecting a species from extinction is a good thing, but doing it on speculative or political grounds can backfire. A poor action can dilute the respect for laws intended to protect truly endangered plants. We have seen this particularly with respect to many of the originally listed CITES Appendix I plants. It does not take a genius to figure out that a species, like *Cattleya skinneri*, that is artificially propagated in dozens of orchid nurseries around the world and is also a common garden plant in Costa Rica, is not truly facing extinction. To pretend otherwise does the truly endangered a disservice and detracts from those species that warrant special attention.

Arguments are often made that it is 'better to err on the side of safety', but in fact that is not always in the best interests of a species. A large number of 'guestimates' about the status or extinction of species has turned out to be false or, at best merely an exaggeration. The loss of credibility that the conservation community faces is real. Everyone believes that large numbers of orchid species are endangered but we must have hard data or the effectiveness of controls loose part of their legitimacy.

CHAPTER 14

Going, Going...Gone?

For all species extinction is the final and natural end point. More than 99.9% of all different life forms that ever existed in the past are now extinct. And all of the species that currently live on the earth can be expected to go extinct at some future time. Extinction usually occurs in one of at least four ways.

1   A species can disappear because it has evolved either gradually or abruptly into a new species. The gradation between the old and new species can be difficult to discern.
2   In a second process a species might be unable to adjust to changing environments and, as a result, all its members die out. These environmental changes could be mild or catastrophic but the end point is the loss of yet another species. Global warming is expected to occur much faster than organisms can evolve new adaptations and this is expected to cause a large rise in extinctions.
3   Hybridization and intermingling of genetic materials between two formerly distinct species into one hybrid swarm, with new characteristics, is yet another way that species might be lost.
4   In the last case, a species is unable to tolerate competition or predation by other species and is vanquished. Extinction caused by man falls into the last category. Most conservation biologists believe that there is currently a spate of extinctions occurring, which is much faster than the normal background rate of species loss.

By now there should be a legion of extinct orchids. Predictions of species extinction suggest that an appreciable percentage of tropical species have been lost by now (Wilson, 1988). Computer simulation models (Koopowitz, 1992) predicted that hundreds of species could go extinct each year. Why then, when I came to write this chapter on extinct orchids did I have so much trouble finding verifiable information on orchid extinction? There are several different possible explanations for the disparity.

It is extremely difficult to be exact about when a wild species disappears into the extinction void. There is usually no one around to witness the last individual winking out. When you go out into the field and you search but cannot find the plant, extinction is usually taken to be the cause of its disappearance. During the last few decades there were many rumors of orchids becoming extinct, often by quite reliable sources. *Paphiopedilum* is one of the most intensely studied and used to be a very intensely collected genus. For many years in the past, *P. delenatii*, *P. sanderianum*, *P. wardii* and *P. rothschildianum* were widely believed to be extinct in the wild. Some other slipper orchid species, thought to be 'extinct' and relayed as such to me personally by various 'authorities' (ranging from taxonomists to plant importers), also included, *P. barbatum*, *P. victoria-mariae*, *P. druryi*, and *P. randsii*. Altogether, that makes approximately ten percent of the entire genus. I was once informed, by one of the most authoritative of sources, that *P. barbatum* was now extinct on Penang Hill. This had been the primary source of that species in the slipper orchid trade. In 1997, we searched for that species there, and found it still exists. True, there were not vast quantities, but the species was present and there were also a fair number of seedlings growing, which gives hope for its future security. Other local growers knew of additional sites on the mountain where that species could be found. *Paphiopedilum barbatum* still exists on Penang Hill.

These supposed losses are not confined to the Asiatic slipper orchids. *Acrolophia ustulata*, *Disa marlothii*, *Laelia milleri*, *Phragmipedium besseae*, etc., have all been thought lost, only to reappear in different localities at later times.

How does one account for the discrepancies between the supposed extinctions and actually species lost? There are several reasons. The most obvious is that there may be more localities for species than are actually known. It is often said that we only explore along the roadsides in the tropics and thus our knowledge of real distributions is quite limited. Often a species may not be obvious unless it is in flower and can be difficult to recognize solely on their vegetative parts. Thus, the plants may continue to exist, but because of their reluctance to flower they simply are not recognized. Another reason is that the whole of the habitat may not get destroyed, and a few remnant plants may persist. Botanists and collectors learn that the site was destroyed and assume that all the members of the population have consequently disappeared. However, a few might survive. The few trees left for shade in Mexican meadows and fields are often festooned with orchids. The life span of individual plants can be many decades but even though the species is not extinct its survival prognosis may be dim. The few survivors may have outlived their pollinators or the remnants are so few that inbreeding depression becomes inevitable and the species is doomed. Such survivors have sometimes been called the "living dead". If the habitat remains, there may be seeds, protocorms or tiny seedlings that have survived and these result in the 'miraculous' reappearance of the species within the previously devastated or stripped out habitat. This is particularly true of terrestrial orchids that can have very long subterranean resting periods or developmental stages.

Extinction occurs not only at the species level, but it also occurs at the population level. *Odontoglossum crispum* populations still persist in Columbia but the populations with the finest forms and largest flowers no longer exist. The extant wild populations of that species seem quite different from the original types and the desirable genes which were originally used to produce

61. *Laelia milleri*, originally known from a single mountain that was destroyed in an iron mining operation, in the Serra dos Ingleses in Minas gerais, Brazil. A few other small populations have since been discovered. This is a species maintained through artificial propagation.

the first hybrids of the species probably no longer exist in the remaining wild populations. We don't know how stable orchid populations are. Ecologists have found that in other plants, populations can sometimes be divided into 'source' and 'sink' populations. A source population produces excess progeny, usually seed, which can be distributed to found new populations. Sink populations never seem to amount to much and within them mortality usually exceeds birth rate. Whether or not a population is source or sink depends on the resources available, These include not only suitable host trees, adequate moisture etc., but also the availability of mycorrhizal fungi and pollinators. Sink populations are naturally expected to go extinct and their loss is of little consequence for the ultimate persistence of a species. It is important however, in an era of limited financial resources, that precious conservation effort should not be wasted on sink populations. Unfortunately, the crucial information on how to distinguish between source and sink populations in orchids has not been researched.

At yet another level, within a population, there may be rare genes (for example the mutations that produce blue colors in *Cattleya* or albinism in *Paphiopedilum* species) and these may be very important horticulturally. Such genes can be very infrequent, occurring only once in several hundred thousand individuals. As a population becomes reduced these rare genes may also become extinct. The opportunities available to the plant breeders consequently become diminished.

The IUCN Extinction Lists

In 1997 IUCN published several lists of plant species that were either known to be extinct or thought to be extinct. The orchids in those lists are reproduced below. Unfortunately these lists probably bear little resemblance to reality and the true nature of orchid extinction.

Unfortunately, these lists were published without adequate review and very poor research and in fact a considerable number of the names should not have been included in the tables. The list has become an embarrassment and once again the credibility about levels of endangerment have suffered. In the first list, *Angraecum carpophorum* is actually a synonym for *A. calceolus*, which while possibly extinct on some Indian Ocean islands, is in fact still a common species in Madagascar. *Pleione lagenaria* is most likely a rare natural hybrid between *P. praecox* and *P. maculata* (Cribb and Butterfield, 1988) and thus its status is irrelevant to species extinction.

On the two lists are three *Masdevallia* species, *M. lynchiphora*, *M. menatoi* and *M. walteri*. All three species are united by the fact that they were discovered

Extinct species – IUCN 1997

Species Name	Region
Acianthus ledwardii Rupp.	New South Wales, Australia
Angraecum carpophorum	Reunion, Mauritius
Bulbophyllum pusillum Thouars	Mauritius
Caladenia atkinsonii Rodway	Tasmania, Australia
Caladenia brachyscapa G.W. Carr	Victoria, Australia
Caladenia pumilla R.Rogers	Victoria, Australia
Calanthe whiteana King & Pantl.	Sikkim, India
Corycium vestitum Sweet	Cape Province, South Africa
Diuris bracteata Fitzg.	New South Wales, Australia
Epidendrum ilense Dodson	Ecuador
Habenaria vesiculosa A. Rich	Mauritius
Masdevallia menatoi Luer & Vasq.	Bolivia
Monadenia ecalcarata G.J. Lewis	Cape Province, South Africa
Oberonia attenuata Dockr.	Queensland, Australia
Pleione lagenaria Lindley	Meghalaya, India
Prasophyllum robustum (Nicholls) M.A. Clements & D.L. Jones	South Australia
Pterostylis valida (Nicholls) D.L.Jones	Victoria, Australia
Zeuxine boninensis Ttuy.	Ogasawara shoto, Japan

Thought to be extinct – IUCN 1997

Species Name	Region
Aphyllorchis gollani Duthie	Utar Pradesh, India
Chlorea venosa Griseb.	Peru
Coelogyne treutleri Hook. F.	Sikkim, India
Dendrobium aurantiacum Reichb. F.	Bangladesh, Bhutan
Eulophia seychellarum Rolfe ex Summerhayes	Seychelles
Habenaria horsfieldiana Kranzlin	Java, Indonesia
Liparis lauterbachii Schltr.	Java, Indonesia
Masdevallia lynchiphora Koeniger	Peru
Masdevallia walteri Luer	Costa Rica
Neottia ussuriensis (Komarov & Nevski) Soó	Primorye, Russia
Paphiopedilum delenatii Guillaumin	Vietnam
Triphora latifolia Luer f.	Florida, USA
Vanda wightii Reichb.f.	Tamil Nadu, India
Zeuxine pulchra King & Pantl.	Meghalaya, Sikkim, India

relatively recently and were in populations restricted to a single locality, said to comprise only a few plants. This is not unusual, approximately three-quarters of all the *Masdevallia* species are known from a single locality (Koopowitz, 1993). One wonders if there had been actual searches for living members of those three species or if their listing was based on hearsay?

The lists also included several other species, which a little research would have shown to be inappropriate for the listing. Among these is *Paphiopedilum delenatii*. At the time the list was published it was already common knowledge that this slipper orchid had been rediscovered and was known to exist in vast quantities. Kumar and Manilal (1994) list *Dendrobium auranticum* as occurring in two different regions of India and they did not consider *D. auranticum* especially endangered. In fact, that name is considered to be synonymous with *D. chryseum* which is a widespread species, ranging from India through Southeast Asia and into China.

Calanthe wighteana, is also listed as extinct, but it is still considered to be endangered in India (Kumar and Manilal, 1994). Its true status is unclear because Karasawa and Ishida (1998) list *C. wighteana* as being of uncertain taxonomic status. It may merely be a synonym for a more widespread species.

Another of the species on the 'possibly extinct' list is *Vanda wightii*. This species, which is also considered as endangered, is listed for peninsular India. Eric Christenson (personal communication) considers that *V. wightii* is a synonym for *V. thwaitesii*. The latter plant had been collected in Sri Lanka in 1861 and was initially placed in *Aerides*, the incorrect genus, but was transferred to *Vanda* as *V. thwaitesii* by Hooker in 1898. The plant was difficult to find and in 1981 was declared extinct (Jayaweera, 1981). Kumar and Kumar (1998) reported finding *V. thwaitesii* in some quantity in Kerala, the southern part of peninsular India. The orchid apparently grows in mango trees and had been mistaken for the closely related *V. tessellata*.

Several species on the IUCN extinct list are terrestrial orchids from Australia. The Australians have paid special attention to their own indigenous orchids and it is likely that those names deserve their listings. But it is a pity that some components of the list were so shoddily researched. The list detracts from the credibility and otherwise good work of that important organization.

Only collected once

It is surprising how many of the extinct species of orchid are only known from their type specimens. These were species collected once, described and then never seen again. We will deal with some of these later on in this chapter, when we discuss the demise of a few specific examples. Rao (1988) discussed the conservation status of the known orchid species of Kodagu in the Western Ghats. Of the 283 species evaluated, 6 were only known from their type collections. A seventh species, *Vanda wightii* was discussed above. Over 2% of the species fall into this category. Among these species is *Acampe congesta* (only found on the Indian mainland in 1836, but also thought to occur in Sri Lanka), *Chrysoglossum halbergii* (described in 1917) and *Oberonii belii* (described in 1912).

Not only rare and extinct orchids fall into this category. *Epipactis veratrifolia* is a widespread temperate terrestrial orchid species ranging from Turkey through Asia and into China. This species was collected once by Lawson in the Nilgiri region of India and not seen again – although it is still common outside the Indian subcontinent. Perhaps the plant Lawson collected was the initial founder for what would have eventually developed into a robust population, but because of the chance juxtaposition of Lawson and the *E. veratifolia* the plant was killed and the species never amounted to anything in that particular locality. There are probably lots of similar 'failed' attempts at colonization in the real world. These little local extinctions occur all the time. Sometimes man just helps them along.

Extinct in the wild?

If an orchid has desirable characteristics, such as large and showy flowers, or belongs to a genus where there is intense horticultural interest, the species may be fortunate to persist in cultivation even after the wild populations have disappeared. There are several species that fit into this category.

Laelia gouldiana

In 1888, H.G. Reichenbach described a species of *Laelia* that bore large flowers of spectacular deep purple coloration. The specimen bore no locality information and Reichenbach speculated that it might be of hybrid origin, possibly between the two well-known species *L. autumnalis* and *L. anceps*. Some forms of the former species approach the depth of color found in the new plant. Nevertheless, the plant was described as *L. gouldiana* and is still often considered to be a natural hybrid. One problem with the assertion of hybrid status is that the plant has spindle-shaped pseudobulbs with stiff erect leaves, unlike either parent and it is hard to imagine what the other parent that mated with *L. autumnalis* might have been. In fact *Laelia* Autoceps, the man-made hybrid between *L. autumnalis* and *L. anceps*, does not resemble *L. gouldiana*

62   *Laelia gouldiana* 'Purple Majesty' HCC/AOS is
widespread in cultivation, although it appears to be
extinct in the wild. (Photo credit: Richard Clark and
the American Orchid Society).

and this also lends skepticism to the hybrid claim.

Despite searches, no known wild specimens of *L. goul-diana* have been found and the species is considered "prob-ably extinct in nature" (Halbinger and Soto, 1997). The species is thought to have been endemic to the Sierra Madre Oriental and the oldest specimen was recorded from El Chico, a mining town in the State of Hidalgo. Searches in the vicinity of El Chico came up empty handed. But the species still exists. These days *L. gouldiana* can be found in a semi-feral state near several other towns in Hidalgo. The plants have obviously been placed on stone fences and mesquite trees, where they form very large clumps and are said to be quite magnificent when in bloom. But the flow-ers on all the plants resemble each other fairly closely and people suggest that all are divisions of one single surviving clone. The semi-feral plants bear no seed pods.

While *L. gouldiana* has been used to make a few hybrids with other members of the cattleya alliance the plants are themselves self-sterile and attempts to breed additional individuals of pure *L. gouldiana* have been unsuccessful. It appears that the clone must be the last survivor of its species. Nevertheless, the plants are also widespread in cultivation around the world. The species will linger on provided that it is artificially reproduced.

What had happened to the other plants of this species? Perhaps the population had dwindled down to one surviv-ing plant, which was rescued because it bore attractive flowers. But the vigor and robustness of this last surviving clone suggests that the species had not gone extinct because it was unable to adapt to changing conditions. Was its habitat destroyed? At this point we may never know the real reasons for its disappearance. We will have to be satis-fied that at least one clone still exists.

Phalaenopsis javanica

Here we have another species that appears to survive solely in cultivation, but this time we know why the species appears to have been driven to extinction in the wild. J.J. Smith described the species at the end of the First World War in 1918 but it had been flowered else-where four years earlier. Two plants, one in Ireland and the other in France, flowered in April 1914 and speci-mens of both were sent to Rolfe at Kew, however he was rather tardy in getting the description published. Perhaps recovery from the Great War was to blame. Rolfe's description only appeared in 1920 and so J.J. Smith's epithet took precedence.

Unlike *L. gouldiana*, above, *P. javanica* lacks gor-geous flowers and has never achieved much popularity. Its role in hybridizing has been minor and it is now grown primarily for its rarity. Relatively few hobbyists grow plants because they are rare or endangered. In fact many growers avoid plants of this nature because they are reluctant to assume responsibility for a species that depends on their own horticultural prowess. Consequently the species is quite rare in the commer-cial trade and its ultimate survival is questionable

Phalaenopsis javanica has a demure little cup-shaped flower, with broad overlapping triangular petals. There never seem to be very many flowers open at once on an inflorescence. Individual flowers are basically ivory-cream, overlaid with generous amounts of mid-brown bars, arranged in longitudinal stripes. The lip is a con-trasting fuchsia-purple. The whole flower is glossy and of thick substance. The flowers have a spicy fragrance.

The species has been used in hybridizing. Approximately 60 grexes were registered with *P. javan-icum* as one parent. Few of its progeny were popular, but among the noteworthy hybrids are *P.* Spice Drops, *P.* Rice Cracker and *P.* Javalin. *Phalaenopsis* Rice Cracker was unique in having flowers about the size and lac-quered brown coloring of Japanese rice crackers. It is a very apt name.

As one might expect from its name the species was found on the island of Java. This plant never appears to have been plentiful in the wild and the last known pop-ulation grew on a coffee plantation. J.B. Comber (1990) related that the species was originally found in west Java, south of Garut, at an altitude between 700 and 1000 m. Another population was discovered in 1975 by an expe-dition from the Bangor Botanic Gardens, on a small mountain south of Cianjur. The plants were growing on trees in a coffee plantation and also on other surrounding bushes and small trees. Comber reported that there were quite a few plants of the species on that mountainside. Unfortunately a well-known Indonesian orchid species trader had heard about the discovery and he sent out collectors, who stripped the mountainside of the entire population of *P. javanica*. Subsequent expeditions were unable to find any plants of that species. No one knows if other populations exist elsewhere. It seems quite possible that that the plant is now extinct in the wild. Here we have an obvious example of a species that was wiped out by greedy commercial collectors.

Once it was realized that this species might be extinct in the wild a demand for plants was generated among *Phalaenopsis* breeders and species collectors. Surprisingly a large number of healthy growing plants appeared on the market and these were avidly sought after. Unfortunately when they flowered they proved to be a hybrid with *P. amboinensis* and had no *P. javanicum* characteristics at all. This in turn has persuaded the few growers still in possession of the species to try and propagate their plants. Perhaps the species will be able to persist in cultivation, even if it no longer exists in its natural habitat.

Paphiopedilum lawrenceanum

Here we have an example of a species that was immensely important in hybridizing and is a notable player in a whole race of economically significant pot-plants. Large numbers of the species were originally collected from their native lands and at least 10 significant clones (Pfitzer, 1902) were named and described. Burbidge, who sent *Paphiopedilum lawrenceanum* to Veitch for commercial introduction, discovered the species in Borneo in 1878. Consignments of *P. lawrenceanum* were sent to Europe in 1888, 1889 and 1894. The consignment in 1889 numbered 1,500 plants (Cribb, 1997).

Birk (1983) remarked that it was found near the Lawas river, near Meringit in Sabah (North Borneo). He said that there had not been any recent importations (by 1983) and that its habitat was not known, except from old descriptions. More recently (Cribb, 1997) also remarked that its exact habitat was a mystery and that plants have not been seen recently. Either the species occurs somewhere yet to be discovered (Cribb suggests Sarawak), or the species is now extinct.

In 1968 another slipper orchid, named *P. nigritum*, was collected in Borneo. Cribb (1997) considered that this was a poor form of *P. lawrenceanum* and if he is correct this would signify the most recent collection of the species. The flower is actually an amalgam of the characteristics of *P. lawrenceanum* and *P. javanicum* var. *virens*. It has the marginal warts on both the upper and lower margins of *P. lawrenceanum*, but the stance and

basal speckling of the petals, and the greenish dorsal sepal found *P. javanicum*. *Paphiopedilum nigritum* appears to have been a natural hybrid. Support for this idea comes from the self-pollination of a clone of *P. nigritum* called 'Dyak Warrior'. This cross, which was made by the famous orchid firm of F. A. Stewart Orchids Inc., produced seedlings whose flowers had a wide variety of shapes and colorings, which suggested that the parent was indeed of hybrid origin.

Paphiopedilum lawrenceanum has strongly mottled leaves and a fairly tall flower stem that usually bears a single flower. Flowers can be quite large and have a relatively flat, rounded dorsal sepal, it has a white background with variable amounts of purple striping. The petals are rather narrow and are usually held horizontally. Both the upper and lower margins of the petals bear black hairy warts. *Paphiopedilum lawrenceanum* var. *hyeanum* is a famous albino flower, without purple pigment. Strictly the name should refer to a *forma* and not a variety, as the albinism was originally confined to a single clone and not a distinct wild population of the species. When crossed with *P. callosum* the grex *P. Maudiae* is made and this is the base for the modern 'Maudiae-type' hybrids, which currently dominate the commercial slipper orchid pot-plant market.

The species, *P. lawrenceanum*, is relatively safe in captivity and both albinistic and colored forms are readily available at reasonable prices. The species is easy to grow, it tolerates a relatively wide range of growing conditions and it is reasonably safe. Signs of inbreeding depression (i.e. the loss of vigor that results from breeding closely related parents) are becoming evident in some of the cultivated stock. If wild populations still exist, it would be worthwhile crossing some of these plants with cultivated material.

Encyclia viridiflora

In 1828 Hooker described a new genus that was related to *Cattleya* and yet did not have the stunning flowers (he called them splendid) typical of that genus. In truth, this new species had decidedly small, dull green flowers. The labellum of the flower enfolded the column and hence he called it *Encyclia*, from the Greek word meaning circumvolute or wrapped around. That character, however, did not distinguish the genus from *Cattleya*. Instead, Hooker pointed to the non-resupinate flowers, the less patent petals and different growth habit. For a long time the name *Encyclia* was out of favor, but today we now use that genus to include those 'epidendrums' which have pseudobulbs. *Encyclia* comprises a very large group of species, spread over a wide geographical range, from just north of Florida down to Argentina. Although there are now attempts to break the genus into a number of smaller taxa it is still an important taxon.

Encyclia viridiflora was the founding species of the genus. William Harrison originally collected the plant near Rio and brought it back to England. He gave it to his sister who flowered the new species in her 'stove' (the term used for conservatories that were used to grow exotic plants). When the plant flowered it was conveyed to Hooker, who had it painted and subsequently described it. The plant had small rounded

63 *Encyclia viridiflora.* The founding species of this important genus has not been seen since its original description in 1828, published in *Curtis's Botanical Magazine.* (Photo credit: Huntington Library, Art Galleries and Botanical Gardens)

pseudobulbs, with two strap-shaped leathery leaves. The inflorescence was a foot high (30 cm) with several branches, each bearing six to eight flowers. The flowers carried their lips uppermost, the petals and sepals were green and the lip a brown-green color with some red markings. It was not really the sort of flower to show off to one's friends. Yet it was new and would eventually prove to be the basis of an important new genus.

The species has not been seen for a long time and Eric Christenson (personal communication) considers it to be extinct. Why was this species lost? It had almost no appeal, except to species orchid growers, and it seems unlikely to have been collected out for commercial trade. We can, however, speculate about the reasons for the species' demise. Some people have calculated that as much as 98% of the original Brazilian Atlantic forested area has been cleared. Much of the cutting has been done to convert land for agricultural use and *E. viridiflora* may have been a casualty of that process. On the other hand, Harrison collected the plant near Rio, over a 150 years ago. That city has expanded since then and has become one of the major cities of the world. Most of what were once nearby hills have been engulfed and are now covered with asphalt and concrete. It would not be surprising if the ever-growing metropolis had eaten up the original locality. All things considered, it is amazing that more species are not known to have gone extinct that way.

Corycium vestitum

In 1772, a Swedish surgeon, Carl Thunberg, arrived at the Cape of Good Hope, in southern Africa. He had been a student of the great Carl von Linné (Linnaeus), inventor of the binomial system of species nomenclature that we still use today. Eventually Thunberg returned to Sweden and succeeded his mentor, assuming Linné's academic position. Thunberg was one of the most important early botanists to explore the plant treasures of the Cape floral kingdom, which is one of the richest in the world.

One of the orchids that Thunberg found in the western Cape was named *Corycium vestitum.* It was collected only once and has never been seen in the wild since. Like *Encyclia viridiflora*, discussed above, there are many other orchid species that are only known from single collections, which may also now be extinct in the wild. Kumar and Manilal (1994) list a number of Indian species that fit into the same category. The reasons for those extinctions are not known and probably bear little relevance to the conservation problems that orchids face at the current time.

The genus, *Corycium*, contains terrestrial herbs that produce a central inflorescence usually bearing large numbers of quite small and insignificant flowers. *Corycium vestitum* differed from other species in the shape of the lip. There are about 24 species in the genus and one must admit that few of them are attractive. The little hooded flowers tend to be greenish, often suffused with brown shades. Several of the species are widespread. Perhaps the most noteworthy among them is C. *nigrescens* which is one of the few orchids that has black flowers.

Descriptions from the single herbarium sheet of C. *vestitum* that is still in existence are of a plant with an inflorescence slightly shorter than a foot (30 cm) tall. It was a robust species with a dense spike of quite small flowers; the petals were 8 mm long and the labellum only 3 mm long. The specimen does not have leaves, so we do not know what they were like. Was this pressed specimen, by chance one of the last of its species naturally on its way to extinction, or does it still linger in obscurity in some hidden part of the Cape?

Epidendrum ilense

This is, in some respects, both a success and at the same time a very depressing story. Originally only three or four plants were found in the wild and many people have referred to this species as an example of one thought to be extinct in the wild. Following its initial discovery, the species was brought to the Selby Botanic Gardens where it was 'meristemmed' i.e. artificially propagated using tissue culture methods. Amid considerable publicity, plantlets were distributed to other Botanic Gardens and orchid hobby growers. The orchid gradually made its way into the trade and has become fairly widely available. Initially all growers understood the endangered status of the species, but with the passing of time and as the species has become more common in cultivation the knowledge of its special status appears to have dissipated.

Approximately 50 plantlets of *E. ilense* were returned to Centinela in Ecuador, for reintroduction to the wild, but their progress was never reported. The reason, of course, was that not one plant had been successfully re-established. Calway Dodson (personal communication) suggests that plants were either attached to inappropriate host trees or someone came along later and removed them. It is also likely that only a small percentage of any orchid seedlings inherit the correct set of adaptations that allow them to survive in the wild. Consequently, when pampered nursery seedlings are 'reintroduced' they are simply not adapted for survival in the wild and sooner or later succumb. This would also explain the abysmal survival rates seen with other attempts at species reintroduction, both for orchids and other plant families.

In the case of *Epidendrum ilense*, two other small populations were found in the wild, one near Santa Domingo, about 40 km from the original site to the north, and another about 60 km to the South. While the species is not yet extinct, Dodson (personal communication) rates its chances of survival in the wild as ranging from "bleak to zilch."

Caladenia atkinsonii and Caladenia pumila

The genus *Caladenia* comprises about 70 species and is centered in Australia, but extends northwards to the islands of South East Asia. The sepals and petals are often elongated, which has given the group the common

64   *Caladenia pumila*. An orchid from Victoria, Australia that has not been seen for decades despite thorough searching. One of the few orchid species that is most likely extinct. (Photo from *Orchids of Victoria*, Precott, 1928)

name of Spider orchids. Usually there is only a single flower carried on a slender stalk, but some may have a raceme with up to six flowers. They are terrestrial orchids with a solitary leaf. The flowers are generally attractive. The Australians have kept pretty good records on locality data of all their terrestrial orchids. The IUCN list contains three Australian *Caladenia* species, namely C. *atkinsonii*, C. *brachyscapa* and C *pumila*. Two of these, C. *atkinsonii* and C. *pumila*, also appear in Dixon and Hopper's list of extinct orchids. The former species was found on the island of Tasmania and the latter on the Australian mainland, in Victoria.

The dwarf caladenia, C. *pumila*, had quite large flowers. A Miss B. Pilloud of Bannockburn, Victoria, discovered the species in 1922 and it seems to have had a very restricted distribution. But although the species was geographically very restricted, plants were recorded as being plentiful in the area. This was a charming species, the plants were dwarf, only between two to four inches tall, but the flowers were relatively large and pretty. The sepals and petals were white but the labellum, also white, had a pink margin and the rows of calli on the lip were also colored pink. The species was painted from life in 1932 (Nicholls, 1969) and a photograph was published in *The Orchids of Victoria* at approximately the same time. When the last flowering occurred is not known, but Nicholls does not mention its possible extinction when he finished his book in 1950. David Jones (1988) recorded that the status of the orchid was

puzzling because it was "locally common" early on, but it then seems to have just disappeared and despite repeated searches could not be found again. The species appeared to have gone extinct.

*Caladenia atkinsoni*i, on the other hand, appears to belong to that select group of orchids which having been once collected and described, is never seen again. The relevance of the extinction of this type of orchid is of no significance for conservation. The third extinct species name listed by IUCN, C. *brachyscapa*, does not appear to be recognized by Nicholls or Jones and the story behind its listing appears to be quite obscure.

It should be clear by now that we have little direct knowledge of the numbers of orchids that have succumbed to extinction in recent years and how much of the loss is actually due to anthropogenic activities and how much is the natural end point we expect for any species. While there may be additional information hidden in various lists and floras that contain the names of species that really have been lost, they are well hidden.

But as we watch the world's forests become decimated it is hard not to believe that land conversion must be driving many species to extinction. Unfortunately we may never truly know the real extent of what we have lost. Wherever there is intense exploration we often find that new species can be found. But at the same time it is clear to anyone who visits the tropics that the forests are being destroyed and it is only logical to assume that unknown species are also disappearing.

CHAPTER 15

Last Words

There is more to orchid conservation than merely saving species and their habitats. There are other aspects of orchids, which have neither been touched upon nor commented about in this book. Collating and writing the information needed for this work has given me insights which I did not expect, and I would like to make some final comments on these.

Orchid sociology

There is an entire sociology of recorded orchid activities and history that extends back over more than 150 years, which is worth preserving. There are records of meetings of societies, which can get lost as office holders change and the societies themselves die or dwindle away. Even published proceedings can be lost, as, one by one, those old books are destroyed or become forgotten. Besides these there is a category of special antique orchid books and pictures. Many of these volumes, not only possess pretty and sometimes magnificent paintings, but are also records of the thoughts and styles of the times. They are also records of some of the magnificent plants, mainly species, which were flowered in the past. There is a regrettable tendency for antiquity dealers to dismember 'picture' books, because they can make more money selling individual plates than the entire assemblage. This is especially true when older works contain hand colored lithographs.

Many of the older books were printed in very limited numbers, often only in the hundreds, and the loss or destruction of any single volume is meaningful in terms of the long-term conservation of the work. Reprints are made, from time to time, of major old works and while this is good they usually fail to capture the essence of those earlier works. We need to cultivate a new consciousness that there is a responsibility that goes along with owning an antique orchid book and allowing or causing its destruction is tantamount to a criminal activity. But there is also an obligation that goes along with those old lithographs and paintings that might be hanging on your walls too. They need to be protected from light with UV absorbing glass and acid free mounting boards.

If one owns precious old books or paintings, provision needs to be made in one's will for their care. Your heirs may not know one botanical artist from another and may not care anyway but if they are singled out then perhaps some appreciation of their value can prevent them from being junked.

As we shift from paper hard copy to electronic recordings there may be increasing resistance to maintaining collections of real books. We see this already in libraries where older books are consigned to storage vaults or sold off. One of the problems with electronic recordings is that one needs a machine to access the material and because both hardware and software technologies change so fast it is most likely that modern orchid works now being placed on compact disk will be totally illegible in 20 years time. Even pages placed on the Internet are not time proof, they can be lost, particularly if servers are changed or become obsolete.

Orchid hybrids

There is another aspect of orchid conservation to which we have given little attention and that is the preservation of important living hybrids and species clones, that have played historic and pivotal roles in orchid hybridization. There are many of these plants such as *Cymbidium* Alexanderi 'Westonbirt', C. Peter Pan 'Greensleeves', *Paphiopedilum* F.C. Puddle, *P.* Winston Churchill 'Indominatable' FCC/AOS, to mention only a very few of a very large number of important breeders. Despite the fact that many of these older clones are hopelessly infected by viruses, they should be preserved. One can never tell when they might become important again. Virus can be cleaned out of plants and virus infected parents can still produce virus-free seeds. It may be impossible to remake those important plants, because the exact species clones used to produce them are probably extinct at this time.

Conservation and sociology

One cannot discuss the conservation of species without acknowledging the aspirations of those other peoples who live in the areas of high orchid biodiversity. It is easy to command or assert that people should stop cutting down their forests, or cease converting savannas to croplands or should not dam a river to fill a valley to provide water and electricity. But there are times when conservation conflicts with the aspirations of native peoples. How does one tell a woman not to cut down a tree for firewood when she has no prospects of getting enough work to afford the fuel for her family's meals? In a world where a small child dies every few seconds from starvation, how can one tell a man not to make a field to grow food for his children if there is no other way to provide them with nourishment? No one has the moral right to do that, unless those people are also willing to provide the where-with-all for making a decent living and the possibility of fulfilling their own various personal aspirations. In the current world, with the prospects of another doubling of the world's population within a few decades, the pressures to destroy the remaining wild life will double too. Is it possible to solve the problem?

Western man has had a long history of ecosystem destruction. The plains of Spain and the rocky countryside of Greece were once forested; large areas of the Sahara desert were formerly rich farmland - it was the granary of Ancient Rome. During the 19th and 20th centuries, the European colonial powers ransacked much of the rest of the world, seizing lands and resources as if it were their divine right. It is difficult with this background to sit back and hypocritically advise the 'less developed' world what they should or should not do, even if one really did know what they 'should' do. The western world's record of ecological altruism is poor.

Pessimism!

While it appears true that fewer species than we expected appear to have become extinct, there are other problems that need to be faced. The gene pool of a species is the sum of all the different genes and alleles that can be found in that species. As populations lose members, because of human activities, one also tends to lose specific genes. The innate gene pool variation becomes reduced and by chance rare alleles are lost. This is genetic erosion. Biologists suspect that it is these rarer genes that allow species to adapt to changing environments. Genetic erosion is detrimental to the long-term prospects of any species and we believe that genet-ic erosion is all too common in reduced populations, even if they are not endangered.

More pessimism

We do not pay enough attention to the effects of pesticides and land conversion on natural pollinator populations. There are real concerns that, even if we are protecting species, we may not be protecting their pollinators. This is particularly important with orchids, where a large percentage of the species have specific pollen vectors.

Optimism!

When I started researching for and writing this book the situation looked hopeless. Twenty-five years ago, many biologists were convinced that by the turn of the millennium as many as one in five flowering plant species would have become extinct. Now that we have entered the 21st century, we find that there is little real concrete evidence of such enormous losses. But we are not in the clear. The forests continue to be cut and the global climate change that only looked like a possibility in 1980 now seems to be a certainty. Why have so few of the orchids gone extinct? In part the answer lies in the fact that although the Earth is, but a small blue planet, it is in fact quite vast and even small remaining percentages of habitat can hold large number of species. Another part of the answer lies in the nature of orchids themselves. They take a long time to die. Many of those that still exist are merely the last remnants of their species, their pollinators have succumbed or the populations are now too small to be viable and so these are merely the living dead – but they can persist or linger for another hundred years before they wink out. Despite this, we now know that we can save most of them if we really want to. It is merely a matter of will and commitment.

Summary

In this book I have tried to review the situation that orchids face as we enter a new millennium. These problems are not peculiar to the *Orchidaceae* but are shared with most of the other plant and animal species in the world. There are a few points that we need to reiterate in order to sum up the situation succinctly. The main lesson to 'take home' is that in nature, orchids need to be integral parts of functioning ecosystems, if they are to continue. We can preserve them in other ways but the easiest and most economical is the natural way, keeping them in healthy and complete ecosystems. The main source of the problem is the ever-burgeoning human population. Even if families can be made smaller the absolute number of people still increases. The average age of individual people is increasing and that adds to the problem. But it is possible to curtail human population growth. We have seen this in modern Western Europe. It is also possible to feed the entire human population, but that should be no excuse to make yet more people, because each person places a pollution and disruption load on the planet and they all add up.

Education is one crucial aspect for dealing with this crisis and with modern mass communication technologies it could be accomplished. The situation is not hopeless, although the current situation is still not seen as a crisis by most of the population. The main reason for this is that man prefers to live in cities, divorced from the real world and thus divorced from nature itself. Man is unaware of the deterioration in the world's ecosystem.

About half of the world's tropical forests have already either been destroyed, severely altered or reduced and much of the rest is still under threat. About 10% of tropical forested area is placed under variable protection and that is probably sufficient to safeguard about half of the wild orchid species. It is possible to save most of the rest but it will require forceful action. Apathy in the future will lead to both further genetic erosion and also increased species extinction.

There is probably no single means of ensuring the continuance of all species. Those that do survive will do so because of a combination of luck, as well as directed action. It seems unlikely that one can rely on institutions or governments for more than passive assistance, because orchids are low priority species, with little direct medicinal or economic importance. Past experience with institutions, their changing priorities and financial resources suggest that such places are poor sites for long-term management of orchid species collections. We have also seen that ideas or plans of action are easy to formulate, but difficult to execute. That should not, however, be taken as an indication that the situation is hopeless. It means that for effective conservation, eternal vigilance must be maintained. The situation is not hopeless, I believe that most orchid species can be saved, either in *ex situ* or preferably in *in situ* conditions.

It appears to be man's nature that he responds best to crisis situations. He seems unable to plan effectively ahead. It is only in bitter life and death situations that effective steps are usually promulgated. Does this mean that we must wait for ecosystems to deteriorate to the levels seen in the Atlantic rainforests of Brazil, the mountains of Malaysia or the forests of Madagascar? One hopes not, but human nature being what it is, that may turn out to be the case.

Because orchids are one of the major hobby plant groups there is a good chance that amateur enthusiasts can bear much of the burden of insuring the continuance of many species. Maintenance in cultivation will be the only hope for many orchid species but that too is fraught with difficulties. We need to guard against artificial selection, which will produce the kinds of overblown, unnatural flat and rounded flowers that orchid judges seem to prefer. We will also need to guard against accidental hybridizing. But the enormous numbers of growers and enthusiasts opens a way to keep large gene pools in existence. It may come to pass that the 'last best hope' for many species will be in *ex situ* private collections where species can be hoarded or passed on from grower to grower.

Unfortunately, it seems unlikely, that sufficient ecological work will be performed in the near future that could give us insight into the management of natural wild orchid populations. Active management of wild orchid species is unlikely at the present time and we just do not have the accurate information that is required. Our best hopes are that sufficient intact ecosystems will remain so that a majority of the species will continue to eke out an existence. It is not too late, we are actually in a fortunate position, surprisingly few species are extinct.

It is surprising how little attention people give to the deteriorating environmental situation. Most educated people these days are divorced from the real world, they live in cities and these concrete cocoons insulate them and they come to believe that their existence is independent of the environment. A recent study suggested that 40% of all human deaths were either directly or indirectly related to pollution and/or environmental factors, exasperated by the human population explosion. If you were forced to cross a street, where you had a four in ten chance of being killed by traffic, you would not accept it passively. You would be on all sorts of committees and working actively to change the situation. The current predicament in the world is no different. Are you simply going to watch the world deteriorate and when you or one of your loved ones dies from pollution-induced cancer or a storm that results from climatic changes brought about by global warming. Will you merely wring your hands helplessly? We cannot save the entire world but we can still preserve a good portion of it. Are you going to do your part?

Bibliography

Aiken, S.R. and Leigh, C.H. (1992). *Vanishing Rain Forests: The Ecological Transition in Malaysia.* Clarendon Press, Oxford.

Alves, R.J.V. (1998). Ex situ Conservation. The importance of private collections in conservation of endangered species. In *Proceedings of the 15th World Orchid Conference.* (ed. C.E. de Britto Pereira), pp.355-357. Naturalia Publications, Turriers.

Batten, A. and Bokelmann, H. (1966). *Wild Flowers of the Eastern Cape Province.* Books of Africa, Cape Town.

Biegel, H. (1976). *Rhodesian Wild Flowers.* National Museums and Monuments of Rhodesia, Salisbury.

Birk, L. A. (1983). *The Paphiopedilum Growers Manual.* Pisang Press, Santa Barbara.

Bokemühl, L. (1989). *Odontoglossum: Monographie und Ikonographie.* Brücke-verlag Kurt Schmersow, Hildesheim.

Bowling, J.C. and Thompson, P.A. (1972). On storing orchid seeds. *Orchid Rev.* **80**, pp. 120-121.

Brawer, M. (1991). *Atlas of South America.* Simon and Schuster, New York.

Foster R.B. and Hubbell, S.P. (1990). The floristic composition of the Barro Colorado island forest. In *Four Neotropical Forests* (ed. A. H. Gentry), pp. 85-98. Yale University Press, New Haven.

Case, F.W. Jr. (1987). *Orchids of the Western Great Lakes Region.* Cranbrook Institute of Science. Bulletin 48, revised edition.

Castle, L. (1886). *Orchids, their structure, history and culture* (illustrated). Journal of Horticulture. London.

Caufield, C. (1984). *In the Rainforest.* Chicago University Press, Chicago.

Collins, N.M., Sayer, J.A. and Whitmore, T.C. (eds.) (1991). *The Conservation Atlas of Tropical Forests.* Simon and Schuster, New York.

Chan, C.L., Lamb, A., Shim, P.S. and Wood, J.J. (1994). *Orchids of Borneo. Vol.1 Introduction and Selection of Species.* The Sabah Society, Kota Kinabalu in association with Royal Botanic Gardens. Kew.

Cochrane,M.A., Alencar, A., Schulze, M.D., Souza, C.M. Jr., Nepstad, D.C., Lefebvre, P. and Davidson E.A. (1999). Positive feedbacks in the fire dynamic of closed canopy tropical forests. *Science* **284**, pp. 1832-1835.

Correll, D.S. (1950). *Native Orchids of North America.* Chronica Botanica Co. Waltham, Mass.

Cribb, P. (1987). *The Genus Paphiopedilum.* Royal Botanic Gardens, Kew.

Cribb, P. (1997). *The Genus Cypripedium.* Royal Botanic

Gardens, Kew.

Cribb, P. (1997). *Slipper Orchids of Borneo.* Natural History Publications, Kota Kinabalu.

Cribb, P. (1998). *The Genus Paphiopedilum. Second Edition.* Natural History Publications, Kota Kinabalu (Borneo) in association with Royal Botanic Gardens, Kew.

Cribb, P. and Butterfield, I. (1988). *The Genus Pleione.* Royal Botanic Gardens, Kew.

Deorani, S.C. and Naithani H. B. (1995). *Orchids of Nagaland.* Devender Singh for Oriental Enterprises, Dehra Dun, India.

D'Alessandro, D. (1987). Orchids of Southern Ecuador. In *Proceedings of the 12th World Orchid Conference.* (eds. K Saito and R. Tanaka), pp. 131-133. Tokyo.

Dodson, C. and Gentry, A.H. (1991). Biological extinction in western Ecuador. *Ann. Missouri Bot. Gard.* **78**, pp. 273-295.

Dressler, R.L. (1981). *The Orchids: Natural History and Classification.* Harvard University Press, Cambridge.

Dressler, R.L. (1993). *Phylogeny and Classification of the Orchid Family.* Dioscorides Press. Portland.

Du Puy, D. and Cribb, P. (1988). *The Genus Cymbidium.* Christopher Helm, London.

Dixon, K. and Hopper, S. (1996). Australia. In *Orchids - Status Survey and Conservation Action Plan.* (eds. E. Hágsater and V. Dumont), pp. 109-118. IUCN, Gland, Switzerland.

Elliott, D. (1995). *Wild Roots.* Healing Arts Press, Rochester.

Endress, P.K. (1996). *Diversity and Evolutionary Biology of Tropical Flowers.* Cambridge University Press, Cambridge.

Falk, D.A., Millar, C.I., and Olwell, M. (1996). *Restoring Diversity: Strategies for Reintroduction of Endangered Plants.* Island Press, Washington, D.C.

FAO (1991). *FAO Yearbook Production 1990.* Volume 44. (FAO Statistics Series No. 99) Food and Agricultural Organization of the United Nations, Rome.

Frankel, O.H. and Soulé, M.E. (1981). *Conservation and Evolution.* Cambridge University Press. Cambridge.

Fowlie, J.A. (1970). *The Genus Lycaste.* Day Printing Corp. Pomona California.

Gelfand, M., Mavi, S., Drummond, R.B., and Ndemera, B. (1985). *The Traditional Medicinal Practitioner in Zimbabwe.* Mambo Press, Gweru.

Gentry, A.H. (1990). Floristic similarities and differences between southern central America and upper and central Amazonia. In *Four Neotropical Forests* (ed. A. H. Gentry), pp. 141-157. Yale University

Press, New Haven.

Gloudon, A. and Tobish, C. (1995). *Orchids of Jamaica*. The Press, University of the West Indies, Kingston.

Grell, E., Haas-von Schmude, N.F., Lamb, A. and Bacon, A. (1988). Reintroducing *Paphiopedilum roth-schildianum* to Sabah, North Borneo. *Amer. Orchid Soc. Bull.* **57**, pp. 1238-1246.

Grieve, M. (1971). *A Modern Herbal. Vol 1 A-H*. Dover Press, New York.

Gruss, O. (1996). *Die Gattung Phragmipedium*. Deutsche Orchideen Gesellschaft, Supplement nr. 4. Hagemann-Druck, Hildesheim.

Halbinger F., and Soto, M. (1997). *Laelias of Mexico*. Orquidea (Méx.) Herbario AMO, Mexico City.

Handa, S.S. (1986). Orchids for drugs and chemicals. In *Biology, Conservation and Culture of Orchids* (ed. S.P. Vij), pp. 89-100. Affiliated East-West Press.

Hansen, E. (1997). The flower of frozen desserts. *Natural History* **4**, pp. 76-79.

Harborne, J.B. (1972). Evolution and function of flavonoids in plants. In *Recent Advances in Phytochemistry*. (eds. V.C. Runeckles and J.E. Watkin), pp.107-141, Appleton-Century-Crofts, New York.

Harrington, J.F. (1972). Seed storage and longevity. In *Seed Biology* (ed.T.T. Kowlowski), pp.145-245, Academic Press, New York.

Hegnauer, R. (1966). Comparative phytochemistry of alka-loids. In *Comparative Phytochemistry* (ed. T. Swain), pp. 211-230. Academic Press, London

Hilton-Talyor, C. (1996). *Red Data List of Southern African Plants*. National Botanical Institute, Pretoria.

Hondelmann, W. 1976. Seed Banks. In *Conservation of Threatened Plants* (eds. J.B. Simmons *et al.*), pp. 213-224. Plenum Press, New York.

Ingram, S.W., Ferrell-Ingram, K. and N.M. Nadkarni (undated) *Epiphytes of the Monteverde Cloud Forest Reserve*. Marie Selby Botanical Gardens, Sarasota.

Jayaweera, D.M.A. (1981). Orchidaceae. In *A Revised Handbook of the Flora of Ceylon* (eds. M.D. Dassanayke and F.R. Fosberg), volume 2, pp. 230. New Amerind. Publ. Co. New Dehli.

Jones, D.L. (1988). *Native Orchids of Australia*. Reed Books, French's Forest, NSW.

Karsawa, K. and Ishida, G. (1998). *Calanthe*. Yasaka Shobo Inc., Tokyo.

Kokwaro, J.O. (1993). *Medicinal Plants of East Africa*. Kenya Literature Bureau, Nairobi.

Koopowitz, H. (1992). A stochastic model for the extinc-tion of tropical orchids. *Selbyana* **13**, pp. 115-122.

Koopowitz, H. and Thornhill, A.D. (1994). Gene banking and orchid seeds. *Amer. Orchid Soc. Bull.* **63**, pp. 1383-1386.

Koopowitz, H. and Ward, R. (1984). A technological solu-tion for the practical conservation of orchid species. *Orchid Advocate* **10**, pp. 43-45.

Koopowitz, H. and Hasegawa, N. (2000). *Paphiopedilum viniferum*, a new species name for a well-known plant. *Orchid Digest* **64**, pp. 148-151.

Koopowitz, H., Andersen, M., Thornhill, A., Nguyen, H. and Pham, A. (1994). Comparison of distributions of terrestrial and epiphytic orchids: implications for conservation. In *Proceedings of the14ᵗʰ World Orchid Conference* (ed. A. Pridgeon), pp.120-124.

HMSO Publications, Edinburgh.

Koopowitz, H., Ngo, T.M., Marchant, T.A., Andersen, M. and Thornhill, A. (1997). Endemism comparisons between zoophilous anthophyta and terrestrial cryptograms in the neotropics. In *Tropical diversi-ty, origins, maintenance, and conservation*, p. 75. Association for Tropical Biology, program and abstracts.

Koopowitz, H., Thornhill, A.D. and Andersen, M. (1993). Species distribution profiles of the neotropical orchids *Masdevallia* and *Dracula* (Pleurothallidinae, Orchidaceae): implications for conservation. *Biodiversity and Conservation* **2**, pp. 681-690.

Koopowitz, H., Thornhill, A.D. and Andersen, M. (1993). A general stochastic model for the prediction of biodiversity losses based on habitat conversion. *Conservation Biology* **8**, pp. 425-438.

Koopowitz, H., Sohmer, S.H., Thornhill, A. and Perez, G. (1998). Deforestation and plant species extinc-tions in the Philippines: *Psychotria* as an example. In *Rare, Threatened, and Endangered Floras of Asia and the Pacific Rim*. (eds. C.-I Peng and P.P. Lowry II), pp. 111-121. Acta Sinica Monograph Series No. 16. Taipei.

Kumar, C.S. and Kumar, P.C.S. (1998). The reappearance of *Vanda thwaitesii* J.D.Hook. (Orchidaceae). *Reedea* **8**, pp. 249-235.

Kumar, C.S. and Manilal, K.S. (1994). *A Catalogue of Indian Orchids*. Bishen Singh Mehendra Pal Singh, Dehra Dun, India.

Kummer,D.M.(1992). *Deforestation in the Postwar Philippines*. University of Chicago Geography Research Paper: No. 234.

Kurzweil, H. (1987). Developmental studies in orchid flowers. I: Epidendroid and vandoid species. *Nordic Journal of Botany* **7**, pp. 427-442.

Laurance, W.F. and Bierregaard, O. (1997). *Tropical Forest Remnants : ecology, management and conservation of fragmented communities*. University of Chicago Press, Chicago.

Lawler, L.J. (1984). Ethnobotany of the *Orchidaceae*. In *Orchid Biology: reviews and perspectives III*. (ed. J. Arditti), pp. 21-149. Cornell University Press, Ithaca.

Ledoux, M. M. (1996). The diminutive *Phragmipedium xerophyticum*. *Orchid Digest* **60**, pp. 122-128.

Leigh, E.G., Rand, A.S. and Windsor, D.M. (1996). *The Ecology of a Tropical Forest: seasonal rhythms and long term changes*. Smithsonian Institution, Washington DC.

Leuer, C.A. (1975). *The Native Orchids of the United States and Canada excluding Florida*. New York Botanical Garden, New York.

Lin, T. (1977). *Native Orchids of Taiwan. Vol. 2*. Southern Materials Center, Inc. Taipei.

Linden, E. (1998). Environment: Smoke signals. *Time* **151**: No. 24, pp. 50-51.

Lovejoy, T.E., Rankin. J.M., Bierregaard, R.O., Brown, K,S. Jr., Emmons, L.H., and Van der Voort., M. E. (1984). Ecosystem decay of Amazon forest remnants. In *Extinctions* (ed. M.H. Niteki), University of Chicago Press, Chicago.

Lugo, A.E. (1988). Estimating reductions in the diversity of tropical forest species. In *Biodiversity* (ed. E.O. Wilson), pp. 58-70. National Academy

Press. Washington D.C.

Mac Donald, N. (1939). *The Orchid Hunters*. Raffar & Rhinehart Inc., New York.

Mace, G., and Stuart, S. (1993-94). Draft IUCN Red List Categories, Version 2.2. *Species*. **21-22**, pp. 13-24.

Mammen, V. and Mammen, J. (1974). Rediscovering *Paphiopedilum druryi* in Southern India. *Orchid Digest* **38**, pp. 31-36.

Mann, C. (1991). Extinction: are ecologists crying wolf? *Science* **253**, pp. 736-738.

McDonald, G. and Duckworth, A. (1994). The uses of orchids in traditional healing. *South African Orchid Journal*. **25**, pp. 75-79.

McMahan, L. and Walters, K.S. (1988). The international orchid trade. In *Audubon Wildlife Report 1988/1989*. (ed. W.J. Chandler), pp. 377-392. Academic Press, San Diego.

Miller, M.A. (1978). Orchids of economic use. *Amer. Orchid Digest*. **47**, pp. 512-522.

Motes, M. R. (1997). *Vandas: Their Botany, History, and Culture*. Timber Press, Portland.

Myers, N. (1980). *Conversion of Tropical Moist Forests*. National Academy Press. Washington D.C.

Myers, N. (1983). *The Primary Source: Tropical Forests and Our Future*. W.W. Norton Company, New York.

National Research Council (U.S.) (1982). *Ecological Aspects of Development in the Humid Tropics*. National Academy Press, Washington, D.C.

Nelson, E. (1967). Das Orchideenlabellum ein Homologon des einfachen medianen Petalums oder ein zusammengesetztes Organ? *Bot. Jahrb. Syst*. **87**, pp. 22-35.

Nicholls, W.H. (1969). *Orchids of Australia*. Thomas Nelson, Melbourne.

Nilsson, L.A., Rabakonandirianina, E., and Pettersson, B. (1992). Exact tracking of pollen transfer and mating of plants. *Nature* **360**, pp. 666-668.

Ody, P. (1993). *The Complete Medicinal Herbal*. DK Publish. Inc. New York.

Pescott, E.E. (1928). *The Orchids of Victoria*. Horticultural Press, Melbourne.

Plucknett, D.L., Smith, N.J.H., Williams, J.T. and Anishetty, N.M. (1987). *Gene Banks and the World's Food*. Princeton University Press, Princeton, New Jersey.

Polunin, Ivan. (1988). *Plants and Flowers of Malaysia*. Times Editions, Singapore.

Preston-Mafham, K. (1991). *Madagascar: a Natural History*. Facts on File, Oxford.

Pritchard, H. W. (1986). Orchid seed storage at the Royal Botanic Gardens, Kew, England. *Orchid. Res. Newsl*. **7**: p.18

Pritchard. H.W. and Seaton, P.T. (1993). Orchid seed storage: historic perspective, current status, and future prospects for long-term conservation. *Selbyana* **14**, pp. 89-104.

Prance, G.T. (1990). The floristic composition of the forests of Central Amazonian Brazil. In *Four Neotropical Rainforests* (ed. A.H. Gentry). pp. 112-140. Yale University Press, New Haven.

Putz, F.E., Leigh, E.G., and Wright, S.J. (1990). Solitary confinement in Panama. *Garden* **14**, pp. 18-23.

Reid, D. (1995). *A Handbook of Chinese Healing Herbs*. Shambala, Boston.

Reinikka, M.A. (1995). *A History of the Orchid*. Timber Press, Portland.

Richter, W. (1965). *The Orchid World*. E.P. Dutton & Co., Inc. New York.

Roberts, J. A., Allman, L.R., Beale, C.R., Butter, R.W., Crook. K.R. and McGough, H.N. (1997). *CITES Orchid Checklist. Vol 2*. Royal Botanic Gardens, Kew.

Roberts, J. A., Beale, C.R., Benseler, J.C., McGough, H.N., and Zappi, D. C. (1995). *CITES Orchid Checklist. Vol 1*. Royal Botanic Gardens, Kew.

Rogers. T., Bohan, G. and Koopowitz, H. (1998). An initial assessment of wild populations of *Paphiopedilum sanderianum* (Rchb.f.) Stein and their reproductive fitness. In *Proceedings of the 15th World Orchid Conference*. (ed. C.E. de Britto Pereira, pp. 415-421 Naturalia Publications. Turriers.

Ruschi, A. (1986).*Orquideas do Estado do Espirito Santo*. Expressão e Cultura, Rio de Janeiro.

Sayer, J.A. and Whitmore, T.C. (1991). Tropical moist forests: destruction and species extinctions. Biological Conservation, **55**,199-213.

Schelpe, E.A.C.L.E. (1966). *An Introduction to the South African Orchids*. Macdonald, London.

Schelpe S, and Stewart J. (1990). *Dendrobiums: an introduction to the species in cultivation*. Orchid Sundries Ltd., Stour Provost, Dorset.

Schoser, G. (1987). The development of an Orchid collection in a botanical garden. In, *Proceedings of the 12th World Orchid Conference*. (K Saito and R. Tanaka eds.), pp.154-155. Tokyo.

Schultes, R. E. and Raffauf, R.F. (1990). *The Healing Forest: Medicinal and Toxic Plants of the Northwest Amazonia*. Dioscorides Press, Portland.

Seaton, P.T. and Hailes, N.S.J. (1989). Effects of temperature and moisture content on the viability of *Cattleya aurantica* seed. In, *Modern Methods in Orchid Conservation: the Role of Physiology, Ecology and Management*. (H.W. Pritchard, ed.) pp. 17-29. Cambridge University Press, Cambridge U.K.

Shafer, C.L. (1990) *Nature Reserves: island theory and conservation practice*. Smithsonian Institute Press, Washington, D.C.

Shung, A. (1992). *Iconography of Wild and Cultivated Orchids in China*. Shu-shing Publ. Taipei.

Stott, P.A., Goldammer, J.G. and Werner, W.L. (1990). The role of fire in the tropical lowland deciduous forests of Asia. In *Fire in the Tropical Biota* (ed. J.G. Goldammer), pp. 32-44. Springer-Verlag, Berlin.

Sweet, H.R. (1980). *The Genus Phalaenopsis*. Orchid Digest Inc., Day Printing Corp. Pomona, California.

Thornhill, A.D. (1996). *Species and population-level patterns of genetic variation in Epipactis gigantea (Orchidaceae), with examination of local genetic and clonal structure in riparian and bog populations inferred from allozyme analysis*. University of California, Irvine. Ph.D. Dissertation.

Thornhill, A., and Koopowitz, H. (1992). Viability of *Disa uniflora* Berg (Orchidaceae) seeds under variable storage conditions: Is orchid gene-banking possible? *Biological Conservation*. **62**, pp. 21-27.

Udal, T. (1994). How resilient is an orchid? *Eulophia*

petersii in drought conditions. *South African Orchid Journal*. **25**, pp. 14-15.

U.S. Fish and Wildlife Service. (1994). *Platanthera praeclara* (western prairie fringed orchid) recovery plan. Technical/agency draft. U.S. Fish and Wildlife Service, Ft. Snelling, Minnesota.

Viana, V.M., Tabanez, A.A., and Batista, J.L.F. (1997). Dynamics and restoration of forest Fragments in the Brazilian Atlantic Moist forest. In *Tropical Forest Remnants: ecology, management, and conservation of fragmented communities*. : (eds. W.F. Laurance and O. Bierregaard) pp. 351-365. University of Chicago Press, Chicago.

Walters, K.S. and Gillett, H.J. (1997). *1997 IUCN Red List of Threatened Plants*. IUCN, Gland.

Warren, R. and D. Miller (1992). Taking Root. Amer. *Orchid Soc. Bull*. **61**, pp. 146-149.

Warren, R. and D. Miller (1994). Practical conservation in Brazil; self-sustainable montane Atlantic rainforest conservation units in Rio de Janiero state. In *Proceedings of the14ᵗʰ World Orchid Conference* (ed. A. Pridgeon), pp. 225-227. HMSO Publications, Edinburgh.

White, B. (1998). Paradise on fire – Chimalapas crisis. AWI Quarterly **47**, pp. 4-5.

Whitmore, T.C. (1991). *An Introduction to Tropical Rain Forests*. Clarendon Press, Oxford.

Wijnstekers, W. (1994). *The Evolution of CITES*. 4ᵗʰ edition. CITES, Lausanne.

Wilson, E.O. (1988). The current state of biological diversity. In, *Biodiversity* (ed. E.O. Wilson) p. 3-18. National Academy Press, Washington D.C.

Withner, C.L. (1977). Threatened and endangered species of orchids. In *Extinction is Forever*. (eds., G.T. Prance and T. S. Elias), pp.314-322. New York Botanical Gardens, New York.

Withner, C.L. (1988). *The Cattleyas and their Relatives Vol. I. The Cattleyas*. Timber Press, Portland.

Withner, C.L. (1990). *The Cattleyas and their Relatives Vol. II. The Laelias*. Timber Press Portland.

Wodrich, K.H.K. (1997). *Growing South African Indigenous Orchids*. A.A. Balkema, Rotterdam.

Wolfe, J. A. (1972). An interpretation of Alaskan tertiary floras. In: *Floristics and Paleofloristics of Asia and eastern North America*. pp. 201-33 Elsevier, Amsterdam.

Wood, J.J., Beaman, R.S. and Beaman, J.H. (1993). *The Plants of Mount Kinabalu. 2. Orchids*. Royal Botanic Gardens, Kew.

Yong, H.S. (1990). *Orchid Portraits: Wild Orchids of Malaysia and Southeast Asia*.Tropical Press Sdn. Bhd. Kuala Lumpur.

Recommended Reading

The following books, while not cited above, provide useful and detailed background information that can be used for gaining additional insight into orchids, forests, tropical ecology, and conservation biology problems.

Achard, F., Eva, H., Glinni, A.,Mayaux, P., Richards, T. and Stibig, H.J. (1998). *Identification of Deforestation Hot Spot Areas in the Humid Tropics*. RCSC-EC-EAEC, Brussels.

Arditti, J. (1992). *Fundamentals of Orchid Biology*. John Wiley and Sons, New York.

Benzing, D. H. (1990). *Vascular Epiphytes*. Cambridge University Press, Cambridge.

Given, D. R. (1994). *Principles and Practice of Plant Conservation*. Timber Press, Portland.

Hágsater, E. and V. Dumont. (1996). *Status Survey and Conservation Action Plan: orchids*. IUCN, Gland, Switzerland.

Koopowitz, H., and Kaye, H. (1990). *Plant Extinction: a global crisis*. Christopher Helm, London.

Lowman, M.D. and Nalini M. N. (1995). *Forest Canopies*. Academic Press, San Diego.

Lüttge, U. (1997) *Physiological Ecology of Tropical Plants*. Springer, Berlin.

Rao, T.A. (1998). *Conservation of Wild Orchids of Kodagu in the Western Ghats*. Navbharath Enterprises, Bangalore.

Richards, P.W. (1996). *The Tropical Rain Forest*. Cambridge University Press, Cambridge.

Whitmore, T.C. and Sayer, J.A. (1992). *Tropical Deforestation and Species Extinction*. Chapman and Hall, London

Index